Bull in Early Indian Art

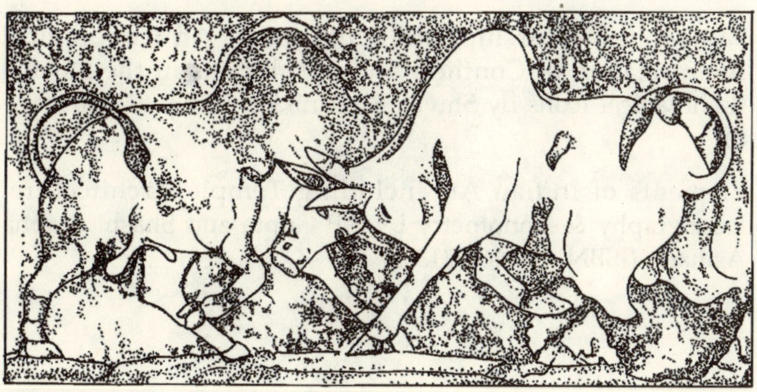

Perspectives in Indian Art and Archaeology
(ISSN 0971-4723)

1. The Splendour of Mathura Art & Museum / Dr. R.C. Sharma (ISBN 81-246-0015-5)
2. Proto-Historic Pottery of Indus Valley Civilisation : Study of Painted Motifs / Dr. Sudha Satyawadi (ISBN 81-246-0030-9)
3. Saptamātr̥kā Worship and Sculptures : An Iconological Interpretation of Conflicts and Resolutions in the Storied Brāhmanical Icons by Shivaji K. Panikkar (ISBN 81-246-0074-0)
4. Elements of Indian Art including Temple Architecture, Iconography & Iconometry by S.P Gupta and Shashi Prabha Asthana (ISBN 81-246-0213-1)

Perspectives in Indian Art and Archaeology, no. 5

Bull in Early Indian Art

(Up to Sixth Century AD)

Bhogendra Jha

With a Foreword by

T.K. Biswas

D.K. Printworld (P) Ltd.
New Delhi

Cataloging in Publication Data — DK

Jha, Bhogendra, 1947 -

Bull in early Indian art.
(Perspectives in Indian art and archaeology, no. 5).
Includes bibliographical references (p.)
Includes index.

1. Bulls in art. 2. Art — India — History. 3. Art, Ancient — India. 4. Bulls in literature. I. Title II. Series: Perspectives in Indian art and archaeology, no. 5.

ISBN 81-246-0255-7
First Published in India in 2004

Published and printed by:
D.K. Printworld (P) Ltd.
Regd. office : *'Sri Kunj'*, F-52, Bali Nagar
New Delhi - 110 015
Phones : (011) 2545-3975; 2546-6019; *Fax* : (011) 2546-5926
E-mail: dkprintworld@vsnl.net
Web: www.dkprint.com

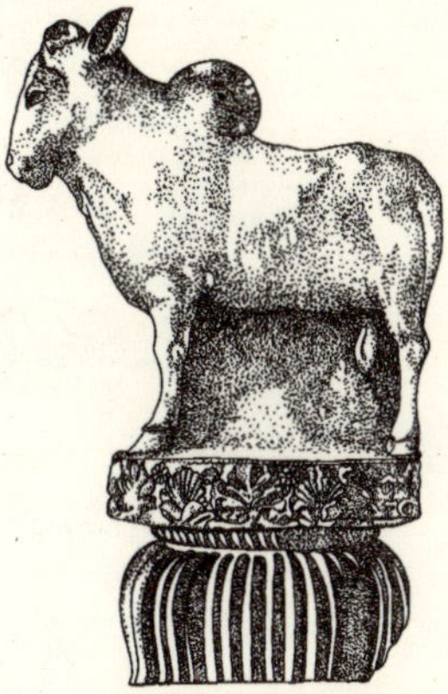

Foreword

ANIMALS played a very significant role in early Indian art and iconography. A careful survey and analysis of Indian art before the beginning of Christian era would show that the depiction of nature was not only favourite with Indian artists of this period, but in fact, it served as a predominant factor in artistic compositions. Human figure were, of course, there but they were there as part of nature. Among the elements in nature, animal portrayals received greater attention. Gods and goddesses, in their iconic shape, did not evolve at that stage. Their presence indicated through their iconoconic and theriomorphic symbols.

Certain select animals were associated with the divinities in Brāhmaṇical Hindu, Buddhist and Jaina religions. However, it appears that men gave much thought before selecting a particular animal and relating it to a god or goddess. The present study takes into account the case study of Bull in early Indian art. The author associated this animal with a number of divinities but, primarily, its association with Śiva in Hindu pantheon, Ādinātha in Jaina pantheon and its relation with the Buddha Śākyamuni were discussed with greater detail. The author did not miss either to discuss it as a secular symbol.

As an animal, Bull evolved in the hoary past. *Bos Guaras* or *Indian Bison* appeared in the Pleistocene period with a heavy built, having a tall hump, a pair of massive upturned horns and a long tail. By nature, it is shy and timid but, if provoked, it can turn wild and dangerous. It is immensely powerful and, among the animals, it is known for its unusual strength. It can carry heavy loads. Its power for sex and its unusual urge for sex were very well-known. Looking into its immense strength and fertilizing powers, along with certain other qualities, men felt a necessity to domesticate this animal. Once domesticated, this animal, as such, served the cause of humanity and helped, in its own way, in the growth of human civilization.

The tremendous possibilities in this powerful animal received its due recognition in all the known ancient cultures and, very soon, the bull could carve a lasting niche in the socio-religious spheres, first, and subsequently, it was reflected in the religious arts of ancient Egypt, Crete, Greece, Rome, Babylonia, Assyria, Achaemenid Persia and, of course, in India. In fact, ancient men found in this animal something magical and divine and, naturally, gave it a respectable position in the society.

Bull served as an animal for drawing ploughshare; it carried heavy loads and was yoked for drawing carts and chariots. Its services were taken also to fertilize cows. Such a useful animal, thus, demanded survival. To ensure the survival of this species, men associated it with various divinities including as symbolic of *Dharma*. Once it was considered as a divine animal, it naturally received immunity from being slaughtered.

Early Indian art was, in fact, a handmade of religion. For its intimate relations with various religion, Bull attracted the ealry Indian artists who modelled this animal in clay, carved it in stone both in relief and in the round and fascinatingly painted Bull in colours. Bull starts appearing in the pre-historic pottery paintings and, among others, was seen painted in the pre-historic rock shelters in India. Subsequently, it continued to appear on proto-historic and in the art of the historic periods in India. What is fascinating in this is that wherever or whenever it was modelled, carved or painted, whether single or in a group, Bulls maintained a sort of aristocratic aloofness and for bringing

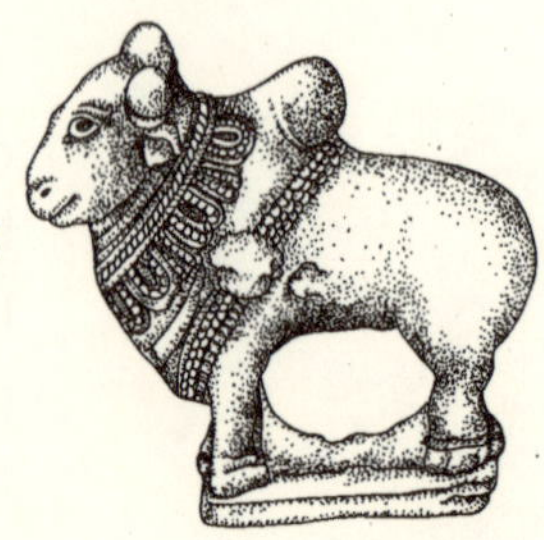

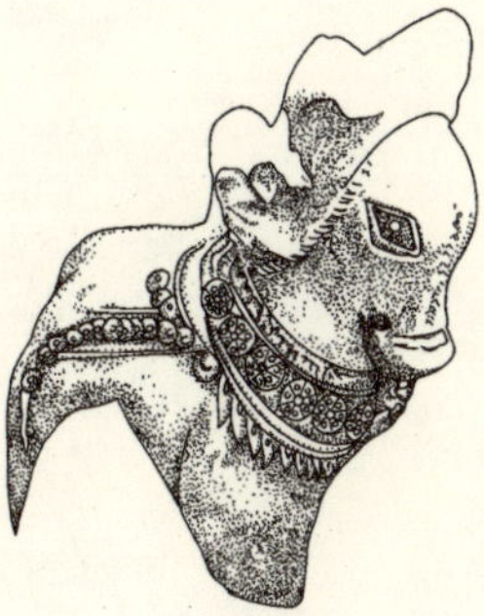

out its bearings and personality, early Indian artists gave greater attention to this animal in their treatments than other animals. As it was a domisticated animal, artists could study it closely and from various angles. Whether standing or seated, whether at rest or in movement, whether walking or charging in high speed, artists composed this animal with evident naturalism and at ease.

A comprehensive study about Bull in early Indian art was awaiting for a long span of time. Shri Bhogendra Jha, therefore, deserves appreciation for working out, for the first time, a comprehensive study of Bull with particular reference to early India. Working with evident and sustained interest, he has gathered exhaustive amount of information both literary and artistic and with such information, he has been successful in projecting the various issues related to this animal; his analysis has been relatively thorough and his conclusions are thought provoking. I firmly belive this book entitled, *Bull in Early Indian Art*, would satisfy the readers, to a great extent, and would raise in them many more questions about this animal, particularly, what treatment this animal did receive after the Gupta period? Perhaps, Shri Jha would engage himself in writing up another book on Bull in post-Gupta and Mediaeval Art. I personally look forward to that.

September 10, 2003 **T.K. Biswas**

DEDICATED

To my parents

Late Pandit Laxaman Jha

and

Late Smt. Parmesvari Jha

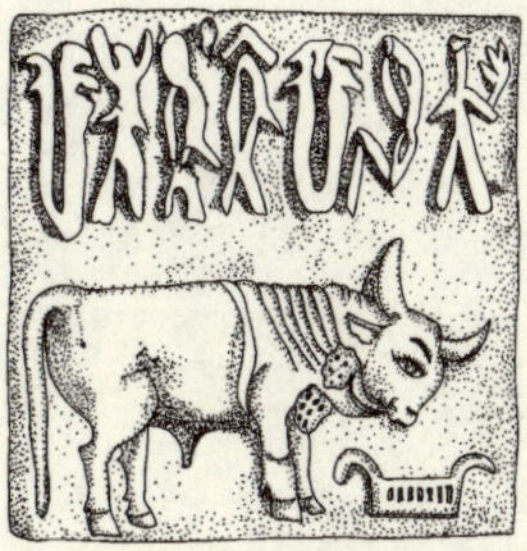

Preface

NATURE played a significant role in early Indian art. With the introduction of icon-worship in or about first century AD, human figures became the pivot of Indian art and the nature receded to the background but it was not divorced altogether. Glimpses of nature were projected on the pedestals on either side of seated or standing images and also on the *prabhā-maṇḍala* of deities.

A survey of early Indian art, from the prehistoric phase down to first century BC, reveals that the art, during that period, was dominated by the depiction of animals and vegetables. Human figures were there but such figures were treated as a part of nature and their role remained, visibly insignificant.

Regarding the role of animals on early Indian art, scholars in the field have worked much less than was expected. Of the works, so far published, mention may be made of the following:

- Asish Sen's *Animal Motifs in Ancient Indian Art*, 1972;
- C. Sivaramamurti's *Birds and Animals in Indian Sculpture*, 1974;
- K. Bharath Iyar's *Animals in Indian Sculpture*, 1977;
- Pratibha Prakas' *Terracotta Animal Figurines in Gaṅgā-Yamunā Valley*, 1985;
- T.K. Biswas', *Horse in Early Indian Art*, 1987;
- K.S. Srivastava's *Elephant in Early Indian Art*, etc., 1989.

The number of research articles on animals has also been insignificant. A few are listed below: O.P. Sharma, "Bull in Indian Art and Literature," *U.P. Historical Society*, vol. V.

(New Series), Part I, 1957, pp. 22-29; O.P. Sharma, "Unicorn in Indian Art and Legend," *Journal of Bihar Research Society*, vol. XLIII, Sept-Dec, 1957, Part III & IV, pp. 357-64; Poonam Chitkara, "Depiction of Cattle Motifs on Amri Pottery," *Puratattva*, No. 9, 1977-78, pp. 92-96; Bisvanath Mukhopadhyay, "Ṛṣabha," *Visvesvarananda Indological Journal*, vol. XVIII, Pt. I & II, 1980, pp. 39-42.

From the above published materials, it is clear that the animals, in general, and bull, in particular, did not receive adequate attention from the scholars in the field. There are, however, a few more articles which deal with certain aspects of bull in Indian art. While writing reports on the results of excavations and explorations of a particular area, oblique references to bull are found. Similarly, in few books small paragraphs are found devoted on bull and that too, within the parameter of a given time and space.

The position of bull in Indian society, its significance in Indian religions and philosophy and its numerous depiction in Indian art have not been justifiably recorded in any book till date. This is the reason why I have taken up to work on bull. Considering the volumes of available material, I have restricted myself to study and analyse the bull in early Indian art, up to the period AD 600.

The investigation involves a systematic evaluation of bull, its origin and evolution, its domestication, its nature, its migration from the place of its origin, the Indian type of bulls, its structure, its power, energy, its sexual urges, its role as a draught animal, its participation in agriculture, its relation with cult of fertility, its acceptance in Indian religions, the philosophical tenets associated with the bull and the various ways and manners in which it was conceived in stone, clay, metal and in colour. In fact, a wholistic evaluation has been undertaken in this book.

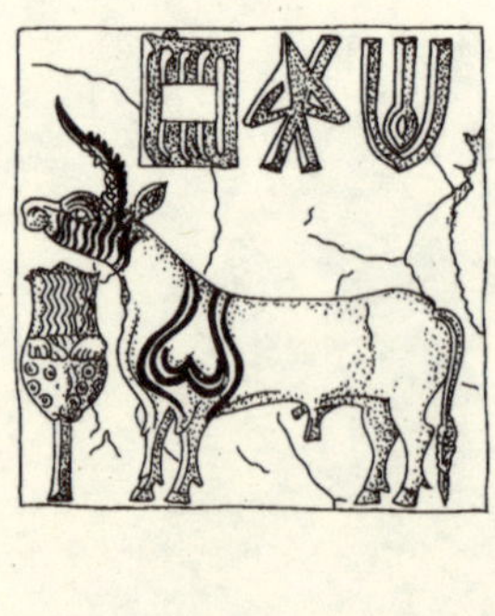

In order to do justice and to work out a clear picture of the bull in early Indian art, the present study has been

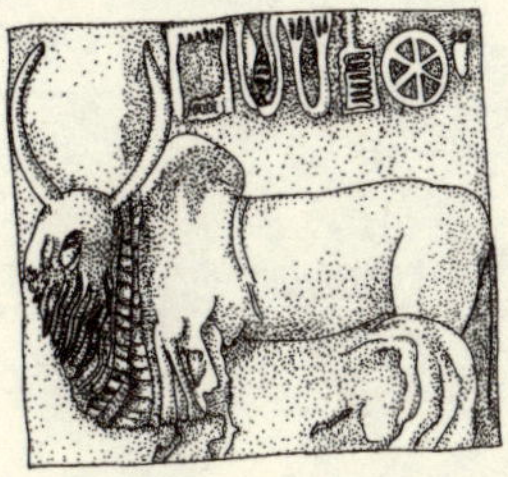

classified into the following chapters:

- Introduction
- Bull in Prehistoric and Protohistoric Art.
- Bull in Early Indian Literature.
- Bull in Early Indian Numismatic and Glyptic Art.
- Bull in early Indian Terracottas.
- Bull in Early Indian Sculpture.
- Conclusion.

In the introduction an attempt is made to study, in brief, about the origin and evolution of the species and, then, its migration to different parts of the world. The type of the bull that entered India is noted. Its physical and psychological characteristics have been recorded. The determination of the age of a bull and its habits, including food, etc., are also discussed.

In the same chapter, the recognition of bulls in ancient world culture has been recorded. The position of bulls in religion and culture of Egypt, Crete, Greece, Mesopotamia, Assyria and Achaemenid Persia has been summarily dealt with.

In chapter 1, a thorough study has been undertaken about bulls in prehistoric art. This includes the depiction of bulls on prehistoric rockshelters and caves in India. The number of bulls painted on the caves of Central India and Uttar Pradesh are not much but the presence of bulls and their relevance and the symbolic role they play have been studied.

The chapter also includes the attempts made by prehistoric clay modellers in working out terracotta bulls. The distribution of such terracotta figurines in India and the nature and peculiarities of each region have been carefully noted. In this connection, analysis of painted bulls on prehistoric potteries and potsherds has also been made.

A detail account is also included in this chapter about

the bull, modelled, moulded or painted in the protohistoric phase of Indian civilizations. The prehistoric bull in terracotta, in copper and bronze, and as these are painted in contemporary potteries, those are carefully studied. In this regard, objects found from Mohenjo-Dāro and Harappā, mainly, and, also, from other protohistoric sites of extended Harappan culture, namely, Rajasthan, Saurashtra, Haryana, Punjab, Uttar Pradesh, Jammu and Northern Maharashtra have been studied with sustained interest. In this chapter, a number of steatite seals and sealings with bull figures have also been taken into consideration and these include seal-sealings found from Harappan sites as well as a few that were discovered in some places in the Gulf countries. Bulls with hump (Brahmāni), bulls without hump, bulls with long and short horns, bulls with hump and legs perforated, bull with stumpy legs, bulls with elongated body, and, in fact, every kind of bulls, including the hybrid and fantastic types, are discussed.

Chapter 2 discusses about the bulls referred in early Indian literature. In this vast chapter, various types of information, supplied by the different texts, are noted. These include Vedas, *Brāhmaṇa*s, Upaniṣads, Smr̥tis, Sūtra, Mahākāvyas, Buddhist Literatûre, Jaina Literature, Purāṇas, Śilpaśāstras and many other texts, such as, *Arthaśāstra*, *Aṣṭādhyāyī*, *Raghuvaṁśa*, *Meghadūtam*, *Kumārasambhava*, *Kirātārjunīya*, *Uttara-Rāmacarita*, *Śiśupālavadha*, etc.

The literature laid bare useful information about bull, its domestication, its use for carrying loads, drawing carts and carriages, its use in cultivation, about the cult of fertility and bull sacrifice, functional types of bull, bull fight, bull racing and betting and, above all, bull's intimate relation with the religions of India. The above information helped me a great deal to explain the meaning and symbolism of bull, as noticed in early Indian art, which, otherwise, I feel, would have remained in obscurity.

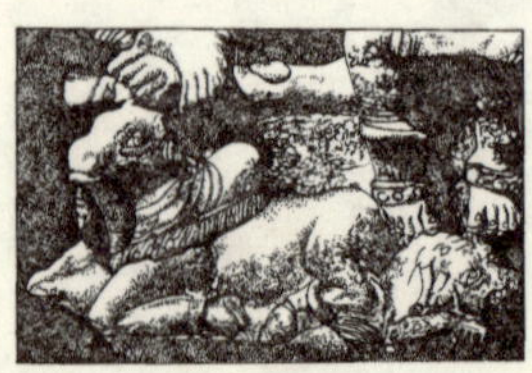

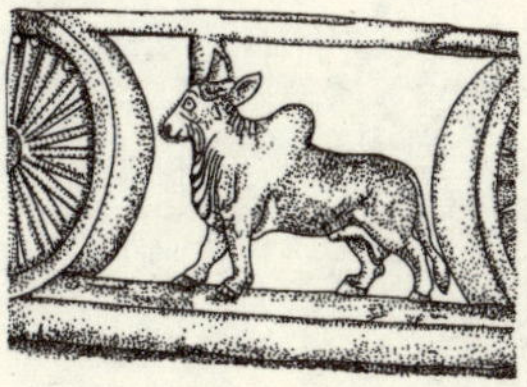

Chapter 3 of this research enables me to consider the depiction of bulls on early Indian coins and on seals and sealings. The bull, as a device, appeared on the silver punch-marked coins, on copper cast coins of the different tribes and localities, the copper and gold coins of the select Kuṣāṇa emperors and on the coins of Skandagupta, issued from Mālwā.

Ancient Indian seals and sealings also incorporated the figures of bull, sometime alone, and, sometime along with other symbols like trident, hill, etc. These seals are generally found at such sites that had been centres of trade and commerce, or of religion or a centre of administration. The seals were made by kings, trade guilds, private persons or by religious establishments. A bull, on coins and seal, according to ancient belief, symbolizes *dharma* or Śiva. Within a minimum space available, the mint masters and seal engravers worked out bulls in seated or standing in their profile and, occasionally, these were frontally treated. This called for high quality of skill and expertise attained by the artists.

Chaper 4 deals in bulls in early Indian terracottas. The discussion includes in-depth studies of pre-Mauryan, Mauryan, Śuṅga, Kuṣāṇa and Gupta terracottas with particular reference to bull. The nature of clay, the treatment of clay, the process of modelling, the application of slip, firing and application of colour differs from one period to the other and these made a deep impact on the depiction of bull. The discussion, in this chapter, includes the artistic and aesthetic analysis of early Indian terracottas. An attempt has been made here with the available examples to examine how these terracotta figures reflect an aspect of Indian culture.

Chapter 5 takes into consideration a thorough investigation of bull in early Indian stone-sculpture, spanning a period between Mauryan (fourth century BC) and Gupta period (AD 600). During the Mauryan period a few ring-stones were made in which pictures of bull appeared. Aśoka, the great Mauryan ruler, patronized the erection of a number of free standing columns. In some such pillars, the figure of bull was embossed on their capital or found relieved on abacus. The pillar capital shows the presence of single bull or double bulls or, even, on a rare occasion, four bulls. The religious affiliation, the symbolism and the delineation of bulls have been discussed in detail.

The art of Śuṅga period (second-first century BC) was predominantly characterized by Buddhist narrative art. In the Buddhist narrative art of Bharhut, Bodh-Gayā, Sāñcī, Amarāvatī and narrative art of a few other sites, such as, Khaṇḍagiri, has been studied, in detail, with particular reference to the presence of bull figures. These narrative panels have been studied with their social, religious and artistic backdrop.

The bull in the Kuṣāṇa art of Gāndhāra and Mathurā was examined with sustained interest, with particular reference, to its affiliation with Hindu, Buddhist and Jaina religions. The bull in the contemporary art of Amarāvatī, Nāgārjunkoṇḍa, Goli, etc., in the Andhra Pradesh, patronized by the Sātavāhanas and Ikṣvākus, has also been taken into consideration.

Finally, the bull in Gupta sculpture has been studied when it became an established religious symbol. The figure of bull in relief or in the round of this period appeared realistically conceived. It appeared in the narrative panels, attached to the contemporary temples and also as mount of a number of divinities. Attention has also been drawn to the bull figure, painted in a number of ways on the murals of Ajantā, particularly, such panels that were painted in the Gupta-Vākāṭaka period. At the end of these discussions, an overall conclusion has been drawn covering the entire span of the chapters, discussed earlier.

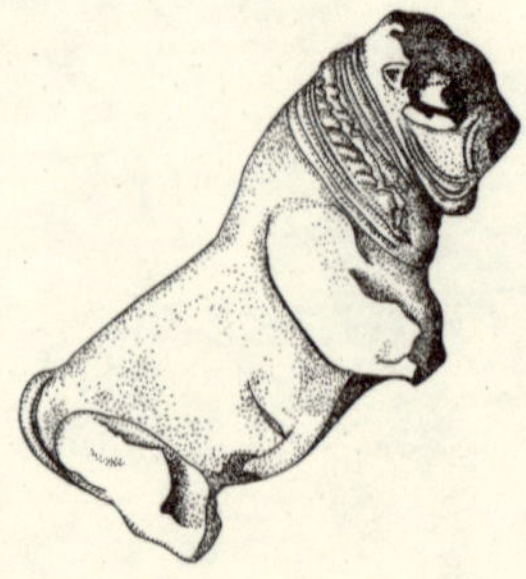

Bhogendra Jha

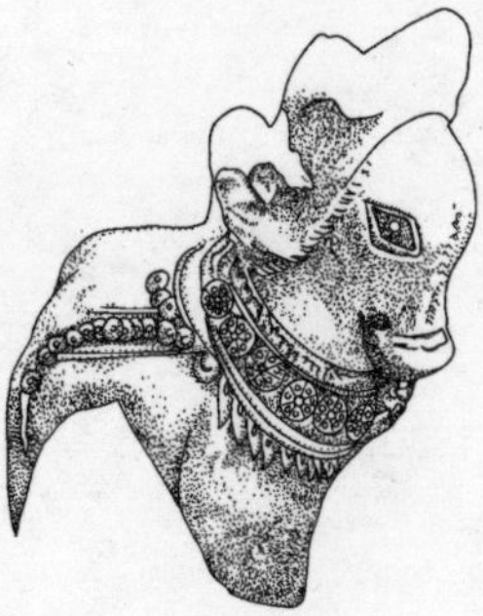

Contents

Foreword by Dr. T.K. Biswas v

Preface ix

Acknowledgements xvii

Abbreviations xix

Introduction 1

1. Bull in Prehistoric and Proto-historic India 8
   - Bull in Prehistoric Art 8
   - Bull in Proto-historic Art 11
2. Bull in the Early Indian Literature 35
3. Bull in the Early Indian Numismatic and Glyptic Art 60
   - Bull on Early Indian Coins 60
   - Bull on Early Indian Seals Sealings 65
4. Bull in the Early Indian Terracotta 73
   - Mauryan Terracotta 76
   - Śuṅga Terracotta 79
   - Kuṣāṇa Terracottas 83
   - Gupta Terracottas 86
5. Bull in Early Indian Stone Sculpture 94
   - Bull in Mauryan Sculptures 94
   - Bull in Śuṅga Sculptures 102
   - Bull in Kuṣāṇa Sculptures 110
   - Bull in Gupta Sculptures 117

Conclusion 128

List of Illustrations 143

Coloured Visuals 149

Black & White Photographs 161

Bibliography 177

Index 189

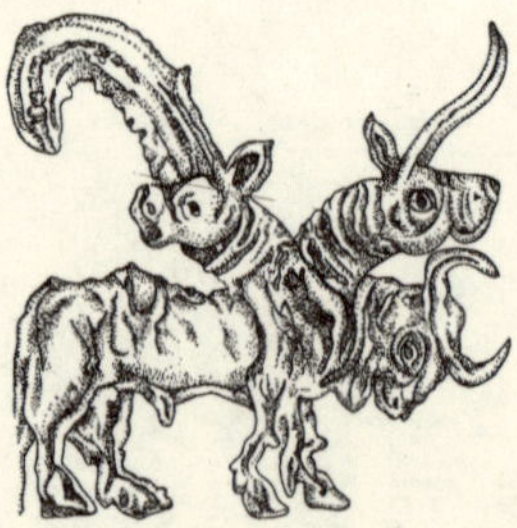

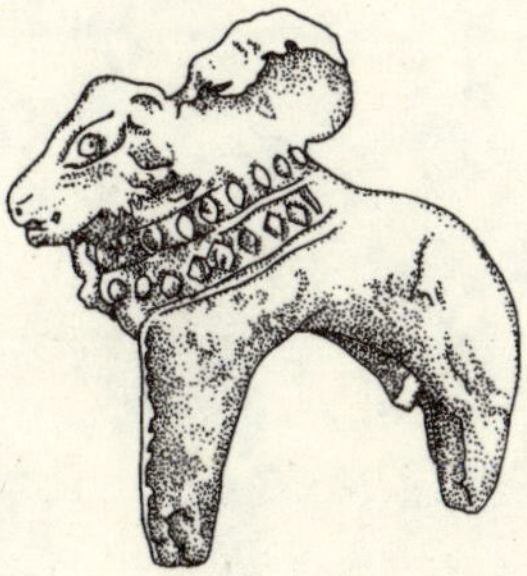

Acknowledgements

I HAVE been working with Bharat Kala Bhavan, the Art & Archaeological Museum of Banaras Hindu University, for over three decades as curator-in-charge of the Archaeological Section. During this period, I have handled thousands of Archaeological materials, including sculptures, terracottas, potteries, seal-sealings, etc. This interaction led me to work seriously on certain aspects of Indian art and I approached Dr. T.K. Biswas, Joint Director, Bharat Kala Bhavan, to suggest me a topic to work. Dr. Biswas, then, suggested to me to work on the topic, 'The Bull in Early Indian Art'. In fact, he not only suggested the topic but also guided me throughout the preparation of this interesting study. But for this generous help, this research could not have taken a final shape. I shall remain for ever grateful to him for his constant guidance and encouragement.

I also acknowledge with thanks the help, the suggestions and advice given to me, with particular reference to the area of my research, by Dr. Deena Bandhu Pandey, Head, Department of History of Art, Banaras Hindu University. I am equally beholdened to Prof. R.C. Sharma, former Director, Bharat Kala Bhavan, besides others, for his suggestions in course of the preparation of this book.

My sincere thanks are due to my colleagues Dr. (Mrs.) Savita Sharma, Dr. T.N. Mishra, Sri S.K. Bhatt and Sri L.D. Vyas. Dr. Sharma helped me, immensely, particularly, about bulls on early Indian coins, and Dr. Mishra and Sri Bhatt gave me interesting facts about bulls on seal sealings. I am grateful to V. Pathak, S.B. Singh and Gopal Ram of Bharat

Kala Bhavan Library, who helped me a lot by supplying the necessary books, journals, magazines, etc., concerning my field of study. I should like to put on record my thanks to R.C. Singh, P.S. Prakash Rao and P.N. Pancholi of the photographic unit of the Bharat Kala Bhavan, who helped me prepare, both black and white and coloured photographs concerning my area of research. Sri R. Ganeshan, Artist, Bharat Kala Bhavan, helped me with the layout of the study paper. My thanks are also due to the staff of American Institute of Indian Studies, Gurgaon, who helped me in various manners during the period of my research. My special thanks are also due to Dr. Ganga Sagar Rai and Sri Arun Kumar Jha of All India Kashiraj Trust, Fort, Ramnagar, who supplied me with the useful textual references concerning my research.

And, last but not the least, I want to express my gratitude to my beloved wife Manju Jha, son J.K. Jha and daughters, Kanchan, Archana and Rachana Jha who assisted ceaselessly in the preparation of this unique work and kept me free from ever so many of the family duties and obligations during this period of strenuous work and research.

September, 2003 **Bhogendra Jha**
Varanasi

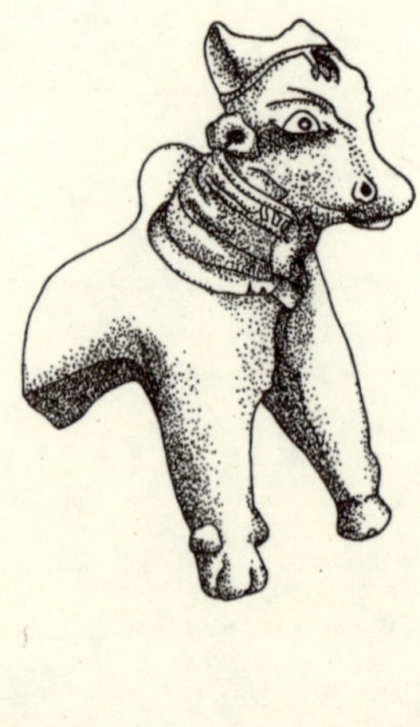

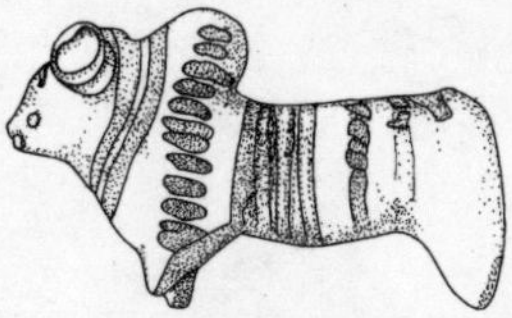

Abbreviations

Acc. No. : Accession Number.

AIIS : American Institute of Indian Studies.

AM : Allahabad Museum.

ASIAR : *Archaeological Survey of India Annual Report.*

ASI-K.R. : *Arachaeological Survey of India — Kondapur Report.*

BKB : Bharat Kala Bhavan.

BMC : *British Museum Catalogue.*

DHI : *Development of Hindu Iconography.*

EI : *Epigraphica Indica.*

Ind. Num. Chro. : *Indian Numismatic Chronicle.*

JASB : *Journal of the Asiatic Society of Bengal.*

JBRS : *Journal of the Bihar Research Society.*

JISOA : *Journal of the Indian Society of Oriental Art.*

JNSI : *Journal of the Numismatic Society of India.*

JRAS : *Journal of the Royal Asiatic Society.*

JUPHS : *Journal of the U.P. Historical Society.*

MFAB : Museum of Fine Arts Bulletin (Boston).

PWMWI : Prince of Wales Museum of Western India.

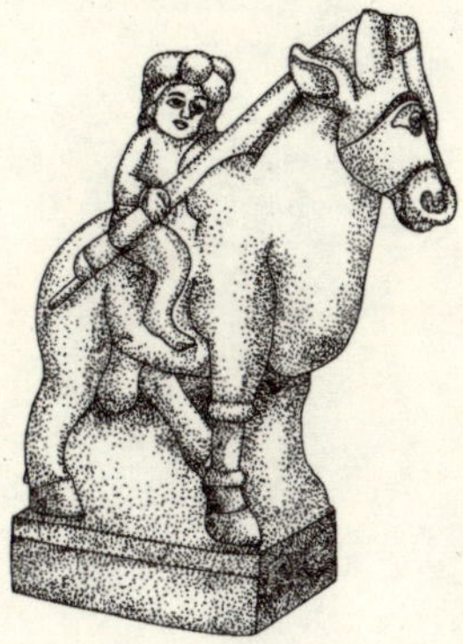

Introduction

The Pleistocene period witnessed the evolution of auroch ancestor of our cattle, which had spread out from Asia and, after the last Ice Age, occupied a vast range from the Atlantic to the Pacific and from the Northern Tundra to India and North Africa. A distinct form of aurochs inhabited India.[1] Bos-Guaras or Indian Bison is known by a number of local synonyms in India. In Hindi, it is called *Gaviya*; in Kannaḍa, it is known as *Kar-kona*; in Tamil, it is called *Katu-erimai* while, in Malayālam, this animal is called *Katu-Pothu*. Originally, it was found in the Indian Peninsula, south of the Himalayas, in most of South-East Asia and the Malayan Peninsula. It frequents forests, places where there are tall grasses, bamboo jungles and, sometimes, in mountain forests.[2]

These animals are large, heavily built with long tails, large moist mouth, muzzles in the neck with a pair of horns. Their back hoofs are fairly developed but there are no foot or face glands. The body-length in old bulls reaches 300 to 336 cm, the tail measures 80 to 92 cm, height at the shoulder is 165 to 190 cm, and the weight is 750 to 1150 kg. The upturned, extremely massive horns, are 60 to 70 cm, longer in adult bulls. Old bulls have a conspicuous, tall hump on the neck and shoulders.[3]

Forests are essential for the existence of this species. They come out to graze early in the morning and continue to graze till about 9 a.m., but it may exceed if the weather remains cool or cloudy. Their food is chiefly grass. They also eat leaves and bark of certain trees. These animals visit salt-lick spots where ground is impregnated with salts and other minerals. It is believed that such earth acts as a medicine to get rid of internal parasites. They are, by nature, shy and timid but they can turn dangerous and destructive, at times. Their defence is their massive size. Their hearing and eyesights are comparatively poor though they have an acute sense of smell.[4] A bull detects when a cow is in heat by sniffing her urine and genitals. While doing this, the bull displays and flexes the nose muscles, or lip-curl reaction which, with the pumping action of the tongue, forces scent to the Jacobson's organ above the palate. In all the bovines, the cow becomes attractive to the bull several hours before she ceases to run away whenever it tries to mount her.[5]

The cult of bull is best known from references to it in the countries like Egypt, near, middle and far East. The bull was prominent as an incarnation or attribute of Egyptian Gods and kings. The Egyptian God, Osyris is said to have invented agricultural instruments and taught men how to harness oxen to the plough. The beneficent career to the Osyris was, however, cut short by the murderous trickery of Tyfon, his own envious and malicious brother. Subsequently, the soul of Osyris was supposed to inhabit the body of the sacred bull, Apis. Egypt remained faithful to the worship of the deified beast (Apis, the bull). Like a few other animals, bulls served a sort of totemic role for one of the earliest political divisions in Egypt and the fighting between different regions is depicted through the fighting animals. Thus, the animal, magic and visual narrative, mark the starting points of Egyptian art.[6] When 'Amon-Ra', the great dynastic God in Egypt, became very popular, he, even, could not wipe out the mystical and popular worship of Osyris during the period of The New Kingdom. Osyris is said to rule over even the paradise and the dead were furnished with objects for the journey and with statuettes, the guarantors who would stand for him in the realms of the God. The cult of Osyris, at one stage, had

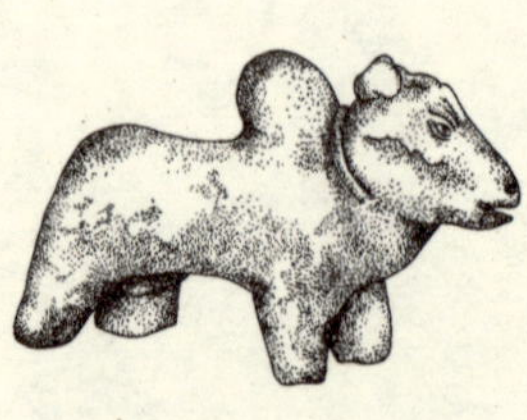

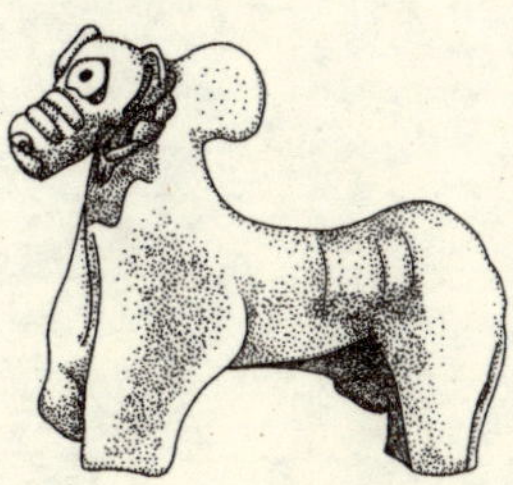

spread from Egypt to Rome. In ancient Egypt, the blood of the sacrificed bull was believed to imbue the earth with life.

The cult of bull appears to have been extremely popular in Minoan Crete. The exacavations and explorations of different sites of Crete laid bare some paintings and artefacts which prove that bull seems to have played a significant role in the religious life of the Cretan people. The paintings and the metals, representing the bull leapers that were found in Crete, has been a point of dispute. Some people think that bull leaping was simply a sport but it appears that the sport became increasingly secularist, in course of time. However, there can be no doubt that there was an underline religious significance attached to it.

In the Minoan and Mycenaean world, generally, the bull-grappling seems to have enveloped the fate of the whole culture, together with the religious traditions with which they were so indissolubly bound up.[7] The bull leaping was a kind of glorification of atheletic excellence, manifesting itself in feats of which the gods themselves were the witnesses. So, too, the participation of women in the Minoan bull-grappling scenes can, by no means, be regarded as a symptom of bondage or of a perverse tyrant's whim. It was rather, as we see, the natural outcome of the religious organization in which the female ministers of the Goddess took the foremost place in the service. At Sparta, where the Minoan religious tradition seems to have had a considerable hold, the girl atheletes continued to take part in the public games. What, in this connection, is specially noteworthy is that the Greek traditions of the bull-grappling feats of Theseus and Herakles clearly acknowledged a Minoan source.[8]

In ancient Greece, young men, made temporary kings, sacrificed bull to Poseidon. The bull is also associated with Dionysus. The Achaian priestesses of earth drank bull's blood as a test of chastity.[9] The blood and, perhaps, testicles of bulls were used in the mysteries of Attis and Cybele.[9] The European references to the sexual prowess of the bull are recorded in the stories of Europa, who was seduced by one, and, of Pasiphae, who herself does the seduction with the help of Daedalus and produced mind-tour with man's body and bull's head.

The word bull is a linguistic accident as it derives from a word probably related to old French *boule,* meaning to trick or confuse. A fragment of a Metope from a temple at Selinus, Sicily, dated C. 590-580 BC, now in the collection of Palermo Museum, shows Europa and the bull.[10] Incidentally, a reference may be made of a Roman relief which probably depicts the *suovetaurilia,* a sacrifice, consisting of a bull, a ram and a pig. These were offered to Mars as an agricultural deity. The said god was worshipped also for his act of increasing the fertility of animals.[11]

The art of early Mesopotamia and Ur exposed a number of beautiful specimens of art which include the colossal winged bulls,[12] and, in the art of Assyria, human-headed bulls were found.[13] A reference has also been made about the bulls kneeling before the sacred tree and the king perfoming a religious ceremony. It may refer to bull sacrifice. Therefore, it can be presumed that the winged bull or human-headed bull must have had links with certain religious notion in the Asiatic West. The recognition of bull as the beast of burden can be established by two wooden four-wheeled wagons, each drawn by three oxen. On the body of such wagon mascots in the forms of bulls have also been found.[14]

The Persian mythology includes fascinating narratives about the bulls. Such narratives also point to its religious association. One of the very important Persian divinities was Mitra Tauro-Ktonos or "slayer of bull." When represented in art, the god is shown as burying a dagger in the heart of the bull and from the heart of the beast's body

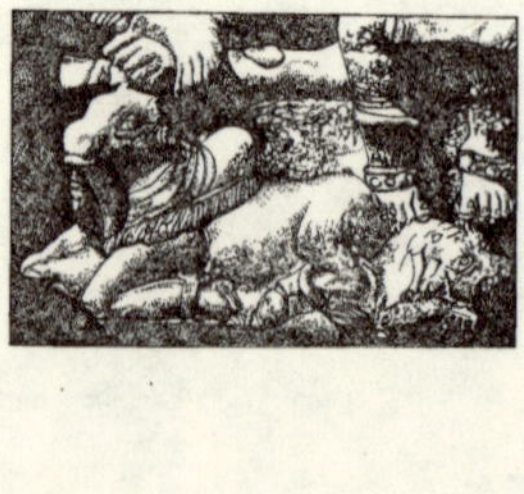

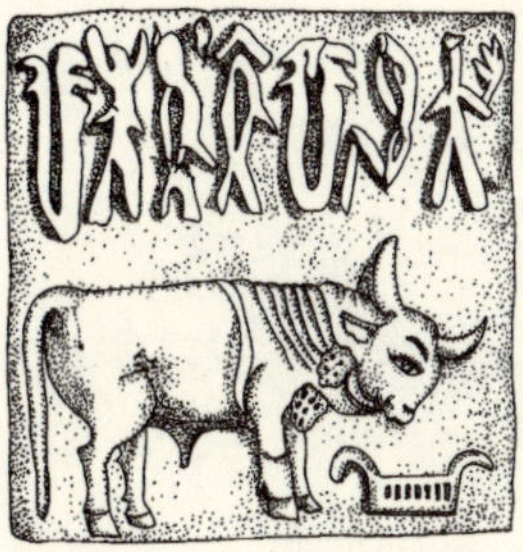

springs every kind of vegetable growth. This is something supernatural or magical.[15] A reference may also be made to Dervaspa, or Ghosht. It is the soul of the bull (Geus Urvan), an object of respect and veneration, which is the guardian of cattle.[16] Achaemenian pillars in certain cases show in the capital two bulls seated back to back. Such pillar capitals with bulls were found from Susa. The Audience Palace of Cyrus, the Great at Pasargadae in ancient Iran, laid bare the remains of animals, including a bull which formed the tops of the columns in its central hall. From the same area, one could notice the upright bull which symbolizes, perhaps, a sacrifical animal to the gods. At Apadana, Xerexes built the portal approach, shown from the staircase of a Mausoleum, where two huge winged man-bulls face the oasis of Marudasht. Two more winged man-bulls at the base of an identical massive wall face the mountains. Such man-bulls in similar pattern appeared in the Hettite and Assyrian civilizations. The upper part of the body in such man-bulls is showing energy while only in the treatment of the muscular legs there is variation with finely carved bone structure. The mane and the tail are mostly decorative. On the top of a Persepolitan pillar, one finds the two-headed bulls with a common figure which was generally carved out of one big stone. The technique by which it was put on top of the pillar is astonishing. The stylization of this symbol is peculiarly Achaemenid. The decorative man-bull with trappings is dexterously carved.

Bulls evolved as a species, long ago, somewhere in the Pleistocene period and during the last phase of interglacial desiccation. It migrated from Asia to different parts of the world. It also, in the same wake, appeared in India. Bos-Gauras (Gaur) or Indian Bisons are large, heavily built, have a long tail, bear a pair of massive upturned horns and have a conspicuous tall hump. Essentially, a grass-eater, these bulls are by nature shy and timid but if provoked these bulls can turn wild, destructive and dangerous. Ever since these bulls were domesticated, men could watch and experience their nature. Bulls appeared to men as extremely powerful and an embodiment of strength. Therefore, these animals were used in cultivation and for drawing the ploughshares. They were also yoked to the carts or carriages for transporting heavy loads and passengers. Their immense power for sex and their unusual sexual urges have also been noted from the distant past. In their unusual strength, power and sexual urge, men found something magical, something divine, at times. In this way, a stage came when the cult of fertility was identified with the cult of bull. The sacrifice of a bull and spraying of blood of sacrificed bulls on earth became a part of fertility rite, and drinking of bull's blood was taken as a test of chastity.

In the ancient world, the cult of bull received recognitions from Egypt, Crete, Greece, Rome, Babylonia, Assyria, Achaemenid Persia and India. Egyptian god, Osyris, was credited to have had the ideas of how to harness oxen. God Apis was a deified bull. During Minoan period, this animal received unique attention. Minos was the son of Zeus (the bull) and Europa. The Greek god, Poseidon, was worshipped with the blood of a bull; the animal was also associated with Dionysius. Winged bulls, human-headed bulls and two bull-heads, having a common body, were all found from the various ancient sites of Middle East and near east and all these point to the magical and supernatural power of the bull, an animal which was endowed with such qualities that made it divinely symbolic.

References

1. David Macdonald, (ed.), *The Encyclopaedia of Mammals*, pt.II, London, 1984, p. 544.
2. Susan Lowery, (ed.), The *Illustrated Encyclopaedia of Mammals*, London, 1979, p. 328.
3. *Ibid*.
4. S.H. Peeter, *The Book of Indian Animals*, p. 204.

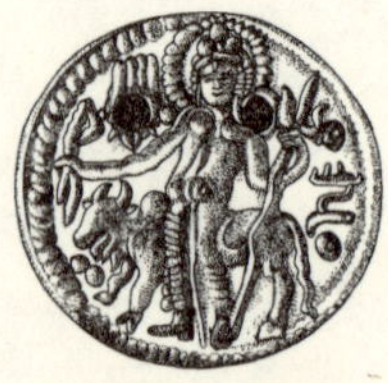

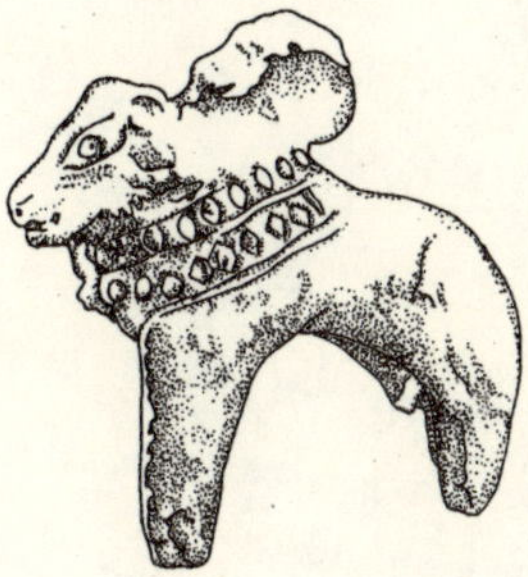

5. David Macdonald, (ed.), *op. cit.*, p. 547.
6. Rene Huyohe, (ed.), *Larousse — Encyclopaedia of Prehistoric and Ancient Art*, London, 1907, p. 116.
7. Jacquetta Hawkus, (ed.), *The World of the Past*, vol. II, New York, 1963, p. 118.
8. *Ibid.*, pp. 118-20.
9. Frank and Waggal, *Standard Dictionary of Folklore, Mythology and Legends*, p. 170.
10. In the Greek mythology it is said that Zeus fell in love with Europa, at first sight, when she was playing with her companions on the sea-shore at Sidon (or Tyre). Disguising himself as a snow white bull he placed himself at the feet of Europa. The other girls fled but Europa climbed on the animal's back. Immediately, it got up, entered the water and swam across the sea. They reached the Island of Crete where he ravished her. Their union led to the birth of three sons, Minos, Serpedon and Rhadamanthys. The god gave her in marriage to the king of Crete, Asterius, who adopted the childern. After his death, Europa received divine honours and was transformed into constellation (*Larousse — World Mythology*, ed. by Pierrerimal, 1965, p. 116).
11. Robert Graves, *New Larousse Encyclopaedia of Mythology*, 1978, p. 202.
12. Jaquetta Haukus (ed.), *op. cit.*, pt. I, p. 398.
13. *Ibid.*, p. 296.
14. *Ibid.*, p. 355 (Discovery on the Tombs by Leonard Wooly).
15. J. Hackin, *Asiatic Mythology*, p. 39.
16. *Ibid.*, p. 42.

1

Bull in Prehistoric and Proto-historic India

Bull in Prehistoric Art

SINCE 1880, about 3,000 caves and rock-shelters have been discovered throughout the country. Among the various animals drawn on the surface of the rock, a number of figures indicate the presence of bull. Conceived in certain cases, realistically, the figures of bulls are always drawn in outline and are not shown with their flesh and bones. In the paintings, the colour used is red.[1] Representations of bulls, both real and mythical, in the rock-shelters have been found from Bhīmbeṭkā and from Rāmguḍiwar Tolkoli in Bādāmī. The idea was, perhaps, to show the deified bull.[2]

The Mesolithic culture of the Period II at Bhīmbeṭkā, dated between 10,000-4000 BC, yielded certain abnormal forms of the bull. Such a bull has been endowed with abnormal face of a rectangular shape with its mouth like that of an elephant. In one place, a bull is shown chasing another animal while a human figure and a crab are shown running ahead of this figure. Since this theme has been repeated at more than one place, it is presumed that it is related to an important event in the life of the prehistoric people. Dr. Pandey finds in it a fight among three tribes, having different animals as their totems.[3] The bull in certain cases appears to be of heavy shape with protruding horns, alert tails with realistic movements in hind legs (BHIM, III *c.* 19). Some such paintings, according to scholars, belong to

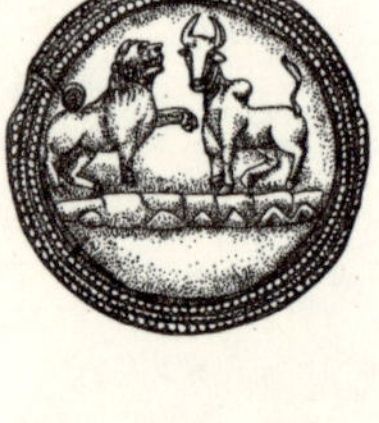

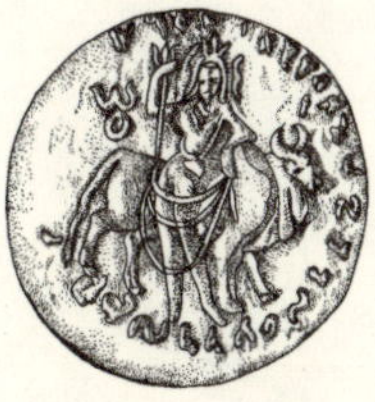

the Upper Paleolithic period (*fig*. 1).

Scientific excavations of prehistoric rocks and cave shelters in India were undertaken by the Department of Ancient Indian History, Culture and Archaeology of the Universities of Allahabad, Dhārwār, Sāgar, Vikram and Banāras. The Archaeological Survey of India and Deccan College, Poona, also participated in reconstructing the history of the Upper Paleolithic culture. Excavations at different places were undertaken by Wakankar, G.R. Sharma, R.K. Varma, Joshi and Khare, P.C. Pant and V. Jayaswal, and they have brought forward useful information of the rock paintings of the contemporary periods. Bhīmbeṭkā, a village about 30 miles from Bhopāl, exposed prehistoric paintings on the wall surfaces just as one finds in the Kaimūr ranges in the Mirzapur district (U.P.). The Neolithic culture of the Vindhya-Kaimūr Range spans between sixth and third millennium BC and is marked by pastoralism. In this period, hunting was practised and animal husbandry was known. The faunal remains from Bagore and Ādamgarh sites suggest the hunting as well as domestication of animals. The hunting scenes are seen on the rock-shelters of even earlier period.[4] In the rock paintings of Uttar Pradesh and Madhya Pradesh, the animal figures predominate but it is very difficult to identify them with any religion. Incidentally, reference may be made of a figure in Monteraga rock-shelter at Pañcamarhī in which a man is shown subduing a lion and a bull and the hero has been compared by Gordon with Gilgamesh. Dr. Jagadish Gupta also supports this identification. This theme, according to some, symbolizes the supremacy of man over the wildlife (lion) and agricultural life (bull).

Trivedi discovered paintings of humped bulls chasing cows in the rock paintings at Thoban in the Mungoli tehsil of Guṇā district, M.P.; painted in dark red pigments, these bulls call for a comparison with the bull found painted at Bhīmbeṭkā and Raṅgmahal.[5]

The rock paintings of Kupgalu and Lal Gairik exhibit a large number of animals. At both the places, among other animals, the horns of bull are shown tied with bows, the symbol of which is not very clear. Recently, on the western course of river, Chambal, in Ujjain, the discovered fragments of pottery are seen painted with bulls, with decorated horns. Most probably, such decorations of horns were connected with some festivals which are not very clearly known. The rock paintings, which were discovered in or around Bellārī, are found painted in five different colours. The animals here are particularly painted in yellow. The painted bulls on the rock at Rāicūr in Hyderabad had been dated to 1000 BC but a careful analysis would show that the painted bulls on these rocks belonged to much later dates. The rock paintings in Mandori in Pakistan show, for the first time, a bullock cart painted between 200 BC and AD 200. The painting shows a large number of animals but the number of bulls is small. Similarly, in the Gombiguḍā near Jamkhaṇḍī in Mumbai, the exposed rock paintings included many animals among which the bulls predominate. These bulls were painted in first century AD.

The Neolithic culture of the Deccan was largely based upon pastoralism and the Indian humped cattle is found to have the same most common characteristics which domestic species possess. This was observed by Alchin when he reviewed the reports on Piklihal excavations (Bellārī).[6] The folk religious culture there, perhaps, included the bull betting, racing and fighting which continue till date.

In the earliest deposits of the Jorwe Culture at Nevāsā, one finds the form of a mother goddess who was associated with bull. This bull was represented in a realistic form, as found at Ināmgāon and Candolī. The holes in the body of the bull as well as in the navel of the headless goddess were intentionally made so that, by inserting a small stick, the goddess could be shown riding on the back of the bull.[7] The storage jars found from Jorwe were decorated either with

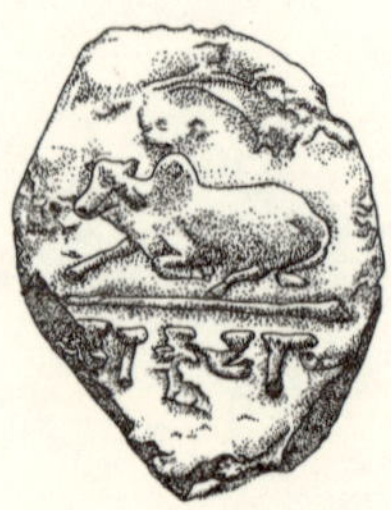

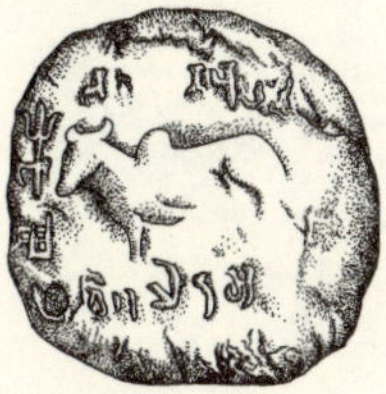

bullock carts or the wheel cart drawn by humped bull. The latter is an interesting evidence that throws light on the means of transport, at that time.

The prehistoric sites of Mehi, Kulli and Ḍābarkoṭ yielded terracotta figures of bulls and the numbers suggest that they were used as religious symbols in shrines.[8] Two sites in North-Western Frontier Provinces yielded through their deposits evidences of horned deities. Such a deity was completely humanized and worshipped by the Harappans.[9] The Ahār culture that reached Kaytha on the Kali-Sin reveals the introduction of a unique bull cult.[10] Bones of domesticated animals, including cow and ox, were discovered by Dr. (Mrs.) Shah, which led Stuart Piggot to conclude, that the Ahārians were non-vegetarians.[11] The Narmadā has laid bare a good idea of the animal world. This can be proved by the discoveries on the Godāvarī and through the stray finds of Pravara. Recently, the Sona river in U.P. yielded large quantities of animal fossils which include the wild ox (*Bos-nomadicus*).[12]

Bull in Proto-historic Art

The chief traits of proto-historic culture are the use of stone or metal craft along with the continuous trend of clay modellings. The motifs and forms, as envisaged in clay, were found associated with the materials for domestic use and for worship besides household decorative items and toys. But some of these were possibly used for popular religious and musical purposes. Besides, their aesthetic appeal, the terracotta figurines of the proto-historic period supply invaluable information for the study of life and culture of the contemporary people. About the first half of the third millennium BC, two significant cultures flourished in North and South Baluchistan. In North Baluchistan, the valley of the river Zhob and in the South a site of Kulli, in Markan coast yielded a fairly good number of terracotta figurines of animals, including bulls. The humped bulls of Kulli sites are found painted with vertical stripes across the body and certain short strokes were noticed down the shoulders and the forehead (*figs.* 5, 6). This, so-called Indian Brahmāni bull appears to have been an object of popular reverence. The terracotta bulls varied from 2-4 inches in length and had stumpy legs with a prominent hump. A number of bulls predominated over the other animal figures. Humped bulls also predominated among the animal figures found from Zhob. It is also interesting to note of the bull figurine from Mehi-Damb which bears a hole through each of its stumpy legs and through the hump. Most probably, terracotta wheels were fitted to axles passed through the leg holes and the hump hole being intended for the string to pull the figure along.[13] Apart from Mohenjo-Dāro and Harappā and some proto-historic sites in Rajasthan, archaeologists, in recent years, revealed over 700 sites with pre-Harappan, Harappan and late-Harappan affiliations. These sites are brought under two regions, namely eastern and southern. The eastern region includes Rajasthan, Haryana, Punjab and some parts of Uttar Pradesh and Jammu while the southern region covers Saurāṣṭra and northern Maharashtra.[14]

The antiquity of terracotta figurines could be pushed back to Neolithic settlements at Mehargarh which is succeeded by Harappan culture, in subsequent phases. But a regular manufacturing of terracotta started from the pre-Harappan habitation. The types of animals differ from site to site depending on the religious faith or ecological familiarity of the population. For instance, there is a total absence of toy carts in the hilly areas of Baluchistan. Similarly, in partially forested areas, one finds the absence of carnivorous animals. Piggot observed, long ago, that figurines of bulls were not found at Lothal or Kālibaṅgan or Surkoṭdar or several other sites from Saurāṣṭra.[15]

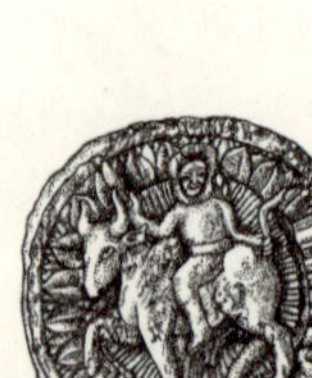

Discovery of plenty of terracotta bull figurines from

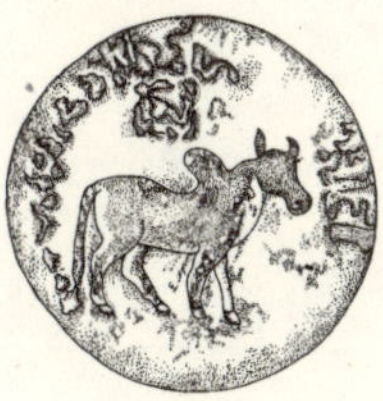

different Harappan sites led some scholars to conclude that they were related to some animal sacrificial offerings. Some scholars, after carefully analysing the figures of bull in subsequent period, concluded that these bulls had definitely certain religious significance. It would be, however, difficult to prove religious association and the matter would remain hypothetical till the letters on the seals are deciphered. The religious connections are mostly drawn on the basis of subsequent faith and religious practices. A reference may be made here that some terracotta figurines of Zhob type, found at Damb-Sadat in Quetta Valley, bearing 'eye' or *yoni* mark, painted on the forehead of the bulls. Were they in any way related to some female deities? M. Toshi, in his reports of Sahari Sokhta, noted that one of the many ox-heads bears rays painted in the middle of its forehead. He found in this a solar or a floral symbol.[16]

The proliferation of representations of Indian humped bulls (*Bos indicus*) on seals and sealings, on terracottas, the typical portrayal of hump, loin head dewlap all go to show a resemblance to the present-day Ongole breed of bulls. The bulls, being a potential sire of generations, might have some relations or symbolism with both wealth and fertility. There are several examples of female figures at Harappā and Mohenjo-Dāro which are in standing pose carrying horn-like headgears or supporting horns with their hands. Marshall found, in such figures, the symbol of fertility.[17] The clay models of bullock carts throw light on the various types of carts used in these days. But such carts are absent in the hilly sites of Baluchistan[18] (*fig.* 17).

At the early Harappan level, interestingly, bull figurines outnumber the female figurines. Most of the bulls are humped, and, in some cases, they are decorated with black straps. In the late Harappan phase, bull figurines continued though their modelling became apparently crude. In Harappan culture, short-horned bull in terracotta occurs, frequently. Such a bull is presented with the head lowered, as if ready to charge. Sometimes, it is shown with garlands around the neck and, occasionally, with a bell suspended from the dewlap. Such Brahmāni bulls were modelled with abstraction in the treatment of hump and dewlap[19] (*figs.* 2, 4).

A few steatite seals from Mohenjo-Dāro depict scenes reminiscent of the Gilgamesh story in Sumerian mythology. Particular mention may be made of a bull-man attacking a horned-tiger which recalls the encounter between Gilgamesh and Enkidu. An interesting Indus steatite seal was discovered from a grave at Bahrein which depicts, for the first time, a unicorn/bull and a peacock and this circular seal bears four letters of Indus script. There is also shown for the first time a peacock along with a bull.[20] (Hammed Town, Bahrein Excavation, 1990 by K.M. Srivastava) Another cylindrical seal from Homa in Syria has been taken to indicate Harappan influence since it depicts a short-horned bull. However, the evidence is too sketchy to think in terms of any direct trade.

Gadd has drawn our attention to 18 seals of the so-called Indus type at Ur and in Babylonia. Of these, at least, six are definitely of Indus style because the script and the motifs are the same. One seal depicts a bull, with a bent-head, which seems to look Indian but the script there is archaic and in cuneiform. Gadd concludes that this might have been made by an Indian merchant residing at Ur.[21] Reference may also be made here of a seal in which a horned, tailed creature, half-man, half-bull has a strikingly Babylonian appearance and resembles the hero 'Eboni' wrestling with the wild beasts (vs 1514). All the seals discussed above establish that the Indus Valley maintained a regular trade relation with countries like Babylonia, Bahrein and Mesopotamia and some such gulf countries.

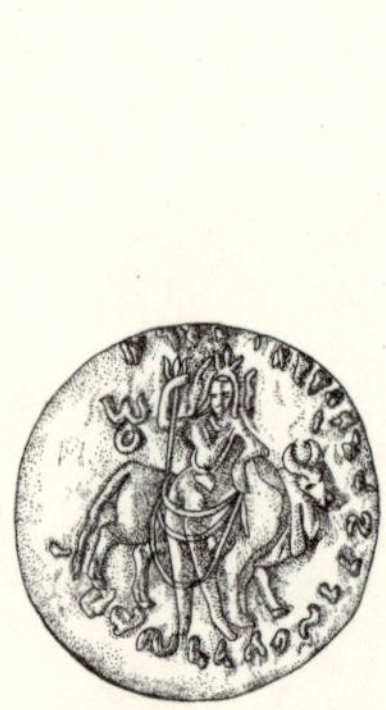

Mohenjo-Dāro yielded seals with peculiar composite forms. A few seals bear a figure of a ram with the horns of

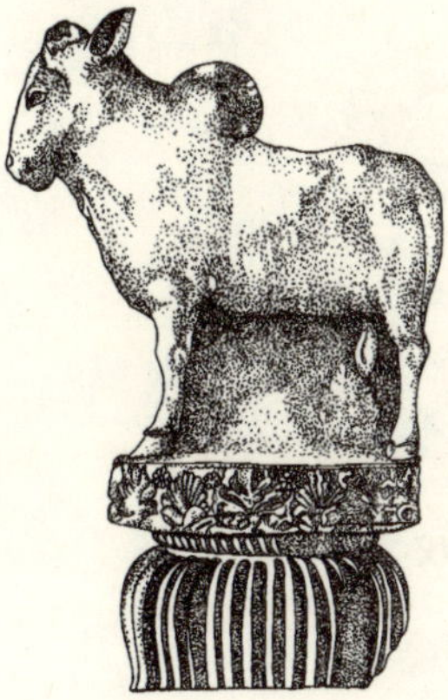

a bull having a human face and the trunk and tusk of an elephant[22] (*fig.* 12). Some seals, on the other hand, are indicating figures of half-human and half-animal. Such a figure has the hoofs, the horns and the tail of a bison. It resembles the figure of Enkidu, the companion of Gilgamesh. In this connection, a reference may be made of a bronze seal, unearthed from Sirkap (Taxila) and Marshall, which explains the bull as Herakles, trampling down a bull-shaped dragon.

When one discusses the maturity of Harappan arts and crafts, one must place, besides the bronze and stone figures, the steatite seals bearing engravings of an exquisite order.[23] Over 2000 seals and sealing impressions have been found from Harappan sites. Made in steatite, these seals were coated with an alkali and, then, fired to produce a white lustrous surface.[24] In general, these seals are square in shape but round ones are not unknown. They bear a perforated boss at the back for handling. It is also interesting to note that, in subsequent periods, one witnesses a superior quality of bronze and stone sculptures but the artists could not produce such seals which could match Harappan ones. It appears that fine burin or chisel was used to engrave animals, human figures and other designs on the seals. The decipherment of the writing on the Indus seals is, perhaps, the most vexing problem for interpreting this ancient civilization. Approxi-mately, the seals bear 400 different signs and they appear as pictographic scripts. Once this language is decoded, the interpretation will be possible with particular relation to the role played by animals. B.B. Lal, while analysing the seals, aptly remarked,

> Who is there who does not get overwhelmed by the grace and majesty of the Brahmani bull with a well grown body, prominent hump, tall in-curved horns, powerful face and a large swinging dewlap. Some doubts have been raised about the Indian characterization of the humped bull. Today, the bulls of the

> Sohan-valley are humped and it may be possible to prove that they were there at Tape Yohy as early as its initial occupation[25] (*fig*.3).

Among the animals on the Harappan seals, the so-called unicorn outnumbered the rest. This animal may have been a bull with two horns, but one horn is noticed in its profile view; it may also be a mythical animal. Agrawala refers to call a unicorn as a 'Śṛṅga-Vṛṣa', that is a bull with horns (*fig*. 13). Another seal shows a composite form of an ox and antelope. Both are associated to Śiva Rudra.[26] But this study is to be accepted with reservation. Indus seals were mostly used for a commercial purpose and served as trade marks, and, according to some scholars, these do not have any magical value.[27] Besides unicorn, the seals also bear short-horn bulls and Brahmāni bulls. The short-horn bulls are very popular in Harappā and are seen commonly on seals and potteries. In most cases, these bulls are also shown on the seals with slight bent-in head as if it is going to charge. In one such seal, a three-headed short-horned bull is shown. One with the face looking down, the second one with face raised towards the sky and the third bent in, was turned round is looking back (*fig*. 22). If two of the heads are removed and remaining face with the tail is a little shortened then it would resemble any normal animal. A close analysis reveals that the seal engraver carved the central head and the body first and, later, on two extra heads were added. Marshall has drawn our attention to a similar seal in which the head, facing the earth, is that of a bison, the second looks like a unicorn and the third one is of an ibex, with horns reversed.[28] Lal wonders if the image denotes the down-to-earth present, the sky-vast future and the left-behind past? Whether such philosophical approach was indeed there in the mind of the Harappan artists or of the person who ordered the seal to be made can, at best, remain a guess. But, sure enough, there was something more in the depiction than just a three-headed animal

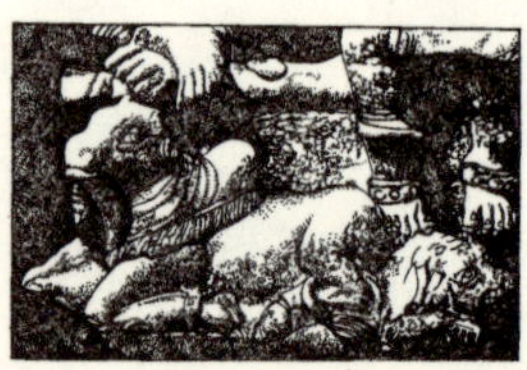

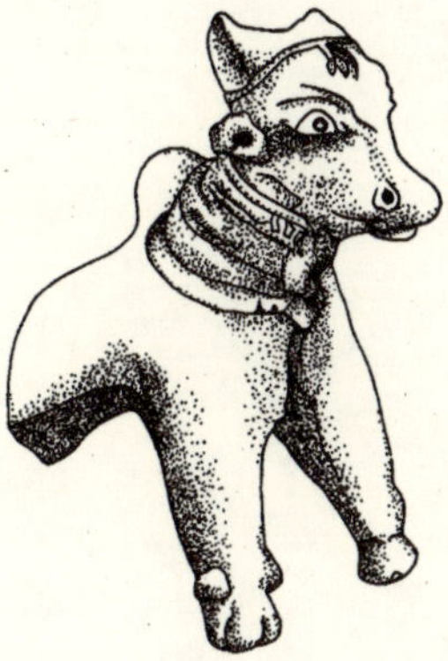

which, in any case, was not deciphered. But it appears also that the animation of a common head was conceived. The first is shown as if grazing, in the second stage, it becomes alert and, then, it looks back apprehending some danger.

Possehl has drawn our attention to a unique seal with an animal figure which Cunningham acquired, long back. When, first discovered, Clark and Cunningham took the animal as representing a humpless bull, and, since the related letters in the seal appeared un-Indian, Cunningham concluded that this was a foreign seal. But, to Possehl, this represents a typical Harappan type.[29] Two more such seals were found, later on, and are now in the British Museum. The Prince of Wales Museum also has, in its collections, seals with the representations of bull. In the catalogue, entitled *Mriga*,[30] the author is of opinion that the humpless bulls were imported to India and were specially bred for the purpose of bull grappling or bull leaping sports. Such a sport was popular in Minoan Crete and, later, at Thessaly.

One of the seals in the Prince of Wales Museum shows a young acrobat grappling the horns of a bull when it seems to charge him. Another seal of the same Museum represents the sacrifice of a bull in which the sportsman is seen, spearing the bull. Many Harappan seals are there which show a bull before an altar, evidently, for the purpose of sacrifice. Several bull figurines of this type have also been discovered from various places at Mohenjo-Dāro, Harappā, Kalibaṅgan and Lothal (*fig.* 4). A clay sealing from Mohenjo-Dāro shows vaulting over the bull. It might have been a popular sport or a part of a ritual, prevalent, at that time.

Huntington draws our attention to a seal showing the kneeling figure with a horned-headdress in front of a deity within a tree, and behind the kneeling figure, there stands a bull whose role is not known. But she thinks that the presence of the bull brings in religious association in the Indus context. A row of figures standing below are seen wearing elaborate headdresses.[31] An Indus seal has raised compelling arguments for relating it with the iconography of Śiva. The figure appears to have three faces, and either wears a tiger skin or has a tiger-like upper torso. He is seated in a yogic posture. He is surrounded by an elephant, a tiger, a rhino and a buffalo. And these are taken to relate the central figure as Paśupati, an aspect of Śiva. The term Paśupati was attributed to Lord Śiva, much later. It is, therefore, within reason to wonder if this actually stood for Śiva-Paśupati (the lord of the animals). Whether it really indicates a *maṇḍala* or a cosmological diagram, is very difficult to say.[32] Sharma studied a seal from Harappā in which a human figure is shown seated on a low dais. The figure has been identified as Śiva since his legs resembled those of a bull.[33] (Mackey, seal No. 222). From Harappā, another sealing represents a seated figure, resembling Śiva (Paśupati) flanked by animals. A tiger, standing below a tree, a bull, a standing human figure and another figure seated near a wooden structure on the reverse side of the same sealing are also observed in the picture.[34]

In the National Museum, New Delhi, there is a seal showing a human being seated in a yogic posture. He is having possibly horns as his headgear. If these are horns then the figure is a composite body, partly human, partly animal or it also could be of a human figure wearing a headdress with horns and, thereby, implicating the figure with certain beastly qualities. The figure could also be a bull-man.[35] Reference may also be made of another interesting seal in the National Museum for which our attention has been drawn by Pupul Jayakar.[36] The seal shows a *śamī* tree along with a half-bovine-half-women figure, wearing horns, and a tiger, with horns. She thinks that the seal, perhaps, is indicative of the moment of the metamorphosis. Incidentally, a reference may be made of certain seals from Mohenjo-Dāro and Harappā about which Chakravarty has drawn our attention.

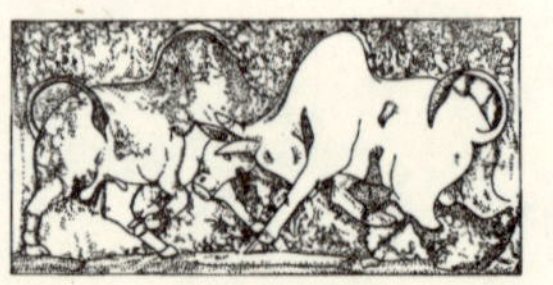

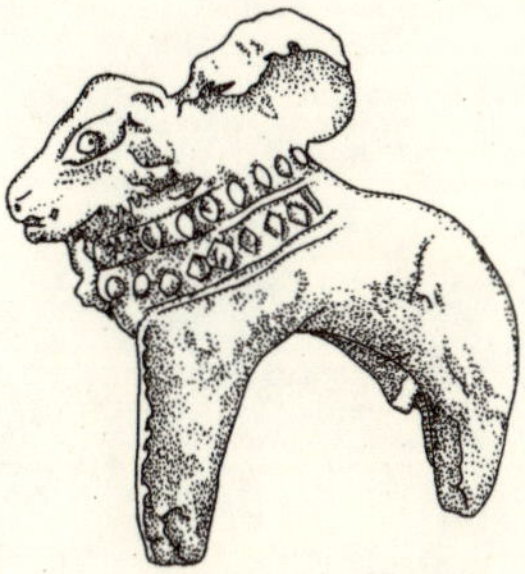

> A bull is teathered inside a building and it is difficult not to connect the three female figures, who seem to be beating symbols or tambourines with some ceremony of worship, the central feature of which is the bull. . . . Neither the texts nor any monuments have so far supplied us with evidence about this curious feature, which is shown by the seals from Mohenjo-Dāro and Harappā.[37]

A bronze seal was unearthed from Sirkap (Taxila) and Marshall explained the bull as Herakles, trampling down a bull-shaped dragon.

The seals of Harappan culture were generally made of steatite stone. These seals are of square shape, with sides measuring 0.75 to 1.25 inches and with a perforated boss at the back for handling and suspension. Occasionally, round seals were also found which are comparable to Mesopotamian seals.[38] The seals were used for sealing and as amulets with representations of creatures, both fabulous and real, and almost invariably accompanied by a number of pictographic symbols. The carving was done with a small chisel and drills working out intaglio designs, engraved with a sun pattern so that the impression appears in relief. The seals were polished with abrasives. The finished seal was given a coating of alkali, which, when slightly fired, imparted a white lustrous surface to the stone. The seals provide a picture of relationship between Mohenjo-Dāro with the ancient near east including Mesopotamia. The greatest number of Indus Valley seals are carved with figures of bulls. The bull's head and body are shown in a profile where its horns, eyes and, sometimes, the hoofs are frontally represented. Rowland takes such depiction as conceptual rather than optical rendering, combining visual and tactile impressions of the subject. He, further, adds that the animal seals are among the world's greatest examples of an artist's ability to embody the essentials of a given form in artistic shape.

> These are not portraits of any individual bull but universal representations of species. The carver imbued his subject with an alive and vital character by his intuitive ability to define everything that is important for the nature of the animal he is portraying. The abstract organization of the folds of the skin and the muscular and bony structure are completely expressive of the massiveness and weightiness of the bull. It is this realization of the essential structure and character of the species that marked the universal character of the work of art which transcends the mere imitation or portrait of a single real animal.[39]

The observations, noted above, by Rowland appears as a very calculated analysis of the seals found from different sites of Indus Valley. What suprises the present scholar is the artistic acumen of the seal engravers. With little space available, they carved the figure of bulls in various ways along with undeciphered inscriptions with the help of a simple chisel and a drill. The steatite is comparatively a softer stone and, therefore, the engravers had to take more precautions during carvings. From the manner in which the bulls are carved on the seals, it appears that the engraver might have studied the animals from a close proximity. Otherwise, such a rendering of the seals could not have been possible. This proves that Saraswati was quite right in his observations, while concluding a series of works on bulls, buffaloes and bisons, engraved on seals.[40] He observes that a humped bull maintains a noble dignity and its mighty body surges with pent-up energy.

The metal casters appear to have taken pleasure in moulding the figure of the bull. Mohenjo-Dāro has thrown light on certain interesting bull-figures in metal. There is the example of a roughly moulded copper-bull, with marked hump. One of its ears is tied to a horn; it is not very clear about the other ear. As a piece of solid casting, the bull

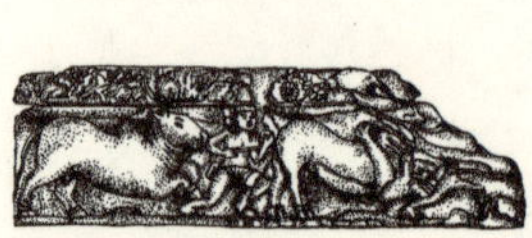

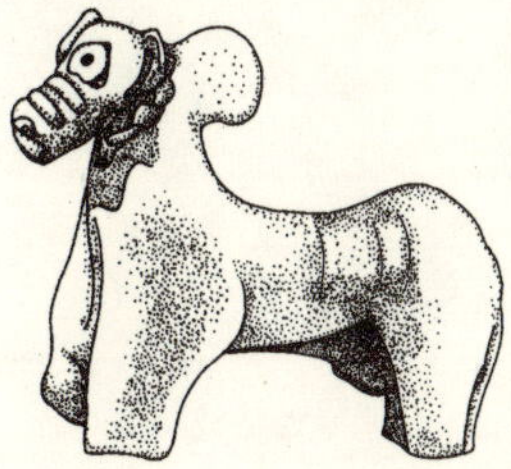

stands on a pedestal with a ring, beneath.[41] A figure of bull also appears on some copper tablets from Mohenjo-Dāro. These tablets include the figures of Brahmāni bull and, most probably, such tablets were used for certain religious purposes. Such a tablet may have been used as an amulet and one who wears this amulet is likely to get protection of the deity of which the animal is associated with.[42] It is interesting to note that the animals on the tablets always face right as if looking back over their shoulders. Among the metal animals, discovered at Mohenjo-Dāro, one finds four short-horned bulls and two Brahmāni bulls.[43] The site museum at Mohenjo-Dāro, once, had a figure of a damaged bull-like animal which was 2.5 inches high, and its sex-organ could not be clearly ascertained because of its bad state of preservation. A horned figure was also found in metal in Mohenjo-Dāro and it is presumed that it represented symbolically a divinity.[44] A copper tablet depicts a very rare variety having spiral horns of a goat. This was found from Mohenjo-Dāro.[45] From the Harappan sites, certain figures of composite creatures — partly ram or goat, partly bull and partly elephant with human countenance — figured on more than one seals and a few stone images. They might have been related to some cult-objects.[46]

Harappā yielded a limited number of animal figures in metal, most of which are in advanced stage of corrosion. However, there are a few which show cases of high skill, attained by the metal-smith. Harappā and Chanhu-Dāro came out with some wheel chariots but, unfortunately, the animals are absent on wheels. The Harappan metals, showing cattle, call for a comparison of the affinities of the animals in chalcolithic Kayatha and also with the terracotta bulls from Quetta and Zhob in Baluchistan.[47] Mackey draws our attention to a short-horn humpless bull which, he consider the finest among the moulded animals. Its standing attitude, its realization of legs and its bulkiness have been very deftly treated. Its massive body is featured by a summary modelling.[48] Mackey refers to another metal-bull from Harappā but its hump is not so well-marked. A tail-like projection at the back of surplus metal has been left unfinished (Mackey F.E.M., pl. LXXIX, 19; p. 308).[49] Vats drew our attention to a unique humped bull from Harappā whose head is found coated with deep red slip on which the decoration is found executed in black. This is the only example of a painted figurine and this was typical of Cemetery-H pottery.[50] The same scholar also pointed to a terracotta head of a bull, he discovered, with the impressions of straw, round the body, and horns, twisted. In another terracotta bull, he discovered the legs were treated in the same way as that of a hare.[51]

Dāimābād happens to be the southernmost site, associated with the Harappan culture. It is situated on the left bank of the Pravara, a tributary of Godāvarī in Ahmadnagar district of Maharashtra. In 1974, the site suddenly came into prominence as a chance-digging laid bare four solid copper figures. These figures comprised a chariot, yoked to a pair of bullocks driven by man (*fig*. 19). The forward projecting horns of the bullocks remind one of the bullocks, found from Chanhu-Dāro. It is important to mention here of the speciality of the found during this period. The alloy did not contain tin as was the case of Harappan objects. Another feature of this metal is that it contains arsenic, which is totally absent in the chalcolithic culture of Jorwe.[52] This chariot appears to have imbibed inspiration from the contemporary clay modellings and evinces remote relationship with the Harappan bronzes. The animals are modelled with rigid forms and they are endowed with wooden stiffness. Some scholars went so far as to identify the bulls in the chariot as *vr̥ṣabha* and the robust and the stylized charioteer as depicting Rudra, who was, subsequently, described in the *R̥gveda* as *rathapati* on a war-chariot (*R̥V*, 2.33.4). This bronze-chariot along with a few more animals have been a chance-discovery. Though it

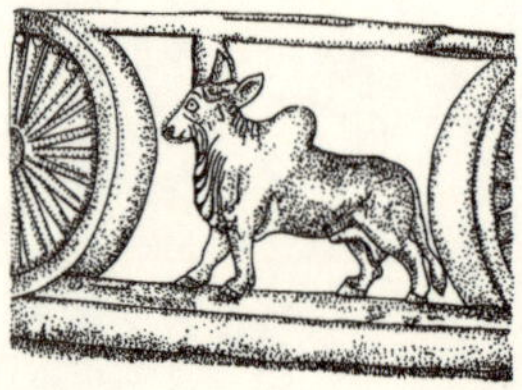

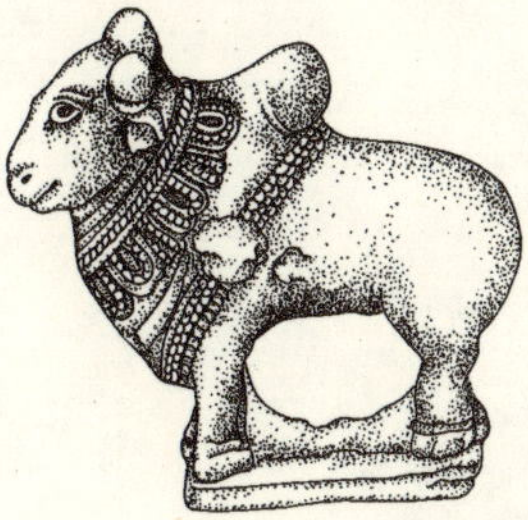

is very difficult to determine its date the site is found to be rich in Chalcolithic antiquities. Dhavalikar, while studying these bulls, observed that the hind parts of the bull look like those of a horse and the bulls generally do not have such tails as found in the case of bronze-bulls. The tail appears also to be that of a horse's tail. In their bodies, the said scholar finds some sort of a horse combination. From certain angles, the bull looks like a unicorn, which was very common on the Indus seals. The carving of the horns are comparable to the horns of bulls, found from the excavations at Kayatha in Ujjain and also of terracotta bulls, found from Chanhu-Dāro.[53]

The excavations at Lothal in Gujarat laid bare an extended Harappan metropolis. The excavations at Lothal exposed a number of metal objects which indicated that the area had an advanced metal industry. Among the small metal figures, one finds the figure of a bull. It appears that the seated bull with crossed legs was favourite the design for an amulet. The figure of bull is moulded here in profile while the face is treated in frontal position. The bull is shown seated with its legs double folded while its head raised-up.[54] Rao has drawn our attention to a four-wheeled terracotta figure of a bull from the Period I-A at Lothal.[55]

Kālibaṅgan, a site on the left bank of dried Ghaggar river (ancient Sarasvatī) in northern Rajasthan, exposed pre-Harappan and Harappan settlements. From this site, the figure of a short-horned bull has been discovered which was cast in copper. This is a Harappan specimen and it was realistically moulded and bears vigour, strength and, in look, it appears, somewhat, reserved. Realistically modelled, this copper-bull appears as if life surging beneath its skin.[56] This bull is comparable to two excellent terracotta bulls from Mohenjo-Dāro, one bull from Lothal in terracotta and one terracotta bull from Kālibaṅgan itself[57] (*fig.* 20). Kālibaṅgan also laid bare terracotta showing bull fight which must have been a source of amusement of the people, there.[58] The same site exposed some terracotta cakes with incised figures of horned human beings and animal-headed human figure. These remind us of the horn deity of Mohenjo-Dāro seal[59] (*fig*. 12).

The faunal remains in terracotta figurines and the seal engravings discovered from the sites of Harappan culture give a graphic picture of an animal world, with which Harappans were intimately acquainted. Dr. Agrawala, who studies these animals from the Harappan sites, observed that, of the total number of animals discovered so far, the number of bull-figures are much more than any other animal.[60] The most conspicuous animal and the most artistically delineated animal have been the bulls. The excavated remains of Indian humped bulls (*Bos-Indicus-linn*) were, perhaps, the descendant of Bosnomedicus of the Pleistocene times in the Harappan sites. Along with these, the humpless varieties were quite handy to the people of Indus Valley (*fig*. 11) who used both the varieties for ploughing fields, for pulling carts and for transporting goods.[61] The clay, as a material, was comparatively cheap and the modelling of this needed less skill than in the execution of stone or moulding in metal. Moreover, the clay has a plastic quality which can be handled without any difficulty. The terracotta figurines of Mohenjo-Dāro and Harappā included both human and animal figures. They were modelled by hands and they used the technique of pinching up and pressing down methods. In very rare cases, one finds the use of a mould. When a figure was made with fine and well levigated clay, a wash or slip was applied. Mohenjo-Dāro yielded a beautiful terracotta bull figure. It expresses its vigour and dash. Its realization is better than any representation of bull in copper or bronze. Dr. Lal also drew our attention to a terracotta bull with a mobile head (*fig*. 21) and appreciated the ingenuity of the artist.[62] Bangdel has drawn our attention to a bull figure in terracotta, which has a schematized hump and a halter

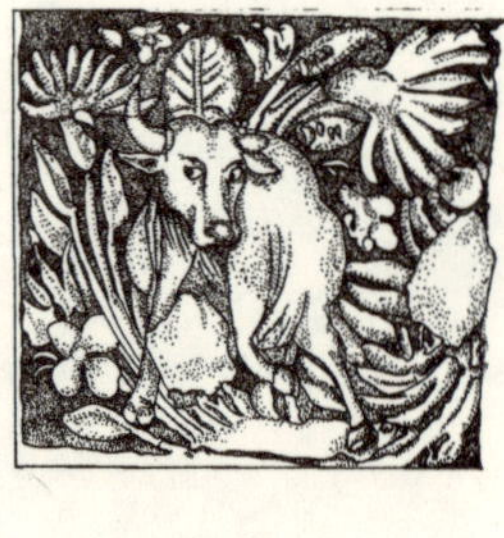

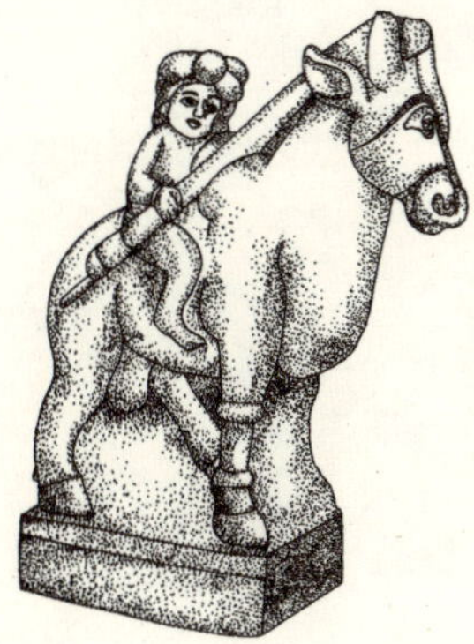

around its neck with rosette in the centre. Its eyes are made with circles of clay with pierced holes for irises. It has a flat tail[63] (*fig.* 5).

Marshall has drawn our attention to an amulet which bears a powerfully modelled young bull in terracotta.[64] Wheeler, in his book, *The Indus Civilization*, observed that

> in the repertory of animal figurines from Ḥarappan sites, the modelling is generally rough and summary, excepting in a few cases of the bulls, which, however, reach a high level of excellence.[65]

Dr. Rao discussed, in his book, both humped and humpless terracotta bulls which are found to be summarily treated. He, however, appreciated some bull figures at Mohenjo-Dāro as remarkable as they exhibit a thick neck and a prominent hump and dewlap.[66] Rao also pointed out two specimens of Brahmāni bulls with prominent dewlap and hump at Lothal.[67] The folds of the hide of the bull are indicated by incised wavy lines. The horizontal performation across its head was perhaps meant for fixing horns. Rao drew attention to another figure at Lothal, with a small hump, elongated body and exaggerated snout. To him, this indicated the arrival of a new species of the bull in later levels of Lothal. Such a bull calls for a comparison with painted bull on the red wares of Rangpur II-C and III. Lothal also yielded figures of gamesmen in various sizes. These terracotta zoomorphic figures are animal-headed, including the head of a bull. Such a figure brings out close similarity between the Harappans and modern chessmen and they can be placed, side by side.[68] Just like Harappā and Kālibaṅgan, Lothal also exposed a few graves. In grave number VI, a jaw bone of a bovine animal, most probably, a cow or bull has been found. Just like the Indus, humpless, elongated figure, Kālibaṅgan also laid bare the terracotta figure of such a type (*fig.* 7). A reference may also be made of a humped, elongated figure of a bull with long inward curved horns with long snouted face (*fig*. 9). A copper amulet with bull-figure of this place has been compared with an etched carnelian bead from Susa-D, and, on Indus seal with similar figure persuaded for a conclusion that Lothal had trade contacts with the cities of the Sumerian and Elamite civilizations.

The prehistoric and proto-historic potters decorated the different kinds of pots with various devices and decorative motifs. Of these motifs, bull played a significant role in their design of ornamenting the body of pots. Different sites in Baluchistan Kulli, which is situated in the foothills of Baluchi mountains, yielded, among many things, pots and potteries. The site maintained a geographical position of significance as it stood on the trade routes between the Indus Valley and the Persian Gulf. It is not surprising that the place would lay bare prehistoric and proto-historic potteries and potsherds. Piggot drew our attention towards the motifs painted humped bull with large "dot-in-circle" eyes seen on its elongated body. Painted in black over red, the bull appears to have been secured to the tree. The bulls are simply depicted with an exaggerated hump and with long horns.[69] Lal also pointed to this type of bull in Kulli.[70] Nindovarī, a site south of Kulli also belongs to a so-called Kulli culture, exposed Kulli style potteries. In the pottery designs of the said site, humped bulls are noticed in the Koṭḍigian style.[71]

Amri in Sindh is an important site which exposed both pre-Harappan and Harappan potteries. One can detect, through its available painted potteries, the evolution of the art of painting from a coarse beginning to a gradually developed form. In the paintings, cattle motifs appeared commonly, but though painted with red colours, no attempt was made to give details of facial features. Apparently, the outline was first drawn and, then, it was filled with colours. In the painted bulls, horns are drawn carefully and smoothly. The hump looks broad and prominent. In relation

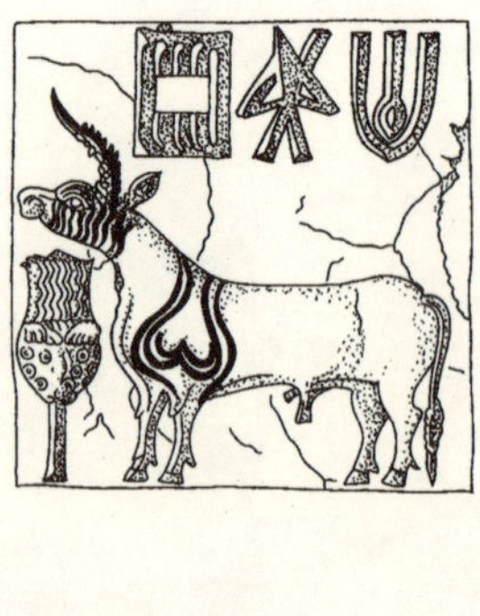

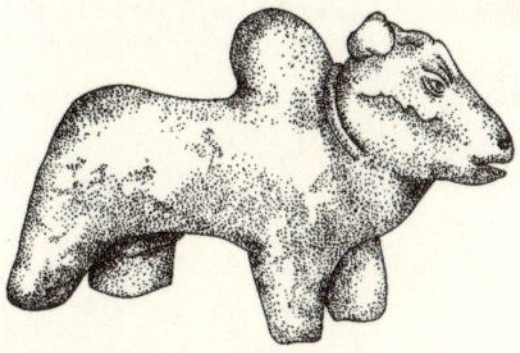

to the body, the tail is, somewhat, smaller and thinner. On such a painting, the painter tried to decorate the body with curved lines. On a pottery fragment from Amri, the body of the bull is found decorated with stripes just as one finds in Kulli. In another pottery from the same place the body of the bull is delineated with black colour and is sketched with red lines. The painted potteries that appeared in the stage 'D', show bulls with realistic appearances. Occasionally, the figure of a seated bull is also painted at Amri.[72] On the painted bulls, from the period I-C at Amri, Lal discovered evidence of Harappan connections.[73] The same observations have also been made by Shendge.[74] The potteries discovered from Zhob also yielded painted humped bulls in black and the figures are compared to the Harappan bulls.[75]

In the Quetta Valley, two sites were excavated by Walter A. Fairservis in 1950-51. These sites are Kile-Gul Muhammad (KGM) and Damb Sadat. The culture of this place was characterized by the presence of microliths and domestication of cattle. This neolithic culture yielded a kind of new pottery named 'Kechi-Beg'. The second phase of the Damb-Sadat, which is comparable to Amri-II, exposed pottery fragments with cattle motifs. The motifs were drawn in black on buff pottery, known as Quetta-ware.[76] On one specimen of a sherd, two bulls are seen drawn together. The humps are shown near the head and the horns are issuing out from the forehead. Their bodies are long and have a long tail but the legs are comparatively smaller. In another example, the hump of the animal is drawn with criss-cross pattern and the animal looks more like a goat. It appears that the painter's first intention was to paint a goat but he, subsequently, changed his idea and included a hump on the back of the animal. Sometimes, the painted bulls on the pottery are shown decorated with wavy lines, spots and vertical lines. Comparatively, the bulls painted on the potteries found at Rana Ghundai in Loralai district have some distinctive features. The bulls in this place appear completely different from bulls of other areas in Baluchistan. The bull's body here appears extremely elongated and stylized. The legs are decidedly long and thin. The hump of the bull is small but the tail is long. The potteries are wheel turned, slipped and painted in black pigments. Mehergarh excavations also brought to light a number of potteries and potsherds. The potteries of this place are of two varieties: one of these being a gray-ware painted with black, which is also called Faiz Mohammad grey-ware, and the other was the black and white type on red pottery. This latter type of pottery is of an earlier date than the types discussed above. The designs on this type of potteries include *pīpal* leaves and humped bulls with large dot-centred eyes and long horns, just like the potteries of Kulli.[77] The same would hold good about the painted potteries from Naushara, where elongated bull, with large dot-centred circular eyes, are found. About 20 km north-west of Kalat is a mound near a village called Togau. This place yielded potteries which are called Togau-wares. These potteries are well fired red-ware often slipped and, sometimes, appear blackish, produced under reduced heat. The potteries, marked Togau-A, show a farely naturalistic renderings of animals or birds. Usually facing left, these potteries are painted in solid black. The paintings include cattle and their figures were simplified, gradually.

Nal, which is situated in south Baluchistan in Jhalwar district, also laid bare a few potteries comparable to Amri I-D type. Such potteries are called Nal Ware. It is of fine fabric, wheel-turned and well-fired. The body colour is either buff or red or even greenish gray. The designs were executed in a variety of colours such as black, blue, yellow and green, and the outlines of the designs being usually in a kind of sepia.[78] On the fragments of potteries, one finds cattle motifs. Of the bulls painted on these potteries two types are noticed. One is very simple and another is decorated and more clear. The first type shows a bull with

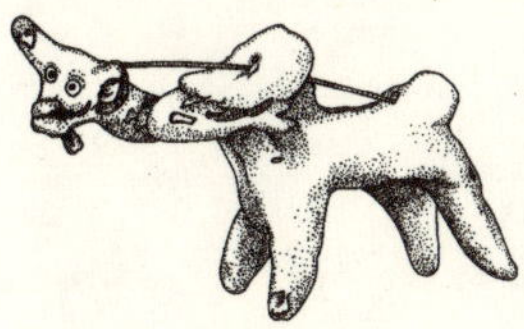

longish body in a walking posture. The other type shows the mature stage of painting with carefully drawn facial parts. The hump is prominent and body of the animal is drawn in lines. The Rahaman Dheri, Tarakai Qila and Gumlā in the north Baluchistan exposed a kind of a horned deity. The Period-II of Gumalā introduced a plain painted pottery, wheel-turned and the area exposed both humpless and humped bulls.

The valleys of the Indus and the Ghaggar (ancient Sarasvatī) and even in Gujarat, there flourished around the middle of third millennium BC a civilization which was named after its culture, the Harappa(n). The most notable sites of this culture are Harappā, located on the southern bank of Rāvī and Mohenjo-Dāro in Sindh. Vats excavated Harappā and brought to light extensive remains of this great civilization. The site was, later, on excavated by Wheeler and he discovered some potsherds which help the archaeologists to solve many riddles and problems. The area yielded black and red potteries on which the figures of bull appear. Vats exposed a number of potteries and potsherds. In one specimen, he observed a bull with a bird-like head, having a curious device around the neck. On a painted band on the body of a jar, he also discovered a bovine animal, probably a bull, with long incurving horns on either side of a beaked human figure. This creature is human, but for the beak and the wavy lines of horns. On the other side of the same jar between the horns of the bull, a trident-shaped crest is noticed. The jar possibly indicates to be a burial jar and it was related to a dead person. It is presumed to be representing possibly the same purpose as the Vaitaraṇī cows do at present.[79] Jalīlpur, which is situated 70 km downstream from Harappā on the Rāvī river, has exposed evidences of pre-Harappan culture and early mature Harappan culture. The Period-II of this place, which laid bare Harappan potteries, there are painted hump-bulls. Kuṇāl, an interesting site in the district of Hissār (Haryana) on the bank of Sarasvatī river, exposed a pottery repertoire, in which the Period I-A produced bi-chrome red ware using black and white colours for painting and the designs included bulls-head with highly curved horns, marked with three parallel lines of white and black colours, alternating in a rhythmic fashion.[80] Bisht, who carried excavations at Banwālī in the district of Hissār, Haryana, drew attention to two interesting potsherds. One of these potsherds has a beautifully engraved figure of a bull, while the other shows a canopied cart with spoked wheels, presum-ably drawn by bulls.[81]

Mohenjo-Dāro, on the other hand, could not produce a good number of painted humped-bulls on its potteries, though the horned-bulls appear, frequently, on the seals discovered in the area.[82] Marshall draws our attention to a round tablet. The one side of the tablet shows a short-horned bull and the other, a rhinoceros.[83] A pottery fragment from Mohenjo-Dāro, shows, from left to right, a file of animals, including a short-horned bull.[84] Another short-horned bull was found standing over a manger.[85] Koṭ-Dījī, located to the east of Mohenjo-Dāro and on the opposite side of Indus, produced not only a forceful terracotta bull but also the potteries of its Period-I, which goes back to *circa* 3000 BC.[86] Bālākoṭ, (Baluchistan, 4000-3000 BC) 88 km from Karachi, and to the west of the Indus delta, brought to light a culture which was characterized by a mixed type of pottery and the paintings of Togau and Amri varieties. Amongst the domesticated animals the cattle outnumbered sheep and goats.

Kālibaṅgan, which is situated on the banks of river Ghaggar in Rajasthan, produced some potteries, termed as Fabric-A. These potteries look similar to the potteries found at Koṭ-Dījī and Rahmān Ḍherī. The faunal motifs on the Fabric-B type of pottery, are painted in black and include among other animals, the bull.[87] The Harappan culture found in Gujarat produced stylized forms of bull, already

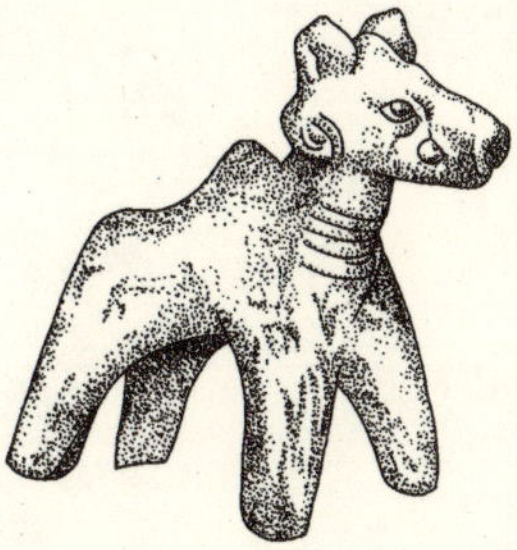

known in the Indus Valley and in central India and the animals are now drawn in an outline.[88] Sali has drawn our attention to the Phase-V in Dāimābād from which a hand-made huge jar was found close to a kiln. This is profusely decorated in applique designs, including figures of bulls.[89] It may also be referred, here, that a pottery fragment, which depicts a scratched-representation of a bullock cart from Ināmgāon, indicates that these vehicles were in use, there. The Neolithic culture of third millennium BC in south India covering an area from south of Godāvarī to Kāverī and the culture of these vast areas laid bare the evidences of the domesticated animals, including the sheep, goat, long and short-horned cattle and buffalo. There are evidences to suggest that in these areas the bullocks were used as draught animals.[90]

References

1. H.D. Sankalia, *Pre-history of India*, p. 148.
2. V.S. Wakankar, *Marg*, Sept. 1975, p. 32.
3. *Ibid.*, p. 29.
4. Vidula Jayaswal, "An Archaeological Evidence for Tribal Tradition in Central India," In *Facets of Indian Civilization — Recent Perspective*, pt. I, p. 46; ed. J.P. Joshi.
5. C.B. Trivedi, "More Painted Shelters from Madhya Pradesh," *ibid.*, pp. 50-51.
6. F.R. Alchin, *Neolithic Cattle Keepers of South India*, p. XI.
7. H.D. Sankalia, *op. cit.*, p. 127.
8. *Ibid.*, p. 86.
9. *Ibid.*, p. 84.
10. *Ibid.*, p. 107.
11. *Ibid.*, p. 104.
12. *Ibid.*, pp. 55-56.
13. S.K. Saraswati, *A Survey of Indian Sculpture*, p. 20.
14. J.P. Joshi, Madhubala and Jassu Ram, 1984, "The Indus Civilization: A reconsideration on the basis of distribution map," in *The Frontiers of the Indus Civilization*, ed. B.B. Lal and S.P. Gupta, pp. 511-30.
15. Stuart Piggot, *Prehistoric India to 1000 BC*, Cassell, London, 1950, p. 86.

16. M. Toshi, "Excavation at Sahari Soktta," *East and West*, no. 18 (1-2), 1968, p. 54.
17. John Marshall, *Mohenjo-Dāro and the Indus Civilization*, vol. I, p. 54.
18. Vibha Tripathi & Ajit K. Srivastava, *The Indus Terracotta* (Pl. XLIX-2; L-1,2,3; L1).
19. S.K. Saraswati, *op. cit.*, p. 11.
20. K.M. Srivastava, "An inscribed Indus Seal From Bahrein," in *Facets of Indian Civilization*, ed. J.P. Joshi, p. 98.
21. S.R. Rao, *Lothal and Indus Civilization*, p. 121 also G.J. Gadd, "Seals of ancient Indian style found at Ur," *Proceedings of the British Academy*, VIII (1932).
22. John Marshall, *op. cit.*, p. 389.
23. B.B. Lal, *The Earliest Civilisation of South Asia*, pp. 171-72.
24. Susan L. Huntington, *The Art of Ancient India*, p. 18.
25. B.B. Lal, *op. cit.*, p. 171 (Pl. L.VI-A).
26. V.S. Agrawala, *Indian Art*, p. 36.
27. S.R. Rao, "Worship of the Bull," *Memoirs of the Archaeological Survey of India*, no. 78, p. 216.
28. John Marshall, *op. cit.*, pl. XIII-24.
29. Gragory L. Possehl, *History of Research on the Harappan Culture*, p. 408.
30. S. Gorakshakar (ed.), "Mriga," *A Catalogue of Animals in Indian Art*, p. 127.
31. S.L. Huntington, *op. cit.*, p. 22, fig. 2.13.
32. *Ibid.*, p. 21.
33. I.K. Sharma, *The Development of Early Saiva Art and Architecture*, p. 11.
34. S.R. Rao, *Lothal and the Indus Civilization*, p. 92.
35. S.L. Huntington, *op. cit.*, pp. 20-21, fig. 2.12.
36. Papul Jayakar, *Earthen Drum*, p. 54, fig. 44.
37. Deepak K. Chakravarti, *The External Trade of the Indus Civilization*, 1990. pp. 109-10.
38. Sir Mortimer Wheeler, *Civilization of Indus Valley and Beyond*, p. 37.
39. Benjamin Rowland, *The Art and Architecture of India*, 1959, p. 17.
40. S.K. Saraswati, *op. cit.*, 1957, p. 20.
41. John Marshall, *op. cit.*, p. 506.
42. *Ibid.*, pp. 400-01.
43. *Ibid.*, pp. 398-99.
44. P.K. Agrawala, *Early Indian Bronzes*, p. 12.

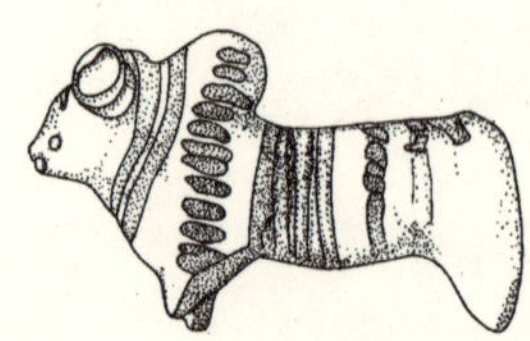

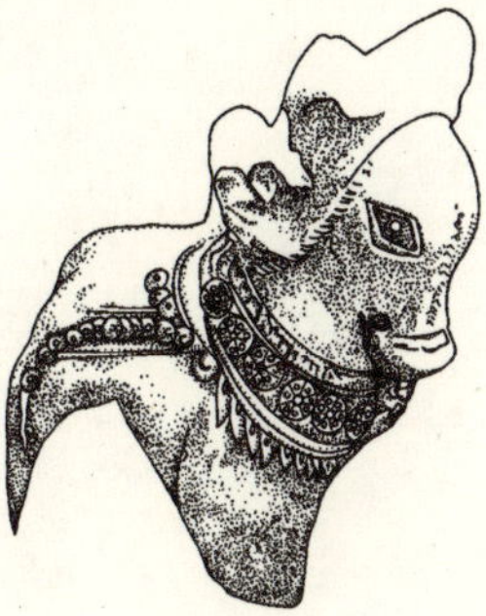

45. *Ibid.*, p. 24.
46. John Marshall, *op. cit.*, p. 66.
47. P.K. Agrawala, *op. cit.*, pp. 18-19.
48. *Ibid.*, p. 17.
49. *Ibid.*, p. 20.
50. M.S. Vats, *Excavations at Harappa*, p. 307.
51. *Ibid.*, pp. 306-07.
52. B.B. Lal, *The Earliest Civilization of South Asia*, pp. 156-58.
53. M.K. Dhavalikar, "Proto Pasupati in Western India," in *East and West*, New Series No. 18 (1-4) pp. 203-11.
54. S.R. Rao, *Lothal and the Indus Civilization*, p. 87.
55. *Ibid.*, 1985. p. 486.
56. B.K. Thapar, "Kalibangan, A Harappan Metropolis beyond the Indus Valley," *Expedition*, Winter 1975, p. 28.
57. S.R. Rao, "Further Excavations at Lothal," *Lalit Kala*, no. 11, pp. 14-30; also *Indian Archaeology, A Review*, 1961-62; Pl. LXXB.
58. Urmila Sant, *Terracotta Art of Rajasthan*, p. 91.
59. *Ibid.*, p. 222.
60. V.S. Agrawala, *Bharatiya Kala* (Hindi), p. 32.
61. B.B. Lal, *op. cit.*, p. 161.
62. *Ibid.*, pp. 171-72.
63. *The Arts of India and Nepal*, The Nasli and Alice Heramaneck Collection, Museum of Fine Arts, Boston, p. 26, pl. 17.
64. John Marshall, *op. cit.*, p. 43 (pl. XCVII, 23).
65. R.E.M. Wheeler, *The Indus Civilization*, 1960, p. 74.
66. S.R. Rao, *Lothal and Indus Civilization*, pl. XX.3-B.
67. *Ibid.*, pl. XIV-G.
68. S.R. Rao, *op. cit.*, p. 113. also, *Indian Archaeology — A Review*, 1962-63, pl. XVI.
69. S. Piggot, "The Chronology of Prehistoric North West India," *Ancient India*, no. 1. pp. 8-26.
70. B.B. Lal, *op. cit.*, p. 53.
71. *Ibid.*, p. 48.
72. Poonam Chitkara, "Depiction of Cattle Motifs on Amri Pottery," *Purutattva*, no. 9, pp. 92-96.
73. S.R. Rao, *Lothal and the Indus Civilization*, p. 169.
74. M.J. Shendge, "The Formative Elements in the Harappan Culture," in *Facets of Indian Civilization*, ed. M.C. Joshi, pp. 147-48.
75. H. Garden, *Bhāratīya Saṁskṛti Kī Prāgaitihāsika Pṛṣṭhabhūmi*, pp. 63-64.

76. B.B. Lal, *The Earliest Civilization of South Asia*, pp. 32-34 and also Poonam Chitakara, *Puratattva*, no. 9, pp. 92-96.
77. See B.B. Lal, *ibid*., p. 43.
78. B.B. Lal, *op. cit*., pp. 52-53.
79. M.S. Vats, *Excavations at Harappa*, pp. 207-08.
80. S.P. Gupta, "The Origin of the Indus Saraswati Civilization," in *Facets of Indian Civilization* ed. J.P. Joshi, p. 132.
81. R.S. Bisht, *Indian Archaeology : A Review, 1986-87 and 1987-88*, pp. 21-27.
82. J. Marshall, *Mohenjo-Dāro and the Indus Civilization*, p. 324.
83. *Ibid*., pp. 396-97.
84. *Ibid*., pp. 395-96.
85. *Ibid*., p. 396.
86. B.B. Lal, *op. cit*., pp. 63-64 and p. 88.
87. Urmila Sant, *op. cit*., pp. 77-78.
88. S.R. Rao, *Lothal and the Indus Civilization*, p. 45.
89. S.A. Sali, "The Harappans of Daimabad," in *Harappan Civilization*, ed. Possehle, p. 179.
90. B.B. Lal, *op. cit*., pp. 27-28.

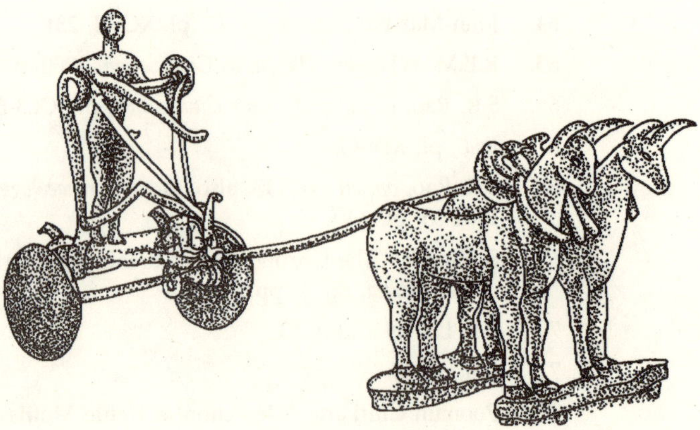

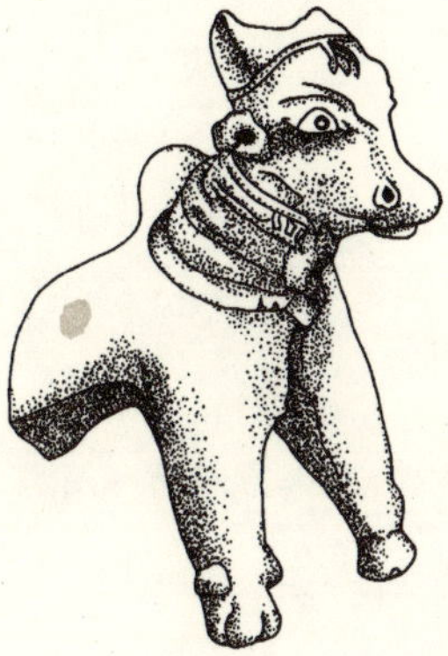

2

Bull in the Early Indian Literature

THE early Indian literature, both religious and secular, emphasized the importance of bull and its significant role in Indian religion and society. Unfortunately, the Indus Valley script remains yet to be deciphered. But the material evidences laid bare, as we have witnessed in the previous chapter, that, among the animals, the bull was given a position with a difference than other animals by the authors of Indus Valley civilization. Likewise, the problem of Āryanization in India is again a matter of dispute. The debates are still on whether the authors of Indus Valley could be recognized as Āryans.[1] If the Āryans were the authors of Indus Valley civilization, then, the Ṛgvedic culture could be an extension of Indus Valley culture and, therefore, bull, which was given notable importance in the Indus Valley, continued to get similar importance in the Vedic period also.

In *Ṛgveda*, the term, *ṛṣabha,* was applied to bull and the term appeared four times (*ṚV*, VI.16.47; VI.28.8; X.91.14; and X.166.1). The term, *ṛṣabha,* denoted two meanings — in general, it means the "great one,"[2] and the other synonyms of the word include *ukṣaṇ* and *vṛṣabha,* of which the latter is an oftquoted one and favourite to the extent that it replaced the term, *ṛṣabha,* on a few occasions. Yāska, the etymologist, is conspicuously silent about the word *ṛṣabha*, but for the term, *vṛṣabha,* he found its root from *vṛṣa,* which means "to shower," in general and to "procreate," in particular (*Nirukta*, 9.22, *vṛṣaṇād vṛṣabhaḥ*). According to B. Mukhopadhyay, the term *ṛṣabha* meant in the *Ṛgveda* as one having motion. The scholar also found an interesting feature in the *Ṛgveda* in which the letter *ṛ* was used as the initial position of a number of words, related to Vedic culture, such as *ṛk* (verse of the *Ṛgveda*), *ṛṣi* (seer), *ṛta* (the cosmic order), *ṛtvik* (Vedic priest), *ṛṣti* (Indra's bolt) and *ṛṣabha* (bull or sound). Incidentally, it may be mentioned that the skin of *ṛṣabha* was used in the drum and, therefore, the supreme sound resides in *ṛṣabha* and, hence, it is considered as the guardian of the demon, killing sound (*asuraghni, Jaiminīya Brāhmaṇa*, 2.404.)

The word, *ṛṣabha,* was also used to denote the second note in the Indian musical system (*Jaiminīya Brāhmaṇa*, 1.122; 3.131). The word, *ṛṣabha,* was used as the epithet of several divinities although there is no reference in the texts of its actual worship. The divinities are Indra, Rudra, Dyaus, Agni, etc. Agni in the *Ṛgveda* was described as resembling to bull that bellows. Rudra is called bull and Agni has been compared with the same animal (*ṚV*, II.33.8; *pra vabhrave vṛṣabhāya svitice*, etc., or II.33.6: *unmā mamaṁda vṛṣabho martvān*, etc.).[4] In the *Ṛgveda* (I.9.1.22) it is stated that the cows were produced by Soma (Indra). Elsewhere, in the *Ṛgvedīya Puruṣasūkta*, all the animals, including bull, are stated to be produced by God Prajāpati.[5] Prof. V.S. Agrawala discovered in the *Ṛgveda* the divine characteristics attributed to bull, and it has been discribed as Mahādeva (*tridhā baddho vṛṣabho mahādevaḥ*, *ṚV*, 4.58,3).[6]

The sexual urge of the bull and its passionate movements have been, metaphorically, referred to in the Vedic literature as *tisrovāca īrayati pravahniḥ ṛtasya dhītiṁ brahmaṇo manīṣāṁ gāvo yānti gopatiṁ pṛcchamānāḥ somaṁ yānti matayo vāvaśānāḥ* — *ṚV*,7.97.34. Although the bull as the symbol of fertility and strength is frequently referred to in Vedic literature and was under worship in several civilizations of the Middle East, there is no clear evidence of a connection between Nandin and any early bull-cult. Nonetheless, Coomaraswamy considers that the bull was

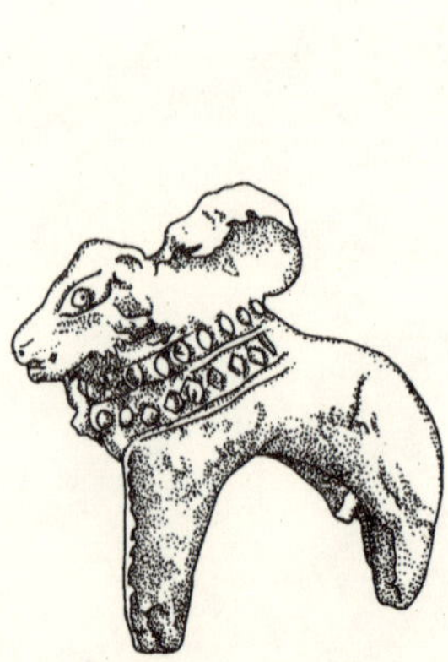

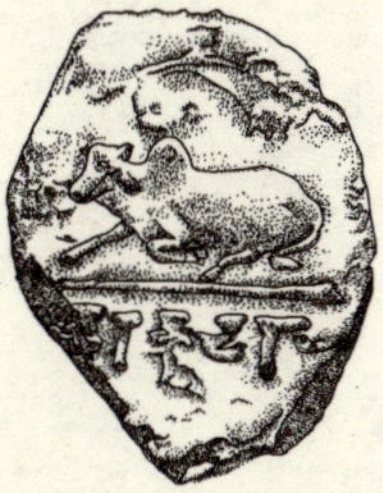

the theriomorphic form of Śiva, which represented anthropomorphically. Herman suggests that the animal-form expresses particular qualities more effectively than is possible, anthropomorphically.

Ṛgveda refers to the great power of bull and its contribution in the economic life of the contemporary India. It has been referred as how the bulls and the oxen are often described as helping in ploughing and drawing carts. The plough was drawn with 6, 8 or even 12 bulls (*ṚV*, VIII.6.48; 101.4). The *Ṛgveda* mentions to the caravan of bullock carts, drawing huge loads of wood from the forests (*ṚV*, 10.146.2; *vṛṣāravāya vadate yadupāvati ciccikaḥ*). The bull has also been referred to in the *Ṛgveda* as drawing chariots (*yadayātaṁ divodāsāya vartirbharadvājāyāśvinā hayantā revāduvāḥ sacano ratho vam vṛṣabhaśca yuktā* — *ṚV*, 1.116.18).

The bulls were sacrificed, occasionally, and, in certain cases, to entertain guests in wedding. The king Divodāsa was called *atithigva,* meaning slayer of oxen for guests and this proves that the bull's flesh was eaten by people. The bull meant for sacrifice, was tied in three ways and these three-fold bindings refer, according to Yāska, to its association with *mantras*, *Brāhmaṇa*s and the *Kalpasūtras* (Yāska, *Nirukta*, XIII.1.7). However, the term for cow, *aghnyā,* denoted that it was never killed or sacrificed in the Ṛgvedic times. The bull was also referred to in the *Ṛgveda* in the context of a composite animal (*vyāla*). The composite body of a *vyāla* included four horns, two heads, three feet, seven hands and was secured by a triple band. "It stood for the Great God himself and the *yajño* and is also explained as Agni or the life force in each living creature."[7] The following are the animals described in the *Ṛgveda* and *Atharvaveda*:

(i) *ṛṣabha* = Bison or bull

(ii) *gavaya* = Bos gaverous

(iii) *go* = Cattle, bullock, cow

(vi) *gaura* = Bos Gauras

(v) *dhenu* = Cow

(vi) *vṛṣabha* = Bull

(vii) *vṛṣa* = Castrated as a bullock.

Sāmaveda compares Indra as a bull. Indra is also called a "Tuvigrīva," having a strong neck (142). The said text also describes the sexual power of Indra like a strong bull which attracts the cows (*Sāmaveda*, 525 and *Ṛgveda* 9.97.7). In the *Śukla* and *Kṛṣna Yajurveda*, there are references to sacrifices, in detail. The sacrifice of five victims namely a man, a horse, a bull, a ram and a he-goat is discussed. These are the essential items of the *Agnicayana*. According to the *Kṛṣna Yajurveda*, the heads of the five victims are to be placed in the first layer of the altar and those of the bull and he-goat to the south.[8] The *Yajurveda* also points to oxen, drawing plough.

The *Atharvaveda* has a number of references to bull and the various aspects of the animal have been dealt in it. In a *śloka*, a reference is found about the domestication of bull (*kāṇḍa* 3, *prapāṭhaka* 5, *anuvāka* 3, *sūkta* 11, *mantra* 8). *Atharvaveda* also refers to *sahasra śṛṅga vṛṣabha*, i.e., thousand horned bull (11.1,12; 13.1,12). It also refers to terms like *nandī*, the bull of pleasures and *vṛṣabha dhenu*, i.e., bull calf. The reference to two-headed bull was first noticed in the *Ṛgveda* (4.58.3). The same expression is also found in the *Atharvaveda* (*dviśīrṣa vṛṣabha*). A reference has subsequently, been also made of the gods of eight directions. Yama, the god of death, is referred to as the presiding deity of the south and he is endowed with a bull (he-buffalo) as his mount. (Goetz. *German Scholars in India*: 1973) *Atharvaveda* (3.6.4.17.5) says that a farmer should follow the bulls at the time of ploughing. It further says that the farmers should keep the ploughing materials separately after the ploughing.

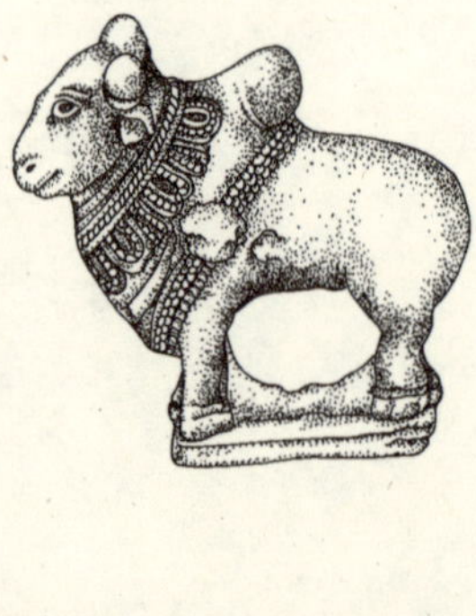

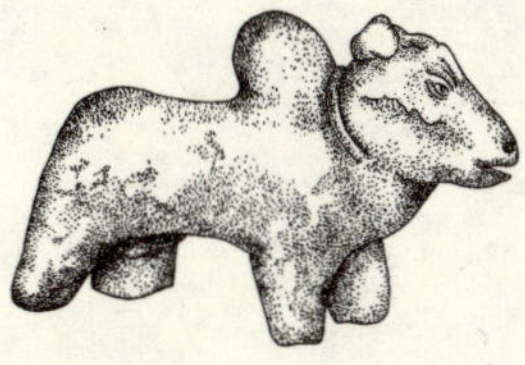

It prescribes that attempt should be made to keep the bull happy and, in case of extreme necessity, the animal is to be controlled by a whip. The bull should be tied with a good rope. The same text (3.5.3.11.8) refers to chariots drawn by bull (*udāsavo ratha iva*). The *Atharvaveda* also refers to a cart drawn by two bullocks carrying the dead body to the cremation ground (18.2.56); the same text mentions to the making of an ox from a bull by breaking its testicles (*muṣkavarho gavāmiva*, 3.5.2.9.2).

The ploughing and drawing carts by the bull have also been referred to in *Śatapatha Brāhmaṇa* and it also has the reference to the sacrifice of ox. The two-headed bull is again referred to in *Śatapatha Brāhmaṇa* (3.2.4.16). Curiously enough, a reference is found in the *Taittirīya Saṁhitā* about a bull of two-and-half years old. In the *Taittirīya Āraṇyaka* a passing reference has been made of Nandī, the bull-form of Śiva. In recitation of Gāyatrī, a reference is found on Nandī (*rudro rudraśca dantiśca nandiḥ samukha evaca*).[9] In the *Īśopaniṣad*, the sun as the lord of procreation is described as appearing in the form of a bull.[10] In the *Bṛhadāraṇyaka Upaniṣad* it is said that *ātman* was divided into male and female, and the female became a cow and the male became a bull and, subsequently, they met and had intercourse, resulting in the birth of horned cattle.[11] The *Aitareya Upaniṣad* (3.3), while analysing the types of life principles (*prāṇa*), mentions bull as being one of the same. There are a number of references to bull in *Sūtra* literature. In the *Pāraskara Gṛhyasūtra*, a reference is made about bull's hide, which was symbolic of fertility and prosperity (1.8.10).[12] *The Kātyāyana Śrautasūtra* gives an interesting information that either the heads of five victims in the sacrifice or their alternatives, made in gold or of terracotta imitations, could be used in the making of the altar. The *Baudhāyana Śrautasūtra* prescribes additional rules that for the purpose of obtaining the heads, the animal should be uncastrated and the heads of all the five victims should be coated with clay

(X.9). In the same passage, a reference was noticed to the cooking of sacrificed bull (*divyantaḥ vṛṣabhaṁ pacante*).

In chapter 8, *śloka* 16 of *Manu-Smṛti*, one finds the etymological meaning of the term, *vṛṣabha*. It says that it is called *vṛṣa* as it rains the success of all desires. *Vṛṣa* is also called *dharma* and one, who kills a *vṛṣa* is called by gods as *vṛṣal*. *Vṛṣa* or *dharma* is described as a four-footed animal and its four feet symbolizes *tapas*, *jñāna*, *yajña* and *dāna*. There are references to the chariots drawn by bullocks in the *Manu-Smṛti*. It says that a chariot should initiate its glorious travel, yoked by two bulls, and such bulls should look good, should have auspicious marks, and such bulls, that can run fast, should not be whipped, frequently. Such bulls should not have damaged horn, defective eyes and injured foot, and its tail also should not be broken (4.67). Manu says that a king should travel in a bullock cart. The bulls, in such a cart, should be well-trained, should run fast, should have auspicious marks and good colours. It further says that one should not ride a bullock cart, which is drawn by such bulls that are hungry, thirsty and ill (4.68). Manu also refers to the fact that if an accident of a bullock cart takes place what the driver should do (8.291-92). He says that, if someone dies under a bullock cart, and, specially, because of the fault of a driver, then, the driver earns sin of a thief. If one of the animals dies due to a bullock cart accident, the driver earns half the sin. Bull has also mentioned as a present (gift) in the list of dowries, as bull had been considered by Manu as a "wealth." According to him, in an *ārṣa* marriage, the father of the bride can demand a pair of bulls for the marriage, (3.29). This statement has been, subsequently, not recognized as a good action. Such a practice was looked down upon by the contemporary society (3.53). Manu cautioned in one place that, during the period of negotiations for a marriage, one should go for a better family than to a family, rich in the collection of cows, bulls, rams and goats (3.6). Bull has also been referred to in

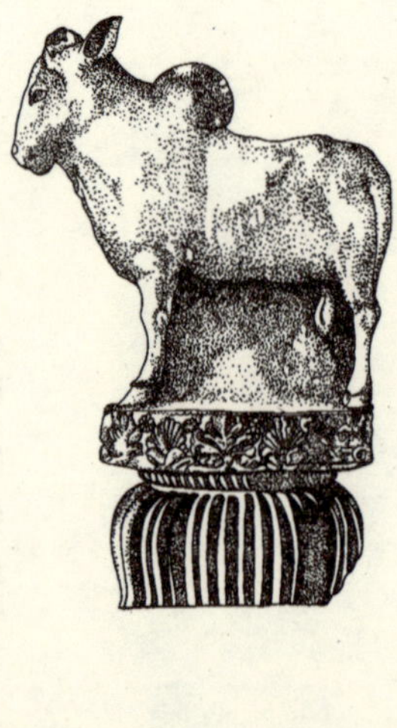

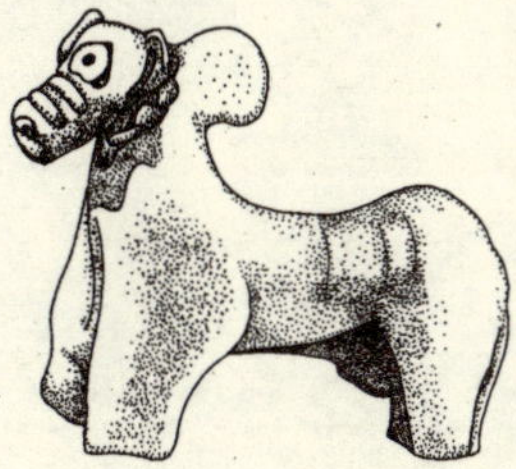

the context of agriculture (8.146). According to Manu, the bulls are not given any punishment even if it grazes the field of paddy or wheat (8.242). Manu further says that the bull, marked on its body with a *cakra* or *triśūla*, is normally used in the sacrifice (*vṛṣotsarga*). According to this text, a person can be freed from the sin of cow slaughter (*go-hatyā*) if he offers a bull to a brāhmaṇa (11.116).

Bull has been described variously in the *Mahābhārata* in terms of its implications. In the *Mahābhārata* (7.173, 30-31), the bull has been described as following:

> *kapardinaṁ vṛṣavartaṁ vṛṣanābhaṁ vṛṣadhvajaṁ* ।
> *vṛṣārpaṁ vṛṣāpatni vṛṣa śṛṅgaṁ vṛṣarṣabhaṁ* ॥ 30 ॥
> *vṛṣāṅkaṁ vṛṣabhodāraṁ vṛṣabhaṁ vṛṣabhekharaṁ* ।
> *vṛṣaudhaṁ vṛṣāsāraṁ vṛṣabhūtaṁ maheśvaraṁ'* ॥ 31 ॥

Further, *Mahābhārata* describes the bull (12.330.24) as —

> *kapirvarāḥ śreṣṭhaśca dharmaśca vṛṣaucyate* ।
> *tasmāt vṛṣākapiṁ prāha kāśyapo maṁ prajāptiḥ* ॥

With reference to this epic, the bull was given to Śiva by ritual skill (Dakṣa).[13] The same epic, while dealing with Maruts, writes about *vṛṣā kapi*[14] (*Mahābhārata* 13.255.12):

> *vṛṣākapiśca śatruśca havanodhe śvarastathā* ।
> *ekādaśaite prathitā rūdraśtribhuvaneśvaraḥ* ॥

In the Droṇa-Parva of *Mahābhārata* (80.1-29) a number of banners of *Mahābhārata* heroes are found enlisted with animals, on both sides. The banner of Kṛpācārya shows a bull (*govṛṣa*), like the great *vṛṣabha* of Śaṅkara. The bull's horns in the *Mahābhārata* are found compared with the prongs of a trident. Śiva is praised in the *Mahābhārata*. At one place, it is stated that he is a bull among bulls. Śiva has been iconically represented as horns of a bull (7.173.30-31). Reference is also made in the *Mahābhārata* of the term, Nandīśvara (13.25.21 — *nandīśvarasya mūrtiṁ tu dṛṣṭvā mucyeta kilmiṣaiḥ*). The term, *vṛṣabha*, was also used as the name of a mountain. (Sabhā-Parva, 2.19).[15] The same text refers to a term called *gomukha* as a *pārṣada*, a companion of Skanda and a Kuṣāṇa terracotta projects such an image.[16] While comparing different means of transport, *Mahābhārata* considered bullock carts as the best among the carts, drawn by different animals (Śānti-Parva, 186.20 — *paṇyānāṁ śobhanaṁ paṇyaṁ vṛṣirāṁ vādyate kṛṣiḥ. vāhūkārāṁ ca sasyānām vāhyeva hayaṁ tathā gavām*).[17] The bull's horn was used as a bugle for auspicious occasions.[18] A word *nīlavṛṣa* is also referred to in the *Mahābhārata* (13.125.73) for a black bull.

The lesser Epic has a number of references to bull. Before proceeding to the forest, Rāma gave presents to the brāhmaṇas. Such presents included different cattles. Vālmīki gave a long list of domesticated animals which includes bulls. Such animals were considered wealth.[19] Vālmīki refers to a number of auspicious animals assembled for Rāma's coronation, which includes *pāṇḍura vṛṣa*. The description of four animals namely elephant, bull, lion and horse are gifted in the *Rāmāyaṇa* exactly in the same order as we find on the abacus of Sārnāth Lion capital. There is a reference where Rāma has been compared as *vṛṣabha* in Raghukula.[20] There is a peculiar reference to Nandin, the bull, in which, it is said, that Nandin has a general appearance of a monkey (*vānara rūpam*). Nandī, described as *karālakṛṣṇa piṅgalaḥ*, is also called Nandīkeśvara. It is called in the *Rāmāyaṇa* as another incarnation of Śiva (*āparatanuḥ*). Nandīkeśvara stopped Rāvaṇa in approaching the abode of Śiva. When Rāvaṇa made some contemptuous remarks regarding his face, the latter felt offended and got insulted and, then, he cursed Rāvaṇa that Rāvaṇa's own race will be destroyed by the monkeys. Nandī, as a mount of Śiva, was first referred to in the *Rāmāyaṇa* (Uttarakāṇḍa, 16.8). The reference of bull in the *Rāmāyaṇa* is found as a metaphor (*yathā candraṁ vinā rātriryathā gāvo vinā vṛṣabha*, Ayodhyākāṇḍa, 14.54). In the coronation of Sugrīva, a reference is found to a term *ṛṣabha śṛṅga*. In Kuṣāṇa period *ṛṣiśṛṅga* meant a sort of bugle

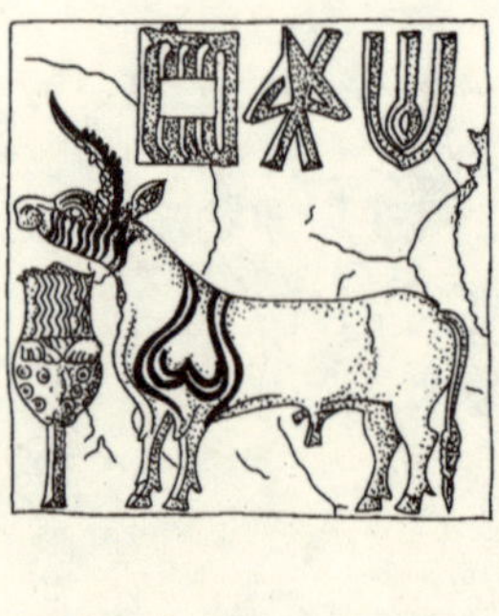

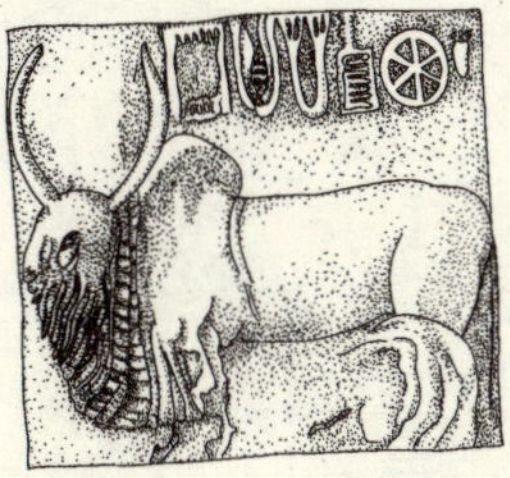

(Kiṣkindhā-kāṇḍa, 26.24).

Mahāmayurī text of third/fourth century AD gives a list of the names of *yakṣas*, which included Nandī and Vardhamāna; we have a reference of Yakṣa Nandī of Nandīnagara. There is also an image of Yakṣa Nandin in Patna Museum.

Bull plays a significant role in the Buddhist literature and art. In Buddhist literature, Buddha is, sometimes, described as 'Śākya-puṅgava', which denotes a bull or an eminent person.[21] The Buddha is stated to have been born in Zodiac Taurus (*vṛṣa-rāśi*). In *Divyāvadāna*, there is a list of 17 auspicious objects, including a bull (*vṛṣabha*). The same text compared Buddha as *vṛṣabha* (*vṛṣabhaiva gogaṇa parivṛto*).[22] Buddhist *Jātaka*s have several references to bull. The bull is endowed in the *Jātaka* in human values for baser passions of the beasts. The reference to bull in the *Jātaka* can be seen in *Cullakaliṅga Jātaka* (301), *Rājovada Jātaka* (334), *Sujāta Jātaka* (352), *Dalhadhamma Jātaka* (409), *Pañca-upāsatha Jātaka* (4900), *Kumbha Jātaka* (512), *Khaṇḍahala Jātaka* and *Chhadanta Jātaka* (514), *Mahākapi Jātaka* (516), *Sandhibheda Jātaka* and *Gaṇḍatindu Jātaka* (520).

In the *Dalhadhamma Jātaka* there is a clear reference to bullock cart for carrying cow-dung. The *Gaṇḍatindu Jātaka* refers to the ox for drawing ploughshare. In the *Mahākapi Jātaka*, there is a reference as to how an oxen, connected with a ploughshare, escaped from its master. The *Cullakaliṅga Jātaka* refers to a spotless white bull and, perfectly, black-coloured bull, which are only visible to the king and to none else. The reference to the choicest bull is made in the *Khaṇḍahala Jātaka*. The references to the four bulls, namely "Yūthapati," "Anoja," "Niṣobha" and "Gavāmpati" are also found in the same *Jātaka*. The *Pañca-upāsatha Jātaka* refers to a glorious white bull, noise of the bull's hoof and beating of bull and the killing of the bull, etc. The *Sandhibheda Jātaka* deals in with the friendship between a lion and a bull and how, diplomatically, other jealous animals turned their friendship into enmity and the eventual killing of the bull by the lion. Incidentally, it is pertinent to mention here the reference of the Chinese traveller, Yuan Chuang, about the Anatatta lake, with four mouths, and also the flowing of the Ganges (King-Kia) through the mouth of a silver ox from the eastern side. (From *Siyu-Ki;* tr. S. Beal, vol. I, pp. 9-17).

In the Jaina literature, among other animals, mention has been made to bulls. A bull is referred to as the attribute of the first of the twenty-fourth Jaina *tīrthaṅkaras*, Ādinātha or Ṛṣabhanātha. It is also said in the Jaina literature that, on the very first night, Marudevī, the mother of Ṛṣabhanātha dreamt of 14 auspicious dreams, including a bull (*vṛṣabha*). Besides this Śvetāmbara tradition, the Digambaras also include a bull in the list of 16 dreams, which Marudevī dreamt of on the day of her conception. However, the interesting fact is that, among the various dreams the first one dreamt of by Marudevī was a *vṛṣabha* and that is why the first *tīrthaṅkara* was also referred to as the one having the good attributes of a bull and the baby, giving birth to, was named Vṛṣabha.[23] It is also interesting to note here that flanking the image of each *tīrthaṅkara* is a *yakṣa* and a *yakṣī*, on either side. Incidentally, the *yakṣa* of Ṛṣabhanātha is even named as Gomukha. The *yakṣa* or the *upāsaka* Gomukha seems to be an adaptation of the bull-mount of Śiva: Gomukha's attributes are also like Śaivites, such as, battle axe, noose, etc. The face of Gomukha *yakṣa* is like that of a bull, Nandī, which is considered, in fact, Śiva himself in his hybrid form.[24] According to Ācārya Dinkara — *svarrābho vṛṣa vāhano dvirad goyuktaścaturthāhubhiḥ* (*Pratiṣṭhādhikārḥ*, 34.1). There is also a reference that on the body of Ṛṣabhanātha, a bull is marked.[25] Tiwari, in his book, draws attention to the figures of certain Jaina *mahāvidyās*. He pointed to an image of Gaurī, which, instead of standing on a mangoose (*godhā*), is shown standing on a bull.[26] The term *vṛṣabha* is also used as a name of a *yakṣa*.[27] Incidentally, in Kannaḍa tradition,

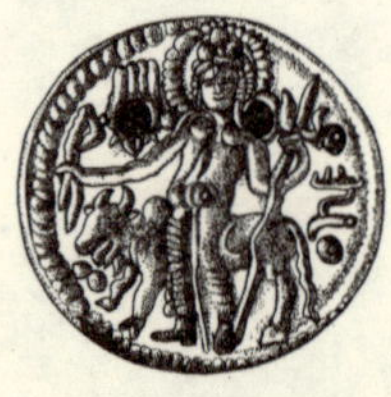

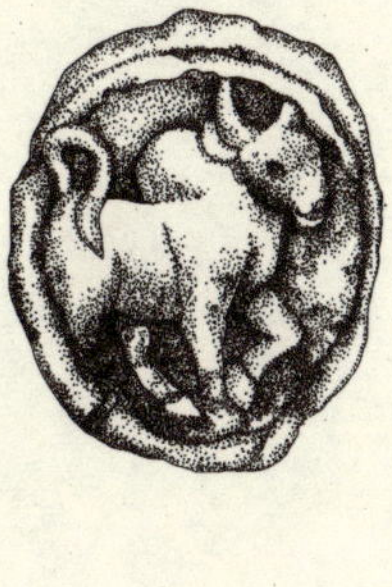

yakṣī, Jvālāmālinī, is provided with a bull as her cognizance (mark).[28] According to *Jīvābhigama Sūtra* (3.1.113), the earth is divided into four *dvīpa*s. The *dvīpa*, which is in the north, is called Gomukha *dvīpa*. In the Jaina literature, the *yakṣa*, Bhṛkuṭi, is found provided with a bull-mount. The *Nirvāṇa-Kālikā* (18.21) called it "Vṛṣabha," while the *Pratiṣṭhāsāra Saṁgraha* takes it as Nandī (5.63). Similarly, Varuṇa, the *yakṣa* of Munisubrata, has also been described in the *Nirvāṇa-Kālikā* (18.20) as having a white bull as his mount (*dhavalavarṇa vṛṣabha vāhanaṁ*). The same thing has been repeated in the *Pratiṣṭhāsāra Saṁgraha* (5.60-61) *vṛṣabhārūḍha varuṇa*. Among the *yakṣīs* in the Jaina tradition (Digambara) Kālī and Sutārā or Caṇḍalikā are endowed with bull-mount. In the *Harivaṁśa Purāṇa* (109.74-103) and *Vāstu-Ratna Kośa* (p. 32) *vṛṣabha* has been described as one of the auspicious marks.[29]

According to *Viṣṇu Purāṇa*, the bull was born from the belly of Brahmā.[30] The same Purāṇa includes the terms like *vṛṣabha* and *ṛṣabha* as proper names of royal beings (I.22.6; II.1.26-31). It may also be referred here that the word *nandīmukha* has been used in *Viṣṇu Purāṇa* in the list of *pitṛgaṇa* (III.13.3-6). The same Purāṇa also narrates the story of the killing of a demon named Vṛṣabhāsura (*Aristrāsura*; V.14.1-14). Curiously enough, there is a single reference in the text which indicates that Indra took to the disguise of a bull and became the mount of King Purañjaya (IV.2.27-32). According to *Vāyu Purāṇa*, Vṛṣabha was considered as the son of Kāśyapa and Surabhi, who was chief of the *gaṇa*s of Śiva.[31] The *Kālikā Purāṇa* (ch. 91) admits of the bull of Śiva as the son of wish-cow (Kāmdhenu).

The *Bhāgvata Purāṇa* gives a list of 22 incarnations of Viṣṇu, "Ṛṣabha" being the eighth. He was, in fact, a righteous king, deified as Viṣṇu.[32] The same Purāṇa, in another place, says that Indra got three sons by divine grace. Their names are victorious (Jayanta), the bull (Ṛṣabha) and liberality (Midhuṣa) (6.18.7). As the embodiment of virility, he is represented in the form of a bull, the perfect male. He became the mount of king Purañjaya and helped gods their fight against enemies (9.6). The *Mārkaṇḍeya Purāṇa* mentions a "Ṛṣabha" as the son of Manu (67.4). In another place, it is stated that, in the eighth *manvantara*, the earth will be ruled by a kinsmen of the sun, and will mark the coming of Ṛṣyaśṛṅga (80.4). The same Purāṇa describes Goddess Māheśvarī as riding on a bull — *māheśvarī vṛṣārūḍhā triśūlavara dhāriṇī* (*Mārkaṇḍeya Purāṇa*, Devīmāhātmya, ch. 8.14). The *Mārkaṇḍeya Purāṇa* makes mention that a house that keeps a bull, a sandle, a lute, or a mirror, can never become the haunt of evil powers (50.82).

Agni Purāṇa refers to eight auspicious things (*aṣṭamaṅgala*) that includes a bull. These auspicious things are necessary for worship. It further prescribes that these eight things are to be placed at the entrance of the assembly hall or other apartments (65.9). The *Agni Purāṇa* mentions of various ways in which earth is obtained, including the anthills, the tip of an elephant tusk and the horn of a stud bull (95.33-34). Such earth are used to purify the head of a king (218.14). The release or gift of a bull is also found mention in the *Agni Purāṇa*. It says that if a person releases a bull on the full moon day of Kārttika and fasts at night, he gets to the abode of Śiva. The gift of a bull is praised in the Purāṇa as — *mahiṣī dānacca saubhāgyaṁ vṛṣadānāddivaṁ vrajet* (211.6). Reference to bull fight is also there in the *Agni Purāṇa* (*vṛṣāṇāṁ yojayet yuddham gītavādyāravairapi*, 292.38). *Bhāgavata* (10.46.13) also describes bull fighting for *ṛtumati* cows. When discussing about agriculture, the *Agni Purāṇa* refers to the plough, drawn by eight bullocks, and says that such a plough is considered as rituals. The plough, drawn by six bullocks, is prescribed by those who make a living, thereupon. The plough, drawn by four oxen, is meant for the evil doers. And those who yoke two oxen in the plough, destroy virtue (152.4).

The *Bhaviṣya Purāṇa* records that the gift of bulls and

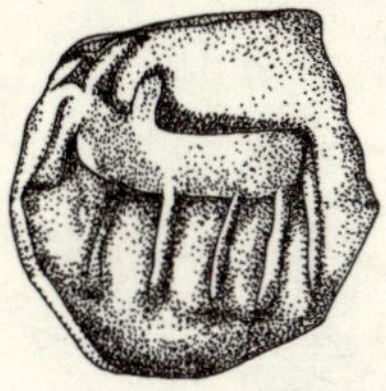

cows was a very common practice. In a ritual pertaining to the Navagraha, the bull is considered as an object of gift (Uttarakhaṇḍa 141.57-59, and 65). It prescribes that the ritual chariot of the sun god should be drawn by two white bullocks (Uttarakhaṇḍa 134.41ff.69). The *Bhaviṣya Purāṇa,* while describing the characteristics of a *yūpa*, says that this sacrificial post may be surmounted by a cow or a bull. The sacrificer acted as a bull during his period. He would drink and eat like a bull; also have sex relations with mother or sister (Madhyamakhaṇḍa, 19-21). For worship of Gaṇeśa, his figure should be prepared, variously. The figure may be made of clay, dug by bull-horn.[33] Finally, a reference may be made here of *Bhaviṣya Purāṇa,* (Brahmakhaṇḍa, 130.17; Madhyamakhaṇḍa, 10.1 ff; 20.9ff.) where a general directive has been given for the construction of a sun-temple. Accordingly, the ground of the temple should be ploughed with white bullocks, while for digging a tank, bullocks of any colour may be used. For preparing a garden or for digging a well, black-coloured bullocks are necessary. But the ground, that is to be used for a sacrifice, pertaining to planets, should not be touched by bullocks (Madhyamakhaṇḍa, 10.1-3). *Bhaviṣya Purāṇa* records (Uttarakhaṇḍa, 131.1ff) that the bull should be released on the full moon day of Kārttika or Māgha or the third segment (*pada*) of Caitra or the twelfth of Vaiśākha. The bull should be partly black and should have feet which is white like a conch. The same Purāṇa prescribes the release of a bull in case of the *śrāddha* of mother.

According to *Skanda Purāṇa*, the *nīlavr̥ṣa* (black bull) was considered Śiva himself, born of Surabhi, the divine cow. It is stated that, being cursed by the sages for being naked, Śiva was in a plight as his organs fell down. He prayed to Surabhi, who hid him in her body and, later, gave birth to him as the *nīlavr̥ṣa.* This Purāṇa identified Brahmā with a bull, like God Rudra, with Śiva (*vr̥ṣo hi bhagavān brahmā vr̥ṣa rūpī maheśvaraḥ*, V.3.181.19). In *Skanda Purāṇa* it is said that one should not circumvent being intervened by a bull or by a pedestal. If he does, he incurs a wrath (1.1.17.259). Like other Purāṇas, *Skanda Purāṇa* also describes the merits of *vṛṣotsarga* (111.213.71). There are certain references to the release of a bull. If a person deceives and abuses his father, he should release a black bull (1.3.6.19;18). It further says that those who performs the marriage of a bull, shall not have a sinful progeny in their family (VI.259.62). *Skanda Purāṇa* also discusses about the auspicious dreams of the riding on a bull being one (II.2.17.136). The same Purāṇa refers to different types of drums in the context of war, such as *dundubhi, tūrya, gomukha,* etc. (I.28.25-26; 46) which are made of bull-skin. The same idea is found in the *Brahmavaivartta Purāṇa* (Gaṇapatikhaṇḍa 33.35). This Purāṇa says that many bulls were born from the body-hair of Kṛṣna, one of which he gave to Śiva to become his vehicle (I.5.46).

Vāmana Purāṇa gave lot of importance to a bull. It takes bull as an auspicious symbol and recommends that one should see a bull before leaving home (14.36). It is further stated that the evil powers do not visit a place where there is a bull. *Vāmana Purāṇa* also notes that everyone should touch the bull prior to beginning his chores (14.36). *Vāmana Purāṇa* describes that the Capricorn should have the shoulders and eyes as those of a bull (*mṛgākhyo makaro brāhmaṇa vṛṣaskan-dhekṣaraṅgajaḥ,* 5.57). It also mentions certain epithets of Viṣṇu such as — *eka śṛṅga* (having only one horn), *vṛṣārcce* (to worship a bull), *sindhu vṛṣa* (the best of oceans), *vṛṣākapi* (the chief or the best of monkeys), *survṛṣaḥ* (the chief or the best of gods), ... *vṛṣāvarta* (turning round by a bull), etc.

The *Matsya Purāṇa* refers to various qualities of a bull and discusses its different types. According to it, a bull should have a prominent hump and should have spacious sides and waists. Its tails should be long and hairy. A white bull, having legs like a cat (*mārjāra pādaḥ*), having eyes like

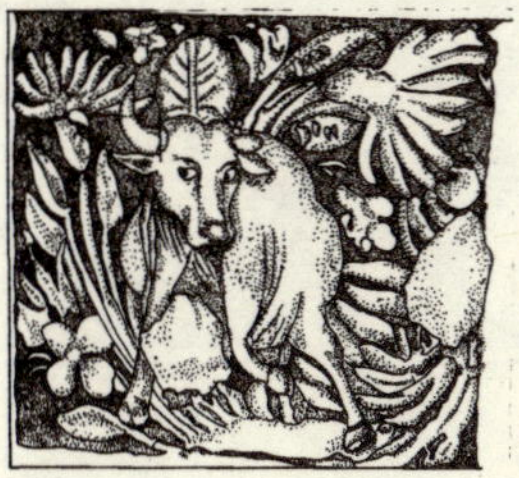

gems, is excellent. The bull, which is brown and yellowish, brownish red, having white feet is also considered as good. A bull having all its feet white or having two feet white and looking dark like a *kapiñjala* bird, is also termed good. Those bulls, whose roar is like a thunder, who are huge with auspicious breasts and have good height and appearance are set apart for praise (205.13). The *Matsya Purāṇa* describes such animals as the mounts of Śiva (260.25-26; 260.23) and a Gaṇeśa (265.36). The Purāṇa recommends that the figure of a Nandī should be placed before a *Śiva-liṅga* so that it could look at the *deva* (Śiva), *deva vīkṣaṇa tatparaḥ* (J.N. Banerjea, *Development of Hindu Iconography*, 1956, p. 536). *Matsya Purāṇa* (259.10-11) prescribes that Śiva could be shown dancing on "Nandī," and goddess Māheśvarī, riding on a bull (*vṛṣasthā*). It may be noted that "Nandī" and "Vṛṣa" are included in the list of Śiva *gaṇas* (265.42). The same Purāṇa refers to Kāśyapa Prajāpati, whose third daughter Surabhi was the mother of all cows.[34] It also records the merit of gifts and the release of a bull. It says that it is auspicious to release the bull at Gayā. It further mentions that the gift of a black bull is equal to *aśvamedha* sacrifice: *yajeta vāśvamedhena nārītvaṁ vā vṛṣamutsrajeta* (22.6). This Purāṇa, while discussing the great gift, refers to *gosahasra pradāna* as reference to a bull made of gold. It says that the bull is none other than Dharma and Śiva. If a golden bull is given as a gift, it will please Umā and Maheśvara (94.6). The Purāṇa says that the gift of a bull that does not belong to a giver, is not permitted. If anybody releases a bull, which does not belong to him, he is precluded from entering Heavens. Instead, he enters hell and suffers (108.22-23). *Matsya Purāṇa* prescribes the types of bulls to be maintained by people of different castes in the society. Such bulls can also be given as gifts. It says that the black bull is good for śūdras, golden for vaiśyas, red for kṣatriyas and white, red, black and grey for brāhmaṇas.

The *Garuḍa Purāṇa* gives a long statement on the release

of a bull (*vṛṣotsarga*) at a *śrāddha* ceremony (11.3.3). It says that when a woman enters fire on the fourth day (after the death of her husband), the funeral rites should be performed along with the "release of the bull" on the *śrāddha* day of her husband (*hutaśaṁ yā samārūḍhā caturthahani pativratā tasya bhartā dive kāryaṁ vṛṣotsargādi sūtakaṁ* (11.16.38). According to *Garuḍa Purāṇa* (11.18.17), the following gods are to be worshipped when performing the rites: "the worship of Amṛteśa" and *mṛtyuñjaya caraṇaḥ*. This Purāṇa (11.11.9.ff.) notes that if one sees himself in a dream . . . mounted on a bull . . . it is all due to the trouble of ghosts. It says that for killing an elephant, one should release five black bulls or a two-year-old calf of white colour (1.105.34). The *Garuḍa Purāṇa* (II.3.32) says that such a release may take place either in a temple or within a cowshed or on the confluence of rivers.

The *Varāha Purāṇa* refers to the custom of *vṛṣotsarga* or the gift of a bull. It also prescribes that, instead of an actual bull, a metal bull may also be offered. Reference are also available of a golden bull and a golden cow in the *Varāha Purāṇa* (211.20). The *Nārada Purāṇa* (XIII.135-37) prescribes that, if anyone wants to please Śiva, he has to release a bull in the month of Kārttika or Āṣāḍha and the day should be a full moon day. The word *mahiṣa* is used in the Purāṇa for a bovine bull and it is to be first marked with the figure of a *Śivaliṅga*, *śivaliṅgāṅkitaṁ kṛtvā mahiṣam yaḥ samutsrajeta*, etc.

In the *Śiva Purāṇa* the bull Nandī's relation to Śiva has been described, in detail. Its father's name was Śīlad Muni. By his meditation, Nandī became the mount of Śiva. The Purāṇa prescribes that the bull should be installed in front of *Śivaliṅga* and the worship of *Śivaliṅga*, without the bull, has been considered illegal.[35] The *Brahmāṇḍa Purāṇa* refers that the bull, meant for sacrifice, is identified with Rudra. It is said that "this lump (body) is created from Śiva, it has attained the state of Śiva; get up, O beast, you are, not unholy; you are, indeed extremely holy. As Rudra is the

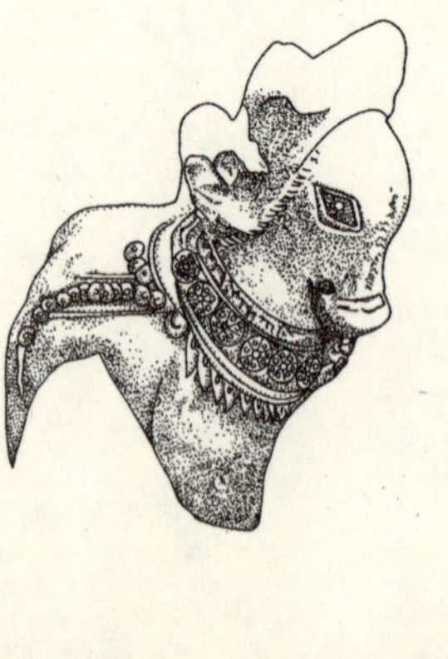

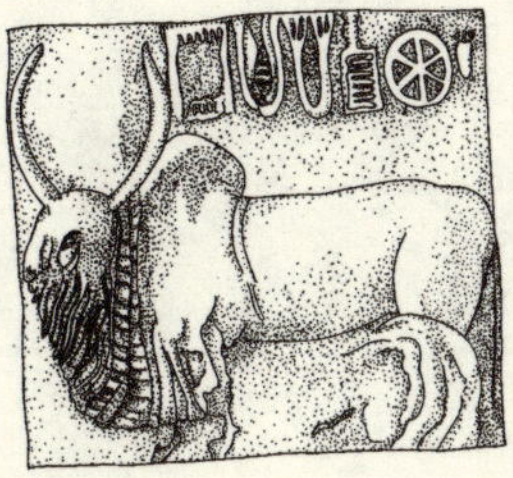

creator of the world and also its end, as he is beyond the world, so you are, Rudra, O Beast" (II.4.6.69-70). The same Purāṇa, while giving the height of various beasts and of the humps, says that the hump of the beast should be of 76 *aṅgula* (*śat saptati aṅgulaiḥ*). The *Brahmāṇḍa Purāṇa* says that the chance meeting of the following beasts, when starting on a journey is ill omen: the alligator, a diseased bull and a fox. In the *Āditya Purāṇa*, Dharma is considered as a minor *avatāra* of Viṣṇu. He resembled a bull (*vāmbhāge tu tataḥ kāryā vṛṣaḥ param rūpavāna*). The limbs of Dharma are said to be *satya* (kindness), *dayā* (mercy), *śānti* (peacefulness) and *ahiṁsā* (non-violence). The Sanskrit word *vṛṣa* means Dharma and that is the reason why Dharma is known as bull. When Dharma is personified, he is conceived as four-handed, carrying a lotus in one of his left hands and a hand placed on the head of a good-looking bull.[36] *Arthaśāstra* classified a bull in six general types such as *vatsa* (that which sucks milk), *vatsatara* (which, no more, sucks milk), *damya* (suitable for "ploughing"), *vahima* (that which can carry loads), *vṛṣa* (for drawing carts) and *ukṣaraṁ* (2.29.47.8). *Arthaśāstra* forbids the killing of a bull. If anybody is found killing a bull he will be fined 50 *paṇa*, gold or silver coins (2.26.44.13). The bull, which draws carts or chariots and runs like a horse, should be fed with more green grasses (2.29.47.39) than any other things. There is an oblique reference to the tradition of bull-fights in *Arthaśāstra.* If someone is found exiting bulls for fight, he should be punished (2.29.47.39). A passing reference has also been made in the *Arthaśāstra* about a hybrid form of a bull and a fish which emerges from the ocean (2.26.44.8).

Pāṇini, in his *Mahābhāṣya,* refers to the different types of bulls. He says, *vālo yuvā vṛddho vatso damyo valīvardo iti* (Bhāṣya, 1.11.13), "The cultivator used to select the type of bull to be maintained and termed them as ox." And it, further, describes how these selected bulls are specially treated so that they could gain further strength (5.1.14).

When such a young ox attains its youth it is called *jātokṣa* and when the dewlaps appear on its neck, it is called *pūrṇakakuda* (5.4.148-49; such oxen are found relieved on some of the sealings of Indus Valley, discussed in the earlier chapter). In their old age, such oxen were called *vṛdhokṣa* (5.4.77). The age of a particular bull or ox was determined by the number of teeth it had. If it has four teeth it has attained four years of age (5.4.141). At the age of four, the two sides of its nose were pierced (3.2.25). The age of a bull or ox was also determined with the horns and the size of the hump (5.1.146.; 6.2.115). Pāṇini further refers that those bulls which were used for drawing chariot were designated as *rathya* or *śakaṭa* (4.4.76), while those that used to draw plough, was called *yugya* (4.4.76) and those which were employed for drawing water from the well for irrigation purposes were called *dhūrya* or *dhāreya* (4.4.77).[37]

In *Pañcatantra,* the story of intense friendship between a lion and a bull is narrated. Their intimacy became a point of jealousy among the other animals in the forest, particularly, to a fox which plans and persuades the lion to kill the friend, the bull. Subsequently, the lion becomes repentant of its own actions and punishes the jackal who misguided him.

A number of references is available about the bull in Kālidāsa's literature. In the *Raghuvaṁśam*, Rāma's shoulder has been compared with that of a bull *vṛṣyanti vṛṣaskandhaḥ* (1.13; 12.34). In *Raghuvaṁśam* "Nandī," the mount of Śiva, has been compared as white and gleeming as Kailāsa (2.35). Elsewhere, in the *Raghuvaṁśam*, the mount, Citrakūṭa, has been metaphorically compared with the various parts of a bull (13.47). In the same text, the bulls playing, with their horns, are compared with the childhood pranks of Raghu (4.22). In the texts of *Ṛtusaṁhāra* (1.27), *Vikramorvaśīyam* (5.17-18) and *Mālavikāgnimitram* (4.15), references to bulls, have been made for similitude or metaphorical implications. In *Meghadūta*, Kālidāsa describes the bull as the mount of Śiva, and its characteristic features. "The bull is as white as

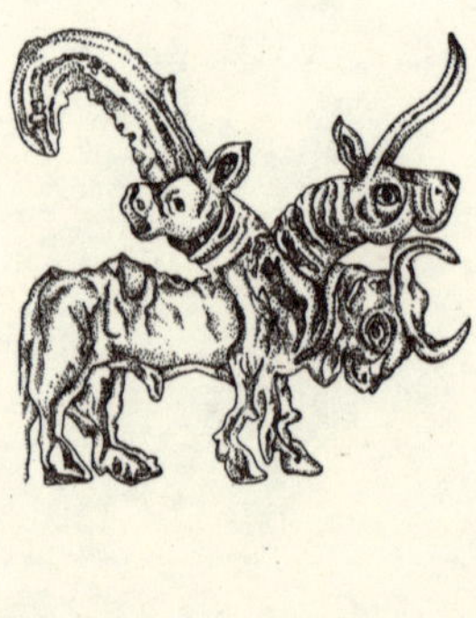

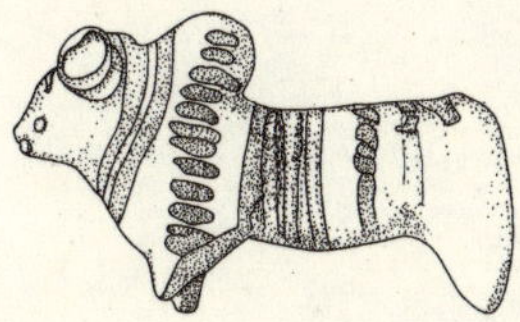

snow with a huge body and soft brown eyes. Its neck is thick; its horns are as hard as diamond and, with their sharp red points, they tear up the earth (1.52). It has broad shoulders, sleek sides and a black tail and is decorated with a golden girth. Its hump resembles the top of a snow-clad mountain." Kālidāsa, in the *Meghadūta,* identified *vṛṣa* with Indra and Kāma and mentions that when the fire from the third eye of Śiva burns Kāma then Śiva mounts on the *vṛṣa* and, for mounting on it, he takes the help from Kumbhodara lion (1.56). In the *Kumārasaṁbhava,* Kālidāsa refers to Śiva mounting on a bull (*vṛṣabhārūḍha haraḥ*) whom Indra salutes (5.80). Nandī is described by Kālidāsa as guarding the entrance of Śiva's abode at Kailāsa with a golden stuff resting against his left forearm and silencing the *gaṇa*s with a finger of his right hand, placed on his mouth (3.41).

Kirātārjunīya, the *mahākāvya* written by poet Bhāravi, refers to bull in a number of *śloka*s (12.20; 18.20; 4.18). He refers to bull-fight which was witnessed by Arjuna and the winner of the two has been compared by the poet as symbolic of pride (*darpa*; 4.11). Bhavabhūti, in his *Uttara-Rām-Carita,* recollects the story of Ikṣvāku, king Purañjaya, for whom Indra took the disguise of a bull and served as a mount (5.27). The bull has also been considered in this text as one of the seven rural animals (*grāmyāḥ paśavaḥ; aṅka* 4; p. 280). The same text also recommends the cooked meat of a bull for entertaining the guests. It further prescribes that the meat should be served along with honey (*madhuparka*). In the *Śiśupālavadha,* there are more than one reference of Śiva, riding on a bull (4.19; 16.58). The killing of bull or cow was considered as sin in this text. But it does not hold good for Lord Kṛṣṇa since he did not kill a bull but he killed Ariṣṭāsura, in the disguise of a bull (15.26 & 35). The text also refers to carts driven by bullocks and it also gives a graphic description of a bull after a heavy meal (5.62-63). There is also a reference to bull-fight in *Śiśupālavadha* (5.64).

Varāhmihira's *Bṛhat-Saṁhitā* refers to a number of terms which are having bearings on bull, such as *vṛṣa, go, gopati, anāduḥ, surabhitanayaḥ* and *ukṣaṇa* (XII.6; XV.16; XXIV. 35; XLVII.76; XLV.62; LXVII.115; XCIV.24; XL.3; XLV.55). The term, *gokula,* (IX.20; XIX.14) means cowherd and the term *goṣṭha* denotes cowpan (LXXXVII.9). The same text (between 61.9-16) refers to different types of bulls, such as, bulls, that cannot carry heavy burden, the bull which is excellent and can carry heavy burdens, the bull whose speed is like that of a horse and the bull which can carry heavy burdens and can travel long distances. The text also refers to bullock carts used for transport as well as for conveyance (VIII.3; XXXIV.5; XLII.21 and LXXXV.74). The chariots, drawn by oxen (*goratha*), have also been mentioned by commentator, Utpala (XLII.34). Oxen were yoked to a plough and used as the beast of burden (LX.9.14.16). Varāhmihira also refers to oxen, with eyes hewed like a bugle, a *mallikā* flower and a water bubble (LX.14). The same text (XLVII.44; LXXXVI.22) refers to a bull-fight and a bull-fighter (*usrakrīḍaka*). Among the animals, the text mentions about the flesh of bull which was consumed (LXXXIV.34-35). Varāhmihira, specially, recommends the ceremonial eating of the fish, the flesh of a buffalo, bull, he-cat, etc. (V.14; VII.16-18, 19,21).[38]

In the *Vsṇudharmottara Purāṇa*, the bull has been described as representing the divine 'Dharma' with four feet (*vṛṣo hi bhagavāna dharmścatuśpādaḥ prakīrtitaḥ*; III.48; IV.1-19). Like the bull, Dharma has four attributes (*catuśpādas*), such as application, defence, rejoinder and sentence. The text also refers to Mahādeva, mounted on a bull (44.14). The text describes about the Sadāśiva aspect of Śiva and the real face of the Tatpuruṣa identified as Nandī.[39] The text gives the iconographic prescription of Nandī. His body-colour should be red as vermilion, he should wear a tiger skin, he should be a three-eyed and a four-handed god (73.15-17). Of the two attendants of Goddess Pārvatī, the text describes Jayā, mounted on the back of a bull (*jayā*

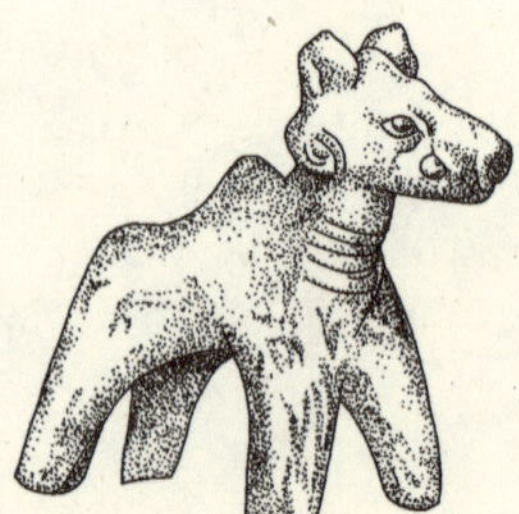

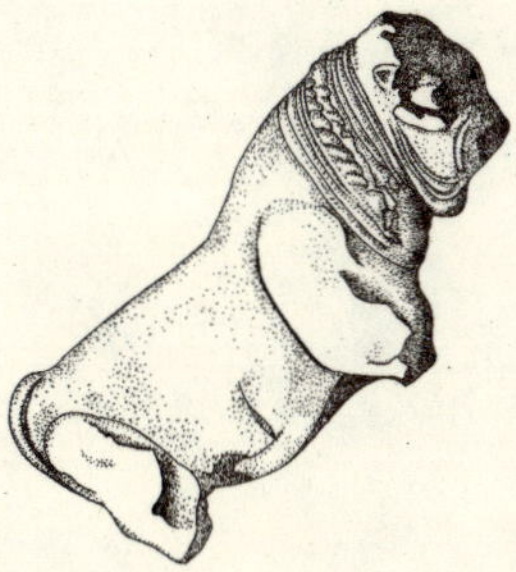

tu vṛṣagā; 67.10). The Purāṇa describes a two-wheel chariot, drawn by ten horses for Sūrya, one of the horses, being called *vṛṣabha* (68.4-5). It also refers to a goddess of the north-eastern wing, very old and white in complexion, who rides a bull (73.38). Īśāna, the lord of the north-eastern quarter, is considered as an aspect of Śiva and he has a bull for his mount. A goddess, called Śiva, is described in *Pratimālakṣaṇa* as 'Vṛṣāsana'. The text also refers to the bulls, with horns holding a treasure (*nidhiśṛṅgānvṛṣāna*, *Citrasūtra*, 43.15-16). The text recommends bull, as the mount for the God, Tumburu (*Pratimālakṣaṇa*, 67.1). In the Citrasūtra of *Viṣṇudharmottara,* it is mentioned that the bulls, lions and other animals, including birds, are to be depicted in their natural surroundings and in close proximity to what is observed in nature (42.46). *Pratimālakṣaṇa* says that the worn-out or old and damaged image of god should be taken away after tying with the rope to the hump of a bull.

In the *Vaikhānasāgama,* while discussing the architecture of the temple, reference to the *vṛṣavāhana* and *vṛṣadhvaja* have been made in the context of the iconographic features of *dvāradevatāḥ* and *parivāradevatāḥ*.[40] *Amarakośa* refers to Indra as "Vṛṣa" (1.42). The writer of this text also refers to the bull while describing Śiva and Vṛṣadhvaja (I.34). He has also the knowledge of Zodiac Taurus (*vṛṣa rāśi*, 3.3.220). The terms, like Nandī and Nandīśvara, also referred in *Amarakośa* (I.21). In *Mānasāra*[41] there is a detailed description of the iconographic features (*lakṣaṇa*) of the bull.

वृषभ लक्षणम्ः

वृषभस्य लक्षणं सम्यगवक्ष्यते विधिनाधुना।
वायोरभिमुखं स्थाप्य (पयेत्) पीठे वाथोत्सवेपि (पपीठे) वा॥ १॥

विमाने मण्डपे वापि चारोपरि परिन्यसेत्।
द्वार तुङ्ग्ग समं श्रेष्ठं त्रिभागं मध्यमं भवेत्॥ २॥

कन्यसं द्विभागं स्या त्रिविधं वृषभोदयम्।
एक हस्तं समारभ्य ए (चै) क हस्तेन वर्धनात्॥ ३॥

नवहस्तात्त मुत्सेधं कन्यसादि त्रयं त्रयम्।
पञ्चविंशाङ्गुलमारभ्य द्विध्वङ्गुल विवर्धनात्॥ ४॥

एक त्रिंसति मात्रान्तं यः (यत्) शुभायादि संभवम्।
वेसेत्सेध समं श्रेष्ठं कर्णान्तं मध्यमं भवेत्॥ ५॥

वाध्वन्तं कन्यसं प्रोक्तमुत्सवं वृषभोदयम्।
पीठायामें त्रिभागैकं पीठतार समं तु वा॥ ६॥

पीठतारं त्रिपादं स्यात्रिविधं वृष भोदयम।
पादादुष्णीष सीमान्तं स्थानकं मान संग्रहम॥ ७॥

स्थानकं शयनं वापि लोहजे वा शिलेऽथवा।
दार्वाभास रत्नेन सुधामृत कट शर्करा (भिः)॥ ८॥

घनं वाप्यघनं वापि कुर्यात्तु शिल्पि (ल्प) वित्तमः।
एवं तु वृषभोत्सेधं पञ्चादशाङ्गुलं भवेत्॥ ९॥

उष्णीषात्तु गलाग्रान्तं दशमात्रं पशस्यते।
तस्याधो वसुभागं स्याद ग्रीवतुङ्ग मिति स्मृतम्॥ १०॥

तस्याधो चो (धश्चो) रू मूलान्तं षोडशाङ्गुल मेव च।
षडङ्गुलं चोरुदीर्घं (दैर्घ्यं) द्विमात्रं जातु तुङ्गकम्॥ ११॥

जङ्घा चोम् (ङ्घाया ऊ) रू समंदीर्घं (दैर्घ्यं) क्षुरोत्सेधं द्विमात्रकम्।
ग्रीवात्तु पुच्छमूलान्तं चत्वारि शाङ्गुलायतम्॥ १२॥

शृङ्गा यामं युगाङ्गुल्यं शृङ्ग्र तारं त्रिमात्रकम्।
तदष्टां शैकभागं स्यात् श्र (च्छृ) ङ्गाग्रस्य विशालकम्॥ १३॥

का (मा) लतारं नवाङ्गुल्यं मुखतारं शराङ्गुलम्।
तत्समं चोच्छयं कुर्यान्ने त्रायामं द्वयाङ्गुलम्॥ १४॥

अत्य (ध्य) र्धाङ्गुलमुत्सेधं निर्गमं सा (चा) र्धमात्रकम्।
नेत्रमध्ये मुखायाया ममष्टाङ्गुल मिति स्मृतम्॥ १५॥

तस्मात्कृकर (काटि) कान्तं स्थात्षण्मात्र तदुहाहुतम्।
शृग (शृङ्ग) मध्यं युगाङ्गुल्यं मालतुङ्गं तथैव च॥ १६॥

नेत्रान्मू (न्ताच्चैवमू) लान्तं वसदमात्रान्तरं भवेत्।
शरांशं श्रोत्रदीर्घं (र्घ्यं) स्याच्छोत्रमूलं द्विमात्रकम्॥ १७॥

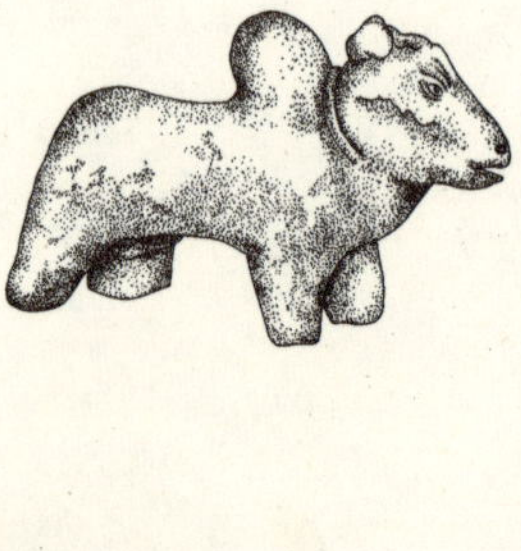

तत्समं विस्तृतं चैव मध्यतारं युगाङ्गुलम्।
शिवाङ्गुला (लय) ग्रविस्तारं यथाह (ना) लमर्धाङ्गुलम्॥ १८॥

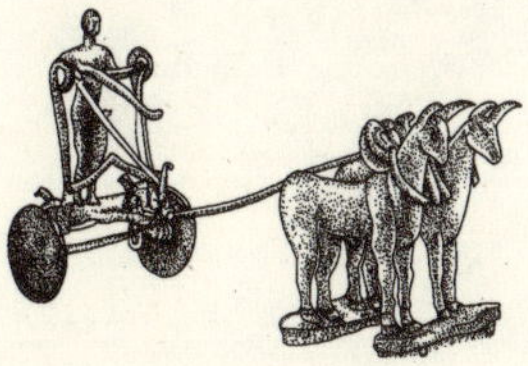

अत्य (ध्य) र्धाङ्गुलं संप्रोक्तं नासिकायाममेव च।
अङ्गुलं सु (पि) र विस्तारं तत्समं नासिकाग्रकम्॥ १९॥

पञ्चाङ्गुलं (लया) स्यायतं स्यादुत्तरोष्ठं त्रिमात्रकम्।
अधरोष्ठं त्रिमात्रं स्याज्जिहवायामं गुणांशकम्॥ २०॥

तद्विस्तारं द्विमात्रंस्यात्तदर्धं तद् धनं भवेत्।
ग्रीवतारं तु पंञ्चाशं मूलतारं त्रिमात्रकम्॥ २१॥

पृष्ठग्रीवस्य मूले तु धनमष्टाङ्गुलं भवेत्।
अग्रं षडङ्गुलं चैव कुर्याद् वासं षडङ्गुलम्॥ २२॥

तदुत्सेधं चतुर्मात्रं ग्रीवात्वे (यां) लम्बनं बुधः।
मूलमध्याग्र विस्तारं वेदवद्ध (न्धु) कलाङ्गुलम्॥ २३॥

घनमष्टाङ्गुलसंयुक्तं कुर्यात्तत्रैव योजयेत्।
ग्रीवस्य (वाया) पुरतो बिम्बं मूल व्यास (सं) द्वयाङ्गुलम्॥ २४॥

हृदया स्निग्ध पर्यन्तं तत्रो (द्) च्चं द्विर्न (द्विन) वाङ्गुलम्।
पृष्ठोच्चं मनुमात्रं स्यात्पृष्ठतारं चतुस्त्रयम्॥ २५॥

पृष्ठोरुमूल विस्तारं दशमात्रं प्रशस्यते।
मध्यमं चाष्ट मात्रं स्यादग्रं तु चतुरङ्गुलम्॥ २६॥

शराङ्गुलं चोरुदीर्घं (दैर्घ्यं) स्याज्जानुतुङ्ग कलाङ्गुलम्।
जङ्घायामं शराङ्गुल्यं खुरतुङ्गं द्विमात्रकम्॥ २७॥

सार्धवध्यङ्गुलं जानुविस्तारं परिकीर्तितम्।
खुरायामं द्विमात्रं स्यात्पुच्छमूलं द्विमात्रकम्॥ २८॥

अपरोरू द्वयोर्मध्ये मुष्क शेषोदरान्वितम्।
स्कन्धतारं षडङ्गुल्यं तस्याधो (धऊ) रूविशालकम्॥ २९॥

मूलं मेदाङ्गुलं प्रोक्त भग्रस्या (ग्रंस्याद्) र्ध गुणाङ्गुलम्।
जानुतारं गुणाङ्गुल्यं तथो (था) जङ्घा विशालकम्॥ ३०॥

सार्घं (चार्घ) द्वयङ्गुलयोर्मध्ये तत्समं तत्खुरं भवेत्।
शेषं युक्तया च संयुक्तं श्वेत वर्णे (न) शोभितम्॥ ३१॥

श्वेत वर्ण निभं भद्रमग्रं हि कृष्ण सधूमवत्॥ ३२॥

वेद पाद खुरैरपि कर्णयोः, श्वेतरक्त समग्र मनोहरम्।
शङ्ख शल्यैः क्षणभ रक्तं च माला, कर्ण बन्धैः कर्णरुद्राक्षमाला॥ ३३॥

अन्यैर्युक्तं किंशुक पुष्पमालैः (लाभिः)
वंशस्योर्ध्वे व्याघ्र चर्माभिरामम्।
मृङ्गकोलकललाट पट्टधृक्
पत्रवल्लि (ल्लीं) बहुरत्न शोभितम्॥ ३४॥

कर्णयोर्वपुर (पुः)पाश्र्व चामरैः
पादनूपुरसभूषणान्वितम्॥ ३५॥

इतिमानसारे वास्तुशास्त्रे वृषभ लक्षण विधानं नाम द्विषष्टितमोऽध्यायः॥

References

1. B.B. Lal, Ṛgvedic Aryans, "The debate must go on" in *East and West*, vol. 48, no. 3-4, Dec. 1998, pp. 439-48.
2. Bisvanath Mukhopadhyay, "Ṛṣabha," in *Visvesvaranand Indological Journal*, vol. XVIII, Parts I-II; 1980. pp. 39-42.
3. O.P. Sharma, "The Bull in Indian Art and Literature," *Journal of the Uttar Pradesh Historical Society*, vol. V (N.S.) p. 25.
4. J.N. Banerjea, *Development of Hindu Iconography*, p. 51.
5. *Tasmādaśva ajāyanta me ke cobhayā dataḥ gāvo he jagyire asmāttasyājātā ajāvayaḥ* II. M.M. Giridhar Sharma Chuturvedi; *Vaidic Vigyan aura Bharatiya Sanskriti*, p. 94.
6. V.S. Agrawala, *Bhāratīya Kalā*, pp. 44-45.
7. V.S. Agrawala, in Forward of the *Vyala figures on the Medieval Temple of India* by M.A. Dhaky, pp. 6-7.
8. *Śatapatha Brāhmaṇa*, VIII.5.2, 18, 19.
9. J.N. Banerjea, *op.cit.*, p. 576.
10. Alain Danielau, *Hindu Polytheism*, p. 93.
11. S. Chattopadhyaya, *The evolution of thematic sects in Ancient India*, Calcutta, 1962, p. 133.
12. R.B. Pandeya, *Hindu Samskaras*, p. 383.
13. Alain Danielau, *op.cit.*, p. 290.
14. *Ibid*, p. 105.
15. V.S. Agrawala, *Bhāratīya Kalā*, p. 102.
16. S.P. Sukla, *Bulletin of Museums & Archaeology in U.P.*, no. 4, December 1969, p. 33.
17. V.S. Agrawala, *Pāṇini Kālīna Bhāratavarṣa*, p. 195.
18. V.S. Agrawala, *Bhāratīya Kalā*, p. 407.
19. K. Bharath Iyer, *Animals in Indian Sculpture*, p. 9.
20. *Rāmāyaṇa*, Balkāṇḍa, Sarga 21, *śloka* 22.

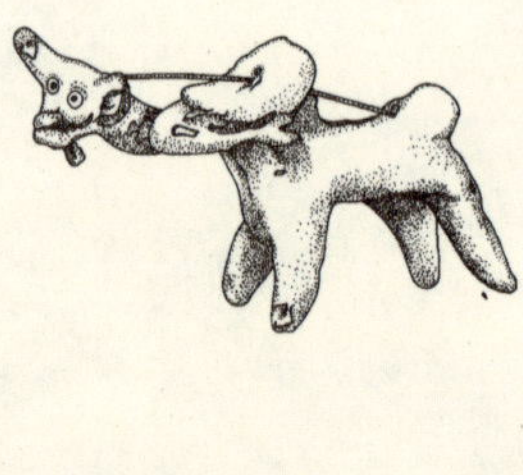

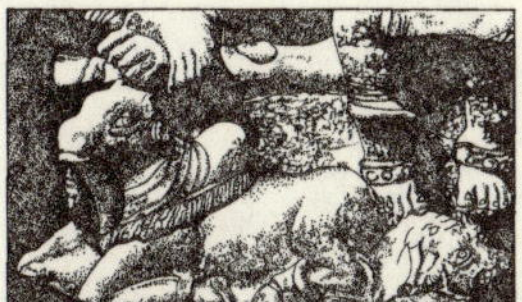

21. Benjamin Rowland, *The Art and Architecture of India*, p. 49, no. 13; *J.U.P.H.S.* (1957-I) p. 28.
22. V.S. Agrawala, *Cakradhvaja*, p. 34.
23. *Āvaśyaka Cūrṇi*, p. 151.
24. J.N. Banerjea, *op.cit.*, p. 562.
25. U.P. Shah, "Beginnings of Jaina Iconography," in *Bulletin of Museums & Archaeology in U.P.*, no. 9, p. 6.
26. *Jain Pratima Vigyan*, p. 149.
27. U.P. Shah (ed.), *Aspects of Jain Art and Architecture*, pp. 26-27.
28. *Ibid.*, p. 3.
29. V.S. Agrawala, *Bhāratīya Kalā*, p. 402.
30. K. Bharath Iyer, *op.cit.*, p. 8.
31. V.S. Upadhyaya, *Bhāratīya Vyaktikoṣa*, p. 118.
32. Alain Danielau, *op.cit.*, p. 165.
33. Sadsiva A. Dange, *Encyclopaedia of Purāṇic Beliefs and Practices*, vol. II, pp. 578-79.
34. V.S. Agrawala, *Matsya Purāṇa — A study*, Varanasi, 1963, pp. 73-74.
35. N.P. Joshi, *Prācīn Bhārtiya mūrti Vigyān*, p. 184.
36. T.A. Gopinath Rao, *Elements of Hindu Iconography*, vol. I, Part I, pp. 265-66.
37. Pāṇini refers to bull of *vahlika* (1.4.10.8) and *kasika* mentions the bull of *kaccha* as *kacchi* (4.2.2.134). And the bulls of Ranka Janapada was called Rankava in the foothills of Raivataka mountains. In Kāṭhiāwār, there still lives certain tribal people who tails cows and bulls. The bulls of this place are very powerful and the cows give more milk than the cows of other areas (see Hunter, *Imperial Gazetteer*, 10.159).
38. A.M. Shashtri, *Varahmihira's India*, pp. 307, 216, 244, 268, 296, and *The Bṛhat-Saṁhitā*, N.C. Iyer, p. 299.
39. *Citrasūtra* of the *Viṣṇudharmottara*, pp. 35-36; Also *Pratimālakṣaṇa*, D.C. Bhattacharya, pp. 4, 114.
40. T.A. Gopinath Rao, *op.cit.*, vol. I, part II, pp. 16, 19, 30, 36.
41. *Mānasara*, Chapter 62; *śloka* 1-35.

3

Bull in the Early Indian Numismatic and Glyptic Art

Bull on Early Indian Coins

THE bull motif appears, frequently, on a series of early Indian coins. The reason is not far to seek. For its wide association with cultivation and transport on the one hand and as a religious symbol on the other, the bull appears to have acquired a meaningful place on coins. From the very inception of its evolution, the bull, for its indomitable courage, strength, virility and muscularity and as a symbol of fertility, has carved for itself a niche in the religions and art of India from the hoary past. The bull was symbolic of *dharma* and this notion was, perhaps, behind the acceptance as a motif on the punch-marked silver coins (*c.* fourth century BC to first century AD) and its continuity is recorded further on the local and tribal coins (*c.* third century BC to third century AD) and on the gold and copper coins of the Kuṣāṇas.

On the series of silver punch-marked coins, the bull appears standing in profile, generally, facing right and rarely, to left. The bulls that are seen on such coins are of humped types. The bull appears on such coins quite crude and bears a somewhat wooden or metallic stiffness (Text *fig*. I.1-2). But, in course of time, their execution received care and sympathy and, therefore, the figure of a bull, in the later series, looks more realistic (Text *fig*. I, 3-8). Sometimes, these coins bear a single bull on their surface and, at times, the bull motif is found associated with a few

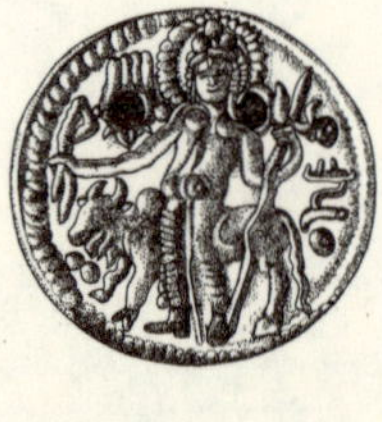

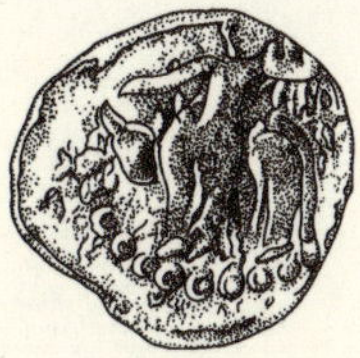

more symbols such as taurine, *yūpa*, etc., or triangle-headed standard, the latter being adjusted at the back of the bull figure. In some of these coins the bull is also seen standing on a five-arched hill, within a frame along with either a fish symbol or the symbol of a taurine (Text *fig*. I).

One of the earliest representations of bull is seen on the punch-marked coins of Kośala *janapada*. A very rare type of such a coin from Singavaran hoard (Andhra Pradesh)[1] depicts a man, possibly a farmer and two bulls, yoked to a plough-share. In this coin, which is kept in the Madras Government Museum, the mint-master very judiciously solved the problem by showing the pair of bulls by placing, one, slightly above the other and adjusting the plough in between. This calls for a comparison with a rock painting from Mirzapur dated *c*. 800 BC[2] which shows a chariot where similar composition is noticed. In another coin, an additional figure of a man is seen. The man could be a cultivator. On another coin, a group of four bulls are depicted in circular motion and such a movement may, perhaps, indicate drawing of water for irrigational purposes or cutting the crops when they become ripened.[3] (Text *fig*. 1,10). The imperial Magadha Mauryan series of silver punch-marked coin project well-built humped bulls (Text *fig*. I).

A series of uninscribed copper coins have been unearthed from the site of Kauśāmbī, dating to *c*. third century BC. These coins have figures of bulls.[4] These are endowed with the figures of bulls, with lanky bodies and upraised heads. The twisted right foreleg of such bulls suggests that the animal is, supposedly, in movement. These bulls are shown facing left before a triangle-headed staff. A group of four *nandīpada* symbols is found at the back of the bull.[5] The figure of bull also appears on some inscribed coins of Kauśāmbī. The obverse of the inscribed copper coins issued by King Parvata[6] shows the bull covering the entire area of its surface. The figure of bull on this coin is crudely executed and is endowed with a wooden stiffness. But the bulls that are seen on the coins of Aśvaghoṣa,[7] Bṛhaspatimitra II,[8] Dhanadeva,[9] Agnimitra,[10] Jyeṣṭhamitra,[11] etc., are better treated and executed with adequate care. These bulls are seen facing left and are endowed with the required strength. The coins of Dhanadeva[12] depict the bulls standing in front of a three-arched hill against a trident motif while the coins of Bṛhaspatimitra II[13] present a three-arched hill within a railing and topped by a *nandīpada* symbol. These coins appear to have certain Śaivite connections.

The uninscribed coins of Ahicchatra[14] are endowed with the figures of bull standing in front of a tree within a railing. The figures of bulls appear also on the coins of Eraṇ,[15] Ujjainī[16] and Taxila.[17] The Ujjainī coin shows a bull standing in front of a tree within a railing. In a few instances, the figure of the bull is seen placed on a pedestal while a few other coins show the bull, depicted with the figure of a deity, facing right, holding something like a pouch or a *kamaṇḍala* in the left hand and a staff, in the right hand. To the left of this deity, a tree within a railing is shown and to his right, the standing figure of a bull is depicted and on its back there appears a *svastika* and Ujjainī symbol.[18] The figure of the bull calls for a comparison with the lanky bull on Kauśāmbī coins.

On the copper coins of Mathurā rulers, Gomitra II (*c.* second century BC),[19] Rāmadatta[20] and Kāmadatta[21] also represent the figure of bull standing to the left. On the Ayodhyā coins of Satyamitra[22] and Āryamitra,[23] Ayohyā (*c.* second century BC), a beautifully executed humped bull is shown standing in front of a spear. Special mention may be made here of the coins of Vāyudeva[24] and Dhanaveda,[25] where the bull is shown standing in front of an object, possibly, a triangle-headed standard on railing. On the coins of Āryamitra, the bull is shown standing in front of a standard occupying the whole area of the obverse.[26] Like

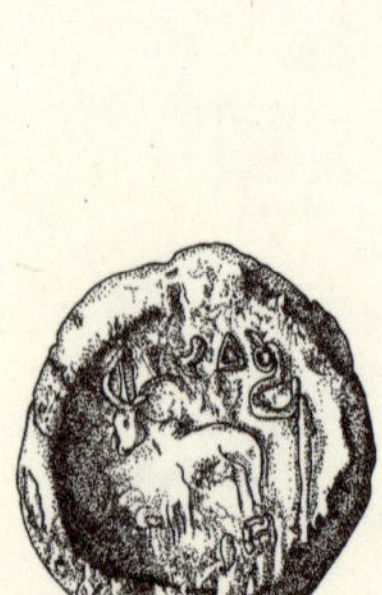

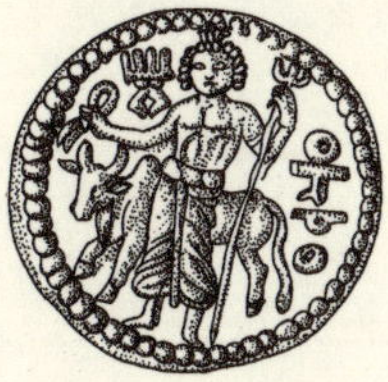

Āryamitra's coins, a well-built figure of a bull is shown standing on the obverse in front of a standard within a railing on the coins of Kumudasena.[27] The coins of Sanghamitra[28] represents the bull standing inside a circle. The coins of Magha and Nāga dynasties also depict the figures of bulls.[29] In comparison to the above-mentioned coins, the figure of bull on the coins of Maghas, is found to be executed, very poorly, and present, somewhat, a metallic stiffness in treatment, while the coins of Mathurā and Ayodhyā bear the natural appearances of a bull and, artistically, belong to the same trend.

The reverse of Auḍumbara coins, (*c.* second-first century BC)[30] bearing the legend of "Amoghabhūti" and Mahādeva represent beautifully engraved humped bulls along with the symbol of *nandīpada* on back. The bull stands here on wavy lines, possibly to indicate a pedestal and also appeared a flower-like design under its neck. The coins of Arjunnāyana (*c.* second century AD)[31] and some coins from Almorā (*c.* second-third century AD)[32] represent a bull in front of a tree within a railing. In the coins of Yaudheyas,[33] the animal is shown standing in front of a *yūpa*-like symbol. The Rājanya[34] coins show the figure of bull inside a rayed circle on the reverse. The well-built figure of a bull, executed with strength and power, can be seen occupying the reverse of the gold coin of Puṣkalāvatī, bearing the legend, Tauras in Greek script and "Uṣabhe" in Kharoṣṭhi script.[35] The Indo-Greek silver and copper coins also represent the beautifully engraved well-built figure of bull. Mention may be made here of the reverse of the silver coins of Appolodotus-I,[36] where appear an artistically engraved figure of a bull with realistic appearance. The folds of its dewlap are marked with deep incisions. The copper coins of Minander[37] depict only the frontal view of its face, realistically engraved on the obverse.

The bull appeared as a mount of Śiva on the gold and copper coins of the Kuṣāṇas. The copper coins of Kujula

Kadphises represent the figure of a humped bull, topped by *nandīpada* symbol.[38] Bull also appears on the gold and copper coins of Vima Kadphises along with Śiva.[39] The coins of Vima Kadphises represent the device in a high relief. The figure of the bull is shown standing to right on these coins. The disposition of the legs suggests the moving posture of the animal. The strongly-built figure of bull reminds the description given in ancient literature, where it is described as a symbol of masculine fertility. The life-like appearances of bull point to the mastery in artistic skills of the mint-masters of the Kuṣāṇa period. The bull, with Śiva, is conspicuously absent on the coins of Kaniṣka I and Huviṣka. After Huviṣka, the Kuṣāṇa ruler, Vasudeva I,[40] reintroduced the device of Vima Kadphises' coins, where the Śiva is shown with his mount, bull. On the coins of Vāsudeva I, the figure of bull appeared as one of the finest examples of art on coins and gave evidence of the artistic maturity, acquired by contemporary artists. The bull is represented with a great sense of supplication and affection towards its lord. After Vāsudeva I, it was also found depicted on the coins of Kaniṣka III and Vāsudeva II and a few other successors of imperial Kuṣāṇas. The representations of bull, however, became quite crude and somewhat ornamental.[41] After the imperial Kuṣāṇas, the bull remained conspicuously absent from the surface of the coins. The device seems to have lost its popularity, at this stage.

Skandagupta (*c.* AD 455-68)[42] was the only Gupta ruler who issued a few silver coins from Mālwā region, where the bull reappeared, once again, as a device where it is shown seated to the left. But the circulation of such coins remained restricted. Handa[43] also referred to a few coins, found from Ropar excavations, bearing the device of crudely depicted humped-bull on the reverse, either standing or sitting to the left, within a beaded border. This occupied the whole of the reverse of the coin and the obverse shows a human figure either standing or sitting to

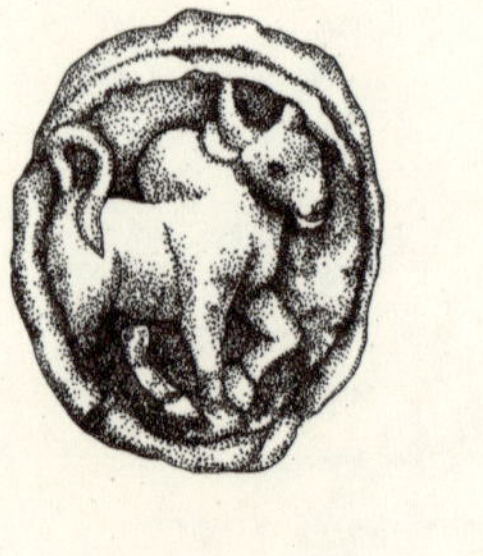

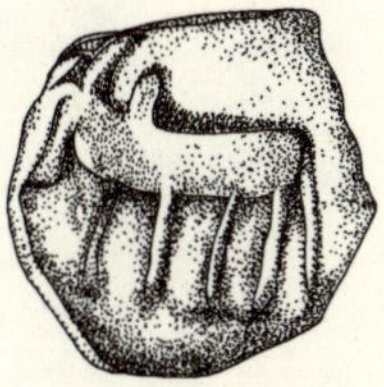

the front, holding a trident in right hand. The coins bears the name of Vidisagupta in Brāhmī characters of *c.* sixth century AD.

Bull on Early Indian Seals Sealings

Seals and sealings provide data which corroborate, supplement and also altar the facts of history. Sealings have been found, in abundance, at sites which were important centres of trade and commerce, religion or administration. The die, in spite of its being baked, and if not already damaged, as a result of wear and tear, was generally destroyed after the death of its owner to avoid fraudulent use. A variety of materials was under use for making seal dies, the most common being the clay. Seals and sealings bear either devices or legends or both. The device, generally, portrays a symbol or symbols, animals and, less frequently, human beings or deities in human form. The seals bear the name of the king, the epithet of the kings, genealogies or the sacred formula. Private seals, generally, bear the names of owners and, sometimes, coupled with their designation or status.

The emblems, in most cases, were indicative of the religious bearing of the owners. The depiction of bull-motif on quite a large number of seals, suggests its evident Śaivite association. In some cases, the device is suggestive of the name, intended to be conveyed by the legend and, therefore, a bull was chosen by Gopa[44] and Gopasena[45] and Nandī also by Dhruvanandī[46] and Viṣṇunandī,[47] on these seals. The Indus Valley seals show the popularity of the bulls, which were earlier discussed, in great detail, in the first chapter of this study. In general, we get seals of rulers from *c.* second century BC onwards from various regions, belonging to different dynasties, indigenous and foreign, depicting the device of bulls. The bull device was used by the Kauśāmbī rulers Pravataka,[48] Jyeṣṭhamitra,[49] Dhanadeva[50] (*c.* second century AD) and Vidiśā rulers Nāgārjuna,[51] Viśvamitra[52] and Jayaka[53] (*c.* first-second century AD). Jyeṣṭhamitra and Dhanadeva are also known from the coins of Kauśāmbī but the device on the seals and sealings and the coins are, however, not identical. A number of clay sealings, found from Rājghāṭ, and kept in Bharat Kala Bhavan and in other museums, bears the figure of a bull standing to the left in front of a *yūpa* and a spear at its back. Bull is the common obverse device in both the cases of, namely, Ayodhyā and Kauśāmbī but Kauśāmbī seals have an additional symbol, a three-arched hill, which is notably absent on Ayodhyā ones. Moreover, the coins of Kauśāmbī, sometimes, bear the title *rājā* (*rājanyo*). A sealing from Rājghāṭ shows a bull, flanked by 'vase' and *paraśu* with the legend *dhanadevasa* in Brāhmī script slightly earlier in date than the last one. Owing to the difference of the device, it is difficult to ascertain whether both the sealings belonged to the same dynasty.

A sealing from Rājghāṭ belonged to Vidiśā king, Nāgārjuna, housed in Bharat Kala Bhavan, bearing the figure of a standing-bull with a *yūpa* to its front and a *cakra* at its back, bearing the legend *nāgārjunasa*.[54] It is dated to *c.* first-second century AD. The bull figure and the *cakra* can also be found on the sealings of Dhanadeva[55] and Abhaya,[56] whose sealings are found from the same site and are identified with the Kauśāmbī rulers. The sealings from Rājghāṭ, bearing the name of Viśvamitra[57] and Jayaka[58] in the collection of Bharat Kala Bhavan, show the figure of bull reclining, with a spear on either side. The legend, above the bull, read . . . *sya mah(a)r(a)ja-sri-vis(a)mitrasya* and *jayakasya* in the Brāhmī script of *c.* first-second century AD, respectively. Perphaps, the king Jayaka belonged to the family of Viyakamitra and Vijayamitra, mentioned in the Shinkoṭ steatite casket inscription.[59]

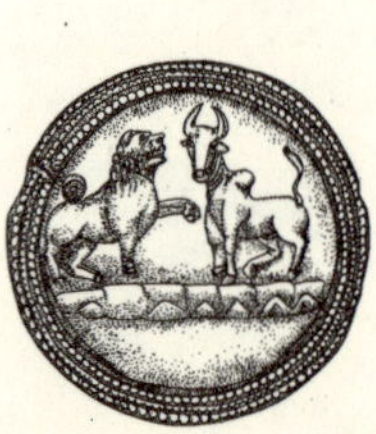

The sealings of Ayodhyā rulers such as Vijayamitra,[60] Śivamitra,[61] Viṣṇumitra,[62] Puṣyamitra,[63] Saṅghamitra[64] (*c.* first-second century AD) also represent the standing posture of the bull. The name Vijayamitra and Saṅghamitra are also

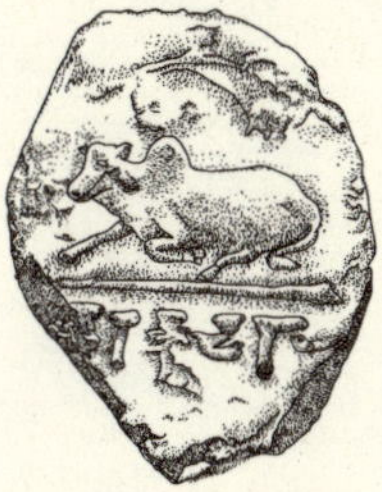

known from the Ayodhyā series of coins. The bull-device is quite common on the coins of Ayodhyā rulers. Paleographically and artistically, these sealings have a trend of Kuṣāṇa period. It is worth mentioning here that a clay-baked lump, bearing the three stamps of the same seal, in the collection of Bharat Kala Bhavan,[65] shows a sitting bull in front of a trident, with the legend *avimukta* (one of the names of Śiva) in Gupta-Brāhmī script. A study of these seals and sealings throws light of the personal religion of the king or of a certain individual. The bull-device was popular mainly on the sealings belonging to the Kuṣāṇa period. The standing-bull can also be seen on the seal and sealings of the kings of the Magha dynasty. A circular sealing from Bhītā, has a bull, standing to the left with a woman standing in the front. Behind the bull is a post or a thunderbolt. Brāhmī legend reads as *(ra)jna vas(i)sth(i) puttrasya sri bhimasena(sya)*, in *c.* second-third century AD character.[66] A number of sealings obtained from Rājghāṭ belong to those of *amātya* Janārdana in the collections of Allahabad, Lucknow and Bharat Kala Bhavan. All these sealings bear a beautifully depicted humped bull, seated to the left, and the legend in Gupta-Brāhmī characters *amātya janārdanasya*.[67] A sealing in the collection of Bharat Kala Bhavan shows a device of bull and the legend *amātya kapilakasya* in similar character.[68] Another identical sealing in the same collection bears the legend of *amātya āryasarma*.[69] However, a good number of sealings from Rājghāṭ bears the figure of a seated bull and the legend of *amacha-hatthikasa* in Brāhmī of Kuṣāṇa character.[70] But the few sealings which bear the same device and the legends, thereon, are *hastikasa*[71] and *hastikasya*[72] without the title *amātya*, respectively. However, it is difficult to ascertain whether these sealings also belong to the same person, as discussed above. Another Rājghāṭ sealing bears the device of a standing bull in front of a *yūpa*, with the legend of *amātya balaka*.[73] The presence of a fair number of sealings with the legend *amātya* indicates the importance of the person in the society. Several clay seals and sealings from Rājghāṭ, Besnagar and Bhītā have been found to be belonging to the class of *daṇḍanāyaka* and *mahādaṇḍanāyaka*.

An artistic seal of this type was unearthed from Bhītā,[74] bearing the legend *daṇḍanāyaka śri śankaradattasya* in Gupta-Brāhmī character. In a sealing of Indian Museum, Calcutta,[75] the bull can be seen standing with a round object between the horns and the legend *daṇḍanāyaka vansa(?)sya* in Gupta character. To the right of the bull is a *śrīvatsa* symbol and on its left a *cakra* inside the circle of the sealing. A few other sealings have bull and the legend in Gupta-Brāhmī characters *daṇḍanāyaka lā asya,*[76] *(daṇḍa)nāyaka kesavadāsa(sya),*[77] *(daṇḍa)nāyaka yajanavi(rya)*[78] (bull reclining to the left), *(daṇḍanā)yaka oni* (?) *masya*[79] (bull recumbent to the left behind it, radiating the circle) and *daṇḍanāyaka crambalasya.*[80] Possibly, the term *daṇḍnāyaka* denoted a judicial officer. It is significant to note here that all the eight *daṇḍanāyaka* sealings from Bhītā, invariably, bear bull *lāñchana*. Apart from being a Śaiva device, the bull is also symbolic of *dharma*. Thus, the bull-symbol is most appropriate for justice. Though the bull, undoubtedly, occurs on the seals of other officials as well, in the case of *daṇḍanāyaka* seals from Bhītā, it occurs constantly. A spherical object is seen between the horns of bulls on certain sealings belonging to the Gupta period.[81] Nothing can be said whether the motif was borrowed from the Sassanians or had an independent origin but it may be suggested that the symbolism, in the present context, conveys the idea of *dharma*, supporting the sphere, a universe (*dhārayati iti dharmaḥ*) and, more so, as a judge upholds the truth and the law.[82] If this argument is acceptable, then, it can be said that the figures in the *daṇḍanāyaka*s of the Bhītā sealings are the representations of judges or *nyāyādhikarī* or *daṇḍādhikarī*. A Basarh sealing, bearing the device of a humped bull, bears the legend *mahādaṇḍanāyaka agniputrasya.*[83] A sealing from Eraṇ simply bears the legend *mahādaṇḍanāyaka siṃghnandī* in

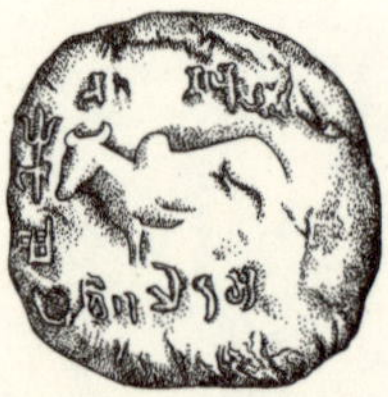

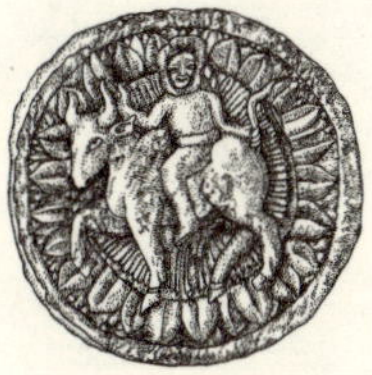

early Gupta script.[84] Jhūsī sealings, with humped bulls and conch to the right, bear the legend *isvaranandisya* in Gupta script.[85] Another example of the seal shows the bull in the centre and a *triśūla*-like object in the front.[86] A sealing from Lachhagir in the collections of Allahabad Museum, representing a bull, recumbent to the right with a trident-cum-battle axe in front of the bull, and a crescent above, undoubtedly shows its Śaivite connection/association.[87] Equally interesting are the Śaiva seals and sealings from Nālandā. The *grāmajanapada* sealings of this place bear a *liṅga* on a pedestal with *triśūla* to the right and bull to the left.[88] A terracotta sealing from Bhir mound, Taxila, bears on both sides the figure of a humped bull standing to left with a *nandīpada* symbol above the hump. A sealing from Kumrahār has the device of a bull and the legend *viṣṇunandī* in Gupta script.[89] The coins were issued by the kings and the republican tribes and rarely by the guilds whereas the seals belonged to all classes of peoples and institutions. Similar symbols were used in ancient times in various forms of art but the resemblance between coins and seals is quite close.

References

1. P.L. Gupta, and T.R. Hardekar, *Ancient Indian Silver Punch-Marked coins of the Magadha-Mauryan Kharsapan Series*, Anjaneri, Nasik, 1985, Series 1 No. 66; Savita Sharma, *Early Indian Symbols, Numismatic Evidence*, pl. 50.
2. D.D. Kosambi, *The Cultural Civilization of Ancient India*, p. 115.
3. Savita Sharma, *op.cit*, pl. 50, F-7. A reference may be seen in the *Bhāgavata* (152.4) for the plough, drawn by eight, six, four and two bulls. P.L. Gupta and T.R. Hardekar, *op.cit*., also P.L. Gupta "Singvaran Hoard, Sonepur Hoard, Dhapewara Hoard, Mahamundi finds," Lucknow Museum (Unpublished thesis) B.H.U., Varanasi, 1952.
4. B.M.C. pl. XII, 5-7; pl. fig. 33.
5. Bharat Kala Bhavan, Acc. No. 619; pl. fig. 34.
6. B.M.C. pl. XX, 10.
7. B.M.C. pl. XX, 6.
8. B.M.C. pl. XX, 2, pl. fig. 35.

9. B.M.C. pl. XX, 12.
10. B.M.C. pl. XX, 5.
11. B.M.C. pl. XX, 9.
12. B.M.C. pl. XX, 12.
13. B.M.C. pl. XV, 2.
14. Savita Sharma, "Uninscribed copper coins from Ahicchatra," in *JNSI*, vol. XLIV (pl. 1-2), 1982, pp. 20-23; pl. fig. 36.
15. B.M.C. pl. XVIII, 23.
16. B.M.C. pl. XXXVII, 10-11.
17. B.M.C. pl. XXXV, 8.
18. B.M.C. pl. XXXV, 15.
19. B.M.C. pl. XXV, 8.
20. B.M.C. pl. XXIV, 10.
21. B.M.C. pl. XXIV, 18.
22. B.M.C. pl. XVII, 10-12; pl. fig. 37.
23. B.M.C. pl. XVII, 18.
24. B.M.C. pl. XVII, 13.
25. B.M.C. pl. XVI, 17.
26. B.M.C. pl. XVI, 18.
27. B.M.C. pl. XVII, 17.
28. B.M.C. pl. XVII, 21.
29. *JNSI*, vol. XLV, 1983, pt. I-II, pl. IV, 1-5.
30. B.M.C. pl. XIV, 16-17; *JASBL*, IX, I, p. 218.
31. B.M.C. pl. XIV, 11-12.
32. B.M.C. pl. XIV, 7-9.
33. B.M.C. pl. XXXIX, 11-13.
34. B.M.C. pl. XXIX, 11-13.
35. J.N. Banerjea, *Development of Hindu Iconography*, p. 118.
36. Bharat Kala Bhavan, Acc. No. 95.3161 pl. fig. 48.
37. British Museum Collection, photo personal collection of Prof. A.K. Narain, pl. fig. 49-50.
38. J.M. Rousenfield, *The Dynestic Art of the Kushanas*, p. 15, fig. 17. We do not have any definite evidence of the personal faith of Kujul.
39. BKB Acc. No. 7173, pl. fig. 53.
40. BKB Acc. No. 8703, pl. fig. 55.
41. Plate. fig. No. 64-67.
42. BKB Acc. no. 95.3162.

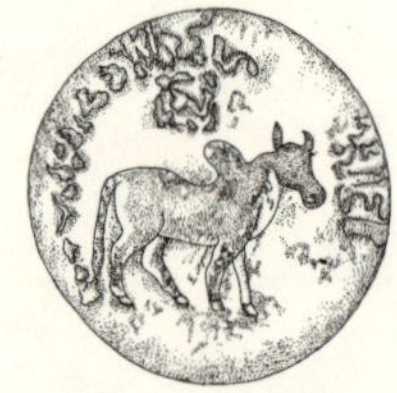

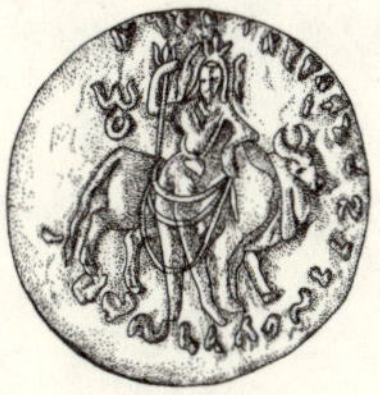

43. D. Handa, *Studies in Indian Coins and Seals*, pp. 139-43, pl. fig. 69.
44. *JRAS*, 1901, p. 108, No. 14.
45. BKB Acc. No. 6076.
46. Deva and Mishra, *Vaisali Excavations*, p. 57, pl. XIX-B, 4.
47. Allakara and Mishra, *Report on Kumrahar Excavations*, 1951-53, p. 104, No. 13. pl. XXX 11-7; Identical sealing form Rājghāṭ in Allahabad Museum No. 192.
48. K.K. Thapliyal, *Studies in Ancient Indian Seals*, pl. IV, 5.
49. *Ibid*. pl. V, 1.
50. BKB Acc. No. 6049.
51. J.N. Banerjea, *op.cit*., p. 189; K.K. Thapliyal, *op.cit*., li, 4,6.
52. *ASIAR*, 1914-15, p. 81, No. 1.
53. K.K. Thaplyal, *op.cit*., pl. III.3.
54. *Ibid*., pl. III.
55. *Ibid*., pl. II-3; BKB Acc. No. 6049.
56. BKB Acc. No. 6331; K.K. Thaplyal, *op.cit*. pl. II, 4.
57. *ASIAR*, 1914-15, p. 81, No. 1.
58. K.K. Thaplyal, *op.cit*., pl. III-3.
59. *Ibid*., p. 31.
60. Allahabad Museum Acc. No. 305; K.K. Thaplyal, *op.cit*., pl. V., 4.
61. K.K. Thaplyal, *op.cit*., pl. V. 6.
62. *Ibid*., pl. V, 2.
63. *Ibid*., pl. V, 5.
64. *Ibid*., pl. V, 7.
65. BKB Acc. No. 21480.
66. K.K. Thaplyal, pl. IV-4; Rājā Bhīmsena of the seals is probably identical with Mahārāja Bhīmsena of Giñjā inscription (year 52). *ASIR*, XXI, p. 119, pl. 30; and Bandhogarh inscription dated in the year 51, E. 9, vol. XXXI, pl. 177, No. 1. coins of that king, bear the legend *rajanyo bhimsenasya* (*JNSI*, VIII p. 16) or *rājā hīmasenasa*, Indian Museum Chronical, III, pp. 12-13, has been found at Kauśāmbī. The combined evidence of Epigraphy, Numismatics and the Seals suggests that the rule of Bhīmasena was extended over the regions of Bandhogarh, Kauśāmbī and Vārāṇasī.
67. Allahabad Museum Nos. 14, 30, 69, 73, 80, 103, 128, 131, 132, 162 & 178: Lucknow Museum Nos. 40, 152; BKB Acc. No. 6367.
68. BKB Acc. No. 6371.
69. BKB Acc. No. 6362.
70. BKB Acc. No. 6369; K.K. Thapliyal, *op. cit*., p. 101.

71. BKB Acc. No. 6233.

72. BKB Acc. No. 6235.

73. In the Department of A.I.H.C. & Arch., BHU, No. 47.

74. *ASIAR*, 1911-12, pp. 54-55, No. 44, pl. XIX; (Thaplyal, pl. IX-3).

75. *Ibid.*, p. 55, No. 1.

76. *Ibid.*, No. 46.

77. *Ibid.*, No. 47.

78. *Ibid.*, No. 48.

79. *Ibid.*, No. 49.

80. *Ibid.*, No. 45.

81. Thaplyal, *op.cit.*, p. 117.

82. *Ibid.*

83. *Ibid.*, pl. IX, 5.

84. *Puratattva*, no. 2, p. 64.

85. Thaplyal, *op.cit.*, pl. XV-6.

86. Allahabad Museum No. 4-7.

87. Thaplyal, *op.cit.*, pl. XV-2.

88. *Ibid.*, p. 149.

89. Altekar and Mishra, *Report on Kumrahar Excavations*, p. 104, No. 13, pl. XXXII, No. 7.

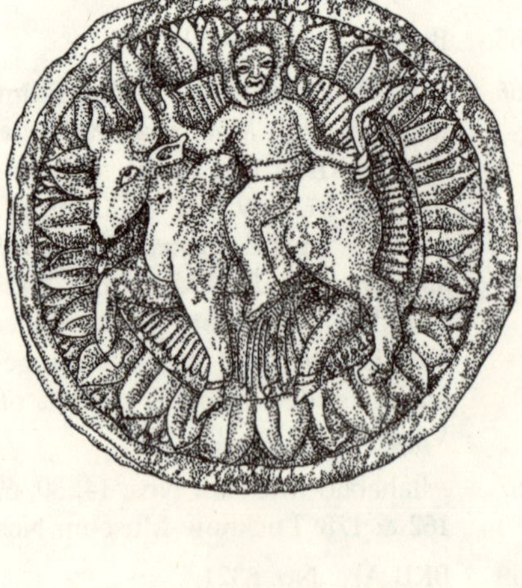

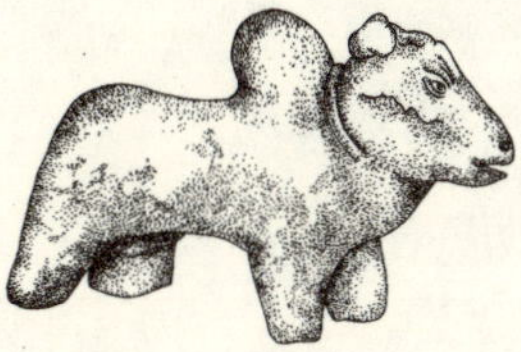

4

Bull in the Early Indian Terracotta

THE decline of Harappan cities in the second millennium BC resulted in a slow process of development of art and craft and in their technological attainments. In this period the production of clay figures suffered immensely. In the north-west, it was totally stopped while the Harappan and non-Harappan regions exposed isolated clay figures. The most common animal-form which appeared in this period was bull. Kayatha yielded some damaged and a few complete figures of bull which are found mostly stylized while a few appeared as of naturalistic types. The stylized bulls are considered as ritual objects. The bulls that are considered naturalistic are those which were represented in totality. Since no efforts were made to decorate the animals, the scholars are inclined to consider them as ritualistic.[1]

Hand-modelled figures of bull appeared in the Neolithic culture of south India. In Piklihal, the archaeologists discovered grey and red fabric bulls. These bulls have resemblances to the grey, red and black chalcolithic potteries. The Piklihal bulls are endowed with prominent forms and humps. Other sites such as Koṭalā Nihaṅg, Bara, etc., also yielded hand-modelled bulls and those bulls are taken as degenerated workmanship of Harappan craftsmen in this area. Non-Harappan chalcolithic clay figurines of central India and Deccan call for a comparison with the terracotta bull, found from Bhagawānpurā sites in Haryana.[2] The excavations at Ahār in Udaipur district exposed a large-horned bull terracotta along with a few other animals.[3]

B.B. Lal draws our attention to the excavations at

Hastināpura and, particularly its Period-II, which is characterized by Painted Grey Ware culture. He discovered from the Period-II remains of crudely modelled clay figures in red fabric, most of which represent figures of bulls. Dated in *circa* 1500 BC, these bulls visibly lack fine workmanship although they were well fired. It appears that the clay that was used was not properly levigated.[4] After an interval of about a century, the Period-IV of the same site, was charaterized by red wares, produced both, hand-modelled and moulded varieties, of humped bulls[5] (*figs.* 86, 87). The excavations at Śrāvastī (Sahet-Mahet), which lies between Goṇḍā and Baharāica in U.P., laid bare from its Period-I a limited number of extremely damaged and mutilated animal figurines. Dated between *c.* 600-300 BC, these damaged animal figures are extremely difficult to be identified. Of these hand-modelled and decorated animals, Jayaswal discovered, at least, two figures of bulls which could be compared with the ill-fired and carbonized bulls of Hastināpura.[6] Other sites which yielded Painted Grey Wares and figures of bulls are Ahicchatra (*fig.* 88) and Atarañjikherā.[7]

According to Gaur, the terracotta objects at Atarañjikherā were not very popular. From the upper levels of the site a few animal figures were found. From the upper phase, a modelled humped bull has been found in a damaged condition. Its hind part and left horn were missing. It has flattened legs and drooping face with a hole for fastening strings. The Period-IV at Atarañjikherā which yields the evidences of Northern Black Polished Ware culture, between 600 to 50 BC laid bare as many as 37 animal figures of which 13 figures of humped bulls predominated over the others. These bulls are found to be well modelled and were treated with a wash or slip to provide with a smooth finish. In some cases, the body is decorated with stamped designs, including *cakra*s, notches, leaves and circles. The *cakra*s appear to be most popular. A few of them

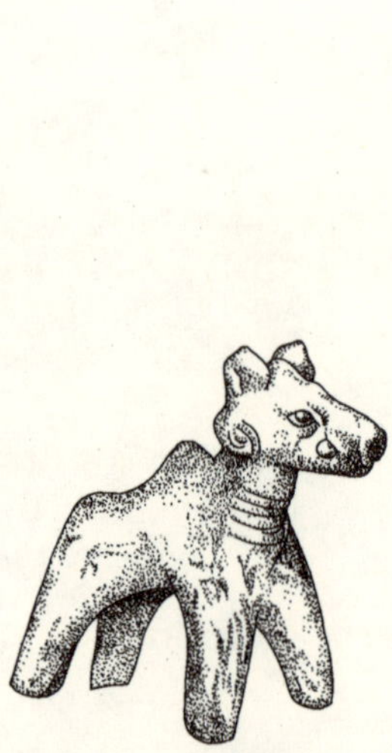

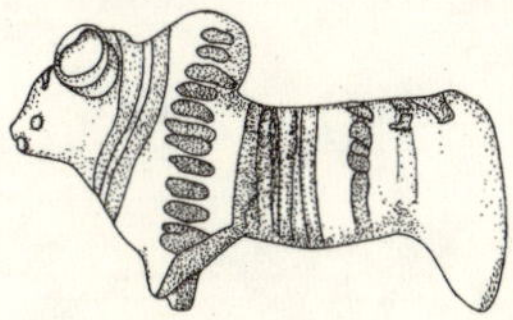

are decorated with pin holes. Some of these bulls are crudely modelled while some exhibit exquisitely modelled figures and prove that, among the modellers, clay-modellers were quite efficient in modelling while others were not as good.[8]

Srivastava, while reporting on Kapilavastu, mentions the discovery of a total number of 347 remains of Bas-indicus.[9] The Period-II of Gunvariā yielded a grey colour terracotta figure of a bull whose hump is seen behind its head. Dated between sixth and fifth century BC, the face of this bull is found painted.[10] Another figure of bull is found decorated with garland around its neck. The garland is decorated in circlets with a dot in relief. Its mouth is projected and there is a hole in the nostrils. It may also be mentioned here that a stamped bull was found from the same site with projected mouth and raised horns. Its hump is seen behind its neck. The figure of the bull is decorated with circlets. These are divided into four compartments. The eyes and ears of this bull are quite natural. There is a hole in the nostril for passing the rope. A stamped bull, stylistically dated to second century BC from the same site and belonging to the Period-III, appears with rope passing through the mouth, while its body is decorated with horizontal lines flanked by star-like patterns.

The pre-600 BC phase in the various sites in Uttar Pradesh yielded hardly any bull. Thereafter, the bull figures were found in Rājghāṭ (Period I-B), Śrāvastī and Mathurā. Rājghāṭ exposed bulls, both humped and without hump-types. The Rājghāṭ, Period I-B, laid bare the pre-urban phase and yielded hand-modelled terracotta animal figures. These specimens are made out of medium to fine levigated clay and are well-baked. The bull figures are found treated in this site with double coats of ochre over the buff slip. A limited number of bulls retains dull red single slip. Some terracottas were also found painted during the post firing stage by the strips and dots of thick white or pink pigments.[11] These bulls were made use of either as toys for the amusement parks for children or they were made to serve for certain social purposes in the contemporary period (*fig*. 89).

The excavations at Narhan (District Gorakhpur), excavated by Prof. P. Singh, exposed from the Period-II of the site which spans between *c*. 800 and 600 BC, a number of terracotta animal figurines, including bull and *nīlgaāī*. An analysis of the terracotta bulls of this site would show that the modellers attempted to attribute sensitive modelling in the figures of the animals and they also kept an eye on the anatomical details.[12] The Period I-A of Bhāgalpur in Bihar exposed the Northern Black Polished Ware culture. The culture is also found associated with the black and red ware people. The Period I-A culture includes a few animal figures including bulls, elephants and dogs.[13] The Sonepur, district Gayā, also provided from its Period-III, Northern Black Polished Wares, human and animal figures, including bulls.[14] Hand-modelled primitive type of humped bulls have also been discovered from Harinārāyaṇpur, West Bengal, and these are dated to pre-Mauryan period (*figs*. 84, 85).

Mauryan Terracotta

A close analysis of terracotta figures, which were made between 600 and 300 BC, reveals that they were exclusively hand-made. The period also witnessed, in certain cases, terracottas with painted surface and applique technique which were adopted for decorative devices. Animal figurines of this period are, in general, made with some kind of decorations. The applique-motif consists of a U-shaped design, formed by applying a band of clay on the forehead and back. This design is, however, found to be restricted to elephants and bulls only (*fig*. 90). Sometimes, punched circlets have also been found on these applique bands. Of the 51 animal figures which were found from Rājghāṭ I-B, 29 were of bulls. While one finds an unusually

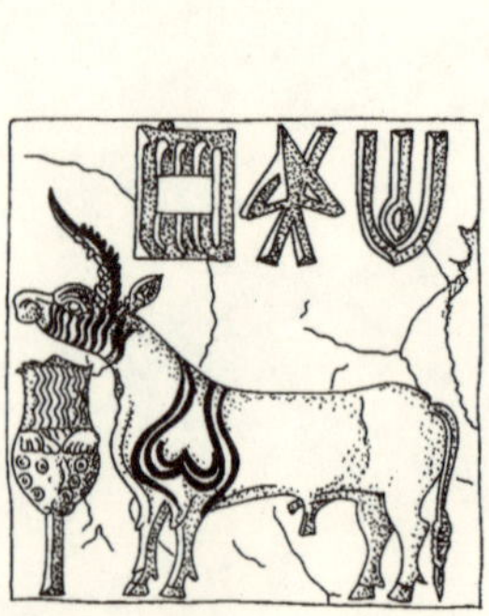

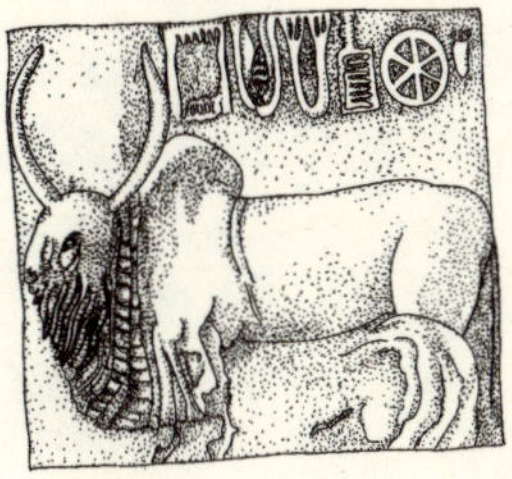

large number of bull figures from I-B, they are completely absent in the preceding I-A phase and succeeding I-C period. The reason is difficult enough to explain. The Rājghāṭ bull of the Period I-B, are made in red colour and, sometimes, betray a thin red slip.[15] The eyes of the animals are shown by deep round dots. In many cases, a strap has been depicted by applying additional clay which is punched in a transverse perforation, apparently, for the cord.[16]

In some other sites, particularly, at Mathurā, the terracotta of this period evinced a developed technique. The modellers used Northern Black Polished fabric and they took more care in modelling. These terracottas are endowed with polished black surface and a grey core. The fabric is, therefore, similar to the well-known Northern Black Polished Ware. But the upper surface of the animal figure does not exhibit the same lusters as are found on the surface of Northern Black Polished potteries. These animals are hand-modelled and solid. The eyes are indicated by holes and, on a few occasions, by the applique method. Sahani draws our attention to a small square terracotta plaque in the Lahore Museum. It shows a circular depression in the middle and is surrounded by four animals in the same order as one finds in the case of the abacus of Sārnāth Lion capital of the Mauryan period. The only point of difference between the two being, unlike the capital, its intervening symbols are a conch, a bow, a wheel and a *triratna* symbol.

Among the terracotta figurines of the Mauryan period, a large number of different kinds of animals, including bulls, have been found from Patna, Buxar, Vaiśālī, Mathurā, Hastināpura and Atrañjikherā. The animals are found meticulously decorated as if they were meant for religious purposes or for some ceremonies. These decorations include applique and punch-marked and incised circlets. Mathurā presents rosette motifs on the body of the terracotta similar to the motifs found on the figures of mother-goddess. But the animals were not only made exclusively for religious purposes but they were made as children-toys. Verma finds, among the terracottas discovered from Chirand, district Sāraṇ (Bihar), a terracotta of humped-bull having a diamond-shaped stamped eyes. Since it was found along with the Northern Black Polished Wares, it was dated to Mauryan period.[17] A similar bull figure is collected in the Brooklyn Museum. This grey hand-modelled terracotta with burnished black slip belongs to Mauryan period between 320 and 200 BC, and it hails from an unknown place in Uttar Pradesh. It represents a bull with its hump. The facial details include diamond-shaped eyes, and the eyes and the mouth are incised and additional incised lines appear also on its neck (*fig.* 91).

Srivastava, while writing his discovery of Kapilavastu, drew attention to, at least, two terracotta figures of bull. One of them shows a straight projected mouth, raised horns and a hump, behind the neck. Dated between fourth and third century BC, the bulls are found decorated in stamped patterns of circles, divided into four compartments, each carrying a dot, all in relief. The eyes and ears of these bulls are naturalistically rendered and there appears hole in the nostrils for putting a rope.[18] From the Period-II of the same site, a terracotta animal in grey colour, with raised head, is, most probably, representing a bull. Its face is painted while its hump is seen projected behind the head.

The excavations at Ahicchatra exposed in its stratum VIII, dated between 300 and 200 BC, some naturalistically treated animal figures, including bulls. These animals were moulded in red fabric and depict stamped symbols of *svastika* within circle. From the same site and from the strata IV and III, a few small bulls were reported and, typologically, these are comparable to bulls of Hastināpura, Period-IV.[19]

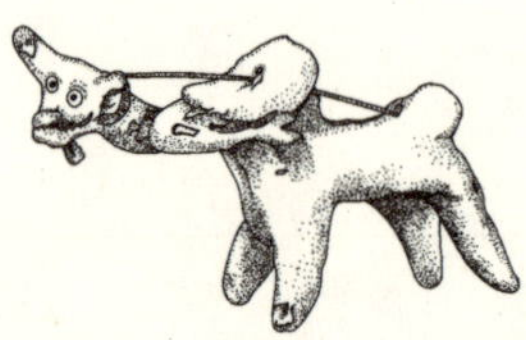

The terracotta figurines of mother-goddess were found from a few sites from Rajasthan along with some votive

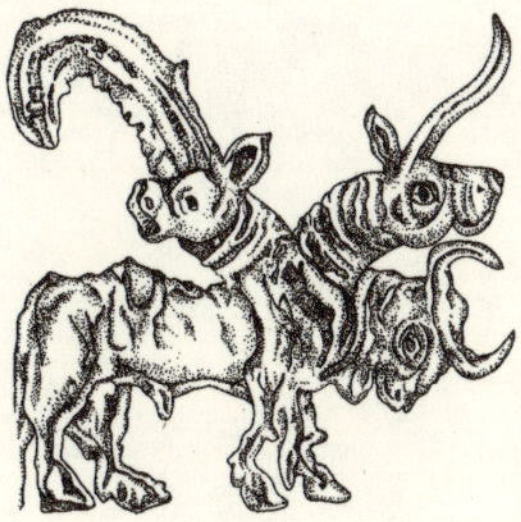

animals. The representation of bull, in this context, is interesting because it was used as a complex symbol, both from the historical and psychological points of view. In ancient Indian religion, the bull was a symbol connected with atmospheric deities, its bellowing sound, associated with the rolling thunder.[20] Sankalia pointed to our notice about the figurines both, with or without hump, from the Mauryan level at Nevāsā.[21]

Śuṅga Terracotta

The period between 185 and 50 BC witnessed certain develop-ments, particularly in the techniques of terracotta productions. This was the period when figures were made in moulds along with the hand-modelled ones. The terracotta figurines that were discovered from the various sites such as Ahicchatra, Hastināpura, Śrāvastī, Kauśāmbī, Bhītā, Rājghāṭ, Vaiśālī and the sites of West Bengal, such as Candraketugarh and Pāṇḍurājār-dibi, etc., exposed not only hand-modelled and moulded figurines but also produced figurines along with Northern Black Polished Wares, fabrics in grey ware and red ware. The period also evinced, in the matter of decoration, the continuity of the earlier motifs as well as the introduction of some new motifs. The animal figurines appeared with incisions and applique decorations and such decorations include circles, oblique, vertical and horizontal lines, additional clay strips and criss-cross hatchings. The only difference with the preceding century was that such designs were more systematically and artistically executed on the body of the animals. In some sites, designs, with wheel and leave patterns, are found. The moulds were mainly used for human figures in the initial period but, at the later phase of this period, moulds were also used to prepare animal figures. In this period, toy-bulls started appearing in Mathurā and Hastināpura. Mathurā yielded many types of animal figures and, among the important ones, were the bulls. Mathurā laid bare to three types of bulls in terracotta — plain red colour humped-bulls with horns and ears, and eyes and mouth made with incised lines; humped- bulls in dark grey colour with incised circlets around the muzzle and neck and the third variety, shown with legs perforated. The latter type is meant for wheeled bull. There are some peculiar compositions where the bulls are placed to the frontal part of a wagon and, in some cases, a composite type of terracotta is found having a head of a bull with the body of a snake.[22]

At Ahicchatra, the terracotta bulls appear right from the Ochre Colour Painted Ware and through the painted grey ware levels but the bull figures of the late Maurya-Śuṅga periods evince a new style and the bulls are found decorated with a different type of punched designs. The decorations on the body of such bulls include circles, incised branches, strokes and punched circles. Humped-bulls, in this site, are rare and the incised lines on the eyes of such bulls are endowed with the shape of lozenges. All the bull figures are hand-made and solid. The bulls may be divided into two types at Ahicchatra:

(i) Red-coloured with red slip on the body and with a hump,

(ii) The bulls with black or grey colour. This variety has four subtypes:

- Bulls with long horn and short mouth,
- Bulls with long horns and elongated mouths,
- Solid bulls with incised lines around the neck, and
- Bulls with horns and ears.

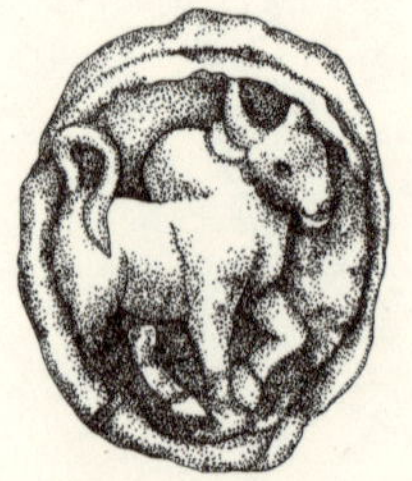

Rājghāṭ laid bare a large number of animal figures in the Śuṅga period. From this place both red and grey colour animals have been found. The red-coloured figures were made of very fine clay, and in some such figures traces of

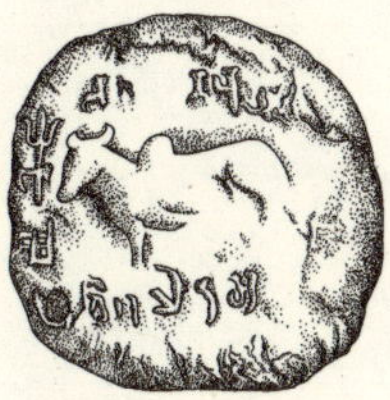

red slip are also found. Of the figures discovered at Rājghāṭ, nearly 20 per cent of animal figurines have ash grey core and are of coarse variety. The decorations on the red animal figures include incised lines, circlets and additional clay strips. Though the bull figures do not appear in the Period I-C at Rājghāṭ, they re-appear in Period-II. This period exposed seven bull figures; of these, except one, all are humped-bulls. All of them have applied bands on the neck while foreheads and tails are punched with deep holes. The muzzles are perforated. On certain parts of the body decorations with incised strokes are noticed. The bull figurines of Period-II in Rājghāṭ, Vaiśālī and Kumrahār indicate that they maintained their appearance in the post Northern Black Polished Ware period. However such figures betrayed plain surfaces and lesser decoration. The material used was also coarse. The excavations at Kumrahār exposed from its Period-II Śuṅga terracottas and two coins with bull figurines which are similar to Kauśāmbī types. A large number of terracotta figurines were discovered in fragmentary conditions from Vaiśālī and, among the animal figurines, representation of bull was also noticed.[23] Such figurines were also noticed from the excavations at Balirājgarh in Madhubanī district, Bihar, from its Period-I which coincide the Śuṅga-Kuṣāṇa period.[24] Period-III of Gunvariā, which is dated to first century BC laid bare the solitary figure of a better finished bull with a long curved face and projected hump. Its ears are also projected. The stumped decorations of the body are of two types — one herring bone and the other star within a circle. The mouth is open and the eyes are naturalistic. A hole has been provided in the nose for passing the rope.[25] The excavations at Tilourakot (Distt. Taulihwa) exposed animal figurines of Śuṅga period, including the bulls[26] (*fig.* 92).

The terracotta figurines of bull have also been discovered from Period-IV which coincide with late Śuṅga and early Kuṣāṇa at Pāṇḍu-Rājār-dibi (district Burdhwān in

West Bengal).[27] Dr. S.C. Kala drew our attention to a number of terracotta bulls and chariots drawn by bulls and a few scenes with bull from Kauśāmbī which are stylistically dated to the Śuṅga period. In Kauśāmbī, the bulls and horses, according to Kala, are adorned with ornaments and reflect a well-developed breed during this period. It appears that, in the Śuṅga period, each famous centre of terracotta art introduced local plastic types of its own while maintaining the general type as prevalent during the period. The fragment of a terracotta at Kauśāmbī depicts a bull with a long tail in relief facing right. A man is seen riding on its back and the neck of the bull has a garland of bells and flowers. Unfortunately, the heads of the man and the bull are missing. A better preserved plaque of this type is in the collection of Bharat Kala Bhavan, Banaras Hindu University, Vārāṇasī. The man riding the bull, in such cases, may be identified as Śiva (*fig.* 93). Kala also speaks about a terracotta tricycle drawn by bulls. The figures of the bulls on either side of the tricycle cover greater part of the tricycle cart (*fig.* 94). The scholar also points out the fragment of a front wall of a toy cart (*figs.* 97, 98). On the top of this there appears three turbaned figures. Below them one finds two bull heads in reliefs. Our scholar compared this terracotta relief with the one seen at Bhaja caves where Sūrya is seen driving his chariot. A unique chariot of Kauśāmbī was also referred to by Kala where a king is riding a chariot drawn by four bulls. The same chariot is seen moving from right to left[28] (*fig.* 95). A reference may be made here of a unique plaque from Rājghāṭ in the collection of Bharat Kala Bhavan (Vārāṇasī). This Śuṅga terracotta plaque shows a pair of fighting men (*muṣṭi-yuddha*), a pair of fighting cocks (*kukkuṭa-yuddha*) and a pair of fighting bulls (*vṛṣabha-yuddha*).[29] It also includes the prizes in the form of four wine containers (*āpāna*) since liquor was an invariable feature in village *goṣṭhīs* or *yātrā* festival in ancient India.[30] It appears, fights like bull-fights and cock-fights were

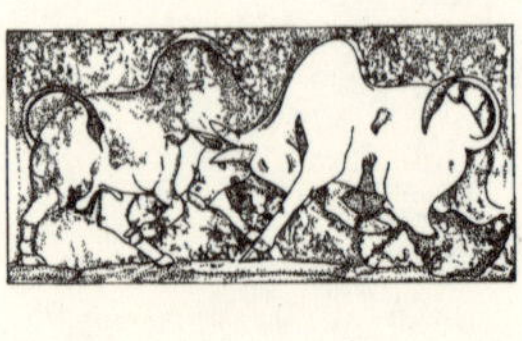

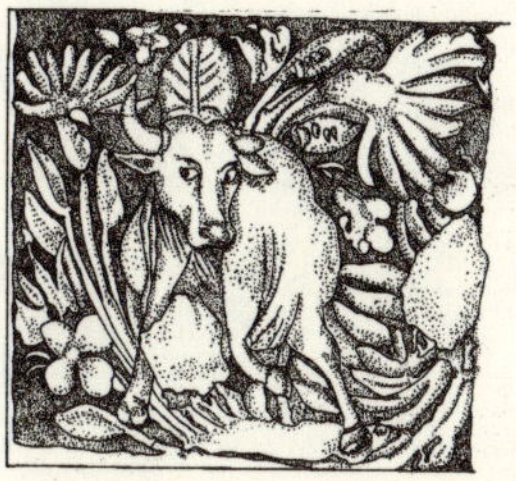

sources of amusements to the common people and the tradition of betting was also involved, in such contexts, (*fig.* 96).

Bhītā yielded a round terracotta plaque of Śuṅga period which depicts a village scene. To the right of this landscape, there appears a bullock cart.[31] This is in the collection of Indian Museum, Calcutta (No. A. AA. 1650-74). Patna Museum has a number of Śuṅga terracottas showing the figure of the bulls (Arch. No. 6678, 4219, 8780, 6088, 4263, etc.). But this museum has a single bull image of Śuṅga period (Acc. No. 7158) which hails from Mathurā. It shows a heavy conventional type of bull, with hump. A band is affixed on the left of his head. The muzzle is holed and the left leg is broken. It is a greyish terracotta.[32]

Dr. Jayaswal, while analysing the technique of terracottas with particular reference to bulls in the Period-IV of Hastināpura dated between second century BC and third century AD, observed that clay for making bulls was, perhaps, acquired from the courtyard or vicinity of the house and such clay was unlevigated. She also informed that the use of pond-bed clay might have also been used. She observed that the terracottas of this phase were allowed to be exposed to sun for a considerable period of time before they were put into fire. Since the terracottas of this phase did not show any cracks, to her, the carbonized and smoky black surface of these specimens was due to their contact with oil and cereals while burning in the fire.[33]

Kuṣāṇa Terracottas

The so-called Kuṣāṇa period, which spans between first and third century AD, is marked by the increase in the production of animal figurines in terms of numbers and varieties. The historical sites such as Mathurā (Period-III), Rājghāṭ (Period-III), Ahicchatra, Bhītā, Kauśāmbī and Vaiśālī exposed a huge number of animal figurines which may be classified and studied on the basis of four major criteria, namely, the frequency, variety of animals represented, decoration and technique. Rājghāṭ yielded 28 animal figurines in the Period-II while in the Period-III it came out with 113 animal figures. The number of animal figures also increased in other sites like Mathurā, Vaiśālī, Bhītā, Kauśāmbī, etc. The general appearance of the bulls looks the same as was in the preceding period but, in the Kuṣāṇa period, the bulls appeared of larger size. Among the animals, the figure of bulls predominated, and at most of the sites in Gaṅgā-Yamunā Valley, one finds humped-bulls. Some bull figures are made with exaggerated hump and thin and pointed mouth[34] (*figs.* 99-102). The figure of bulls are generally found decorated, particularly, in Rājghāṭ and Vaiśālī. The decorative motifs include leaf pattern, wheel and sun symbols, etc. The decoration, generally, appears around the neck while the middle part of it was kept plain. In this period, a new change is noted in the technique. The clay modellers used double-mould. Some scholars took this technique as of foreign origin. But the period also throws some hand-modelled forms which look coarser because of the inferior quality of clay used. The period mostly witnessed red colour figures; only in Rājghāṭ, a few grey colour figures were made. In this period, we find terracotta figures with moulded face having hand-modelled body. The period also produced hollow figures while a few animals have been noticed, having holes in their legs. The moulded face with modelled body was restricted to human figures and to a few monkey figures. The animals were mostly made in hollow figures. The wheeled figures, in this period, became quite popular with holes, appearing on their legs. The animal figures of this period are characterized by the use of paint on the surface, large size, and some, with movable heads. Double moulds were used for making animal figures in round shape. In such cases, the figure is moulded in two halfs and then joined. Use of double

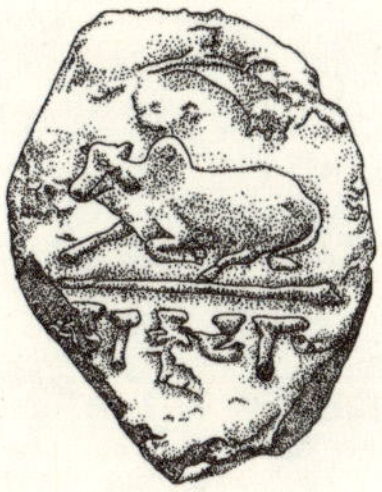

moulds is reported from Mathurā, Ahicchatra, Kauśāmbī, Rājghāṭ, Vaiśālī, Kumrahār, Koṇḍapur, etc.

Kauśāmbī yielded a few bullock carts datable to Kuṣāṇa period. In Indian Museum, Calcutta, there is a toy bullock cart (Acc No. A-20838, AAA/1682-74). This bullock cart is shown drawn by a pair of bulls and these animals are shown in relief. A reference may be made of another toy cart in terracotta in the same museum (A 22515). Dated in the first-second century AD, this cart shows a grotesque face having two horns on the sides of its head. And his legs are shown by the side of the cart.[35] There is a terracotta figure, cow-headed, in the State Museum, Lucknow and this figure has been identified with *gomukhī yakṣī*. In the same museum, there is a stone bull-headed (*gomukha yakṣa*) accompanied by a standing female in human form.

Bhītā exposed Kuṣāṇa image of Śiva-Pārvatī and a bull or Nandī shown as the mount of Śiva (*fig.* 104). The figure is in Indian Museum, Calcutta and is dated to third century AD (No. A 103080, AAA/1624-74). Excavations at Narhan has laid bare a number of bull figures between its Period-II and V. Most of the bulls are humped bulls. Some bulls are shown here standing and some are shown in movement. About 11 of these figures, discovered at Narhan, show that they were hand-modelled and fired red under oxydized condition. Most of the figures are devoid of any ornamentation, applique or incised.[36] Dr. Jayaswal reported two types of bull figures from Period-IV at Hastināpura which spans between second century BC and third century AD. There is a group of bulls, red slipped, decorated specimens with skilled modelling. The other group represents archaic bulls with strikingly small features. This group can be divided under four subgroups:

(I) Baked,

(II) Semi-baked with smoky surface,

(III) Fired and carbonized, and

(IV) Red slipped well baked.

Discussing technique behind these terracottas, the scholar is of the opinion that the small archaic bulls from Hastināpura were used as ritual objects while the bulls with skill-modelling were used as children-toys.[37]

Koṇḍapur, a village of Kalabgur tehsil in Meḍak district, Hyderabad, exposed a number of figurines made of Keoline, a soft grained clay of white colour. These figures were made in double moulds.[38] Dated between first and second century AD, these Sātavāhana terracottas include a considerable number of animal figurines, including bull[39] (*fig*. 103).

Gupta Terracottas

Between fourth and sixth centuries AD, the political history of India was dominated by the powerful rulers of Gupta dynasty. The period is also taken to represent as a golden period of Indian history. The period attained the height of excellence in various cultural activities. The art and literature of the period acquired all the characteristics and height of skillful achievements and, therefore, the period is rightly called the classical period. Like other branches of art, the period also witnessed the expertise and excellence in the field of terracotta productions. Specimens of terracotta art of the Gupta period have been brought to light from the various historical sites such as, Mahāsthān, Maināmatī, Pahārpur (Bangladesh), Raṅgmatī, Gokul, Kasīā, Sahet-Mahet, Bhītarī, Mathurā, Ahicchatra, Rājghāṭ, Sārnāth, Kośam (Allahabad), Bhītā, Bhītargāon, Sankisā (U.P.), Kurukṣetra, Basenagar, Barapal, Mīrpurkhās, Jhukar, Raṅgmahal, Hanumāngarh, Muṇḍa, Pīr-Sultān-Kī-Ḍherī (Rajasthan), Apasad, Nālandā, Vikramaśilā and Kumrahār

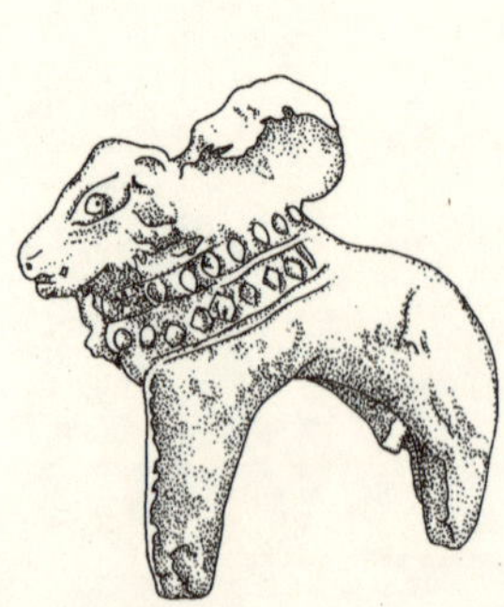

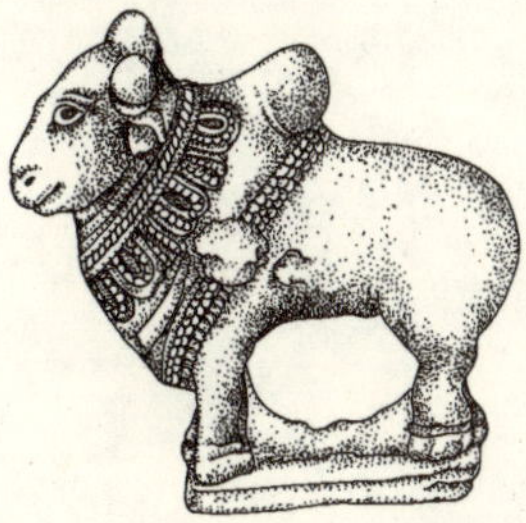

(Bihar).[40]

The terracottas of Gupta period were produced in various techniques. Unfortunately, the contemporary texts are silent in indicating the technique of terracotta art. Technique of terracotta is found to have been discussed in later texts such as *Matsya Purāṇa* (Ch. 258-263), *Śukranītisāra* (Ch. IV.4.72) and *Hari Bhakti Vilāsa* of Gopāla Bhaṭṭa (18 *vilāsa*). It appears from these texts that the technique of terracotta, discussed in these texts, was already in practice in the Gupta period.[41] The technique of the Gupta period includes modelling by hand, use of single mould, use of double mould, finishing and baking and, in certain cases, use of paints.[42]

The exposed terracotta objects from the various sites of Gupta period included a large number of animal figures. For example, the Gupta terracottas from Rājghāṭ, alone, laid bare 137 animal figurines. At Ahicchatra, the number of animal figures also increased but neither Kauśāmbī nor Mathurā could produce large number of terracottas in this period. Of the animals, the figure of bull appeared with different features. The period produced archaic bull, a kind of toy-bull, seated or standing on a pedestal, humped-bull with realistic anatomy, bull, without hump and having transverse hole, bull, with cylindrical neck and bull, with rider. The archaic type of bull figures are found to be solid and hand-modelled and they were crudely executed (*figs.* 105, 106). The hump in such a case is noticed over the head and they are found endowed with flaring legs. Such bulls were discovered from Kumrahār,[43] Bhītarī, Rājghāṭ and Ahicchatra. The toy-bulls are found to be made with double moulds. And such figures are found from Rājghāṭ (*fig.* 108) and Ahicchatra. Made in very fine levigated clay, a few toy bulls are found painted in black and white. The humped-bulls were found from Rājghāṭ, Ahicchatra and Bhītarī. Made in solid clay, their bodies are found plain and smooth (*fig.*107). The large size heads of the bull were meant to be fitted into the hollowed body. Rājghāṭ (Period-III) discoveries found 66 full figures of Gupta period, of which 42 are of crude variety and are characterized by applique decorations around the neck and, sometimes, on tails. These crude bulls are without hump.[44] The decoration of the Gupta animal figures includes only floral designs.

Ahicchatra in its Gupta phase, exposed a few bull figures which are found to be plain, red in colour and made from moulds. A few humped-bulls have also been found at Ahicchatra. They are moulded, red coloured, plain and are endowed with naturalistic treatment of anatomy. The same area produced, at least, seven solid hand-made bull figures. Some of these bulls bear surface decorations by incised circles, lines and dots.[45] The Period-III at Śrāvastī exposed the existence of a few ill-fired humped-bulls comparable to Hastināpura type. Such conical humped-bulls appeared on the lower level of the period.[46] The unique brick temple at Bhītargāon are found embellished on its exterior wall with decorative bricks. Such decorations include a number of mythological narratives. This signifies that the modellers in clay (*puśta kāraka*), potters (*kumbhakāra*) or brick masons (*iṣṭaka vardhakin*) achieved acme and expertise in this art. A terracotta brick panel of the said site in The State Museum at Lucknow depicts Kṛṣṇa killing the bull Ariṣṭāsura or Vatsāsura. While Kṛṣṇa was playing with cowherd boys and girls, his maternal uncle Kaṁsa sent a demon in the form of a bull to kill Kṛṣṇa. But in the duel, Kṛṣṇa knocked the demon down and killed him. This panel skillfully represents the theme. Unfortunately, the face of Kṛṣṇa is mutilated but the artist appears to have given vigorous bodies both to Kṛṣṇa and Vatsāsura and was successful in capturing the tense atmosphere of this powerful drama.

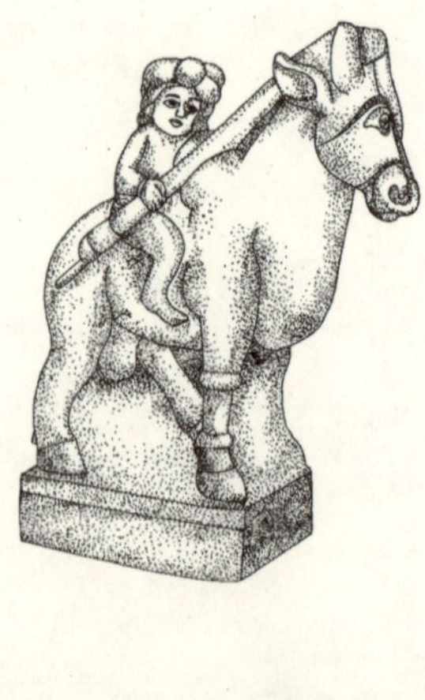

Moulded bricks of Gupta period were also very popular in Rajasthan and are found in the historical sites of Sambhar, Nagar, Nagarī, Muṇḍa, Pīr-sultān-kī-ḍherī, Sūratgarh and

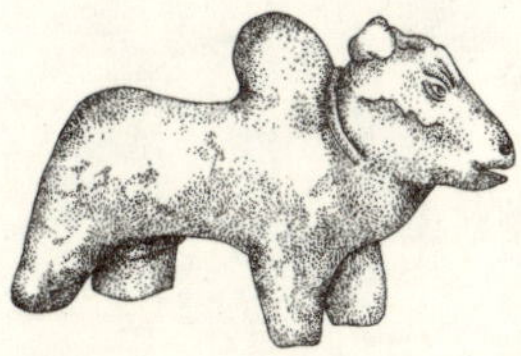

Raṅgamahal. In Sambhar, one finds the depiction of humped bulls. Nagarī also produced terracotta tiles with various animals, including bulls, in their naturalistic renderings.[47] Muṇḍa also exposed a few bull heads of very fine workmanship. The most interesting terracotta plaque from Raṅgamahal depicts a three-faced Śiva seating cross-legged with Pārvatī on his mount Nandī, the bull (*fig*.110). Another terracotta plaque from Raṅgamahal shows Kr̥ṣṇa as lifting Govardhana. On the Govardhana mountain, there appears trees and animals which include cows and bulls. And these animals are depicted in such a way that they seem quite peaceful and unconcerned of the great drama which was under enactment by lord Kr̥ṣṇa[48] (*fig*. 111). A terracotta bull has also been discovered from a place called Belwā in the Sāraṇ district of Bihar. It represents a heavy humped-bull delineated in abstration. Its hump is unusally large. A rope is seen around its neck. It has a small. tail. Its sex-organ is also comparatively large and pellets are found used for eyes. It is covered with red slip. This terracotta which is now kept in Patna Museum also reveals traces of black paints (*fig*. 112).

The above discussion takes the form of a survey of terracotta bull figures from post-Harappan period down to the period of the Guptas (fourth-sixth century AD). The survey has brought to light that, in the period of our issue, a large number of animal terracotta figures have been discovered mostly from the north Indian sites. Among the animal figures, the figure of bull predominated in some of these sites in terms of its number. A close analysis of these bull figures shows that most of the bulls are humped-bulls (*Bos-indicus* or Brahmāni bulls). Its basic utility in agriculture and in commerce made it more popular than other animals. In a later phase, bulls were associated with Śiva and thus they became symbolic of the all-pervading holiness. The study found that some of the bulls were used as children-toys while some were shown as means of transport and a number of them have been depicted as beasts of burden. In the initial stages of terracotta art, the bulls were of hand-made varieties with applique decorations. In the same period the clay was not properly levigated and the execution was visibly crude. In course of time, the moulds were introduced. Some of the figures were partly moulded and partly finished by hands and tools. Subsequently, double moulds were introduced in the making of bulls. Although moulds were introduced, the tradition of hand-modelled bulls continued even later. The introduction of the moulds came into being in the historic phase and in the terracotta art of Maurya, Śuṅga, Kuṣāṇa and Gupta periods. The clay-modellers tried to catch the spirit and the sculptural mannerisms of the period and, thereby, they were unique in their approach. In the Gupta period, the introduction of relieved tiles and decorated bricks became very popular with which the exterior walls of the temples were decorated and such decorations included narrative panels. This was not noticed in the terracotta art of the pre-Gupta period. Some of the bulls of this period were applied with a kind of a slip before firing and some of the bulls appeared with the application of colours, particularly, red after firing. There are bulls which are sun-baked, some are ill-fired while others are evenly-fired. Most of the bulls look red but there are ample evidences of greyish and black-coloured bull figures, particularly, from the Mauryan level of few sites in northern India. The terracottas of the Śuṅga phase were allowed to be exposed to sun for a considerable period of time before they were put into fire and, therefore, the terracottas of this phase did not show any cracks. The carbonized and smoky black surface of some specimens of this period was due to their contact with oil and cereals while lying in the fire.

The body of the bull is, often, found decorated. Initially, the decoration was done with applique method but, later on, the decoration was done by incision or

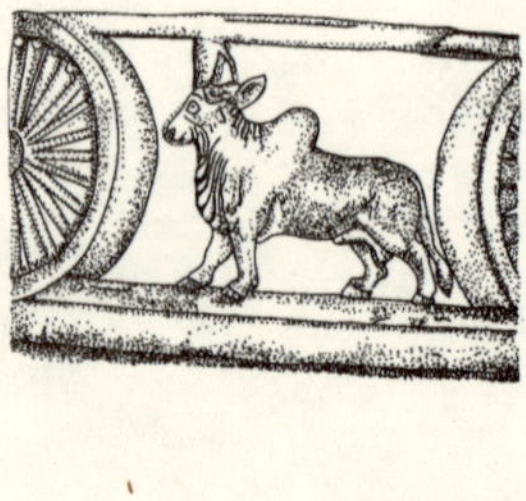

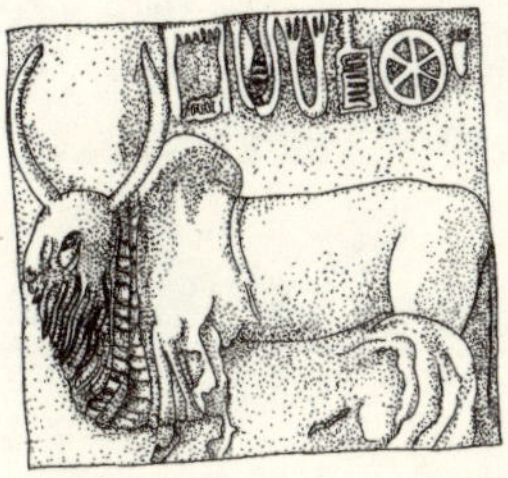

stamping or by scratching. The decoration includes circlets, dots, floral designs, *triśūla*, parallel lines, *cakra*s, notches, etc. The period also witnessed both varieties of bulls, humped and humpless. A careful analysis of these two types would reveal that the clay-modellers were more comfortable and were at ease in the making of humped bulls with which they were more familiar than the humpless ones. It may be noted here that the humped-bulls were of indigenous origin and were more in number. The artists studied them for a long time and could attribute, in their figure, more naturalism and realistic plasticity in body formations. The humpless bull is of non-Indian origin and, therefore, the artistes could not produce such figures with required perfection as they did in the case of humped ones.

The study also reveals that, with the time, the terracotta clay modellers gained experience and technological perfections. A comparative analysis of bull figures, produced in the Śuṅga, Kuṣāṇa and Gupta periods would show that in technique and treatment, the figure of bulls, produced in the Gupta period was superior to the bull figurines produced in the Śuṅga-Kuṣāṇa periods. The Gupta modellers not only used a better quality of clay but they prepared it with technological acumen and produced the figures of bulls with superior anatomical details whether standing, seated or in movement.

References

1. Vidula Jayaswal & Kalyan Krishna, *An Ethno-Archaeological View of Indian Terracotta*, pp. 111-12; and also see K. Samir Mukhopadhyaya, "Terracotta toys in Ancient India and their display in modern museum," in *Calcutta Review*, vol. III, nos. 1 & 2, pp. 158-59.
2. *Ibid*., pp. 111-12.
3. H.D. Sankalia, "Excavation at Ahar, District Udaipur," *Indian Archaeology, A Review*, 1961-62, p. 50.
4. B.B. Lal, "Excavations at Hastinapura," *Ancient India*, nos. 10 & 11, 1954-55, pp. 32-50.

5. Pratibha Prakash, *Terracotta Animal Figurines in the Ganga Yamuna Valley* (*600* BC *to 600* AD), pp. 41-43.
6. V. Jayaswal and Kalyan Krishna, *op.cit.*, pp. 120-21.
7. R.G. Gaur, *Excavations at Ataranjikhera*, p. 8, Pl. XXXII-A.
8. *Ibid.*, pp. 366-68 (pl. LXXX-modelled, pl. LXX-6 moulded).
9. K.M. Srivastava, *Discovery of Kapilavastu*, p. 259.
10. *Ibid.*, pp. 192-93, Pl. LXXXIV-A; pl. LXXXIV-B.
11. V. Jayaswal and Kalyan Krishna, *op.cit.*, pp. 121-23.
12. P. Singh, *Excavations at Narhan*, p. 19.
13. V.S. Verma, "Importance of Chirand," in *JBRS*, vol. 45, Part 1-4, 1959, p. 320.
14. *Indian Archaeology, A Review, 1991-92*, p. 5.
15. Pratibha Prakash, *op.cit.*
16. *Ibid.*, pl. IV. B; fig. 3,5.
17. V.S. Verma, *op.cit.*, p. 320.
18. K.M. Srivastava, *op.cit.*, p. 193.
19. V. Jayaswal and Kalyan Krishna, *op.cit.*, p. 120.
20. Urmila Sant, *op.cit.*, pp. 165-66.
21. H.D. Sankalia, *Pre-History and Proto-history of India and Pakistan*, 1974, pp. 381-91.
22. M.C. Joshi and C. Margabandhu, "Some Terracottas from recent excavations at Mathura - A study," in *JISOA*, vol. VIII, 1977, p. 2, pl. IV, fig. 20.
23. Nisha Verma, *The Terracottas of Bihar*, p. 21.
24. *Indian Archaeology — A Review, 1974-75*, p. 10.
25. K.M. Srivastava, *op. cit.*, p. 193, pl. LXXXIV-B.
26. *Indian Archaeology — A Review, 1961-62*, p. 74, Pl. LXXIX.
27. *Indian Archaeology — A Review, 1962-63*, p. 43, Pl. LXXIV. B-I.
28. S.C. Kala, *Terracotta Figurines from Kausambi*, pp. 55, 134, 315, 40, 71, 74.
29. A. Dange, *Encyclopaedia of Puranic Belief and Practices*, p. 240; The author quotes the *Agni Purāṇa* (292.38) that records the tradition of bull fight for the general weal or cattle (*go-santi*).
30. V.S. Agrawala, "A unique Terracotta plaque from Rajghat" vide *Prince of Wales Museum Bulletin*, no. 2, 1953, pp. 82, Pl. 85.
31. M.K. Dhawalikar, *Master Pieces of Indian Terracotta*, p. 54, Pl. 35.
32. P.L. Gupta, *Patna Museum Catalogue*, p. 332, S.No. 181.
33. Vidula Jayaswal, *op.cit.*, pp. 149-51.
34. Pratibha Prakash, *op.cit.*, pp. 103-05.
35. Suman Mathur, *Art and Culture under the Kushanas*, p. 110.

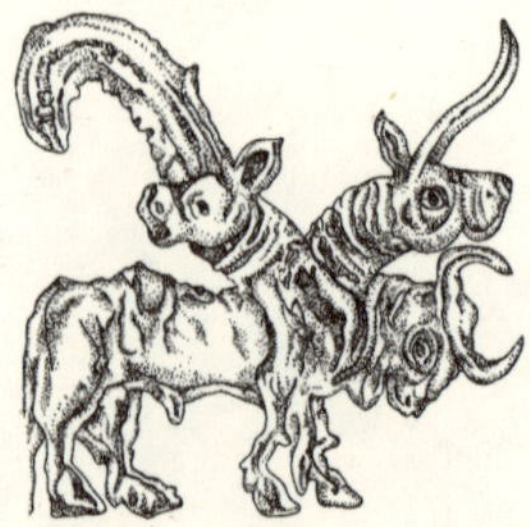

36. P. Singh, *op.cit.*, pp. 152-54.
37. Vidula Jayaswal & Kalyan Krishna, *op.cit.*, pp. 116-17.
38. The Sātavāhana terracottas were made of highly refined white clay with properties similar to keoline. Keoline is not geologically indigenous to the Indian sub-continent and, therefore, this identification is technically wrong. See Amy G. Poster, *From Indian Earth*, p. 114.
39. K.M. Ahamad, "Antiquities and Archaeological Remains of Kondapur," pp. 11-12; Proceedings of the Hyderabad Archaeological and Historical Society (Special meeting held on August 10, 1941); Also see V.S. Agrawala, *Indian Art*, p. 137.
40. Urmila Sant, *op.cit.*, p. 183; Also see C.C. Dasgupta, *Origin and Evolution of Indian Clay Sculpture*, p. 213.
41. S.K. Srivastava, *Terracotta Art in Northern India*, pp. 18-19.
42. Pratibha Prakash, *op.cit.*, pp. 133-34.
43. A Gupta terracotta humped-bull of heavy type with a rope around its neck and with a small tail was collected from a place called Belwā which is now in the Patna Museum collections. See Shere, *Terracotta Figures from Patna Museum*, Pl. 9.
44. Prathibha Praksh, *op.cit.*, pp. 122-24.
45. *Ibid.*, p. 137.
46. V. Jayaswal and Kalyan Krishna, *op.cit.*, p. 121.
47. Urmila Sant, *op.cit.*, p. 173.
48. *Ibid.*, p. 176.

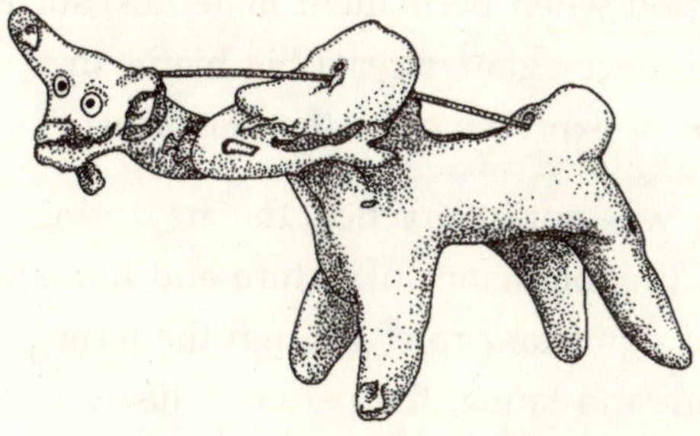

5

Bull in Early Indian Stone Sculpture

Bull in Mauryan Sculptures

THE Mauryans ruled from about 324 BC to 185 BC. The empire was founded by Candragupta I and the last ruler of the dynasty was king Bṛhadratha who was killed by the founder of Śuṅga dynasty, Puṣyamitra Śuṅga. The greatest ruler of the Mauryan dynasty was Aśoka, who is reported to have ruled the kingdom from 272-232 BC. He had his capital at Pāṭaliputra but he extended his empire, practically, throughout India. Initially, he conquered many places through war but, after the subjugation of Kaliṅga, he launched his campaign of righteous war or *dharma vijaya*. The examples of Mauryan art, so far exposed, were, mostly, produced during the time of Aśoka and were largely, patronized by him. The period witnessed a new turn because this was the period when permanent materials, such as stone, was introduced, once again, after a big hiatus in a wider scale as a medium of expression for the plastic art.

Since image-worship was not in practice, the art during this period revealed the predominance of nature and human figures did not play any significant role. Though the term nature includes both flora and fauna, the period is justly famous for the productions of numerous animal figures in stone, including bulls. In the art of northern India during this period one finds the plastic realizations of the figures of bull in various manners, including, both secular and religious, with symbolic implications. During the Mauryan period, through the excavations and explorations, a number

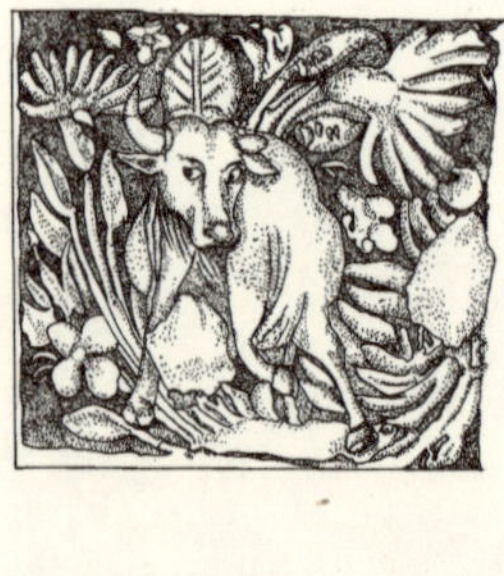

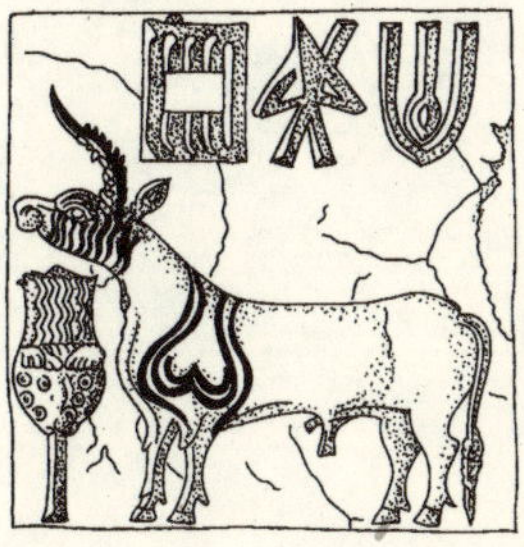

of ring stones and stone discs have been discovered from north-western part of India to as far as east Pāṭaliputra. One such ring stone is in the collection of the Archaeological Museum, Mathurā (No. 2471) with a diameter of 9 cm. The ring stone shows a full blown lotus flower with four animals, namely, a lion, an antelope, a bull and a stag, adjusted in four directions. There are also four female figures badly eroded holding different attributes. It is very difficult to explain the symbolic importance of all these animals and female figures. Yet it can be presumed that this ring stone, like other ring stones, is an example of something religious. The animals may refer to theriomorphic symbols of deities or all of them represent different aspects and are related to the concept of mother-goddess.[1] Another ring stone, which was discovered from Murtajiganj (Patna), has also been referred to by Agrawala which bears on it four animals, just like the abacus of the Sārnāth lion capital, including a bull.[2] This ring stone which is in the collection of Patna Museum (Acc. No. Arch. 10724) is made of soapstone and shows a humped-bull.[3] A similar ring stone was also discovered from Ganvariā (Kapilvastu) on which there are two concentric rings. The outer ring is wider and is intricately carved with four animals, including a bull just like the abacus of the lion capital at Sārnāth. So far as the bull is concerned, within a very limited space available on such ring stones, the sculptor with a mild depth executed the animal with characteristic details and with great care and, therefore, it appears nearly realistic. Srivastava rightly observes that only a religious zeal and devotion could produce such a work of art.[4] Patna Museum has a few mutilated pillar capitals with bull figures. Made in buff stone, a pillar capital has been found from Kumrahār, Patna (Acc. No. Arch. 11154). This capital shows four bulls, adorned, having a socket in the centre, most probably, to affix a wheel above (*dharmacakra*). The capital is endowed with the so-called Mauryan polish. V.S. Agrawala referred to the fragments of a bull capital found in Sadar *galī*, Patna, about which P. Mukherji reported earlier. Dr. Agrawala also referred on the basis of Mukherji's report, the existence of six Aśokan pillars at Pāṭaliputra and on the capitals of these pillars there appeared lion, elephant, bull and horse.[5] In the same Museum, there is another example of a pillar capital with four bulls (Acc. No. Arch. 10974). The heads of the bulls, except for one, are missing. This capital was discovered at Lohānīpur (Patna) and it shows the body of the two seated bulls (*fig*. 113).[6] Mr. Pandey, while surveying a number of places in the Hājīpur (Vaiśālī) subdivision in Bihar, discovered the capital of a pillar with four bulls. They were lying down on the cart road to the south of the village Salempur. It consists of two pairs of bulls reclining back to back within a square block. This block is adorned with honey suckle designs. Made in Chunār sandstone, this capital was found in a badly damaged condition. The heads of all the animals were found lost and the legs were badly injured. Mr. Pandey was unable to find any clue to the pillar to which this capital was attached but he firmly believed that the pillar in question might have been the one which Aśoka is known to have erected at the site of Nirvāṇa Stūpa of Ānanda, which he locates at this place.[7] Saraswati studied this sculpture carefully and found that each of these animals is characterized by an archaic look and represents a lower level of artistic conception, compared to the animals on edict-bearing columns. To him, the capital may be related to the pre-Aśokan days.[8] To Mr. Chanda, this bull capital of Salempur offers certain amount of stiffness and the acanthus above the bull stylized and, therefore, he compares this piece with reliefs of Śuṅga period.[9]

The capital of a pillar showing a single bull standing was found from Rāmpurvā in Bihar (*fig*. 114). This sculpture is now collected in the President House in New Delhi. This capital originally topped an Aśokan pillar. The capital consists of three component parts, viz., a bull at the top, a round decorated abacus in the middle and an inverted lotus

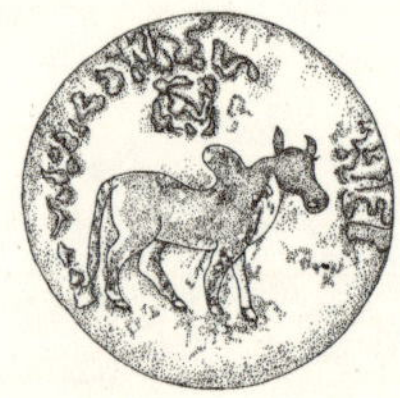

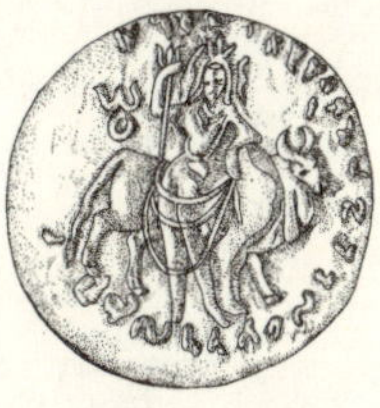

below. Sir John Marshall, while analysing this capital of Rāmpurvā observed that the figure of the bull at the top does not fit judiciously with the components below. This view has been challenged by P.K. Agrawala. To him the bull has been proportionately conceived and harmoniously adjusted with the other parts of the capital.[10] The bull at the top stands with its full weight on earth, appears quiet and maintains a restrained dignity. To Ray, its modelling is vigorous but not conventional; its plastic realization and linear adjustment are fully matured but not schematized; a dynamic naturalism gives it potency and strength. In aesthetic vision and treatment, it, perhaps, reflects the legacy of the art of the bulls of the prehistoric Indus Valley.[11] Huntington also holds the same view. To her, the bull on Rāmpurvā capital reminds her of seal engravings with bulls from the Indus civilization, suggesting, thereby, a continuity of the same tradition. As in the Indus seals, Huntington says that the species of Rāmpurvā bull is the Bos-Indicus. The proportions of the animal, its bone and muscle, structure and other features of its anatomy have been so carefully rendered by the sculptor that the uncarved matrices beneath the body left for structural purposes do not detract from the effect of naturalism.[12] The Rāmpurvā bull is rendered with all the tension and accentuations of muscles, of veins and bones, that a vigorous movement brings into play.

Ray, while carefully analysing the Rāmpurvā bull, observes that the Rāmpurvā bull, perhaps, represents the continuation of an indigenous art tradition, practised in wood, presumably, through centuries. He also referred to the literary references in this connection in the *Arthaśāstra*, the *Manu-Smṛti*, the *Aṣṭādhyāyī* of Pāṇini and in certain early Buddhist texts. To him there must have existed in pre-Mauryan Indian art of wood carving and clay modelling that carved and modelled free and round figures like Rāmpurvā bull.[13]

The symbolic role of the bull on this pillar, in particular, or bull, in general, in other Aśokan pillars has been explained by scholars in different ways. To R.P. Chanda, this bull symbolizes the Nandī, the mount of Śiva and, therefore, to him it was a Vṛṣadhvaja.[14] To Smith, the bull represents as the mount of Virūpākṣa, the guardian of the west. To some, the bull refers to the Buddha theriomorphically because the Master was born on Zodiac Tauras. Some scholars also connect the bull with the first Jaina pontiff (*tīrthaṅkara*), Ṛṣabhanātha, but a careful analysis would probably take us to believe that the bull, whether on the top or on the abacus, represented symbolically, the Buddha.[15]

Incidentally, a reference may be made of an information supplied by the Chinese travellers Fa-hien and Hiuen Tsang. When Hiuen Tsang was at Jetavana in Śrāvastī, he noticed that the eastern gate of the Jetavana *vihāra* was flanked by two Aśokan pillars. Of these two pillars, the left one was crowned by a wheel and the right one by an ox. He also saw a *stūpa,* enshrining the relics of the Buddha made by Aśoka.[16] A reference may also be made of a massive but mutilated stone animal figure, with head and foreleg missing. It was found at Manhai, Kośam. This was earlier identified as the figure of a bull, but on a closer examination of the genital organ, Prof. G.R. Sharma identified it as a figure of horse.[17]

F.O. Oertal, the executive engineer of the Archaeological Survey of India, discovered the famous lion capital at Sārnāth in 1904 when he was engaged in clearing the debris close to the western wall of the main shrine (*fig.* 115). This pillar capital has been considered undoubtedly the finest pieces of sculpture, so far discovered in India. Conceived of four parts, the bottom has a pitcher covered with lotus petals with double-curved contour. On the top of it is a round abacus or drum (*aṇḍa*) depicting on its body, between four wheels the figures, viz., a lion, an elephant, a bull and a

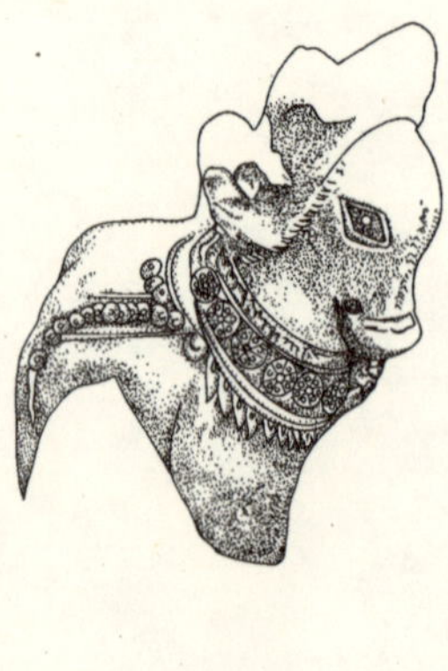

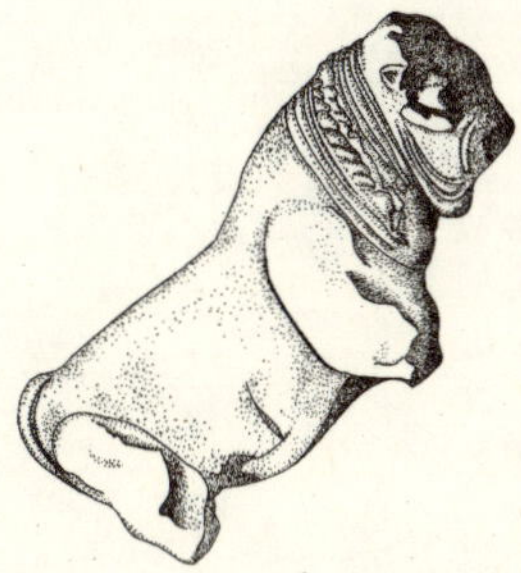

horse.[18] On the top of the abacus there appear four magnificent lions sitting back to back and these were topped by a wheel. Ever since its discovery, the scholars were looking for the iconographic explanations of the capital. T. Bloch was the earliest of scholars to explain the four animals on the abacus; to him the animals represent theriomorphically the four Hindu deities, namely Sūrya, Indra, Śiva and Durgā, and he found in these the subordination of the Hindu deities to the Buddha. Here the bull stood for Śiva. This identification was not accepted by many scholars.[19] Foucher found in these animals the four great events of Buddha's life. The bull symbolized Buddha's birth in Zodiac Tauras.[20] Sahani suggested that these animals, were connected with the imaginary four outlets of Buddhist Anatatta Lake. The four mouths of this lake were guarded by a horse, a dragon, a bull and an elephant.[21] Sahani further says:

> . . . . It is interesting to note that the Archaeological Section of the Central Museum at Lahore contains a small square terracotta plaque showing a circular depression in the middle surrounded by the same four animals, arranged in the same order. This plaque, according to some scholar's stood for, a true representation of the Anatatta lake and must have been used for worship.[22]

Vogel took these four animals on the abacus as merely ornamental motifs. To Huntington, the symbolism of the four animals remains unclear. She, however, feels that these had directional significance.[23] Khandalawala holds the same opinion and he thinks that the four animals on the abacus are guardians of four quarters. To him, Vaiśravaṇa, the guardian of north rides on lion, Dhṛtarāṣṭra the guardian of east, rides on an elephant, Virūdhaka, the guardian of the south, rides on a horse and Virūpākṣa, the guardian of the west, rides on a bull. And he thinks that these animals therimorphically represent the four guardian deities who carried to the four ends the spirit of Aśoka's *dharma*.[24] Agrawala took these four noble animals (*mahā ājāneya paśu*) and the *dharmacakras*, the continuation of *puruṣa* (*cakra*) the divine Purāṇic power and the animals as *paśu* and each pair of a *cakra* and an animal symbolizes *puruṣa paśu*, half-human half-animal. The former stands for divine power and the latter for material body — *yodyagyum tanvan avaghnan puruṣaṁ paśuṁ*, (*R̥V*. X.90.15).[25] Raychoudhary drew our attention to *Cakkavattisihnāda Sutta* and he found that the animals and the wheel on the abacus represent the royal chariots of Aśoka as symbol of monarch's conquering efficacy. The wheel of this chariot rolled over his dominions. The horse-driven chariots were quite common. The classical historian Nearchus noted the use of elephant for drawing chariots. On the authority of Megasthenese, historian Strabo referred to the use of bull for chariots. Chariots, drawn by oxen on either side, were found in Pāṭaliputra during the Mauryan period.[26] The animals depicted on the Sārnāth abacus are of two types — the elephant and the lion are wild animals, not fit for *yajña*, whereas the bulls and the horse are domestic animals which are called *yajñīya*. Thapalyal, after carefully analysing the capital, came to the conclusion that it served as a symbol which could satisfy the people of various likings and various attachments. Aśoka made the pillars both for religious and secular purposes and the symbolism of the animals were also at once religious and secular. He further says that Aśoka had respect to all the sects and he enjoined on his subjects to respect the religious beliefs other than their own. The animals on the abacus may represent as a secular symbol of vigour, patience, service and tolerance for inspiring people. The animals and the wheels may also be taken as representing the Buddha, the *dharmacakravartī* as well as the Aśoka, the *rājā cakravartī*. So the wheel symbolizes Buddha and also the jewel wheel (*cakraratna*) of a *rājā cakravartī* ruler. The animals on the abacus may also represent the four directions and indicate the spread of

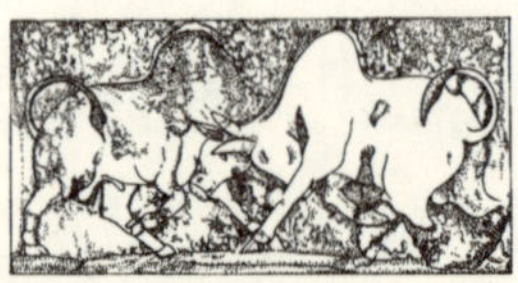

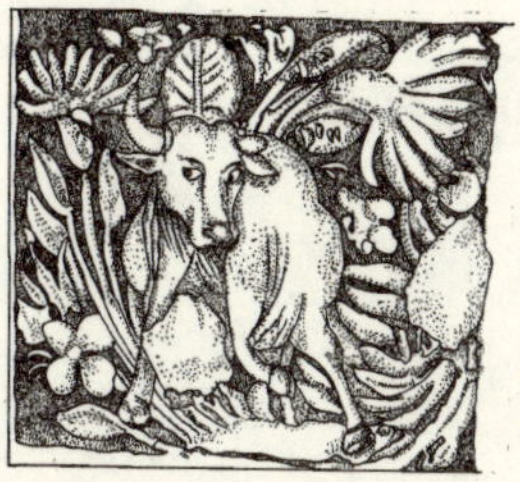

Buddhism in all the four quarters. And, secularly, they represent the might of a *cakravartī,* king in all the four directions. Of the four animals, bull and elephant appeared from the period of Harappan civilization whereas the appearance of lion and horse, on the other hand, was new. Thus, it indicates, perhaps, Aśoka's love and respect for both, the old and the new traditions and these four animals may be connected theriomorphically with Hindu, Buddhist and Jaina divinities.

The bull on the Sārnāth abacus is shown as walking. It is a humped-bull with a long tail, its ears are alert and the eyes in its profile are very expressive. The figure has been very naturalistically delineated and the abstraction is noticed only in the treatment of its dewlap. The artist was quite successful in portraying the ups and downs and the movement of muscles of a walking bull in such a manner as if he watched a moving bull from a close distance. The figure has been carved in relief and it is carved on the bend of the abacus and in conformity with the rolling wheels. Its movements have been very deftly conceived. Professor Ganguly observed that "the wheels on the abacus of the capital are given a flat surface but the areas on which animals are shown are convex in shape" and, as such, certain problems appeared before the sculptor which he seems to have overcome easily by making the animals appear taking a turn while in motion (including the bull). This is a clever device revealing a maturity on the part of the sculptor. Kramrish took the Mauryan art as the Gangetic aftermath of the art of Indus Valley. She tried to hint at that the impact of Indus Valley tradition, particularly, in the treatment of bull and elephant on the Sārnāth abacus.[27] Ray observed that the art of Indus Valley remained chronologically unrelated and unexplained and the two arts belonged to two different aesthetic vision and imagination.[29] Ray further said that "Indus Valley may have bequeathed but distant and faint memories." Prof. Ray, while analysing the animals, artistically, observed that the scholars often go for a comparative analysis of the Rāmpurvā bull with the bull on the abacus at Sārnāth. But to him, there is not much similarity in the art form and style of these bulls. The Rāmpurvā bull is standing erect as if it is standing with all attention to face a forthcoming situation whereas the bull on the abacus at Sārnāth is in movement and, apparently, not as alert as the Rāmpurvā bull is.

Bull in Śuṅga Sculptures

The last Mauryan ruler is known to have been killed by Puṣyamitra Śuṅga. The latter, thereafter, eastablished the Śuṅga Dynasty which covered a period from 185 BC to 75 BC. Thereafter, the Kaṇvas ruled up to 30 BC. Since the content and nature of the narrative art of this period remained the same, the sculptures made from 185 to 30 BC is generally described under a common caption of Śuṅga sculptures. The period witnessed brisk activities in stone sculpture with particular reference to the Buddhist theme. The contents of the sculpture are found relieved on the gateways and railings of Buddhist *stūpa*s. One of the earliest *stūpa*s of this period was discovered by Alexander Cunningham in 1873 in a village called Bharhut in central India. Bharhut is situated, six miles north-east of Uchahara and nine miles south of the Satnā railway station on the Jabalpur Railway zone. It is nearly 120 miles to the south-west of Allahabad. When Cunningham visited this place, he saw the entire complex in ruins. Therefore, the remaining parts of the gateways and the railings of Bharhut were sent to the Indian Museum, Calcutta. The Museum at Allahabad, Bharat Kala Bhavan in Vārāṇasī and the National Museum, New Delhi and a few museums, abroad, have a number of dispersed pieces from Bharhut in their respective collections. Dated in the second century BC, this *stūpa*, its railings and gateways were made of red sandstone quarried from a local hill, called Lāl Pahār. On the railings and gateways of Bharhut, one finds the

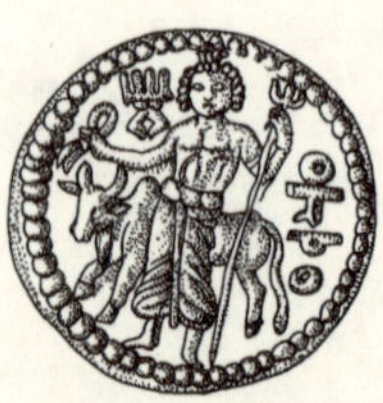

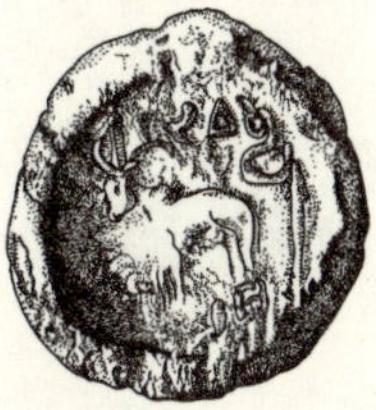

depiction of different kinds of animals both realistic and fantastic. Prof. Agrawala says that the cult of four great animals found a gushing admittance in the concept of *stūpa.* The *Niddesa* refers to Hasti-Vrata, Aśva-Vrata, Go-Vrata, Suparṇa Vrata, amongst others, and the Bharhut *stūpa* shows these animals freely sculptured in a religious atmosphere.[29] Among the animals, the unknown sculptors of Bharhut represented bulls in different ways. Agrawala draws our attention to the tall pillar of a gateway at the top of which there appear two-winged bulls (*sapakṣa vṛṣa saṅghāta*).[30] Bharhut has laid bare through its reliefs a number of *Jātaka* stories but there are instances which do not appear to be directly taken from *Jātaka* stories but were taken from the *Mūlasarvāstivādī Vinaya*. One of these shows,

> a bull had fallen into a swamp and as its owner had not been able to free it from its predicament before the night halt, he placed a snare consisting of a noose in front of it to protect it from the attack by wild animals. During the night, a jackal climbed on to the trapped bull's back to devour its flesh. The bull, however, tossed it through the air with its horns, so that it was caught in the noose in front of him. In a mocking rhyme, the bull then asked the jackal, struggling in the noose, why it was putting on such a performance. The jackal replied that it was not putting on an acrobatic performance but was in the process of ascending into Indra's heaven.

The relief shows the bull in the swamp and the latter is indicated by waves and tall water flowers. The jackal is shown twice, once flying, thrown in the air in front of a pole and second time, beneath it squatting on the ground with its paws bound together by the noose. This panel is seen relieved on the railing of Bharhut, collected in Indian Museum, Calcutta.[31] In the Indian Museum, one finds on a railing post, the story of the purchase of Jetavana park (156). Prince Jeta demanded the price for the park with as many coins as would cover the park. Thus we find a bullock cart loaded with coins and the unyoked bullocks resting on the ground. The narrative is labelled with an inscription — *jetavana anātha pediko deti koti santhatenaketa* (Anātha-piṇḍika dedicates Jetavana, purchased with a layer of crores).[32] The two bulls are shown very naturalistically and they are shown in a relaxed position after their toils with heavy loads of coins. They are shown quite indifferent to the drama enacted just above them (*fig.* 116). In a peculiar composition, the unknown sculptor of Bharhut also depicted the composite body of a bull and fish (*vṛṣamaccha*). Such a motif represents marine and water symbology and served as a part of the *stūpa* symbolism[33] (*fig.* 117). *Aṅgavijjā* refers to *gomaccha,* a type of composite animal just discussed.[34] In the Vedic tradition the bull was connected with the cycle of water life. This may explain the fish tail in the hind part of a bull.[35] The relief, showing the *Sujātā Jātaka,* includes the profile of a dead bull who is being offered a bunch of tender grass by Sujātā with the prayer in vain to come to life (*Jātaka* No. 352). It is probably the solitary example of relieving a dead bull. This humped bull is shown with emaciated body and closed eyes. The sculpture could not visualize the body of the dead animal lying and, therefore, it appears seated with folded legs within a meandering lotus creeper (*fig.* 118).

The ruins of a *stūpa* railing of the Śuṅga period (first century BC) was also found at Bodh-Gayā in Bihar. A small portion of the railing is in the collection of Indian Museum, Calcutta, while a bigger portion of the railing is *in situ.* Among the animals, the bull is also found represented on the railing of the place. A panel, that depicts two side pillars, is crowned by two bulls. Bodh-Gayā also shows a ploughman ploughing the field with a goad in his hand to drive the pair of bullocks and has a long wooden beam in the middle to which the oxen were yoked.[36] This panel proves that in second-first century BC, regular use of

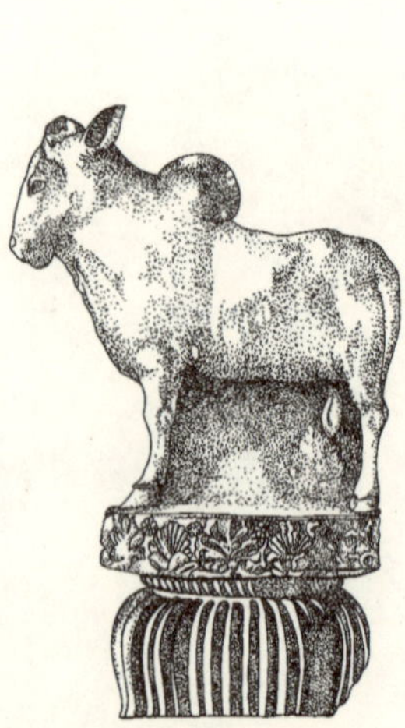

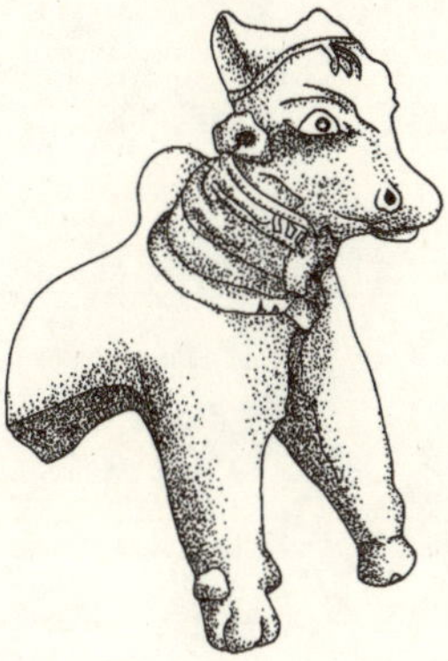

bullocks was made for cultivation purposes. In another medallion, a standing mounted-bull along with an infant-bull are found accommodated. Though badly eroded, the matured bull appears quite alert as if it is getting ready to face certain unforeseen eventualities. In the middle of another pillar, within a round medallion, a full blown lotus has been carved and on the centre peripheral of the lotus appears a humped-bull. The way the bull has been depicted against something like a hollow, leads us to take it as symbolizing Buddha's birth in Zodiac Taurus.[37] Coomaraswamy points out a few friezes showing real and fantastic animals. At least, in one of these, there are two bulls shown running violently from right to the left. Nowhere in Indian art, neither earlier nor later, the figures of running humped-bulls are shown.[38] This conclusion, however, does not hold good, since examples of running bulls have been discovered, elsewhere, also, such as at Amarāvatī.

During the reign of the Śuṅgas and the Sātavāhanas, a number of *stūpa*s were constructed, of which the best preserved is Stūpa No. I at Sāñcī. At the top of a hillock at Sāñcī, there are three *stūpa*s of which the Stūpa No. II is earlier in date and Stūpa No. III is considered as the latest at the site. Sāñcī is only 5.5 miles from Vidiśā (modern Bhilāsā) on the confluence of river Vidīśā (modern Beas) and the Betravatī (modern Betavā). It was the capital of Eastern Mālwā and it is situated on the highway from Mathurā to Pratiṣṭhāna on the Godāvarī. The Stūpa No. II at Sāñcī shows, among other animals, bulls. Seated bulls are also noticed on the top of the pillar at Stūpa No. I. Among the architraves of Stūpa No. III, there appears the figures of bulls. There is only one reference of a bullock cart in Sāñcī sculptures, which appears in the inner face of the eastern pillar and, that too, in a lower panel. It shows two bullocks yoked to a two-wheeled cart. The body of the cart is shaded with a vaulted roofing (*apavṛta*). The tails of the bullocks seems tied on a side of their body with a rope probably to prevent them from flexing the dirt and mud on way and, thus, save the passangers from being besmeared with it. Bullock cart is also found in the sculptures of Bharhut (Indian Museum No. 95) and Mathurā. Although there is only one relief of a bullock cart at Sāñcī it does not mean that the use of such a cart was less popular in Śuṅga India[39] (*fig.* 121). Bull was one of the six animals used for drawing vehicles, as has been referred to in the *Mahāniddesa.*[40] In Sāñcī, the bull is shown in the reliefs both as drawing the vehicle as well as carrying the passengers on its back. Two seated bulls are noticed with riders each on their back. Such bull-riders are found on southern, eastern and northern gates of Stūpa No. I at Sāñcī (*fig.* 122) and on the small gateway of Sāñcī Stūpa No. III. The bulls at Sāñcī are all humped and call for a comparison with the Indus bulls, engraved on seals. The Sāñcī bulls are of typical Indian breed and remain popular through a long span of time. It may be mentioned here that to make the ride a matter of pleasure the bulls were endowed with some sort of saddles like those found on the back of the horses and elephants, including trapings and jewelleries. The traping included the nozzle-strips which after passing through the nostrils were fastened around the head. A rope was attached to it as a rein. Instead of a stick, the bull riders on the eastern gateway at Sāñcī hold a lash in their hands. The adorning of bull is also noticed at Sāñcī. One finds on the neck of the bulls broad necklaces (*graiveyaka*) of many pearl strings.[41] Sometimes a bridle, consisting of a band, is found on the forehead of a bull. In a few cases the humps of the bulls were found decorated. The western gateway of Sāñcī Stūpa No. I exposed the depiction of unicorns with riders or grooms standing at their site.[42] On the northern gateway at Sāñcī, the places where the lower most architraves cross each other, there are on either side, two seated bulls shown with riders. The bulls are humped and each have a pair of long twisted horns. On each side, one of the figures of the

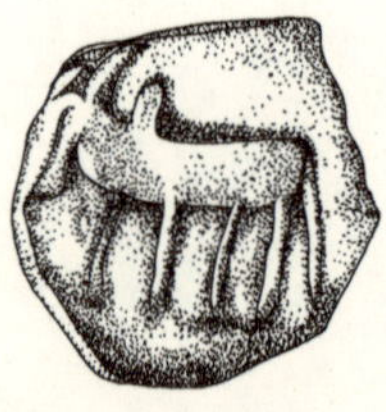

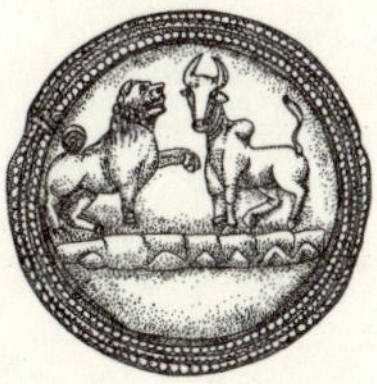

bull oversects the other bull and, therefore, only the fore part of the bulls at the back is visible. Similar compositions are also noticed on the eastern gate of Sāñcī Stupa No. I but, in this case, the figures of bulls, with riders, are carved on the uppermost architrave where it meets with the pillar on either side.

In the Śuṅga Mathurā one finds a few figures of bulls made in spotted red stone and these are found normally on the fragments of coping stone (*uṣṇīṣa*). Among these a few are winged bulls. A cross bar in Mathura Museum (Acc. No. 2322), carved with a full blown lotus medallion showing a spirited bull with a rider on its back, who holds the tail of the animal with his left hand (*fig.* 123). Allahabad Museum (A.M. 65) has in its collection the fragment of door lintel from Kauśāmbī (district Allahabad) and it is stylistically dated first century BC. The lintel shows the figure of a Gajalakṣmī (*fig.* 124). It is interesting to note that she is flanked to the left by a walking bull and to the right by an elephant. The bull wears a garland. It is said that "primeval bull is the consort of the mother-goddess." It is further said that in the Vedas, the bull manifests for Indra, the god of rain and, thus, gets associated with the cycle of water of life.[43] It may be referred here that the arch above the goddess Śrī Lakṣmī, relieved in the Ananta Gumphā at Khaṇḍigiri, near Bhuvaneśvara (Orissa), includes, among other animals, a bull.[44] The Śuṅga rock-cut reliefs at Bhaja has in its eastern part of its *mukha-maṇḍapa* one full and one half pilasters on which a couple is shown riding on a bull.[45] In the Nahapana Vihāra at Nāsik, there is an octagonal pillar placed on a *pūrṇa kumbha* and the latter is placed on a four-tiered basement. On the abacus of this pillar one finds pairs of addorsed bull (*vṛṣasaṁghāta*) over whom is an impressive entablature covered by a parapet with superimposed rail design. Huntington noticed in Vihāra III (Gautamīputra Gufā) at Nāsik, the recumbent bull figures and bull capital on the pillar.[46]

In Andhra Pradesh, the bull, was found relieved on the Buddhist *stūpa* railings discovered at Amarāvatī, Goli, Nāgārjunakoṇḍa and Candavaram. In the State Museum at Hyderabad, four sculptures are there that hail from Candavaram in the district of Prakāśam. Of these, on the stone panels (Nos. 244 & 246) a number of animals are found relieved, including bulls. Nigam connects this bull as symbolic of *vṛṣabha rāśi* in which Buddha was born.[47] Ganguly's *Andhra Sculpture* points to a series of fragments in low relief, found from Amarāvatī and dated to 100 BC; these are relieved with a number of animal figures, some with wings and recall analogous figures at Bharhut and Bodh-Gayā. He says that the fragments of casing slabs from Bhaṭṭiprolu, Jaggayapeṭa and Amarāvatī of the Archaic period (*circa* 200-50 BC) offer five complete examples and various fragments of pillars[48] and they have caryatids (*yakṣas* and *yakṣīs*). The capital of the pillar includes, among other elements, winged bulls, horses and elephants, which are comparable with such figures, which were found relieved in the cave architecture of western India. The animal figures at Amarāvatī, including bulls, appear invariably on friezes. The animals appear with three varieties of horizontal panels; such panels include both domestic animals such as bulls and also mythical animals with wings and fantastic types. The second way of depicting the animals appeared as purely decorative and the third method of relieving the animals had been to delineate a narrow strip placed at the bottom of the lotus on the pillars of the rails. Amarāvatī also projected in one of its reliefs the story of the gift of Jetavana by Anāthapiṇḍika. Though the relief is partly destroyed, the remains that survived can help in reliably identifying the scene. On the left of the panel at Amarāvatī appears the part of an ox-cart fully ladened and on the right a walkman squatting on the ground and laying coins on the ground.[49] In the Government Museum, Madras, there is a fragment of a coping stone from Goli (Andhra Pradesh) which shows the story of *Vesantara Jātaka* (*fig*. 125). The

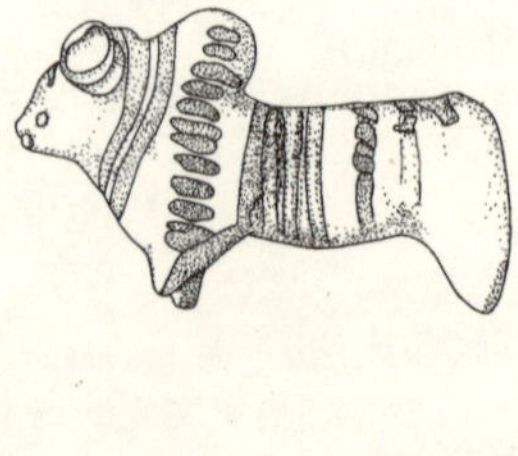

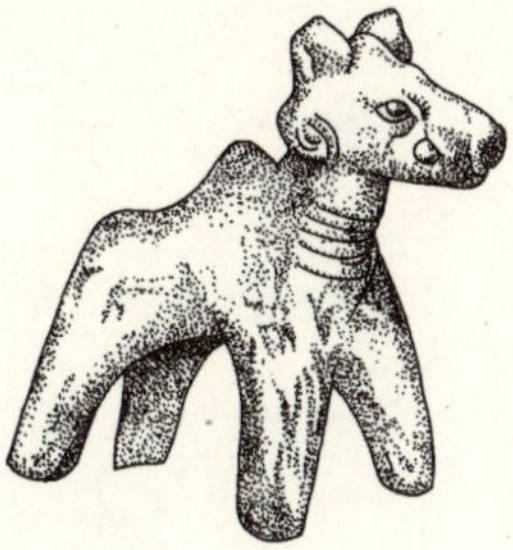

Jātaka has been relieved in detail. In the continuous narration at its third stage shows the banished prince Vesantara who sets out in a wagon drawn by bullocks. It also includes the scene where the two brāhmaṇas desiring the bullocks from the prince as gift.[50] In the next scene Vesantara and his wife are shown drawing the cart which was earlier drawn by bulls and their children are shown seated on the cart.[51] Such an event led Ramachandran to infer that car, carts and chariots (the latter of primitive types) represented on the relieves were quite common at Goli and also at Amarāvatī.[52] The relief sculptures from Nāgārjunakoṇḍa (Andhra Pradesh) depict domesticated animals like horses, goats, bulls and cows. Longhurst and Ramachandran drew our attention to two interesting Buddhist panels, one showing the offering of food to the Buddha after enlightenment and other showing Trapuṣa and Bhallika visiting Buddha. In both the panels there is a depiction of bulls and such bulls may be compared with the bulls found at Bharhut, Sāñcī, Gāndhāra and Amarāvatī. Nāgārjunakoṇḍa exposed the remains of a moonstone on whose border there appears a bull. This bull is somewhat generalized and abstract and yet it retains the natural form.[53] The people not only domesticated bulls but they also used the horns of the bulls in the manufacture of various articles. Bullock carts, with solid or spoked wheels, were used for travelling while the wagons were used for the transport of goods. This is evident from the relieved sculptures of Nāgārjunakoṇḍa. The wheel varieties include cart and carriages. The carts were used for short journeys and the carriages were used for carrying goods. The bullock carts are, perhaps, the oldest and the commonest vehicle in India. An excellent example of it is found in a relief, illustrating Sujātā, feeding the Buddha. The solid wheels were used for carts during the Ikṣvāku period. In this connection, a toy-cart, depicted in the panel illustrating the gift of the earth, shows such a cart. The type of bullock cart depicted in Nāgārjunakoṇḍa relief is still in vogue in

Andhra Pradesh, including the solid wheels. Below the nearly-complete lotus medallion at Panigiri (Andhra Pradesh) dated third century AD appears within a rectangular frame a walking humped bull and a walking elephant and a knelt down human figure with left raised-hand in between. The bull, in profile, appears quite agitated (*fig.* 126).

A few fragments of Buddhists railings from Amarāvatī, dated first century AD, were reportedly found in the Indian Office Library, London. In one of these fragments within a bordered horizontal panel, there appears the profile of a running bull with its face in frontal view.[54] It has a pair of small horns and a pair of alert ears while there appears evident abstraction in the treatment of its dewlap and in the movement of its long tail. Curiously enough, one of its horns is tied with a long rope but it is difficult to say what was on the other end of the row. Whether it was controlled by a man or it was tied with a pole, it is a matter of conjecture only. But, in any case, the humped-bull is seen trying to get itself freed and that dramatic tension has been very faithfully delineated on the face of the animal (*fig.* 119). The inner face of a coping stone from Amarāvatī, which is now in collection of British Museum, shows a bull with leaping forelegs behind a running man. The bull has a weighty body. It is humped and it has a long tail dangling down. Carved in profile, a few parallel lines on the neck show its stylized dewlap. Unfortunately, the details of its horns are not seen. It appears that, with its raised forelegs, the bull seems to be attacking the man in its front in a running attitude[55] (*fig.* 120).

Bull in Kuṣāṇa Sculptures

The so-called Kuṣāṇas were related to Yueh-Chih race of Central Asia. Yueh-Chihs were forced to leave from Tun-Huan and Kan-Shu by another group of people called Hsiung-nu. The Yueh-Chih migrated to Ta-Hsia to the north

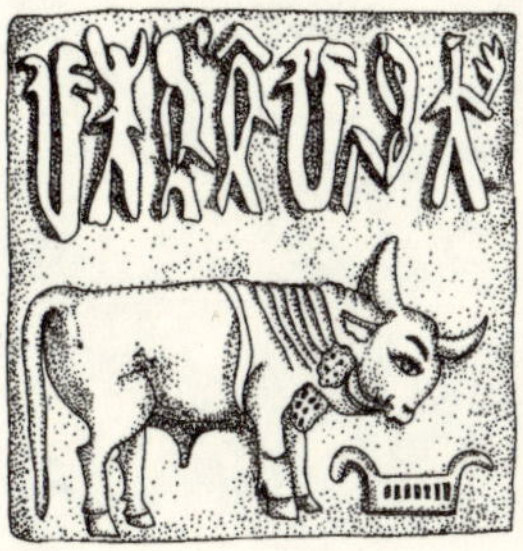

of Oxus river. These tribal Yueh-Chihs were then divided into five hsi-hou. One of the five was Kuli-Huang who destroyed the other hsi-hou and established their authority in the regions of Wakhan, Badakshan, Chitral, Kafiristan, etc. The earliest known Kuṣāṇa king was Miaos. The term Kuṣāṇa has come from the word Kuei-Shuang and the most powerful ruler of Kuṣāṇas, outside India, was Kujula Kadphises. He extended his empire up to Western Bactria, Kabul and Chi-pin including Kashmir. He is known to have ruled over Gāndhāra to the west of the Indus and the Taxila to the east of the river. He turned the kingdom, founded by Minos, into an empire. He was succeeded by Wima Kadphises and the latter was followed by Kaniṣka I, the greatest ruler in the line. Kaniṣka I founded an Era in AD 78. In India, the Kuṣāṇas had their capital at Taxila. After Kaniṣka I, came Vasiṣka, Huviṣka, Vāsudeva I, Kaniṣka II, Kaniṣka III and Vāsudeva II. In the second half of the third century AD, the Kuṣāṇa empire virtually collapsed because of the rise of the Sassanians. The Kuṣāṇas, who entered through the north-western passage into India, extended their territory as far east as Pāṭaliputra. In order to rule this vast territory during Kaniṣka I's time (Year 1-23) another capital was built at Mathurā.[56]

When the Kuṣāṇas entered India, they first established themselves in the so-called Gāndhāra region. The Gāndhāra was divided into two parts; the Eastern Gāndhāra with its capital at Taxila while the Western Gāndhāra had its capital in Puṣkalāvatī (modern Charsadda). Thus, the ancient Gāndhāra region was situated, encompassing the three river valleys of Swāt, Kabul and Indus. This vast area laid bare extensive ruins of Buddhist shrines. A number of dilapidated *stūpa*s have been discovered which were embellished with a large number of narrative panels. The territory was exposed to different foreign contacts, namely the Persian, the Greeks, the Śakas, Pahalavas and Kuṣāṇas. The influences of these regions led to the growth of an eclectic centre of art, popularly known as Gāndhāran art. Most of the Gāndhāran sculptures were found to be made either in black or bluish schist stone and the theme of the majority of the narrative panels is related to Buddha or his religion. Some images and motifs are of alien in nature. Because of the huge demands, in the later period of the Gāndhāran art, images were made through the medium of stucco or clay. Among the innumerable sculptures, there are instances where the unknown sculptors are seen to have composed certain fascinating aspects of bull, the animal under discussion. The bull appears on Gāndhāran art not occasionally but frequently. Bulls are seen as being used for ploughing or pulling the carts. An excellent example of a bullock cart was found along with two merchants offering food to the Buddha. The bullock cart depicted in this panel consists of a vaulted roof of a bamboo work for protecting the occupants from sun and rain. Two bulls are yoked on this cart and they are partially visible; this panel is now in the collection of Peshawar Museum (No. 799) and it hails from Takht-e-Bahi (*fig.* 127). In the Peshawar Museum (No. 1739) there is an image on the base of which a cultivator is shown engaged in ploughing the land with the help of a pair of humped-bulls. The cultivator is holding in his left hand something like a staff while on his right hand he is seen manipulating the ploughshare. The bulls are shown as if in movement and they were carved in profile. The profile of the bull on the left almost guarded the figure of the bull on the other side. In spite of this oversecting, one can see a part of its face and its legs including some parts of its body. This sculpture hails from Sahri-Bahlol and is now kept in the Peshawar Museum. This panel proves that ploughing with oxen was in vogue from Pāṭaliputra to Gāndhāra regions[57] (*fig.* 128). There is also a fragment of a panel from Peshawar that shows the bulls kneeling down and licking the feet of Buddha. The exact identification of it is still in dispute but the humped-bull has been depicted here as showing its reverence and this proves that Buddha could influence not

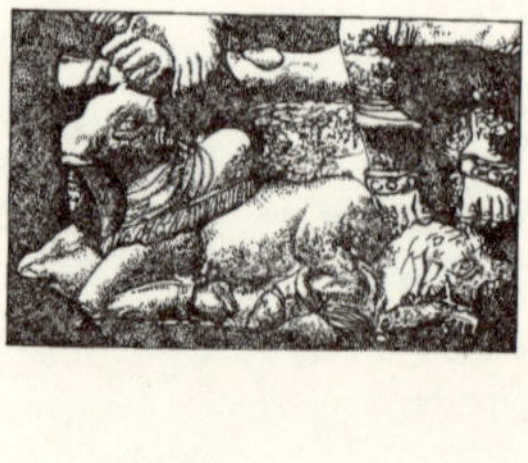

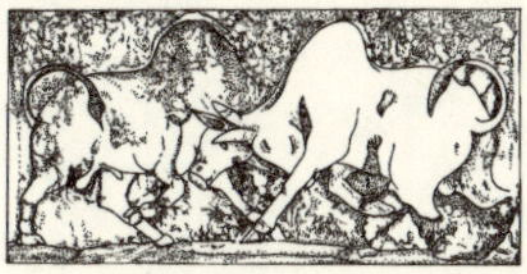

only men but also animals.

Gāndhāra has also laid bare certain mythical animals and there is one such depiction of a Marine bull (*go-maccha*) which is in the collection of Lahore Museum (No. 83A). It shows the forepart of a bull with coiled body or coiled tail of a dragon accommodated within a triangular panel.[59] A green steatite tray, which hails from Helmond area in Afghanistan, dated first century AD, and which is now in the collection of British Museum, shows the tray with a lion and the bull confronting each other (*fig*.129). The lion is shown, in profile, facing right while the bull is shown in three-quarter view and faces the left. Each animal is depicted in a fairly naturalistic way although the details of their body are not shown. The mane of lion and the dewlap on the bull's neck are marked by a few simple incised lines. However, both the animals are endowed with strong muscles, denoting, thereby, their strength. Their tails are held up and the hind legs are bent as if the animals are getting themselves ready to charge each other at any moment.[60] Prof. Vasudeva Saran Agrawala noted the presence of capitals with addorsed bulls.[61] The bull capitals are generally noticed on the top of Indo-Corinthean pilasters and call for the comparison with Persipolitan bull capitals.[62] Prof. Agrawala refers to Kapiśī where the cultural traditions of the east and the west met. The area laid bare to some specimens which came from the Roman world, including the narrative of the abduction of Europa by Zeus in the disguise of a bull.[63] Similarly, the figures of Satyr are endowed with a body of a bull to symbolize masculinity. In Gāndhāra, a few figures of Śiva has been discovered. Particularly, a reference may be made of a piece, which was found from Charsadda. This Peshawar Museum object shows a three-headed god possibly indicating Brahmā, Viṣṇu and Maheśvara. The central figure of Śiva is shown against the body of Nandī.[64] Shortly after the rules of Bactrian Greeks, the period of Indo-Parthian and Kuṣāṇas witnessed the introduction of anthropomorphic figure of Śiva although his theriomorphic form of bull was not altogether forgotten. The Kuṣāṇa coins bear, in all, evidences of Śiva in human figure along with bull and generally with the coin legend, "Oesho" or Maheśa.

Mathurā in the Kuṣāṇa period evolved as a very interesting site of Indian art. Its importance lies in the fact that at Mathurā one finds the parallel growth and development of Buddhist, Jaina and Hindu sculptures. The sculptures were made mostly in spotted white red sandstone of Sīkrī and Rūpbās. This great centre of art, Mathurā, paid serious attention, in this period, in the iconic developments of Buddhist, Jaina and Hindu images. It also gave similar importance to the depiction of Indian flora and fauna. The depiction of bull, in particular, finds its notable place in the art of Kuṣāṇa-Mathurā. The bull has been shown here in various ways — as a beast of burden and also as drawing chariots and carriages. It is also shown as the mount of divinities and, in many cases, its fantastic forms have also been delineated. Thus, we find in Mathurā the association of bull with reference to religious and secular connections.

In Patna Museum collection, a bull appears on the fragment of an *āyāgapaṭṭa* dated in the second century AD (Acc. No. Arch. 5811). A humped-bull is noticed on this piece just to fill the corner of inner square. The bull on this red mottled sandstone serves as an auspicious symbol. The bull is included in Jaina pantheon as one of the auspicious items of the dream and, therefore, it finds its place on an *ayāgapaṭṭa* which is nothing unusual.[65] A reference may be made to a Kuṣāṇa terracotta, housed in the State Museum, Lucknow (G. 385) and it shows a bull-headed male (*gomukha yakṣa*) standing with a female. This bull-headed male is considered as the attendant of Ṛṣabhanātha, the first Jaina *tīrthaṅkara*. The bull-headed *yakṣa*, most probably, owes its origin to such figures as the companions (*gaṇas*) of Śiva.[66] A

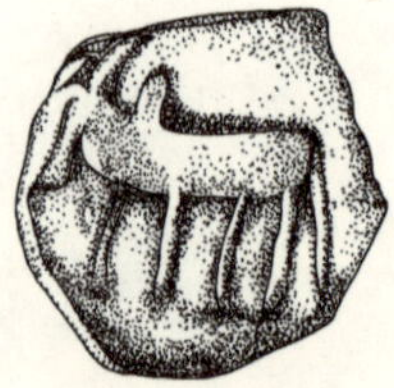

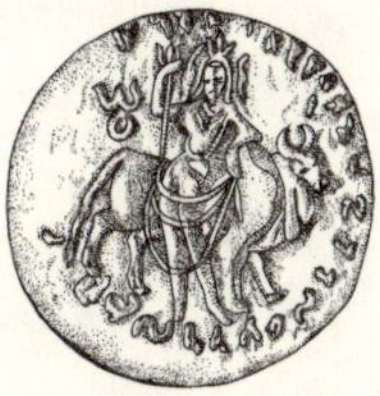

unique stone sculpture was found and reported by Dr. Fuhrer from the Jaina site at Kaṅkālīṭīlā at Mathurā. It shows a double-faced rider on a bull (*fig*. 150). Its execution is, somewhat, rude and it bears an archaic appearance. The rider holds in his right hand a broken shaft which was either a spear or a trident. This image has been identified by scholars as representing Śiva. Smith observes that, although the sculpture was discovered from a Jaina site, its identification as Śiva is correct because the Jainas never ignored the existence of Hindu gods.[67] In the State Museum, Lucknow (No. J.510), there is the fragment of a cross bar which shows human-faced bull. There is another composite figure of bull-horse (*uṣabha turaga*) which reportedly occurs in Mathurā.[68] The figure of the bull is found on the fragments of coping stones in the railing of Kuṣāṇa Mathurā. Prof. V.S. Agrawala also refers to figures of bull with fish tails in Mathurā. Dr. R.C. Sharma refers to the fragment of an epigraphic record where the figure of a bull is found carved at the end of the epigraph. Dr. Sharma felt that the figure of the bull was added to the slab at a later part of time but Kṛṣṇa Deva raised an interesting point and said the letter *ra*, which cuts the tail and hind parts of the bull, is indicative of its existence prior to the epigraph. The headless figure of the bull also suggests that the slab was of a larger dimension (Acc. No. 79.20).[69]

In the State Museum Lucknow, there is a fragment of a *toraṇa* tympana and on the reverse side of it, one finds three examples of a carriage drawn by a pair of humped-bulls (*fig*. 131). The said panel also includes carriages drawn by a pair of horses. Therefore, it could be said that both horses and bulls were yoked for drawing carriages in Kuṣāṇa Mathurā. The bulls in these carriages are carved in relief and they are being driven by a rider. It is through the movements of the legs, one can say that the carriage was drawn not by one but by a pair of bulls. Among the three carriages, one, at least, shows a partial view of the face of the second bull, which, in the other case, is found completely guarded by the figure of the bull.[70] In the Kuṣāṇa period not only *liṅga* or *mukhaliṅga* but Śiva in his anthropomorphic form (*vyakta*) is found to have been represented. In the Mathura Museum there is an image of Śiva standing before the Nandī, the latter stood as the symbol of Kāma. In the same museum there is another image of the Kuṣāṇa period which shows Śiva with Pārvatī and to the right of Pārvatī there appears the bull Nandī. The said sculpture, that hails from Kośam, bears all the characteristics and mannerisms of the period. Incidentally, a reference may be made of an intaglio in the Indian Museum, Calcutta, belonging to the late Kuṣāṇa period. It is found carved in Gāndhāran style, in which Śiva is shown with three faces and four arms. He is seated on his mount Nandī in the most comfortable (*sukhāsana*) pose.[72]

Bharat Kala Bhavan has also in its collections two fragments of cross bars hailing from Mathurā which are stylistically dated to Kuṣāṇa period. One of these is a double-sided (Acc. No. 22561). On one side, against a plain medallion, a walking humped-bull with a long tail is found relieved. Carved in profile, the right foreleg of this bull is held up and the posture of the other three legs shows that it was in movement. The four scratched lines on the neck of the bull indicate its dewlap (*fig*. 132). The other side of this panel depicts within a circular medallion a bull with a fish tail. Somewhat crudely executed, the humped-bull is shown here with a pair of alert ears and impressive eyes (*fig*. 133). The fragment of the second medallion (Acc. No. 23962) shows a walking bull with raised right foreleg. The sculpture is badly eroded. However, it has a prominent hump and its tail raised up. In course of excavations at Vaiśālī, Dr. Altekar discovered two pots containing gold and silver objects. Of the gold objects, mention may be made of two humped seated bulls which bear the plastic qualities of bulls, made in stone[73] (*fig*. 134). M.V.N. Krishna Rao discovered a life size highly decorated figure of a bull

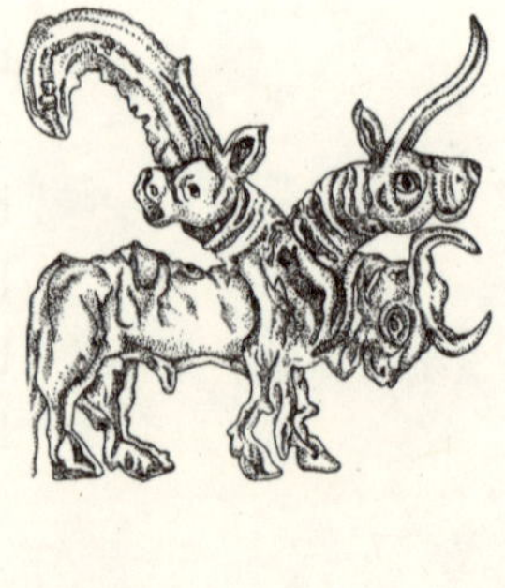

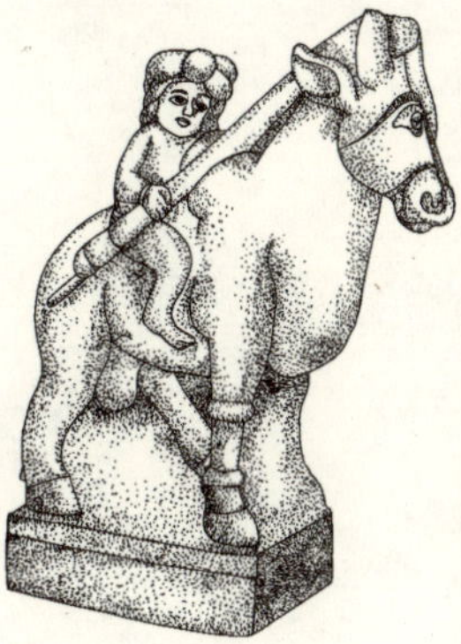

(ears and horns mutilated) from the Amarāvatī temple. This sculpture is in round shape and stylistically, assigned-made, and assigned to Sātavāhana period. Its size (1.30 m high), beauty and style led Sharma to conclude that it could be classed next only to the Mauryan bulls. It bears realistic modelling and a dignified stance. About a century later, a reclining humped bull was probably made at Nāgārjunakoṇḍa in which the Nandī is shown engaged as looking at a nearby *Śiva-liṅga* (*deva vīkṣaṇa tatparaḥ*).[74] Robert Knox, in his observations on Buddhist sculptures from the great *stūpa* of Amarāvatī, draws attention to a panel showing the continuous narrative of *Vesantara Jātaka*. While passing by a hermitage on a bullock cart, yoked with two bulls, the prince Vesantara meets a brāhmaṇa who asked the bullock cart as a gift to which the prince readily agreed. The panels show the movement of the bullock cart down below and that the cart was in movement, has been indicated with the movement of the legs of the bull yoked to the right of the cart. Both bulls are humped but the bull on the left only projects his head and the other part of the body are guarded by the cart. The visible bull to the right has its tail tied up so that it does not clash with the movement of the wheel.[75] It is interesting to note that the rider on the seated bull appears on the top of the pillar in *caitya* hall at Bedśā in Western India. The seated bull appears quite majestic in its profile form with three quarter profile showing the face (*fig.* 143).

Bull in Gupta Sculptures

In the Gupta period (fourth-sixth century AD), bull received the full recognition as a religious symbol and, therefore, this animal appeared in various places with intimate relations to certain deities of the three major religions of India. The period also witnessed the development of many mythological stories in which the bull found a mention. In Mathura Museum, there is a panel (D-47) which depicts

Lord Kṛṣṇa holding the mount Govardhana by his raised left hand and to his right and left, cows and the cowherd boys are shown standing. Kṛṣṇa has been referred to as Gopāla and Govinda and the very name, connects the lord with bovine animals. In a *toraṇa* panel at Mandor in Jodhpur state, Kṛṣṇa is shown as Govardhandhārī and at the bottom of the panel a few cattles were shown, including bulls. Dated in the fifth century AD, the cattle are shown in this panel in different poses and postures.[76] In the Mathura Museum (No. 44.3118.; 44.3129) there are two fragmentary pieces of a bracket depicting two events of the life of the Buddha, namely Enlightenment and Great demise made in red sandstone and stylistically, dated in early Gupta period. These two pieces were collected locally from Swāmī Ghāṭ (Mathurā). Just below these two Buddhist scenes there appears in both the fragments a pair of humped- bulls seated back to back on *padmapīṭha*. Their necks and the humps are found adorned with garlands. The way these bulls are shown seated on lotus persuades one to take them as animals with divine attachments (*fig*. 135). A fragment of a pillar capital of the Gupta period shows a pair of bulls seated back to back and, in the middle, there appears a *kīrtimukha* from whose lower jaw a pendant dangles down. Thus, the tradition of showing bulls on the capital of a pillar from the Mauryan period appears to have continued till the period of the Guptas.[77] There is a small fragment of a red sandstone piece in Bharat Kala Bhavan on either side of which there appears a bull and a lion. The humped-bull is shown in front covering the body of the lion behind while on the other side the lion covers most of the portion of the bull. It is very difficult to explain why such combination of a wild animal and a domesticated animal is shown in one square format. Do they represent the mount of Śiva and Durgā questions may arise (Acc. No. 21826) (*fig*. 136-37).

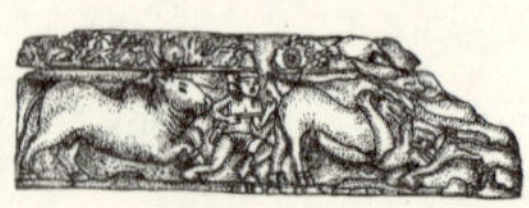

The Viṣṇu temple at Deogarh (Jhānsī) has in its south wall a *rathika bimba* which accommodates the narrative of

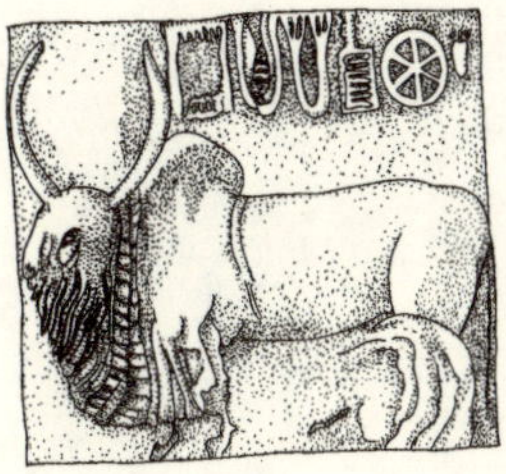

God Viṣṇu reclining on the body of a cosmic serpent, Ananta or Śeṣa. On the upper part of this narrative, four divine figures of Indra's heaven have been carved out, of which Śiva is shown with his spouse Pārvatī seated on a bull and soaring through the space. Most probably, this is the first instance where a bull is seen soaring in the void (*fig.* 138).[78] The Śiva temple at Bhumara which is dated sometimes in fifth-sixth century AD is built in red sandstone. A damaged Candraśāla of Bhumara accommodates within its shallow niche, the figure of Śiva on a seated bull.[79] The piece is badly mutilated and its detailed analysis is not possible but, since it is a Śiva temple, its stylized *caitya* windows can very easily accommodate Śaivite themes. Curiously enough, on the dado of the same temple there appears the composite figure of Nandī, the bull in which the torso is human and the head in profile is that of a bull[80] (*fig.* 139). Within a mutilated niche in the same temple there appears only the head of a bull.[81]

The caves of Bādāmī also depicted a few aspects of Śiva. There is a beautiful figure of Ardhanārīśvara who is holding a *vīṇā* and is flanked on either side by emaciated Bhṛṅgī and Nandī as bulls and a few *gaṇa*s are shown dancing[82] (*fig.* 140). There is also a figure of Hari-Hara in the lower cave temples at Bādāmī in which the composite god is flanked by bull-faced human figure of Nandī and Garuḍa on either side.[83] The Cave No. I at Bādāmī depicts a 16-armed *nṛtya mūrti* of Śiva and the bull, Nandī, standing calmly to the left.[84] A *vṛṣa vāhana mūrti* of four-armed Śiva hails from Aihoḷe. The god is shown reclining on his mount Nandī and the front right hand of the god displays the *varada* pose and placed on the horns of the vivacious bull, and the later gives a vigorous look.[85]

The excavations at Atarañjikhera exposed a mound towards the south where there is a modern Śiva temple having an ancient *Śiva-liṅgam* and the images of Nandī and Gaṇeśa, all belonging to *circa* sixth century AD. The massive bull is shown seated on a severely plain pedestal. Its prominent hump is adorned with a necklace made up of small bells whereas its neck has a beautiful chain with a bell hanging. Unfortunately, the face of this animal is badly mutilated.[86] The bull is also noticed in a horizontal row of animals relieved on the walls of *caitya* hall at Kānherī which is 16 miles north of Mumbai.

In the sixth century AD, in the temple of Vijayawāḍā, one finds below the seated Śiva in *lalitāsana*, a seated bull, Nandī. It is reasonably stylized and profusely ornamented with beaded chains (*fig*. 141). The image of Umā-Maheśvara from Illeśvaram, dated in the sixth century AD, shows a small figure of Nandī, below the feet of Lord Śiva[87] (*fig*.142).

The Ajantā paintings, which were produced in the Gupta-Vākāṭaka period, evinced a great sympathy in the delineation of animals. Among the animals appeared on the Ajantā murals, mention may be made of a bull fight in the Cave No. I. It appears that in the drawing of fighting bulls, the painters of Ajantā excelled others. The fighting and the charging of the bulls have been very faithfully rendered in this painting[88] (*fig*.144). In Cave No. I there is also a very fascinating narrative in which the painter depicted an encounter of five demons with men tending cattle in the jungle in the realm of king Maitrabala. The cows here bear the customary incision in their ears. While the demons were painted in their evident frightening and demonic shape, the cattle are shown either standing or seated and each one is indifferent of the high drama enacted in the upper part[89] (*fig*. 146). In Cave No. I, the unknown painter illustrates the figure of an agitated bull placed amidst flowers and plants in such a way as if to suggest that it has lost its way and, therefore, it is shown charged with nervous tension. It is a splendid example of how conversant the artist was with the techniques of fore shortening (*fig*.145).[90] In Cave No. XVII, a painted pillar shows a bull inside a medallion. In Cave No. XVI at Ajantā, a bullock cart is shown and this is being

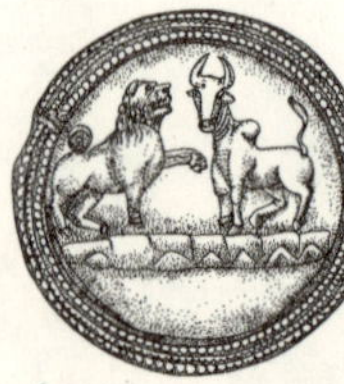

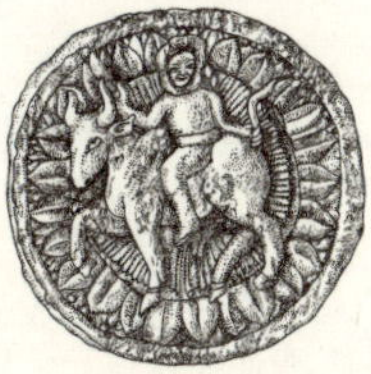

drawn by a pair of humped-bulls. In the same cave a man is seen ploughing with two bulls, and, in both the cases, the bulls are humped with powerful bodies. This scene has been found to be related with a narrative where an attempt is made to take the *bodhisattvas*' mind off the idea of renouncing the world. The king sent him to inspect his villages where the *bodhisattva* saw the miserable conditions under which the ploughmen worked and the torments to which the drought-bullocks were subjected to. When, in answer to his questions, he learnt that the village formed part of his father's possession, he set both the ploughmen and the bullocks free. Thereafter the *bodhisattva* sat down into the shade of a rose apple tree to meditate. The episode is found to be painted with encounters, in the foreground of which a farmer is seen ploughing with two humped-bullocks.[91]

The figure of bull appears to be very popular among the bead-makers in ancient India. A number of ancient sites exposed huge quantities of beads in different types of stones such as agate, carnelian, quartz, amethyst, malachite, lapis-lazuli, garnet and jasper. The beads are, generally, small in size and are perforated, in general. They were used either for making a necklace of a chain or used as amulets. It is, however, difficult to say if these amulets were used with some religious implications or taboos. There has been a general belief that the amulets were used to ward off evil eyes. A close analysis would show that most of the animal-beads were made in the initial centuries of the present era. The carving shows that some artists became quite competent in capturing the realistic look of the animals on small pieces of a stone. Some of these beads and amulets are conceived in the round and some are conceived in relief with flat base. Whatever the case may be, it appears that in rendering the figures of bull with its hump, dewlap and horn, the artist executed them with evident naturalism. In the following lines a reference is being made about a few beads carved in the form of a bull.

At the time of carving, the sculptors were careful enough to the various veins and natural colours of the related stone. Figures of bull were modelled in different natural poses and actions to give them a life-like appearance. These beads are found from Taxila, Sahri Bahlol, Kauśāmbī, Chainpur-Bhabhua, Masona, Rājghāṭ, Bairat, Koṇḍapur, etc., and are collected in Bharat Kala Bhavan, Vārāṇasī, Allahabad Museum, State Museum Lucknow, National Museum, New Delhi and Prince of Wales Museum Mumbai. The bull-shaped beads, discussed below, are all showing humped-bulls, except one. Generally, the figures are endowed with a perforation above the front legs. Of the bull figures, those that are found carved on agate are found surging with life and seem more natural than those made from carnelian. The lines in the agate are so carved as if they are painted as bands, garlands or dewlap of the bull. Of these, mention may be made of a bead, used as a pendant from Taxila. The pendant is hung by tail and is datable to third century BC. A carnelian amulet of this shape from Bhir Mound, Taxila, is also notable.[92] There are three carnelian bull-amulets from Sahri Bahlol.[93] These are kept in the Garden collection. In south, about 12 specimens in terracotta were recovered from the excavations at Koṇḍapur in the old Hyderabad state and are assignable to the Sātavāhana period (100 BC-AD 200).[94]

A crystal-bull-amulet from Kauśāmbī is preserved in the Allahabad University Museum (*fig*.147). It was found during the course of Kauśāmbī excavations in 1949-50 and it is datable to the first century BC.[95] From Kauśāmbī, three bull beads of deep red carnelian are housed in Bharat Kala Bhavan. Each of these bulls has an unusual long face. One of these (Acc. No. 2/5411 of Bharat Kala Bhavan) bulls is made of red coloured stone (*fig*. 148), while another is made of deep red carnelian (Acc. No. 2/5414) (*fig*. 149). The third, the deep red carnelian bull (Acc. No. 11/668), has a performation on its foreleg. Its hump is very prominent. Its

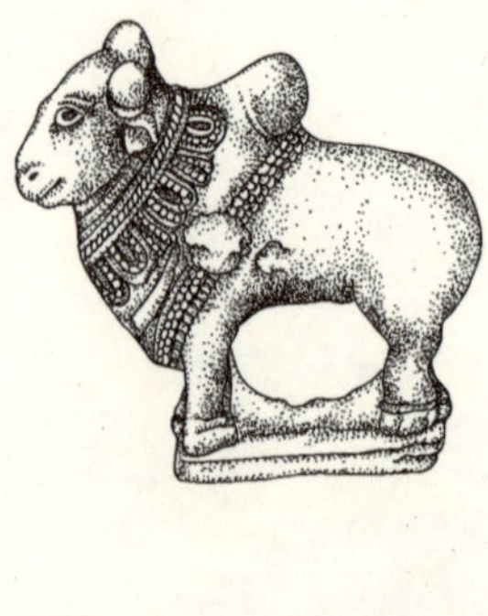

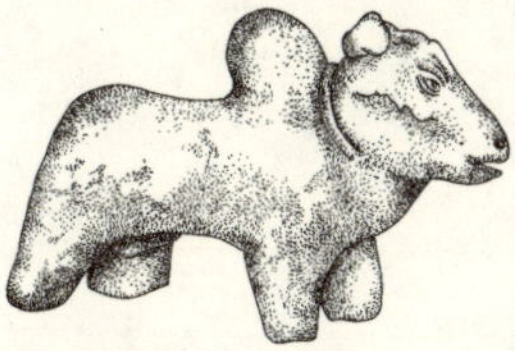

left horn is prominently shown (*fig.*150). There is a bead showing the bull from Kauśāmbī which is made of banded agate. It has a hump and two horns and two perforations on the front legs. It is housed in the Allahabad Museum and can be dated to the Kuṣāṇa period.

A bull made of red stone with white spots is stored in Bharat Kala Bhavan (Acc. No. 1201). This bead presents a seated Nandī figure on a base with a thick garland around its neck. The posture of Nandī is quite like the colossal Nandīs, placed before the Śiva temples. However, the face in this case does not appear natural and the modelling of the head differs from others. The figure is perforated under its belly and stylistically made, belonging to the Kuṣāṇa period (*fig.* 151).

There is a good example of a bull, made from banded agate in Bharat Kala Bhavan. It is full of life and looks like a painted bull (Bharat Kala Bhavan Acc. No. 11/430) (*fig.* 152) with a pointed mouth. A bull figure from Kauśāmbī is found made of banded agate. Though poorly modelled the bull's hump is clearly shown and is housed in Bharat Kala Bhavan (Acc. No. 2/4520) (*fig.* 153). A rare piece of the same agate is housed in Bharat Kala Bhavan (Acc. No. 11/607) (*fig.* 154) where the bull has been depicted very traditionally. Its lines are used as bands for the hump and dewlap. The bull is shown very powerful and stands majestic. The bead is having an unbroken gliding outline that moves smoothly towards the delicately rendered tail. Though the head is missing, its form calls for a comparison with the Brahamāni bulls noted on the seals from Mohenjo-Dāro or the Aśokan bull capital of Rāmpurvā.

The above research on bulls on the stone sculptures of early India, spanning between fourth century BC to sixth century AD, reveals that the said animal received adequate attention and became a favourite item to be relieved on the stone. The animal appeared in the secular seen as being used in transporting loads, drawing carts or carriages, yoked in ploughshare for cultivation and also as a participant of a pastoral landscape. Fighting bulls appeared also as a popular theme and it was included as an interesting pastime.

The physical power, the strength, the vigour and the sexual prowess of the animal were given adequate attention and recognition and behind these qualities, men found something extraordinary and, therefore, the animal was given soon a religious recognition. The bull was accepted as a symbol or cognizant of deities in Hindu, Buddhist and Jaina religions. It appears as the mount of Śiva, became theriomorphic symbol of the Buddha and was recognized as the cognizant of the *tīrthaṅkara* Ṛṣabhanātha. This animal also got references in a number of mythological narratives. Thus, the sculptors of this period depicted this animal in conformity with the various situations. Since the animal was domesticated much earlier, the early Indian sculptor studied the animal from a close proximity and, in comparison with other animals, its bearing, its appearance, its movement and its tension have been better projected, as has been noted in the foregoing lines.

References

1. V.S. Agrawala, *Indian Art*, pp. 77-78.
2. V.S. Agrawala, *Bhāratīya Kalā*, p. 112.
3. P.L. Gupta (ed.), *Patna Museum Catalogue*, p. 346.
4. K.M. Srivastava, *Discovery of Kapilavastu*, p. 235.
5. V.S. Agrawala, *Indian Art*, p. 96.
6. *Indian Archaeology — A Review*, 1957-58, Pl. XCIII.
7. Archaeological Survey of India, Annual Report, Eastern circle, 1918-19, p. 45.
8. S.K. Saraswati, *Survey of Indian Sculpture*, pp. 25-26.
9. R.P. Chanda, The Beginning of Art in Eastern India with special reference to sculptures of Indian Museum, *Indian Museum Bulletin*, July, 1975, Pt. II, p. 31. also see A.R.I. East Circle 1918-19, p. 19.
10. P.K. Agrawal in *Rajbali Pandey Smriti Grantha*, pp. 280-81.

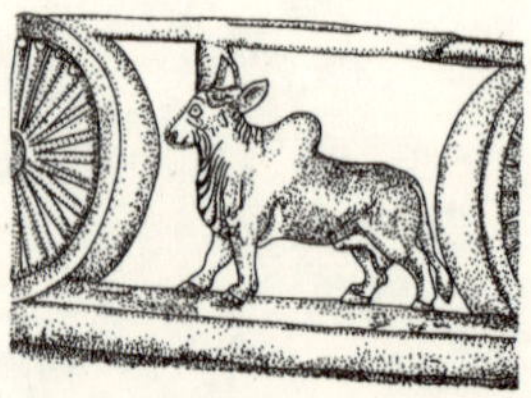

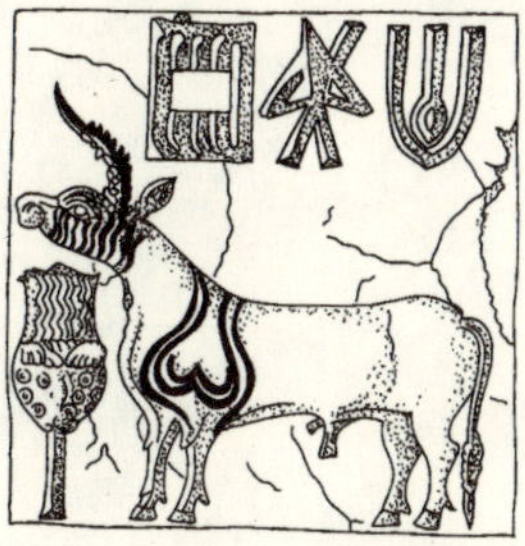

11. N.R. Ray, *Maurya and Sunga Art*, p. 97, fig. 9.
12. S.L. Huntington, *The Art of Ancient India*, p. 45.
13. N.R. Ray, *op.cit.*, pp. 44-45.
14. R.P. Chanda, *op.cit.*, p. 29.
15. T.K. Biswas, "Sarnath Lion Capital: Its Historians," *Citi-Vithika*, vol. 3, no. 1-2, 1997-98; pp. 41-54.
16. Debala Mitra, *Buddhist Monuments*, p. 76; See also Agrawala, *Indian Art*, pp. 93-94.
17. Nihar Ranjana Ray, *Maurya and Post-Maurya Art*, p. 106, fig. 14.
18. Prof. V.S. Agrawala found on a steatite plaque with four animals from Akara, now in the Indian Museum (Calcutta); these four animals are shown on a shallow dish (*Chakradhvaja*, p. 35).
19. T. Block, *ZDMG*, LXII, 1908, p. 653-56.
20. A. Foucher, *The Beginnings of Buddhist Art*, p. 21.
21. Dayaram Sahani, *Catalogue of the Museum at Sarnath*, p. 41.
22. V.S. Agrawala, *Chakradhvaja*, p. 73.
23. S.L. Huntington, *op.cit.*, p. 47.
24. K.J. Khandalawala, "Herald in Stone, etc.," published in *Buddhist Iconography*, Sambhota Series 11, Delhi, 1989, pp. 31-35.
25. V.S. Agrawala, *Chakradhvaja*, p. 40.
26. H.C. Raychoudhuri, *The Aśoka Chakra — Its Symbolism, Studies in Indian Antiquities*, Calcutta, 1958, pp. 219-22.
27. S. Kramrich, *Indian Sculpture*, 1981, p. 9.
28. N.R. Ray, *Maurya and Post Mauryan Art*, 1975, p. 1.
29. V.S. Agrawala, *Indian Art*, pp. 141-42.
30. *Ibid.*, p. 130, fig. 58.
31. A. Cunningham, *The Stupa of Bharhut: A Buddhist Monument*, 1879, pl. 27, fig. 10; B. Barua, *Bharhut Book III*, 1937, pl. 80, fig. 109. A.K. Coomaraswamy, *La Sculptures de Bharhut*, 1956, pl. 28, fig. 70.
32. Dabala Mitra, *Buddhist Monuments*, pp. 257-58; See also N.R. Ray, *Maurya and Post Maurya Art*, pp. 110-14; V.K. Mathur, *Art and Culture under the Sungas*, p. 50.
33. V.S. Agrawala, *Indian Art*, pp. 141-42; fig. 67a.
34. *Ibid.*, p. 222.
35. B. Barua, *Gaya and Bodhagaya*, fig. 57.
36. A.K. Coomarswamy, *La Sculptures de Bodhagaya*, Pl. 9.
37. *Ibid.*, pl. 48, No. I.
38. A.L. Srivastava, *A Life in Sāñcī Sculptures*, pp. 77-78.
39. G.P. Majumdar, *Conveyances in Indian Culture*, vol. II, 1935-36,

no. II, p. 277.

40. A.L. Srivastava, *op.cit.*, p. 83.
41. O.P. Sharma, "Unicorn in Indian Art and legend," in *JBRS.*, vol. XLIII, Pt. 3-4, p. 364.
42. Sadashib Gorakshakar (ed.), "Mriga," *Animal in Indian Art*, p. 142; Also see R.R. Tripathi, *Masterpieces in the Allahabad Museum*, p. 7, also Pramod Chandra, *Stone Sculptures in the Allahabad Museum*, Pl. XXX.
43. V.S. Agrawaala, *Bhāratīya Kalā*, p. 227.
44. *Ibid.*, p. 235.
45. S.L. Huntington, *op.cit.*, pp. 168-69.
46. O.C. Gangoly, *Andhra Sculptures*, p. 42.
47. *Ibid.*
48. *Ibid.*, p. 86.
49. Dieter Schlingloff, *Studies in Ajantā Paintings*, p. 246, fig. 24.
50. *Ibid.*, p. 224; also see Debala Mitra, *Buddhist Monuments*, p. 274.
51. O.C. Ganguly, *op.cit.*, p. 93; Also see M.L. Nigam, *Sculptural Art of Andhra*, pp. 77-78.
52. K. Krishna Murthy, *Nagarjunakonda, A Cultural Study*, p. 245; also see Nihar Ranjan Ray, *Maurya and Post Maurya Art*, p. 125.
53. H. Zimmer, *The Art of Indian Asia*, pl. 38-D.
54. Douglas Barrett, *Sculptures from Amaravati in the British Museum*, pl. XXXVIII.
55. Savita Sharma, *Gold Coins of Imperial Kuṣāṇas and their Successors*, Varanasi, 1999, pp. 1-7.
56. Krishna Murthy, *Gandharan Sculptures : A cultural study*, p. 120.; Also see Francive Tissot, *The Art of Gandhara*, fig, 288, 289.
57. Harold Ingholt, *Gandharan Art in Pakistan*, Pl. 180.
58. *Ibid.*, p. 393.
59. Stanislaw, J. Czuma, *Kushana Sculptures; Images from Early India*, 1985, p. 150, Pl. 68.
60. V.S. Agrawala, *Indian Art*, pp. 273-74.
61. Suman Mathur, *Art and Culture under the Kushanas*, p. 37.
62. *Indian Art*, p. 267.
63. Suman Mathur, *op.cit.*, p. 18.
64. P.L. Gupta, *Patna Museum Catalogue*, p. 21.
65. S.P. Sukla, "Some Interesting terracottas in the State Museum, Lucknow," in *Journal of Museum and Archaeology*, no. 4, pp. 32-33.

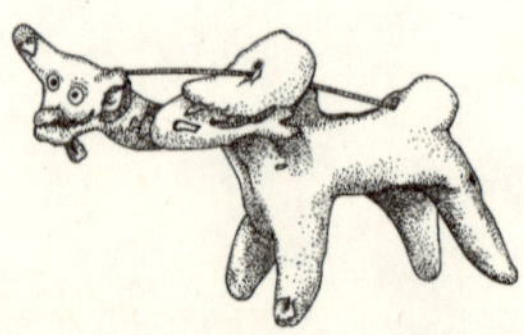

66. V.A. Smith, *Jain Antiquities of Mathura*, Pl. CII.
67. N.P. Joshi, *Life in Ancient Uttarapath*, p. 13, fig. 6.
68. R.C. Sharma, "New Inscriptions from Mathura," in *Mathura the*

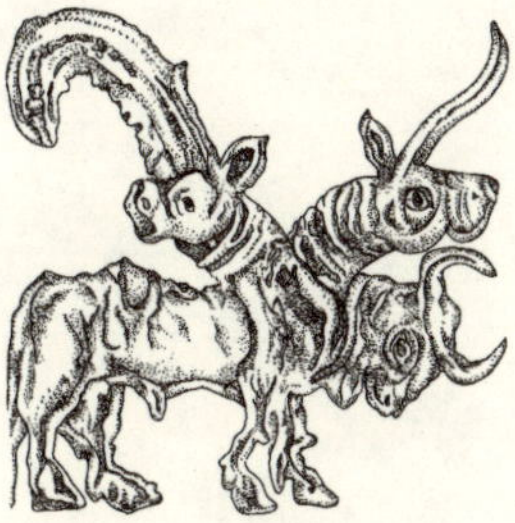

Cultural Heritage, p. 311, Pl. 31.1.A.

69. V.S. Agrawala, *Master Pieces of Mathura Museum*, Pl. V, fig. VI.
70. V.S. Agrawala, *Indian Art*, p. 257; And also see Kanchan Chakrabarti *Society, Religion and Art of the Kushana India*, p. 18; And also see Suman, *Mathura, Art and Culture Under the Kushanas*, p. 18.
71. J.N. Banerjea, *Development of Hindu Iconography* (1956), p. 469, Pl. XXXIV-1.
72. *Indian Archaeology — A Review*, 1958-59, p. 12, Pl. XB.
73. I.K. Sharma, *The Development of Early Saiva Art and Architecture*, pp. 77-78, Pl. 87.
74. Robert Knox, *Amaravati; Buddhist Sculpture from the Great Stupa*, p. 102, Pl. 42.
75. A.K. Coomaraswamy, *History of Indian and Indonesian Art*, New York, 1965, pl. 166.
76. *Memoires of the Archaeological Survey of India*, no. 4, p. 125.
77. Stella Kramrisch, *The Art of India*, Varanasi, 1987, pl. 57.
78. R.D. Banerjee, *MASI*, no. 16, Pl. 13-C-Temple of Bhumara.
79. *Ibid.*, Pl. 10-C.
80. *Ibid.*, Pl. 9-C.
81. A unique Ardhanārīśvara image is collected in Jhalwar Museum in which the figure is flanked by a bull and a figure of Kārttikeya on a Peacock, *Marg*, vol. XII, no. 2, March 1959, p. 18, fig. 11.
82. R.C. Majmudar, *Classical Age* (1962), p. 440.
83. J.N. Banerjea, *op.cit.*, p. 414, Pl. XXXVI, fig. 2.
84. *Ibid.*, p. 468, Pl. XXXIV, fig. 3.
85. R.C. Gaur, *Excavations at Ataranjikhera*, p. 3, Pl. III.
86. M.L. Nigam, *Sculptural Art of Andhra*, Pl. XIV; XVI.
87. Ajit Mookerjee, *Art of India*, p. 29.
88. Dieter Schlingloff, *Studies in Ajantā Paintings*, Pl. cover page.
89. A. Ghosh, *Ajantā Murals* (reprint), 1987, p. 47, Pl. 30.
90. Dieter Schlinghoff, *op.cit.*, p. 28, 1, 22.
91. Mareswara G. Dixit, *Prince of Wales Museum Bulletin*, no. 2, 1953, Pl. XV, b, fig. 6.
92. *Ibid.*, Pl. XV, b, fig. 10.
93. M.G. Dixit, *Some beads from Kondapur*, Hyderabad, Archaeological Series, no. 19, Pl. VI. fig. 264-73.
94. Mareswara G. Dixit, *Prince of Wales Museum Bulletin*, no. 2, 1953, Pl. XV, b, fig. 7.
95. Kamal Giri, "Animal and Bird Beads," in *Chhavi*, vol. I, pp. 312-23.

Conclusion

THE early genesis of the bull, the "auroch," evolved somewhere in the Pleistocene Age. During the inter-glacial dessication, the species migrated to different parts of the world from Asia, including India. The species in India was named Bos-Gauras (Gaur — the Indian bison). When the animal approached human dwellings, it was captured and domesticated. On its domestication, people could study it from close proximity. Its heavy structure, its tremendous power and energy, its movements and tension were closely watched. Its sensuousness and unusual sexual urge were subjects of studies as well. Men appreciated this animal as it maintains an aristocratic aloofness and majesty when it stands among other animals.

Bull received universal approbation from a hoary past. In Egypt, the God Osyris taught men how to harness oxen to a plough for cultivation. Ancient Egyptians worshipped Apis — the deified bull. Egyptian maintained a strong belief that the blood of a sacrificed bull could imbue earth with life. King Minos of ancient Crete was the son of Zeus (in the disguise of a bull) and Europa. The most favourite athletic item of bull grappling or leaping in Crete, to some, was a religious rite. The tradition of this game became equally popular in ancient Greece where Herakles and Thessaly became legendary heroes of bull leaping. The young kings of ancient Greece sacrificed bulls to appease god Poseidon. The Greek God Dionysus was identified with the bull-cult. To prove their chastity, the Greek priestess drank bull's blood. God Zeus, in the disguise of a bull, abducted Europa and took her to the island of Crete and there they gave

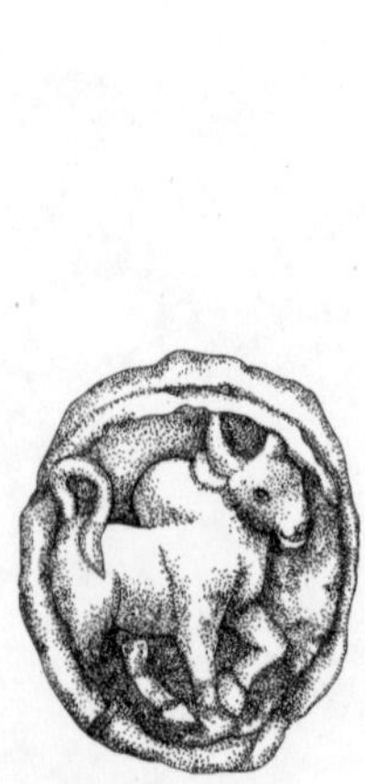

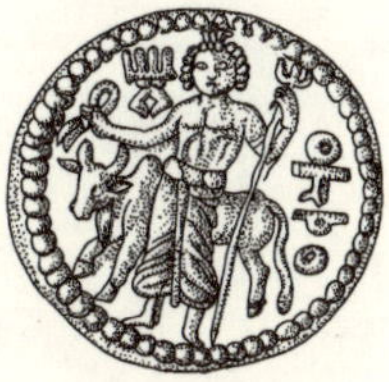

birth to three sons. Mesopotamia laid bare to a number of colossal winged bulls and, in Assyrian art, examples of human-headed bulls were noticed. Assyria also recognized the sacrifice of bulls. In ancient Persian art, the examples of human-headed winged bulls or two heads of bulls with a common body were found. Persia knew about Mitra Tauro Ktonos, the slayer of bull who buried a dagger in the heart of the bull, and from the flowing blood vegetables sprang forth.

In the repertoire of Indian art, a bull appeared, for the first time, on the walls of prehistoric caves and rock-shelters that date back roughly to *c.* 10,000 BC. The purpose for such rock paintings remains a mystery. The prehistoric people painted the caves, most probably, to overcome the dullness of the dark rock-shelters. To others, these rock paintings had something to do with the fundamental principle known as sympathetic magic. The primitive magicians knew, for instance, "that food allys hunger and the sleep banishes weariness." According to some, good luck in hunting and successful procurement of food were the fundamental incentives in the beast-symbolism and so were the ideas of fecundity. Animals were painted as totems, as a protective symbol, and to other animals served as the insignia of different tribes.

The prehistoric caves and rock-shelters of Central India and Uttar Pradesh exposed the paintings of a variety of animals, including bull. The painted bulls are seen as standing, seated, chasing or in charging attitudes. Most of the bulls painted are in abstractions but there are instances of bulls conceived in evident naturalism. The latter became possible with the time and experience gained and also with intimacy men had with the animal. Of the painted bulls, some are endowed with a kind of rectangular face while some are seen with elephantine mouths. In most cases, the figures are drawn in red lines and are seen devoid of bone or flesh. In certain areas of rock paintings, one finds the popularity of bull-fights, bull races or bull bettings. A rare theme on such a rock painting shows a prehistoric man subduing a lion (symbolic of wild life) and a bull (symbolic of bio life).

Bull became a very favourite theme to the prehistoric and proto-historic clay modellers, metal moulders and potters. Terracotta bull of these periods were hand-modelled, horned and of humped-types. The proto-historic clay modellers also produced a number of bulls without hump. This type was introduced to India at a later date. Of the horned types, one finds both long-horned and short-horned bulls. A few terracotta bulls are found painted with vertical stripes and with short strokes. Some terracotta bulls of this period are found endowed with "eye" and *yoni* marks on their forehead (cf. Damb Sadat bulls). The bull, at Sahri Sokhta, bears on its forehead painted rays. The terracotta bull of Mehi Damb presents holes on the legs, perhaps to adjust a wheel, and its holed hump was meant for putting through rope to draw chariot. The short-horned bulls are generally made with their heads lowered down and they appear ready to charge.

The steatite seals found from Indus Valley (Mohenjo-Dāro and Harappā) included the figures of bull in various ways. A rare seal from Harappā deals with the fight of a bull-man with a horned-tiger. This reminds of the legendary heroes, Gilgamesh and Enkidu. Indus Valley-type seals, discovered at Bahrein, Homa and Babylonia, speak of ancient India's trade relation with the Gulf countries. Certain seals from Mohenjo-Dāro came out with composite figures (such as the body that of a ram, horns of a bull, face of a man and tusk and trunk of an elephant). Another seal depicts half-human and half-animal (the hoofs, horns and tail of a bison). A bronze seal delineates a bull (Herakles), trampling a bull-shaped dragon. A number of seals of Mohenjo-Dāro project figures of unicorn (one-horned). To some, this animal stands for a bull in profile and, that is

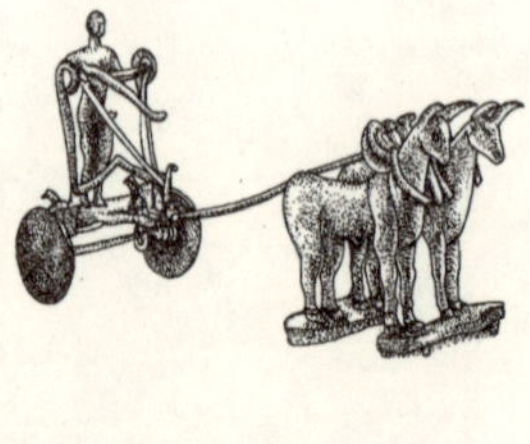

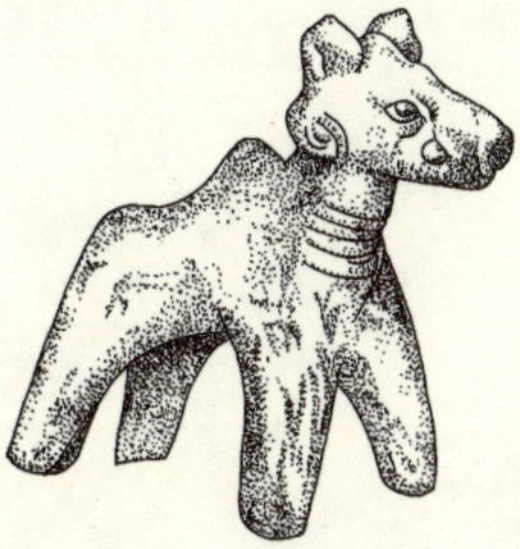

why, it looks one-horned (*śṛṅgavṛṣa*). Another seal depicts a short-horned three-headed bull. Do these heads imply the animation of a common head or do these heads signify down to earth the present, the skyvast future or the left-behind past? In these proto-historic seals, the body of the bull is always shown in profile while the horns and heads are frontally treated. The seal engravers opted for conceptual and not optical forms of these bulls and, therefore, these figures do not project the portraits of bull but conform to the universal representation of the species.

The period witnessed a few metal-bulls. A solid casting example of a bull is found placed on a pedestal. The bull also appears on certain copper tablets which were possibly used as amulets. In such a tablet, a short-horned bull is noticed and its horns are spiral. Harappā produced a short-horned humpless bull that calls for a comparison with such a bull in terracotta from Kayatha. A Harappan metal-bull is found coated with red slip and black decoration. This is a solitary example of its kind. Dāimābād yielded a metal chariot, drawn by a pair of bulls with a human rider. Lothal laid bare a nice seated bull having its legs double folded while Kālibaṅgan presented a realistically moulded bull, surging with life.

The prehistoric and proto-historic potters decorated their potteries with many fascinating devices, including the figures of bulls. A fragment of a pottery from prehistoric Kulli shows a painted bull secured to a nearby tree and its eyes appearing as a dot in circles. On a careful study of a pottery fragment from Amri, it appears that the figure of the bull on its surface was first painted in line and, then, it was filled with colour. This period witnessed figures of bulls whose body was coloured in black and hatched in red lines. The potteries from Zhob show humped bulls painted in black. On the black or buff pottery fragments of Quetta, one finds painted bulls. The decorations of such bulls included wavy lines, spots, vertical lines and uncertain cases, the humps bear criss-cross lines. At Rana Ghundai, the potters preferred to paint stylized and elongated body of bulls. Wheel turned potteries were slipped and painted in black. Mehergarh red potteries are found painted with bull figurines in black and white. These bulls are humped and have long horns but their eyes are found painted as large dots. The red, buff and greenish gray potteries of Nal are found with bull figures with designs in black, blue, green or yellow and the outlines are done in sepia. These bulls are elongated having prominent hump. Their faces are carefully drawn and are shown in walking posture. The black and red potteries of Harappan culture also laid bare painted bulls with bird-like heads. Some of the painted bulls are endowed with long curving horns. A solitary example of a potsherd is painted with a trident between two bull horns. Painted bull head is also found on the potsherds, found from Kuṇāl and Banwālī. One potsherd shows a painted canopied wheeled cart, presumably, drawn by bullocks. The basic purpose of the paintings on potteries was to decorate the same but the way the bulls are painted led scholars to infer that these figures were not shown as merely a decorative appendage. These painted bulls meant something more. Some potteries were connected with burial customs and some were apparently related to a bull cult with particular reference to the cult of fertility.

Early Indian artists modelled, moulded, carved and painted bull in various ways. The meaning, significance and symbolism and the contextual relationship of bull figurines, as depicted by the Indian artists, can largely be understood if one peeps through the pages of literature. The direct, indirect or oblique references in traditional literature came forward to solve many riddles of bulls delineated in various mediums throughout the centuries.

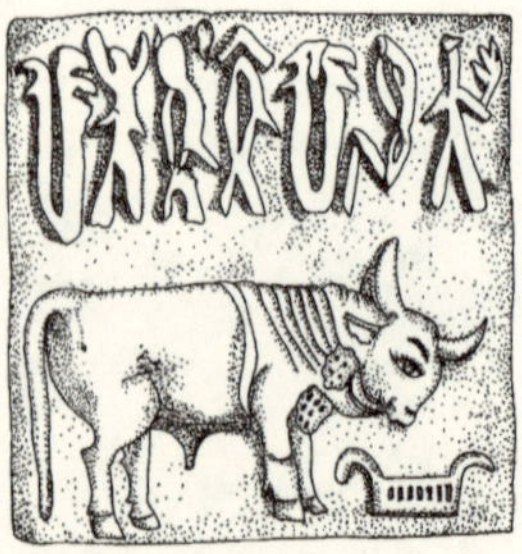

The Indian term *ṛṣabha* for a bull does not only refer to mean the animal at issue but the term means "a great one," it denotes the "supreme sound," "the second notation of

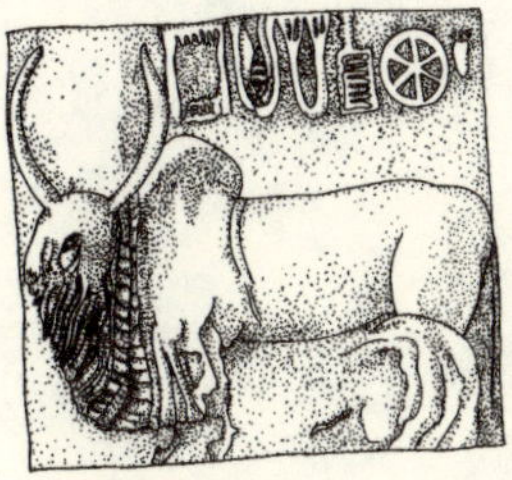

music," etc. Besides these, *Ṛgveda* takes the term to mean as "having motion," "to shower," "to procreate" and denote Mahādeva. The animal was also identified with deities like Rūdra, Agni and Dyaus. Though there are references to bulls in the *Ṛgveda* in connection with ploughing, drawing carts, carriages and chariots yet the text endowed the animal with certain divine sentiments. The bull was recognized as symbol of passion and sexual urge but it was also sacrificed to entertain guests. Thus it appears that by the time of the compilation of *Ṛgveda*, the animal attained importance in the society both as a secular and as a religious animal.

The power of sex in bull and its power of procreation was so much astonishing that in the *Sāmaveda*, Indra's power of sex was compared to that of a bull. The authors of *Atharvaveda* referred bull in more detail. Its use in ploughing fields, its power to draw carts, chariots, etc., were repeated. But the said text refers that even for carrying dead bodies, the bullock carts were in use. The text prescribed that the bulls be kept happy and, occasionally, if it does not behave properly it could be whipped. Interestingly, it refers that how an ox was made from the bull by breaking its testicles. The text refers to the domestication of bulls. The fantastic forms of bulls was noticed in the *Ṛgveda* where it was associated with Vyāla. In the *Atharvaveda*, there are references to two-headed bulls with a common body (*dviśṛṅga*) or thousand-horned bulls. The *vṛṣavyāla* and the double-headed bull also provoked artists to compare such forms. *Śatapatha Brāhmaṇa* knew about this fantastic double-headed creature. In *Atharvaveda*, Yama is found identified with a bull while the *Īśopaniṣad* mentions that the Sun god assumed the form of a bull. The *Bṛhadāraṇyaka Upaniṣad* describes that how *ātman* divides itself and becomes two, a bull and a cow and how the union of a bull and a cow gave birth to horned-cattle.

In the *Sūtra* literature, various aspects of bull sacrifice have been discussed. The *Kātyāyana Śrauta-Sūtra* refers that instead of a real bull, an alternative image of a bull in terracotta or gold may be used in sacrificial ritual. The *Baudhāyana Śrauta-Sūtra* prescribes that, after the sacrifice, the five decapitated heads be coated in clay and the bull's head be placed to the south of first layer of the altar. It further says that not an ox but a bull has to be sacrificed. The *Pāraskara Gṛhyasūtra* says that the bulls hide symbolizes fertility and prosperity. According to Manu, bulls can shower the success of all desires. It further informs that the *vṛṣabha* is symbolic of *dharma* and the four feet of the animal symbolize *tapas, jñana, yajña* and *dāna*. Manu recommends that, for sacrifice, such a bull should be used which bears on its body the mark of either a *triśūla* or of a *cakra*.

According to the *Mahābhārata,* Lord Śiva received the bull as his mount from Dakṣa, expert in the ritual skill. The said epic declared that Śiva was bull among bulls. It also takes the horns as symbolic of bull. Bull, in the text, is described as the companion of Skanda. The greater epic also refers to a rare variety of black-bull (*nīlavṛṣa*) and mentions that the horns of a bull were used as bugle. Likewise, there are references to bulls in the *Rāmāyaṇa*. Rāma has been described there as *vṛṣabha* of Raghukula. Elsewhere, the bull is referred to as an incarnation of Śiva (*apara-tanu*). The *Rāmāyaṇa* includes *pāṇḍura-vṛṣa* among the auspicious presents which Rāma gave away during his coronation.

In Buddhist literature it is said that the Master was born in Zodiac Taurus (*vṛṣa-rāśi*). The term *sākya-puṅgava* denoted the Buddha. *Divyāvadāṇa* described Buddha as a Vṛṣabha. The bull was also considered as an auspicious animal. References to bulls are found in a number of *Jātaka* stories. The Anotatta Lake, according to the Buddhist text, had its eastern mouth in the form of a bull through which Gaṅgā came out. The Jaina literature mentions that before the birth of the first *tīrthaṅkara,* Ṛṣabhanātha, his mother, Marudevī, dreamt of a bull. His attributes were, therefore, those of a

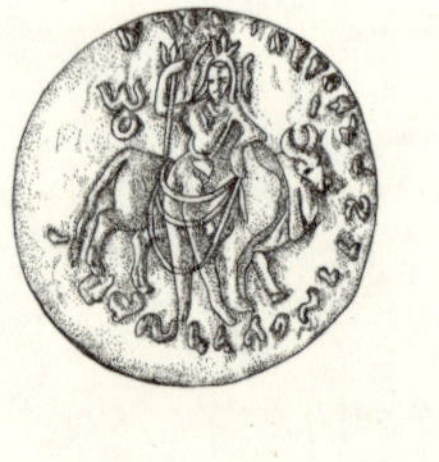

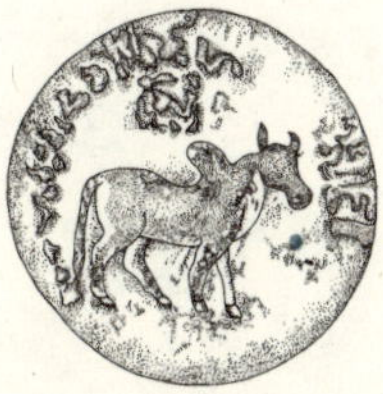

bull. It is said that his body bears the mark of a bull. The Jaina tradition refers to a bull-headed *yakṣa*. This *gomukha yakṣa* became an attendant of Ṛṣabhanātha.

Purāṇas supply useful information about the bull and its association with the region and culture. According to *Viṣṇu Purāṇa*, the bull was born from the belly of Brahmā. This Purāṇa mentions that once Indra took the disguise of a bull and became the mount of king Purañjaya. *Vāyu Purāṇa* gave a different origin of bull. According to this Purāṇa, the bull was born to Kaśyapa and the wishing cow (Kāmadhenu). *Bhāgavata Purāṇa* takes Ṛṣabha as the eighth incarnation of Viṣṇu. It is also elsewhere mentioned in the same text, as the son of Indra. To *Mārkaṇḍeya Purāṇa*, the bull is the son of Manu.

Agni Purāṇa includes bulls among the eight auspicious signs. It says that the earth collected from a bull's horns is auspicious. Like *Bhāgavata*, the *Agni Purāṇa* mentions its awareness about bull fight. The text also says that the plough, drawn by eight bullocks, is ritualistic and the plough that is drawn by six bullocks is connected with smooth living. Evil doers use ploughs, drawn by four bulls and ploughs, drawn by two bullocks, destroy things. According to *Bhaviṣya Purāṇa*, sacrificial *yūpa* or the post should carry on its capital a bull. *Skanda Purāṇa* connects Brahmā with bull. Bull is the mount of Gaṇeśa, says *Matsya Purāṇa* and mentions its knowledge about a golden bull. *Varāha Purāṇa* prescribes that the alternative metal bull may serve the purpose in a sacrifice in the place of a real bull. *Brahmāṇḍa Purāṇa* summarily discussed the *tāla-māna* of bull figures while, to *Āditya Purāṇa*, the bull is symbolic of *dharma* and its four feet denote *satya* (truthfulness), *dayā* (mercy), *śānti* (peacefulness) and *ahiṁsā* (non-violence).

Six types of bulls are discussed in the *Arthaśāstra*, including *vatsa* (that sucks milk), *vatsatara* (that no-more sucks milk), *damya* (that is fit for ploughing), *vahima* (that carries load), *vṛṣa* (that draws a cart) and *ukṣaṇam* (ox). The said text prohibits killing of bulls and fines were recommended if someone killed a bull. It also refers to a hybrid bull-fish. The *Mahābhāṣya* classified bull as per age. It refers to the determination of the age of a bull by studying its number of teeth and the size of the horn and hump. It also refers to bull called *rathya* or *śakaṭa* (bull yoked to chariot), *yugya* (fit to be yoked with ploughshare), *dhūrya* or *dhāreya* (bull for drawing water), etc.

Bṛhat-Saṁhitā discusses various types of bulls such as those that carry heavy loads, those that are used for transport, such bulls that run fast, the bull fights, etc. The *Viṣṇu-dharmottara* mentions bull as *dharma* and its four feet denote plea, defence, rejoinder and sentence. The same text describes about bull mount for Śiva, for Īśāna and relates the animal with Tatpuruṣa. It maintains that horns of a bull holds a treasure. *Mānasāra* gave a long iconic description of the bulls.

The figures of bulls appeared also on the surface of early Indian coins. It appeared first on the silver punch-marked coins which were issued roughly between fourth century BC and first century AD. Attempts have been made by scholars to interpret the symbols that appeared on punch-marked coins in terms of religion. The bull was accepted as symbolic of *dharma* and, therefore, it found its place on such coins. It is interesting to note that earlier the date of this coin, cruder the figure appeared. Bull appeared, sometimes as a single symbol and at times, with a few more symbols, such as, taurine, *yūpa*, etc.

The figure of a bull continued to appear on the local and tribal coins during the period spanning between third century BC and third century AD. These are copper cast coins and the bulls appeared with some other motifs such as three-arched hill, *svastika*, trident, *nandīpāda*, tree within railing, etc., in which its evident Śaivite association has been

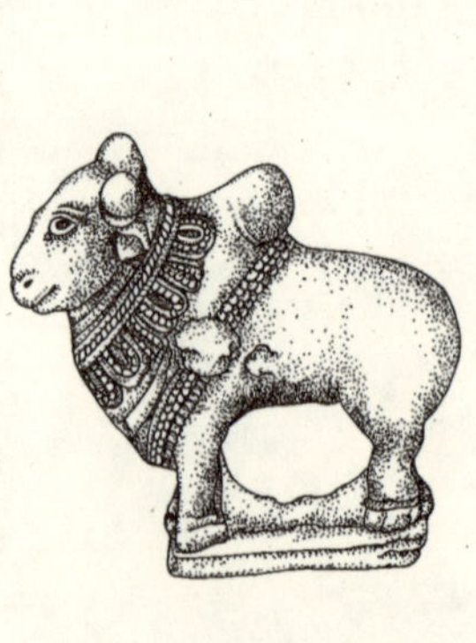

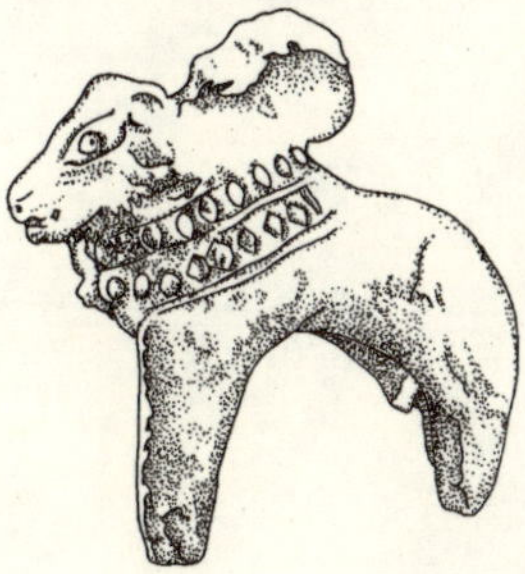

pointed out. Such coins are reported from Kauśāmbī, Ujjain, Eraṇ, Mathurā and Taxila. The animal also appeared on the coins of Maghas and Nāgas. The coins of the Auḍumbaras, Yaudheyas and Rājanya also incorporated the figure of bull on their coins.

The Puṣkalāvatī gold coins include not only the figure of bulls but also legends mentioning *Tauras* in Greek and *Usabhe* in Kharoṣṭhī. The silver coins of Indo-Greek ruler Appolodotus depict on their reverse realistically conceived bull figures while the copper coins issued by Minander included the frontal views of a bull on their reverse.

The bull as mount of Lord Śiva appeared beautifully on the gold and copper coins of Kuṣāṇa kings. A bull topped by *nandīpada* symbol appeared on the copper coins of Kujula Kadphises. Powerfully conceived figures of bull appeared on the coins of Vima Kadphises. Curiously enough, this device is found conspicuously absent on the coins of Kaniṣka I and Huviṣka. The animal found introduced, once again, on the coins of Vāsudeva I, Kaniṣka III and Vāsudeva II. The finest realization of a bull is noticed on the coins of Vāsudeva I but it became cruder in the cases of coins of succeeding rulers. Among the Gupta rulers, a few silver coins of Skandagupta (*c.* AD 455-68) issued from Mālwā depicted seated bull figures. It appears that most of the Gupta rulers were inclined to Viṣṇu, Lakṣmī or even to Durgā, Kārttikeya and Gaṅgā and, therefore, these deities appeared on their coins and the representations of Śiva were pushed to the background.

The figures of bull appeared also on some ancient seals and sealings of the historic phase. Such seals were found at such sites which remained important centres of trade and commerce, administration or religion. A few persons used bull motif because the animal was related to their name such as Gopa, Gopasena, Dhruvanandī, Viṣṇunandī, etc. The figure of bull started appearing from about second century

BC. The figure of bull was favourite to Kauśāmbī rulers and these were found from Kauśāmbī, Ayodhyā and Rājghāṭ. The Mitra rulers of Ayodhyā also opted for bull on their seals. Most of these seals are stylistically dated to Kuṣāṇa period when the bull became a favourite theme. In most of the cases, the presence of bull indicates its association with Śiva. A clay baked lump bears three stamps of the same seals and each shows a sitting bull in front of a trident with the legend *avimukta* in Gupta-Brāhmī script. The term *avimukta* denoted Śiva.

A few seals appear as official or administrative seals. A Bhītā sealing bears a legend *daṇḍanāyaka Śrī śaṅkara-dattasya* and it depicts a bull, a *śrīvatsa* symbol, a *cakra*, etc. The term *daṇḍanāyaka* denoted a judicial officer. The bull being a symbol of *dharma* was projected in such sealings. Similarly, a Basārh sealing depicts a humped bull with the legend *mahādaṇḍanāyakasya agniputrasya*. Yet another sealing found at Eraṇ reads *mahādaṇḍanāyaka siṁhanandī* in early Gupta script. Thus, it appears that the bulls that appeared on ancient seals and sealings are either related to Śiva or Dharma or as its term coincided with the names of the authority that issued these.

There are a sizeable number of bull figures made by the clay modellers of the historic phase. In the early historic phase hand-modelled figures of bull appeared from a number of historical sites. Such terracotta bulls were found at Hastināpura. Made in poorly lavigated clay, humped bulls of crude workmanship were produced. Similar figures were also unearthed from Śrāvastī. Atrañjikhera laid bare terracotta bulls along with NBP wares. The bulls found from this place are of humped variety, and are well modelled with wash or slip having smooth finish. The bodies of such bulls are marked with *cakras*, circles, leaves patterns and notches. Gaṇvariā produced grey-coloured terracotta bulls with humps behind their heads. Rājghāṭ in Vārāṇasī, in its early phase, produced hand-modelled

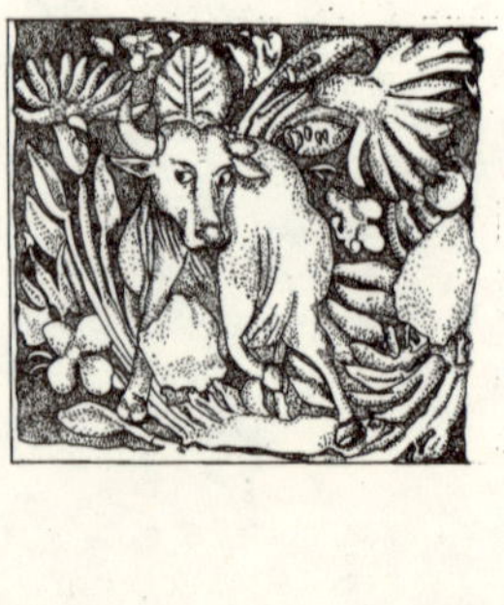

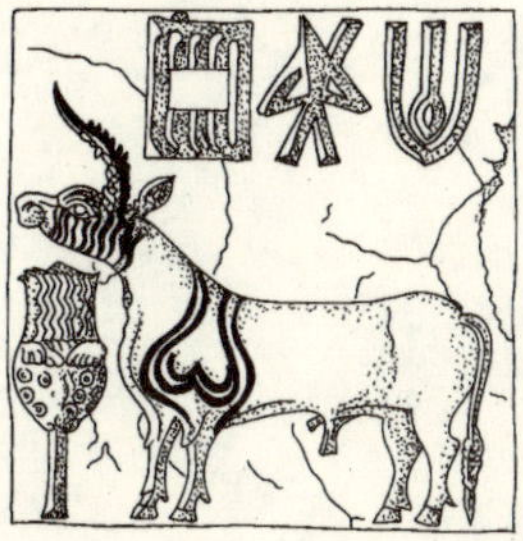

figures of bull with double coats of ochre on buff slip. A few bull figures show the use of a dull red single slip. Narhan (Gorakhpur) produced a few bulls with matured modelling and with anatomical details.

The terracotta bull figures of the Mauryan period were, in general, hand-modelled, at times, seen painted and are endowed with applique designs of bands with punched circles. Some bull figures of this period from Rājghāṭ were made with red colours or red slip and the eyes of the animal indicated with deep round dots.

During the Śuṅga period, both hand-modelled and moulded figures of bull appeared with incisions and applique designs. Grey-coloured humped bulls appeared from Mathurā. The figure of some such bulls appeared with perforated legs, presumably, to adjust wheels. The terracotta bulls of this period, that were discovered from Ahicchatra, bear on their bodies punched circles, strocks, incised branches, etc. Ahicchatra produced a variety of bulls, at this time, such as a bull with red colour or red slip with hump, bull with black or gray colour having long horn and with short mouth or bull with long horn and elongated mouth, etc.

The Kuṣāṇa terracottas that were discovered from Mathurā, Rājghāṭ, Bhītā, Kauśāmbī, Vaiśālī, etc., included bulls in large numbers. Larger in size, such bulls are, at times, made with exaggerated hump and thin pointed mouth. The bodies of such bull figures bear wheel or sun-symbol on their necks. The period yielded both hand-modelled and moulded, figures, generally, appeared with red colours but, occasionally, a few figures are endowed with gray colour. A few bulls have moulded face while their bodies are modelled. The use of double moulds also detected with the intention to show such a figure in the round. Curiously enough, a few bulls have mobile heads and holes in the leg.

Terracottas, belonging to the Gupta period, were found from a vast area covering from Mīrpurkhās (Sind) to as far east as Bangladesh. The period witnessed the production of bull figures in various manners. Realistic humped bull with hole on the hump, bull without hump, bull with cylindrical neck, bull with rider, etc., were produced by the clay modellers of the period. Both hand-modelled types and moulded ones are found to be made in this period. Bull, made in double moulds, were quite common and were painted in black and white. Moulded bricks were also produced at Bhītargāon, Raṅgmahal, etc. Such bricks depict figures of gods, goddesses and semi-divine beings along with popular mythological scenes.

Like other medium of expressions, the sculptors of ancient India exposed their abiding interest in sculpting bull in stone or moulding the same in metal in the historic phase. After a long hiatus, since the disintegration of Indus Valley civilization, the Mauryan sculptors introduced, once again, the use of permanent materials in their artistic creations.

The Mauryan period introduced a number of ring stone or stone disc and the examples of these were found from north-western part of India to Pāṭaliputra in the east. On these stone rings, the figure of bull appears either shown against a lotus or with a few other animals. The association of bull, in this context, is not very clear but it appears to have had certain religious connections.

Stone figure of bulls or two bulls or even four bulls appears on the capital of Mauryan columns. The place of eminence that was given to bull persuades scholars to look for its relevance. To some, it served on a pillar as a secular symbol while, to others, it had definite religious association. The patron of these columns was Aśoka who is known to have imparted both the notions through this animal motif. What is interesting to note is that the figures of bulls (at Rāmpurvā, Sārnāth, etc.) recorded unmistakably the artisitc

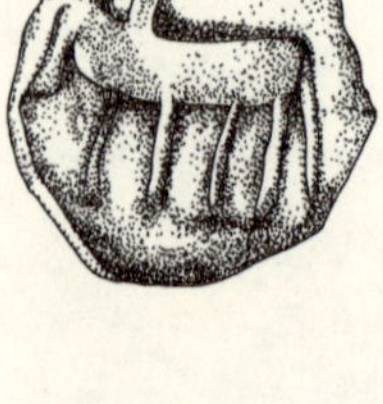

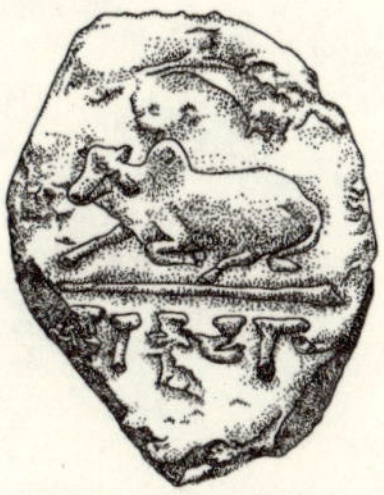

excellence achieved by the stone cutters as they, effortlessly, depicted the bulls either standing or in movement and in both the sculptors proved their expertise.

In the Śuṅga period, the consents of art were of narrative nature and predominantly Buddhist. In the narrative reliefs of Bharhut, Bodh-Gayā, Sāñcī and Amarāvatī of this period, time and again, the bull was presented either as a therio-morphic symbol of the Buddha or shown, associated with *Jātaka* stories. And while delineating the latter, the artists could not avoid showing secular backdrop of the period. Therefore, riding on bull or riding on bullock cart or carriage driven by bull or tilling of land by ploughshare with bulls appeared on a number of occasions. The period also witnessed the representations of hybrid, fantastic figures of bulls such as winged bulls, bulls with fish tail, etc.

The above tradition continued in the art of Mathurā and Gāndhāra, in the Kuṣāṇa period and also in the art of Andhra Pradesh patronized by the Sātavāhanas and Ikṣvāku rulers. The use of bulls for ploughing and drawing carts were projected in a number of panels found in different sites at Gāndhāra. The area also produced Marine bulls or bulls with the tail of a dragon. The Corinthian pilasters are crowned by bull capitals. Gāndhāra also produced bulls as the mount of Śiva. Kuṣāṇa Mathurā projected bulls with its relationship to Hindu, Buddhist and Jaina religions. The association of bulls with secular activities are also noted from the said period. The presence of bulls is noted in the art of Amarāvatī, Nāgārjunakoṇḍa and, exclusively, in connection with the Buddhist narrative art. From the way the actions, tensions and movements of bulls were projected, it is sufficient to prove that sculptors of Andhra Pradesh excelled in this art their other contemporary schools.

Bulls received its full and established recognition as a

religious symbol in the Gupta period. In association with Śiva, in particular, and a few other deities in the Hindu religion, in general, the bulls were projected in various ways in conformity with the contents and theme. The sculptures of this period were largely hand-made for religion and, therefore, the delineation of secular scenes became comparatively microscopic. But whether associated with Śaiva or Vaiṣṇavite themes or with Jaina affiliations, the sculptors evinced hardly any difficulty in the rendering of bull figures. The period also witnessed how the bull, a down to earth animal, was raised to the status of a divine celebrity.

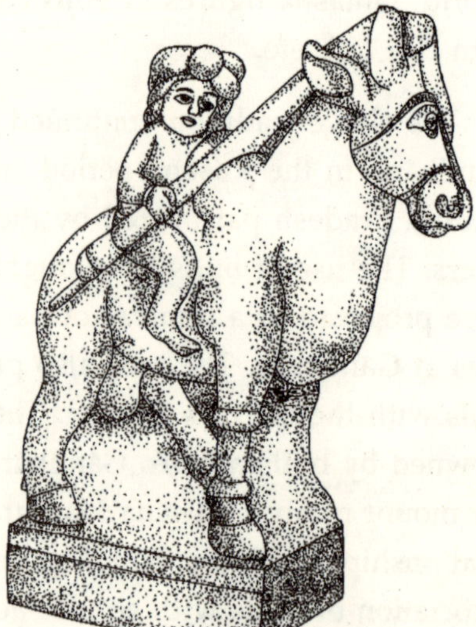

List of Illustrations

1. Prehistoric rock paintings, Mirzapur (U.P.).
2. Seal from Harappā (Vats, pl. XC 1-241).
3. Steatite sealing with Brahmāni bull, Indus Valley.
4. Steatite seal, Mohenjo-Dāro, National Museum, New Delhi.
5. Painted bull, terracotta, Indus Valley, Nasli Hiramaneck collection, M.73.4.4.
6. Painted bull terracotta, Kulli.
7. Humpless bull, terracotta, Kālibangan.
8. Humped bull, terracotta, Lothal, Bharat Kala Bhavan collection (No. L. 1333).
9. Bull, terracotta, Kālibangan.
10. Humpless bull, terracotta, Indus Valley, Bharat Kala Bhavan (No. DK 7627).
11. Bull, terracotta, Mohenjo-Dāro, National Museum, New Delhi.
12. Sealing with composite animal motif, Lothal.
13. Unicorn, steatite sealing, Lothal.
14. Painted bull, terracotta, Kulli.
15. Bull, terracotta, Ahar (Dist. Udaipur).
16. Painted bull, terracotta, Chanhu-Dāro.
17. Bullock cart, terracotta, Indus Valley.
18. Brahmāni bull, terracotta sealing, Kālibangan.
19. Bullock cart, copper, Dāimābād.
20. Bull, bronze, Kālibangan.
21. Bull with movable head, terracotta, Indus Valley.
22. Bull with three heads, seal impression, Mohenjo-Dāro.

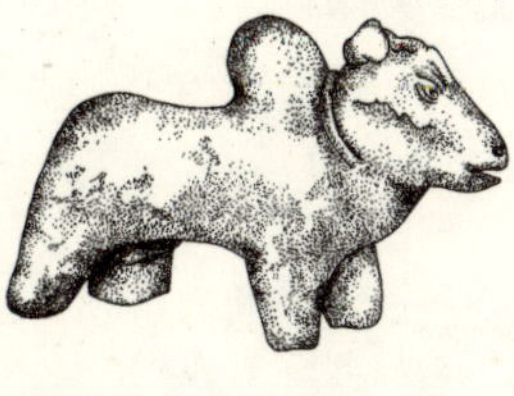

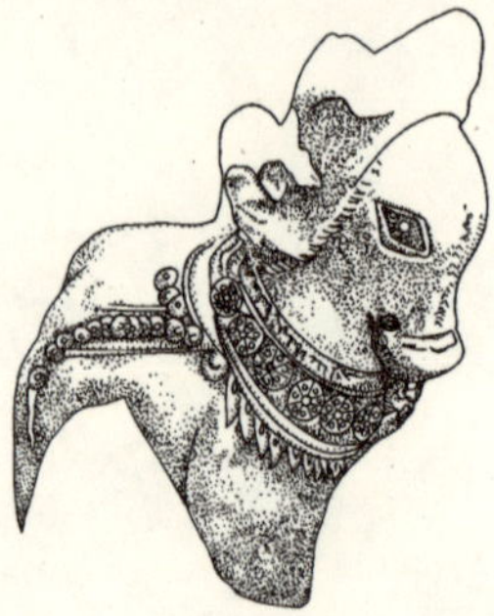

23. Humped bull, Harinārāyaṇpur, State Archaeo-logical Gallery, West Bengal.
24. Humbed bull, terracotta, Indus Valley, Bharat Kala Bhavan (No. 1528).
25-32. Silver punch-marked coins, BKB.
33-36. Uninscribed and inscribed copper coins, BKB.
37-42. Inscribed copper coins from Mathurā and Ayodhyā, BKB.
43-47. Copper coins from Magha and Nāga Dynasty, BKB.
48-52. Silver and copper coins of Indo-Greek and Śaka-Pahlava rulers, BKB.
53-68. Copper and gold coins of Kuṣāṇas.
69. Silver coin of Skandagupta, BKB (No. 95.3162).
70. Clay sealing of King Dhanadeva, Rājghāṭ, Kuṣāṇa, BKB (No. 19688).
71. Clay sealing of King Abhaya, Rājghāṭ, Kuṣāṇa, BKB (No. 6331).
72. Clay sealing, Kauśāmbī, Kuṣāṇa, Allahabad Museum (No. S/R 526).
73. Clay sealing, Jyeṣṭhamitra, BKB (No. 6394).
74. Bull on seal, Candraketugarh, Śuṅga, State Archaeological Gallery, West Bengal.
75. Clay sealing, Viṣṇumitra, BKB.
76. Clay sealing of Sarapaksha, Rājghāṭ, Gupta, BKB (No. 6199).
77. Oval clay seal of Haribhaṭṭa, Rājghāṭ, Gupta, BKB (No. 6230).
78. Clay sealing of Kumāradatta, Rājghāṭ, Gupta, BKB (No. 6063).
79. Clay sealing of Kumāranandī with bull, Rājghāṭ, Gupta, BKB (No. 6064).
80. Clay sealing with bull, Rājghāṭ, Gupta, BKB (No. 21332).
81. Clay sealing with bull, Taxila, Gupta, BKB (No. 478).
82. Clay sealing of Avimukta having three impression of

same seal, bull seated to left, Rājghāṭ, Gupta, BKB (No. 21480).

83. Oval clay sealing having inscription 'Caraka caran', bull seated to left, Rājghāṭ, Gupta, BKB (No. 6311).

84. Humped bull, terracotta, Harinārāyaṇpur, West Bengal (No. 04.289).

85. Humped bull with pointed mouth, primitive or hand-made, terracotta, Harinārāyaṇpur, West Bengal (No. 04.280).

86. Red slipped bull, terracotta, Hastināpura, period IV.

87. Carbonized bull, terracotta, Hastināpura, period IV.

88. Bull, terracotta, Ahicchatra, stratum, VIII.

89. Humped bull with black slip, terracotta, Mauryan, Rājghāṭ, BKB (No. 2598).

90. Humped bull with black slip, terracotta, Mauryan, Rājghāṭ, BKB (No. 2490).

91. Humped bull with black slip, terracotta, Mauryan, U.P., Brooklyn Museum (No. 73.99.53).

92. Bull, terracotta, Tilaurakoṭ (Nepal).

93. Bull with rider, (Śiva), terracotta, Śuṅga, Kauśāmbī, BKB (No. 22579).

94. Running bull, terracotta, Kauśāmbī, Śuṅga (R.C. Tondon collection).

95. King standing on chariot, yoked by four bulls, terracotta, Kauśāmbī, Śuṅga, Allahabad Museum, (No. 5072).

96. Terracotta plaque with bull fight, Śuṅga, Rājghāṭ, BKB (No. 4827).

97. Terracotta toy cart with two bulls, Śuṅga, Rājghāṭ, BKB (No. 22579).

98. Terracotta toy cart with two bulls, Kuṣāṇa, Kauśāmbī, BKB (No. 3496).

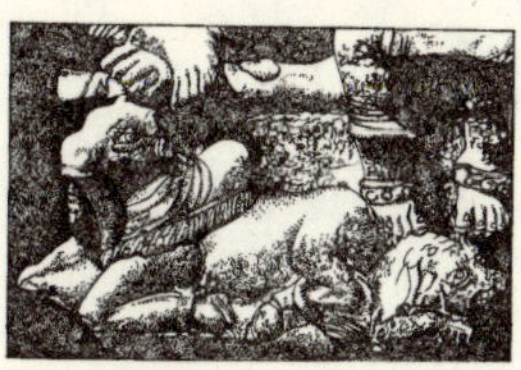

99. Terracotta bull with pointed mouth, Kuṣāṇa, Rājghāṭ, BKB (No. 2537).

100. Terracotta bull, Kuṣāṇa, Rājghāṭ, BKB (No. 2529).

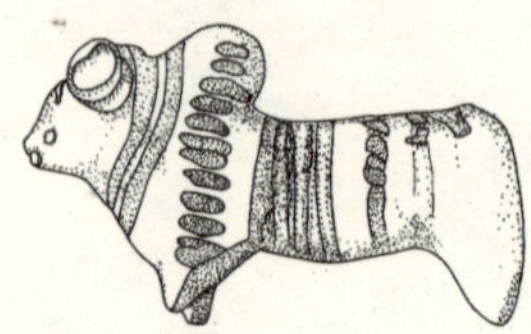

101. Terracotta bull with red slip and incised decorations, Kuṣāṇa, Rājghāṭ, BKB (No. 2512).

102. Terracotta bull with hole on the nostrils, Kuṣāṇa, Rājghāṭ, BKB (No. 2503).

103. Terracotta Nandī prepared by double moulds, Kondapura (Andhra Pradesh), first century AD, ASI-K.R. (No. 5408).

104. Śiva on Nandī, terracotta, Kuṣāṇa, Bhītā, Indian Museum, Calcutta (No. A. 103080).

105. Terracotta bull with pointed mouth, Gupta, Rājghāṭ, BKB (No. 2532).

106. Terracotta bull with hump on the head, Gupta, Rājghāṭ, BKB (No. 2518).

107. Terracotta bull made by double moulds, Gupta, Rājghāṭ, BKB (No. 2514).

108. Terracotta seated Nandī on pedestal prepared by double moulds, with white colour, Gupta, Rājghāṭ, BKB (No. 2432).

109. Terracotta seated Nandī on pedestal, prepared by double moulds, Gupta, Rājghāṭ, BKB (No. 2432).

110. Three-headed Śiva seated on Nandī, terracotta, Gupta, Rangamahal, Golden Jubilee Museum, Bikaner (No. 228).

111. Kṛṣṇa lifting Govardhan Giri, terracotta, Gupta, Rangamahal (Urmilasant, Pl. XLIV).

112. Terracotta humped bull, Gupta, Belwa (Sāran, Bihar), Patna Museum (No. Arch. 300).

113. Bull capital, sandstone, Lohānīpur, Patna, Mauryan, Patna Museum, (No. 1937).

114. Bull capital from Rāmpurvā (Bihar), Mauryan, Rashtrapati Bhavan, New Delhi.

115. Bull on the abacus of lion capital, sandstone, Sārnāth, Mauryan, Sarnath Museum.

116. Purchase of Jetavana, Bharhut, Śuṅga, Indian Museum, Calcutta, (No. 156).

117. Vṛṣabha Maccha, Bharhut, Śuṅga, Indian Museum, Calcutta.

118. Sujātā and the Ox, Bharhut, Indian Museum, Calcutta.

119. Fragment of a railing with bull, Amarāvatī, first century AD, Madras Museum.

120. Rail coping with bull, Amaravati Museum (No. 99).

121. Bullock cart, Southern gate, Śuṅga, Sāñcī.

122. Bull with rider, right side Eastern Gateway of Stūpa No. 1, Sāñcī.

123. Bull with rider, buff stone, crossbar, Śuṅga, Mathurā, Mathura Museum (No. 2322).

124. Door lintel, Kauśāmbī, Śuṅga, Allahabad Museum (No. 65).

125. *Vesantara Jātaka*, Goli (Gunṭūr) *c*. 250 AD.

126. Carved floral scroll, Panigiri (Andhra Pradesh), *c*. third century AD.

127. Bullock cart, detail of a high relief, schist, Takhta-e-Bahi, Peshawar Museum, (No. 799).

128. Plough pulled by two oxen, detail of a high relief, schist, Sahari Bahlol, Peshawar Museum, (No. 1739).

129. Tray with a bull and lion, green steatite, early Kuṣāṇa, Gāndhāra, Helmand Area, Afghanistan, British Museum, London (No. 1913.10-22.2).

130. Bull with double-faced rider, Mathurā, *c*. second century AD, State Museum, Lucknow (No. J. 642).

131. Toraṇa Tympanum, Kaṅkālīṭīlā, Mathurā, State Museum Lucknow (No. J. 555).

132. Running bull on crossbar, Mathurā, Kuṣāṇa, BKB (No. 22561).

133. Seated bull on crossbar, Mathurā, Kuṣāṇa, BKB (No. 22561).

134. Bull from Vaiśālī, gold, Kuṣāṇa (IAR 1958-590).

135. Bracket showing two bulls seated back to back, red sandstone, Swāmīghāṭ (Mathurā), Early Gupta, Mathura Museum (No. 44.3118).

136-37. Double-sided plaque with bull and lion, Mathurā, Gupta, BKB (No. 21826).

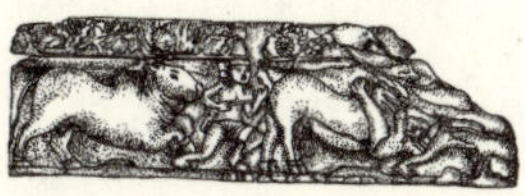

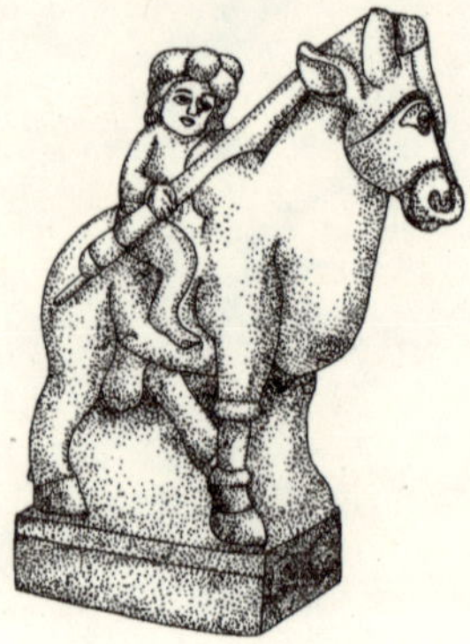

138. Śiva-Pārvatī seated on a bull, stone, Deogarh, U.P., Gupta.

139. Bull-faced man on the Doda, Śiva temple, Bhumara, Gupta, (MASI-4).

140. Śiva on Nandī, *c.* sixth century AD, Vijayawada Museum.

141. Ardhanārīśvara with bull, Bādāmī, Cave I, late sixth century AD.

142. Umā-Maheśvara and Nandī, Yaleśvaram, *c.* sixth century AD.

143. Bull capital in the *caitya* hall, stone, Bedsa (Mumbai) Kuṣāṇa.

144. The fighting bull, Ajantā, Cave No. I, early sixth century AD.

145. Bull in tension, Ajantā, Cave No. I, early sixth century AD.

146. Painting with bull, Ajantā, Cave No. I, early sixth century AD.

147-154. Stone Beads.

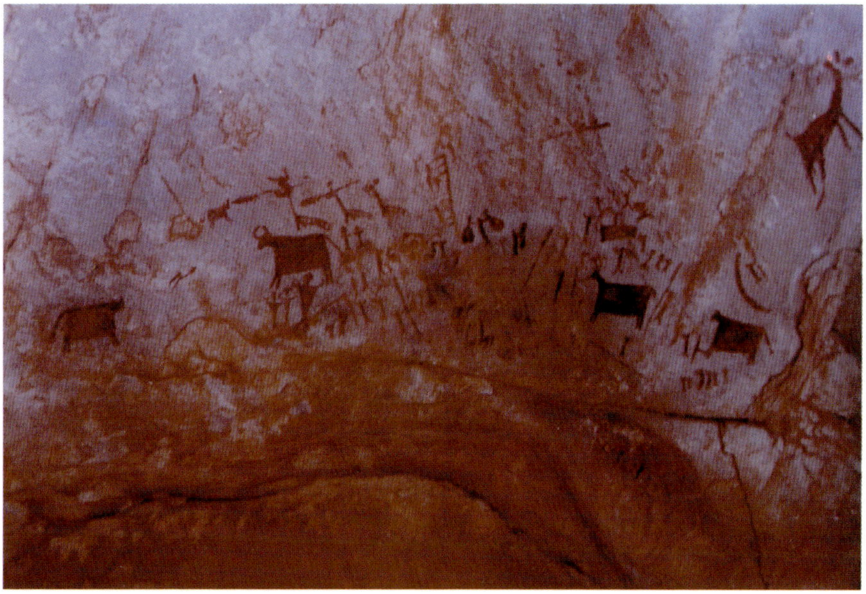

fig. 1

fig. 6

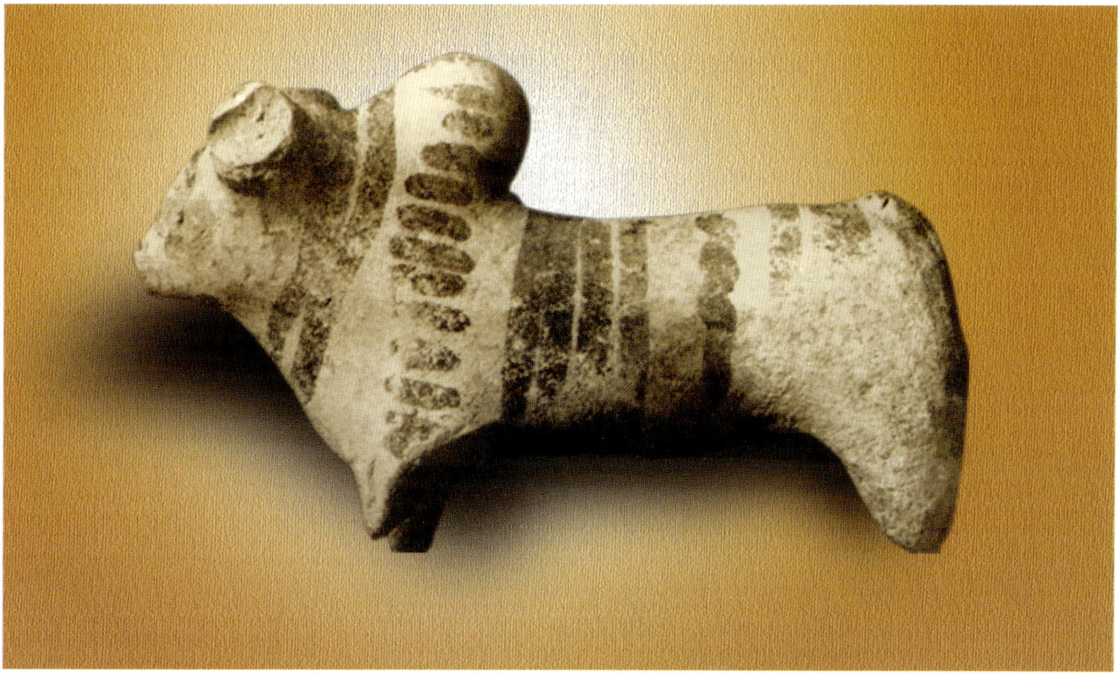

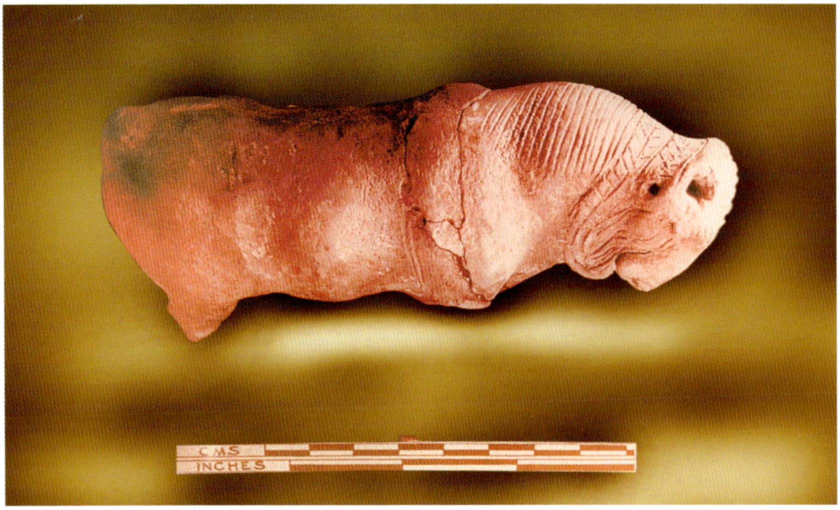

fig. 7

fig. 8

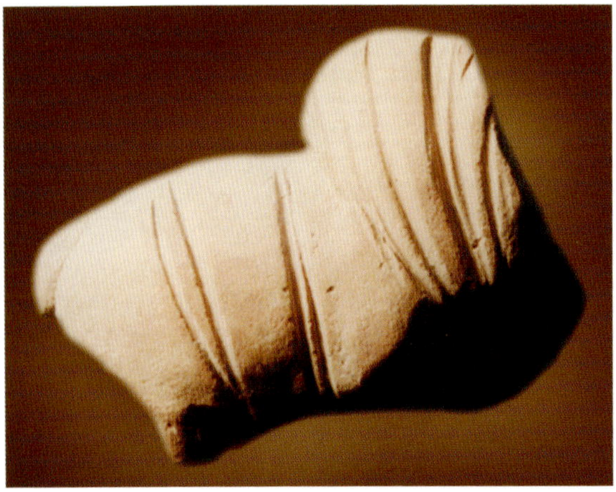

fig. 10

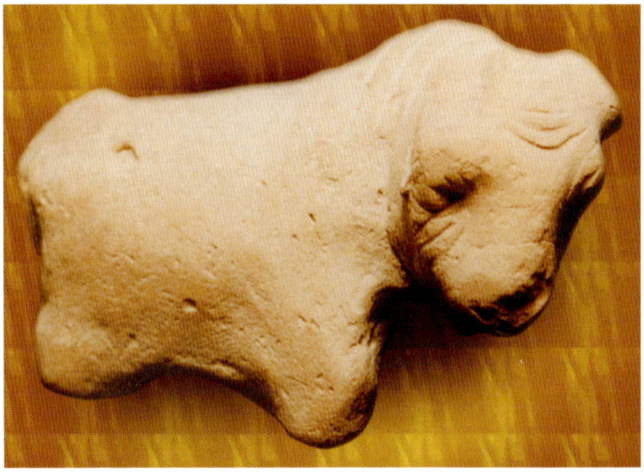

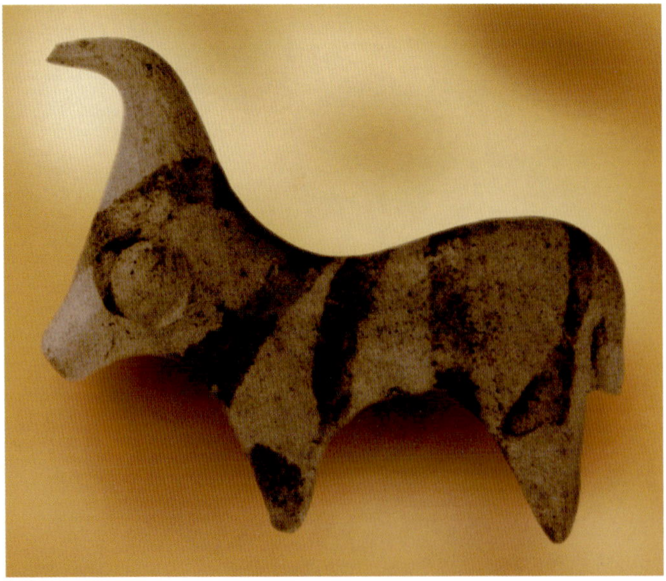

fig. 16

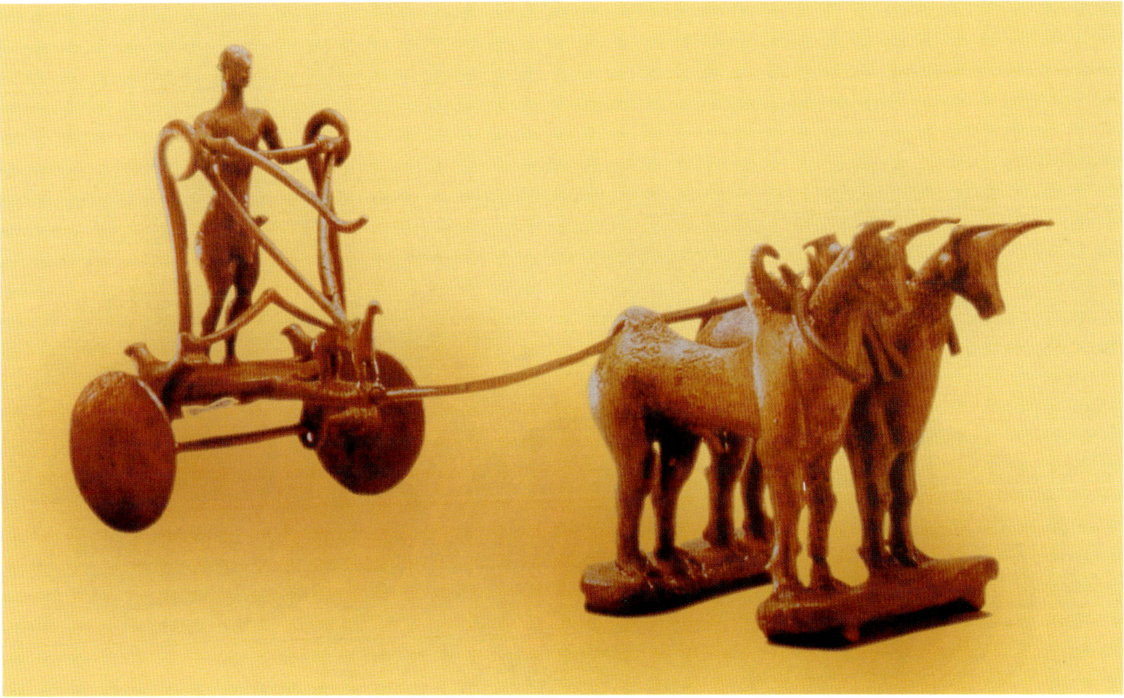

fig. 19

fig. 20

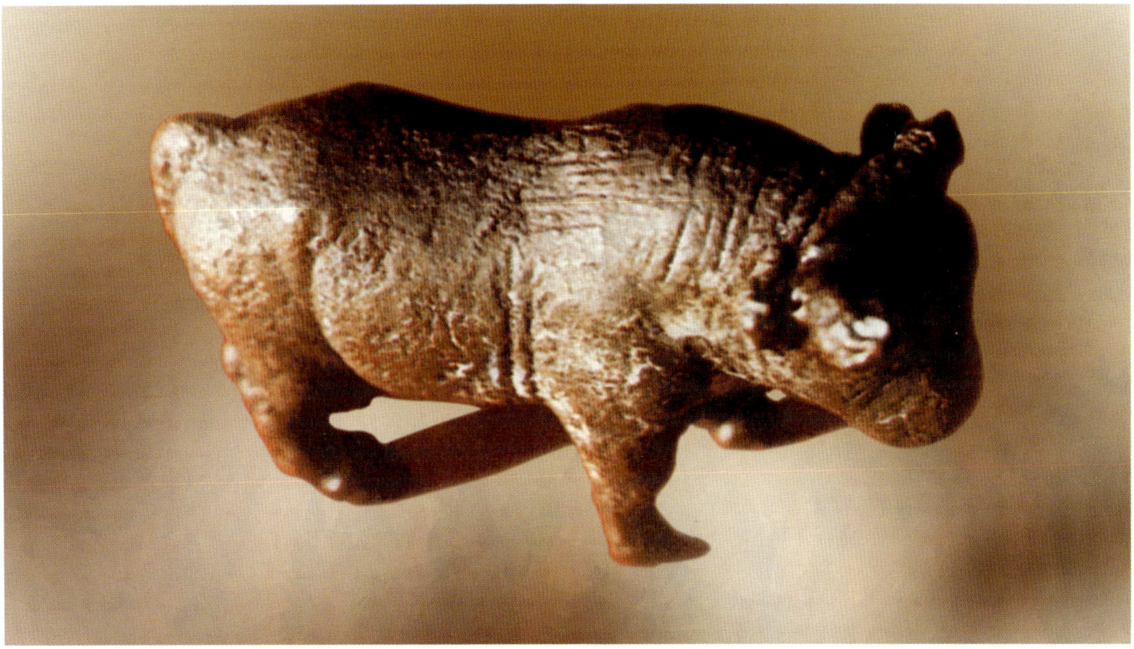

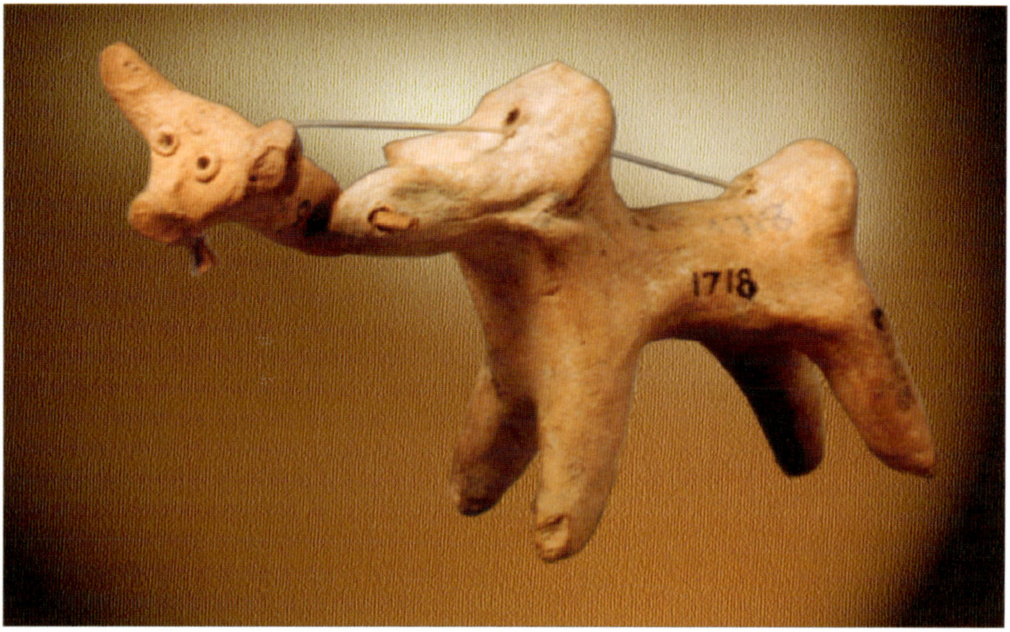

fig. 21

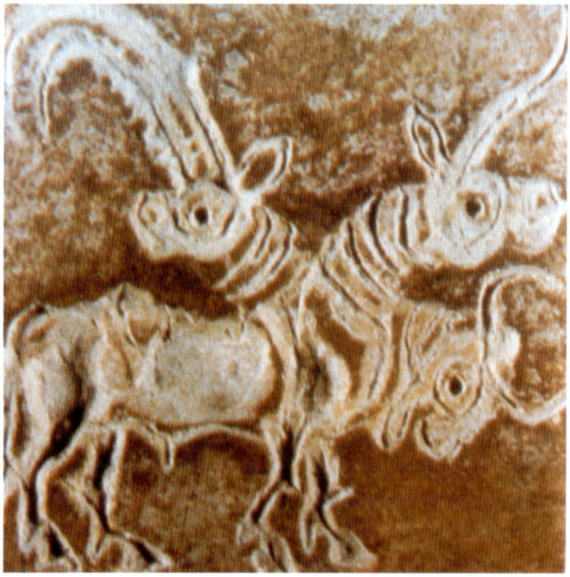

fig. 22

fig. 24

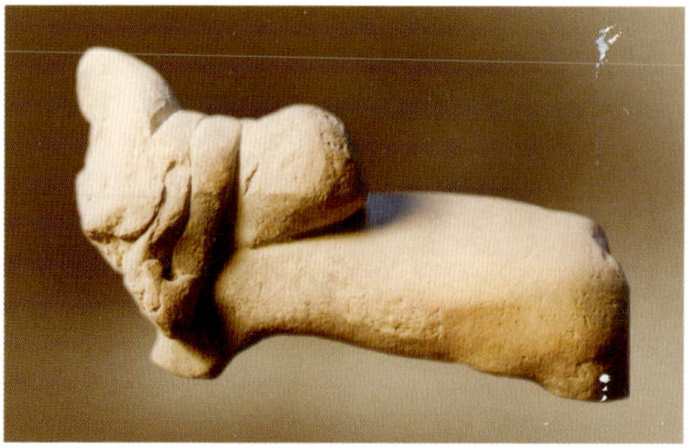

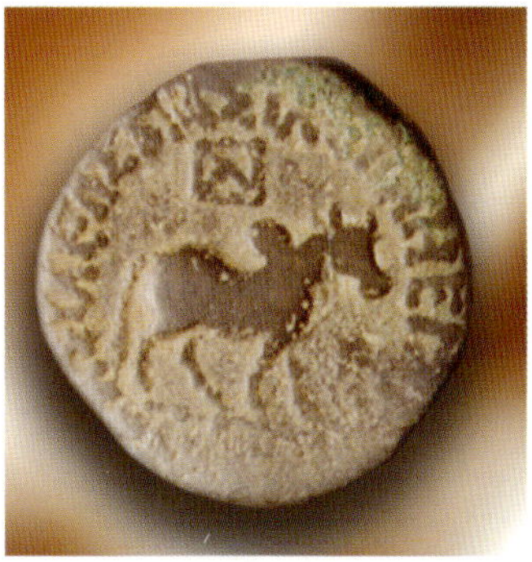

fig. 51

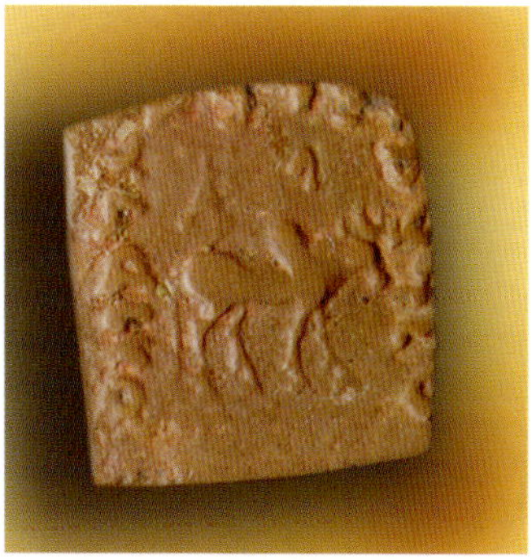

fig. 52

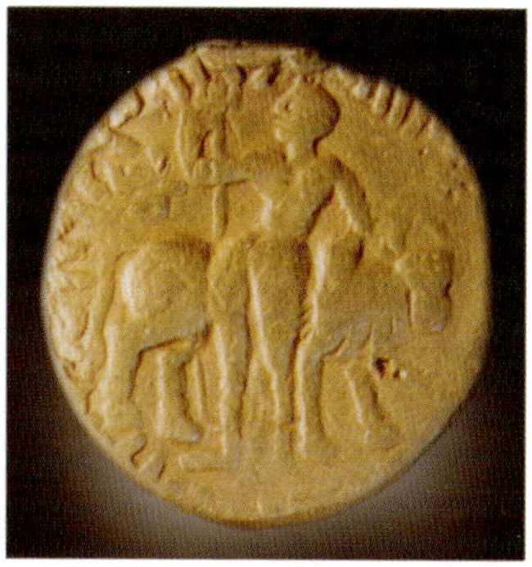

fig. 54

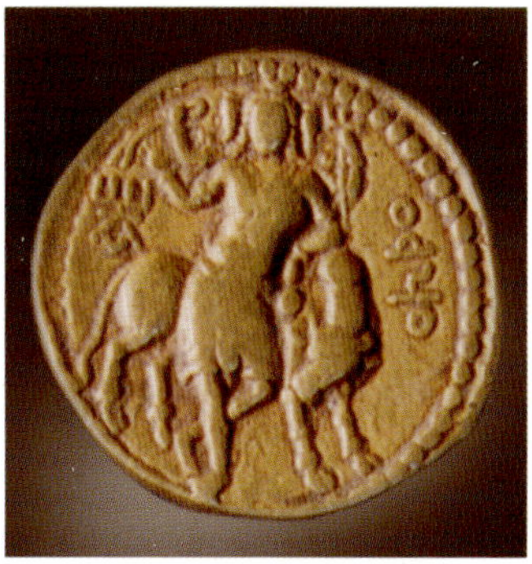

fig. 55

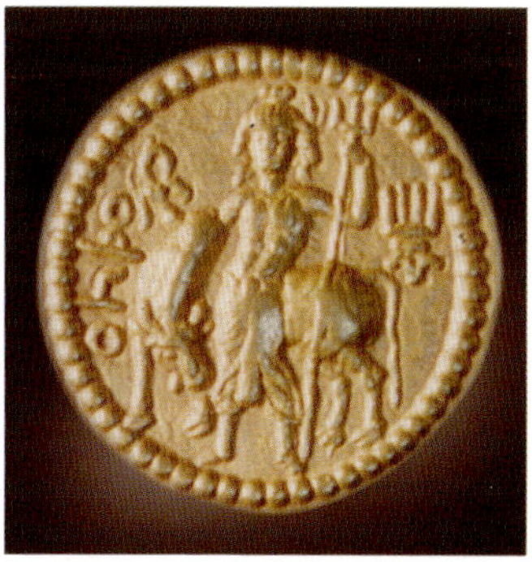

fig. 56

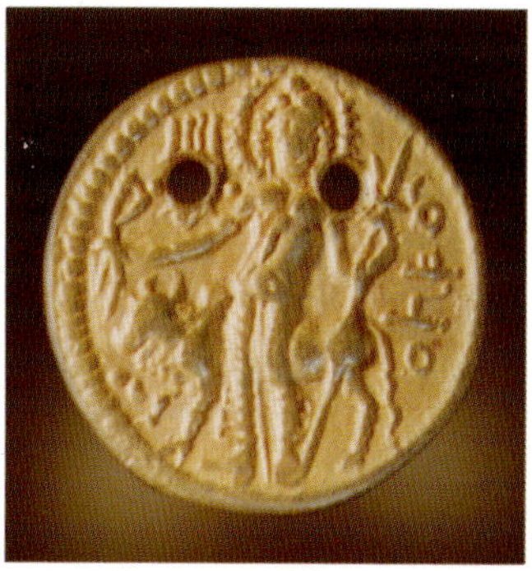

fig. 57

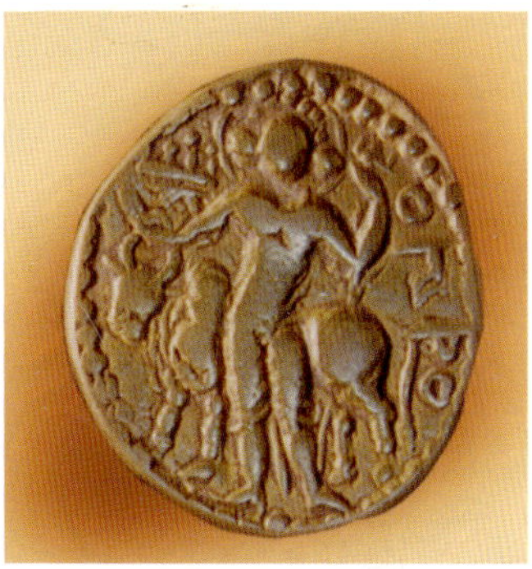

fig. 58

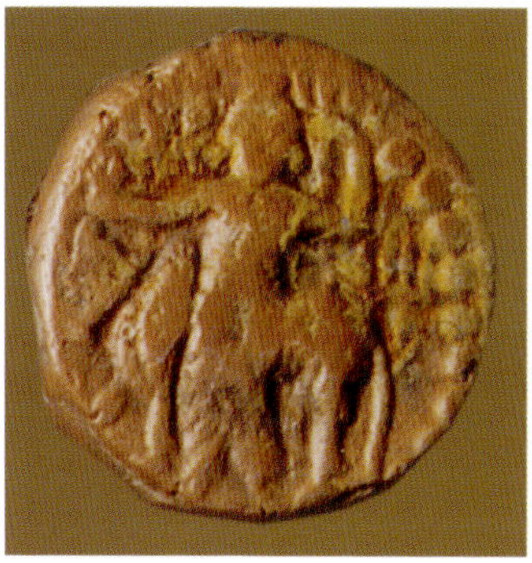

fig. 59

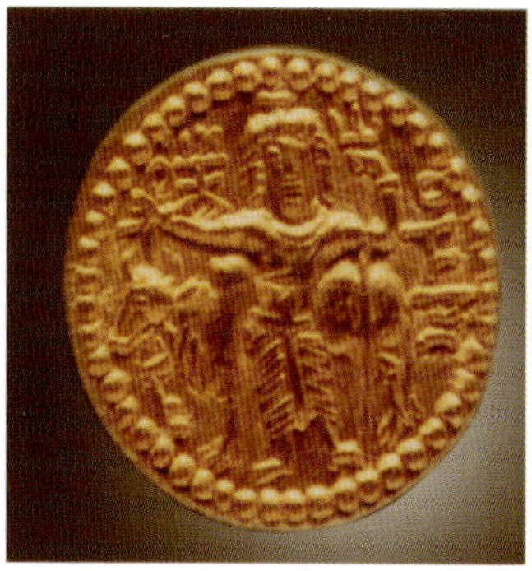

fig. 60

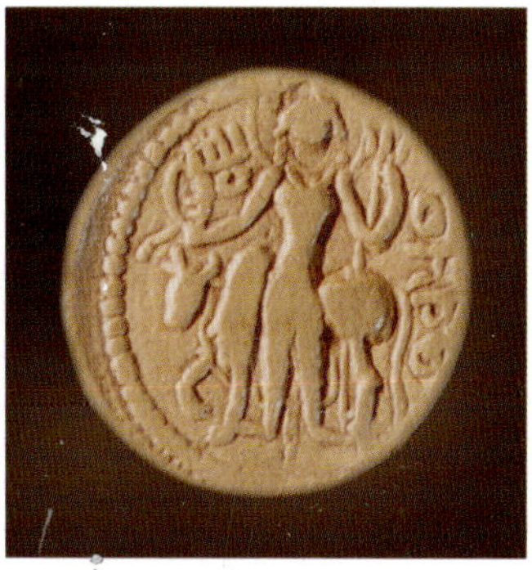

fig. 61

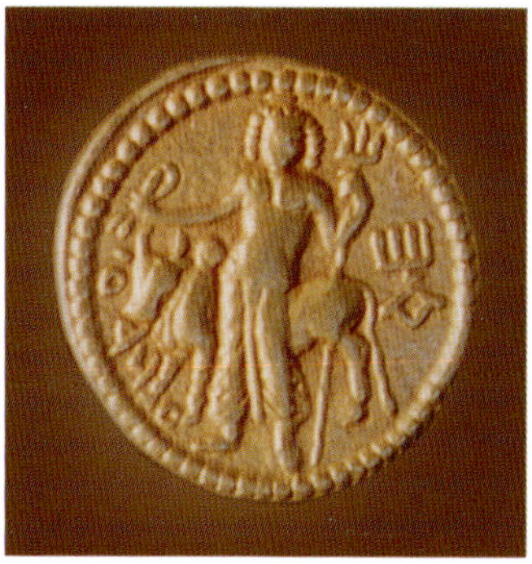

fig. 62

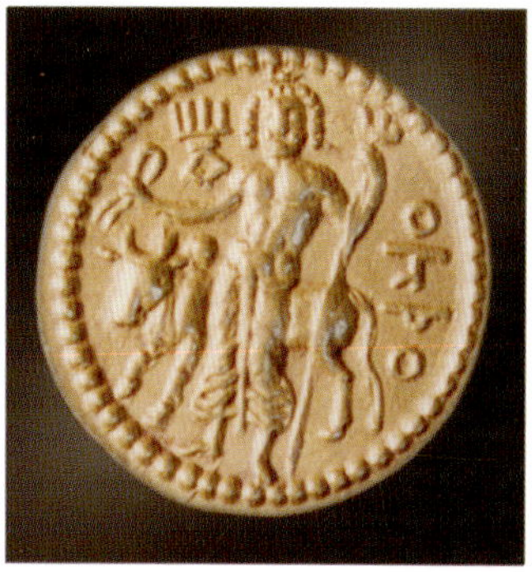

fig. 63

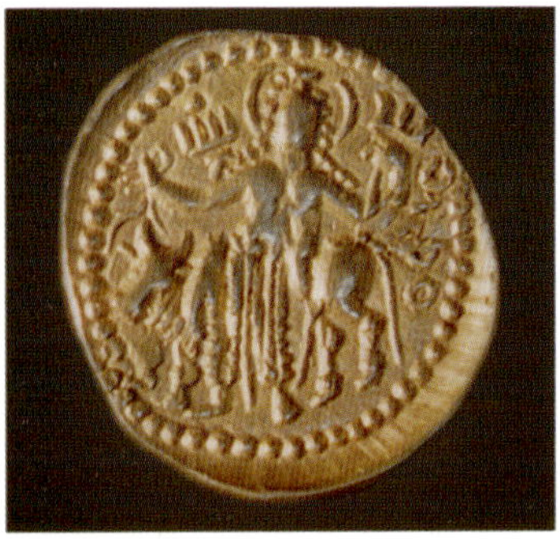

fig. 64

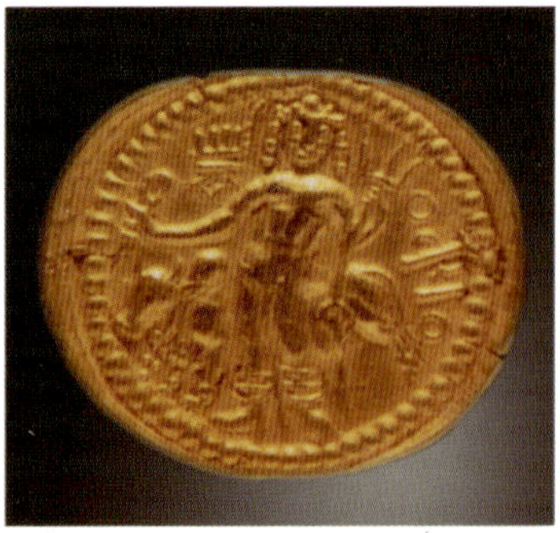

fig. 65

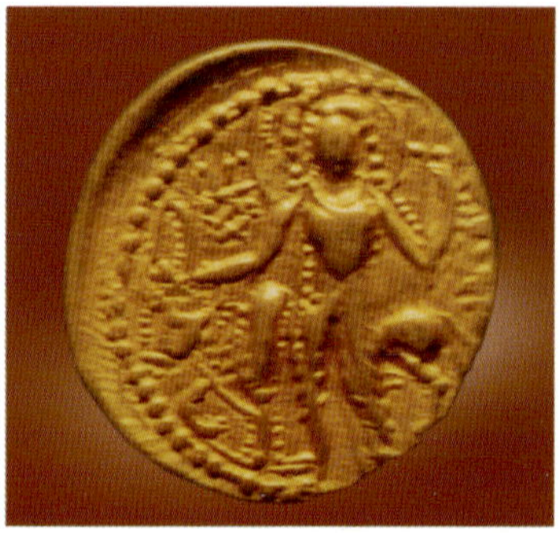

fig. 66

fig. 67

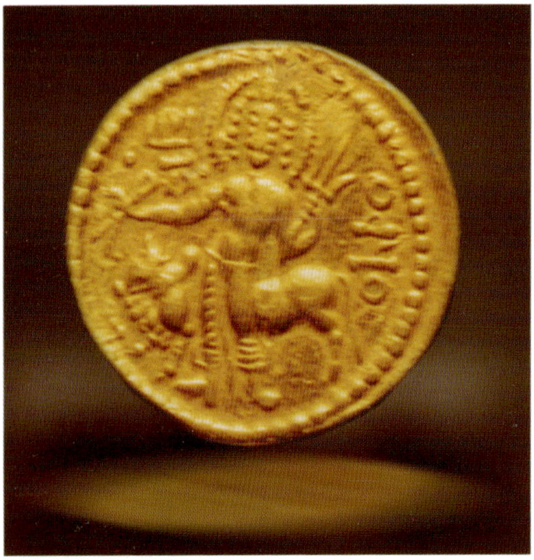

fig. 69

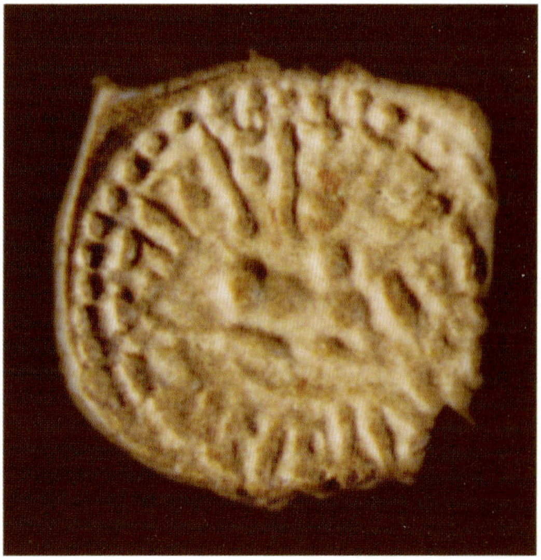

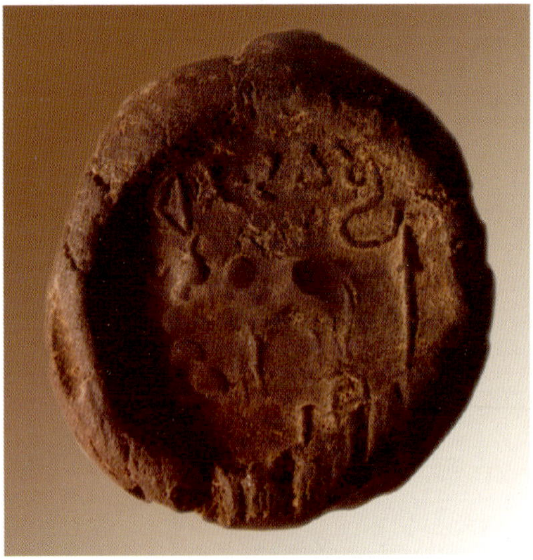

fig. 70

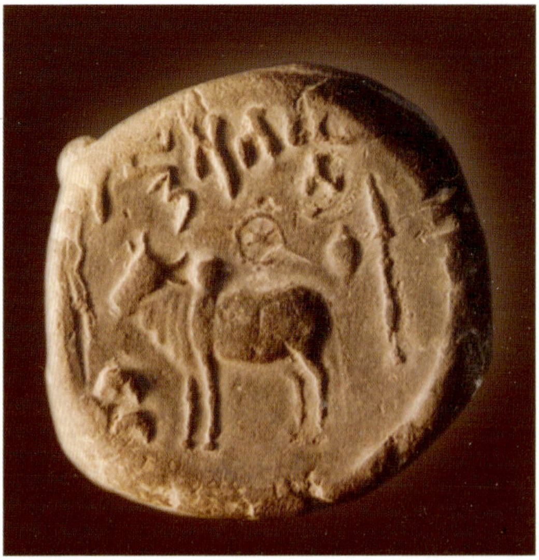

fig. 71

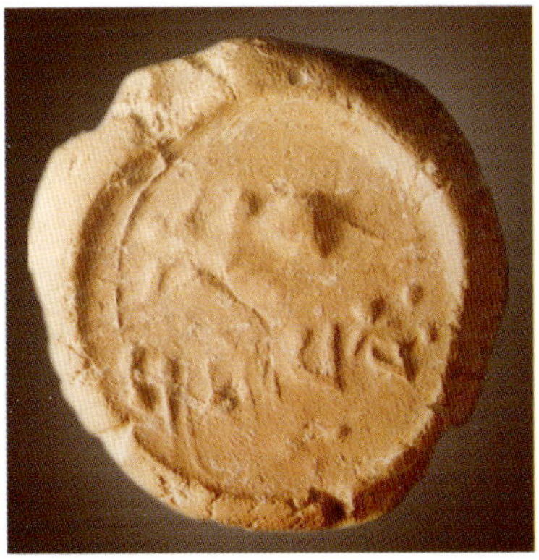

fig. 76

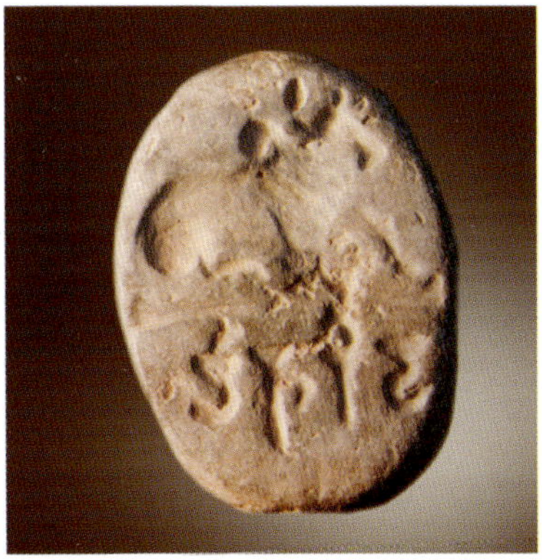

fig. 77

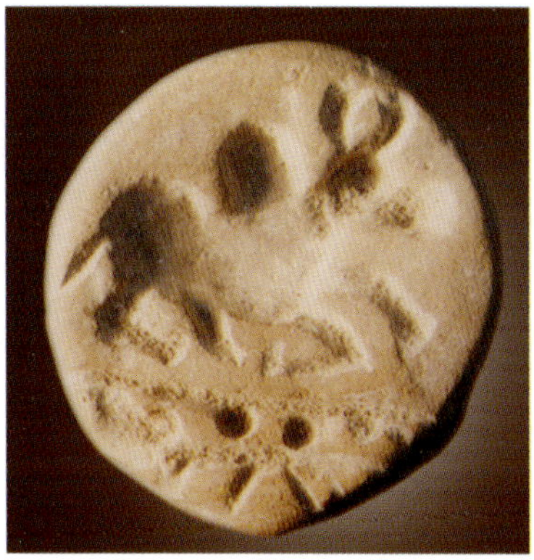

fig. 78

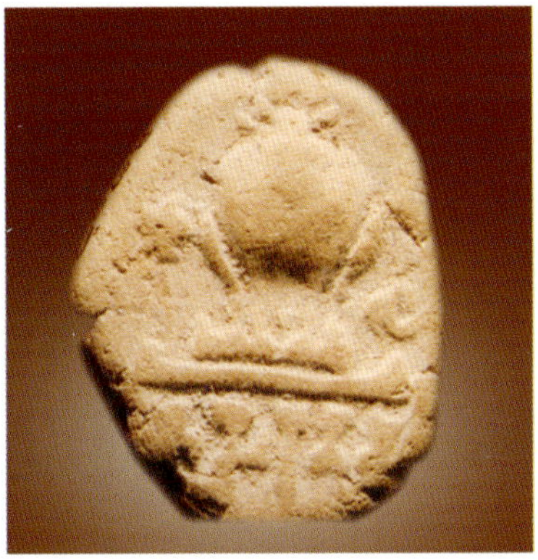

fig. 79

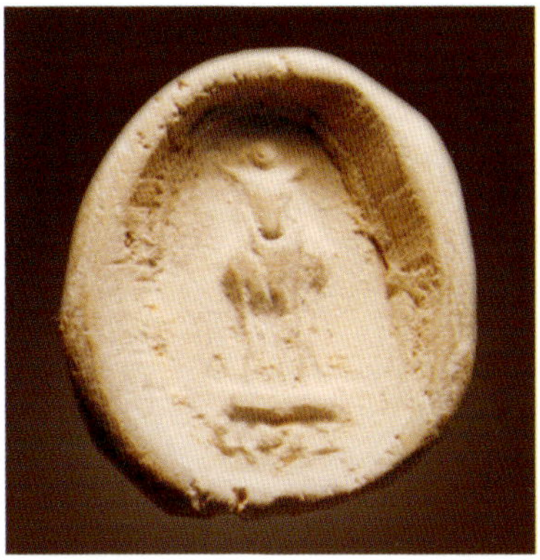

fig. 80

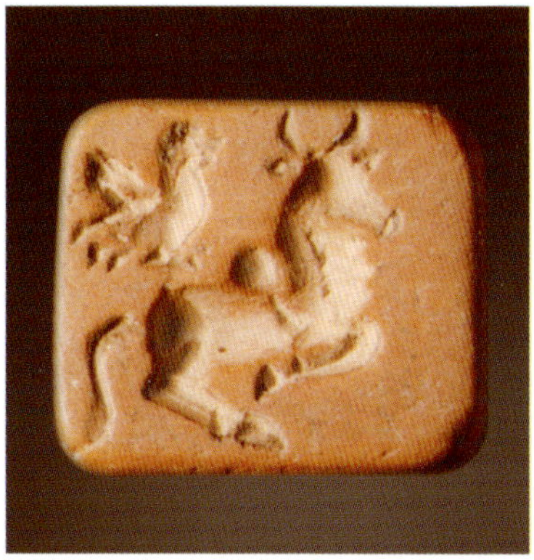

fig. 81

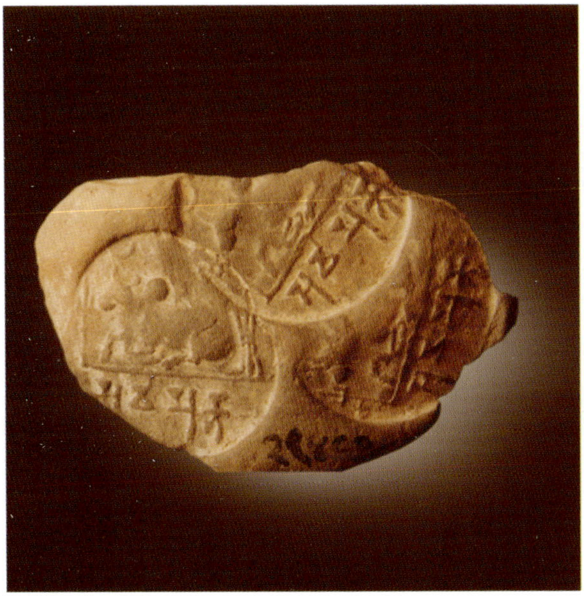

fig. 82

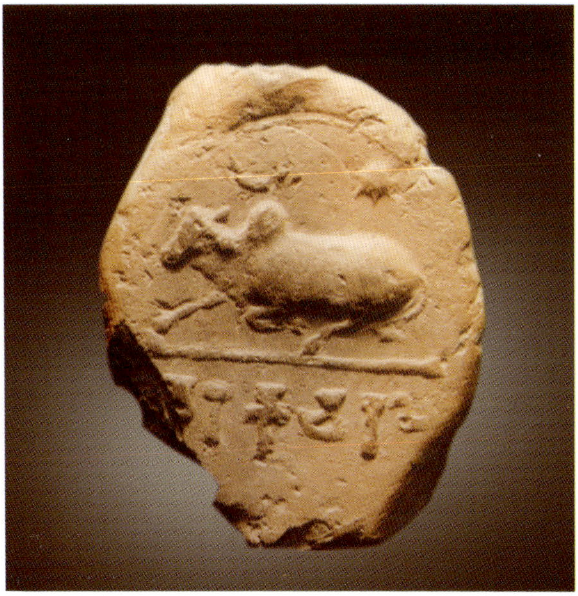

fig. 83

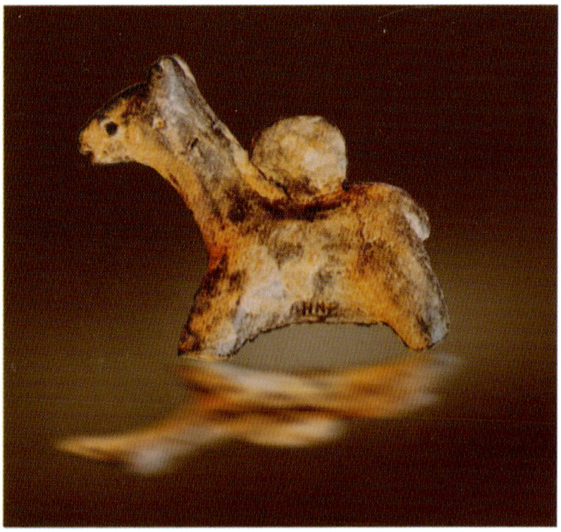

fig. 84

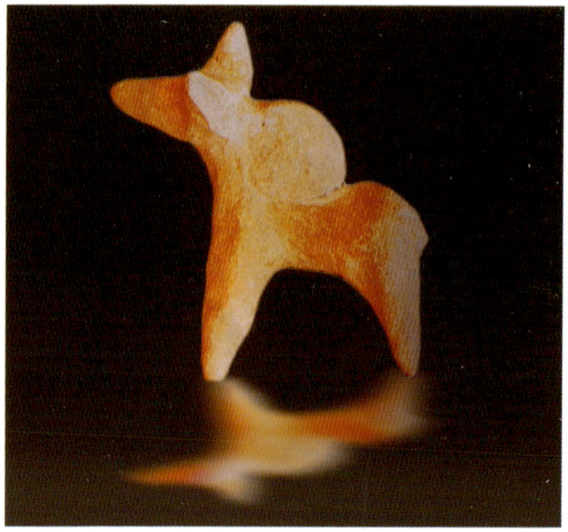

fig. 85

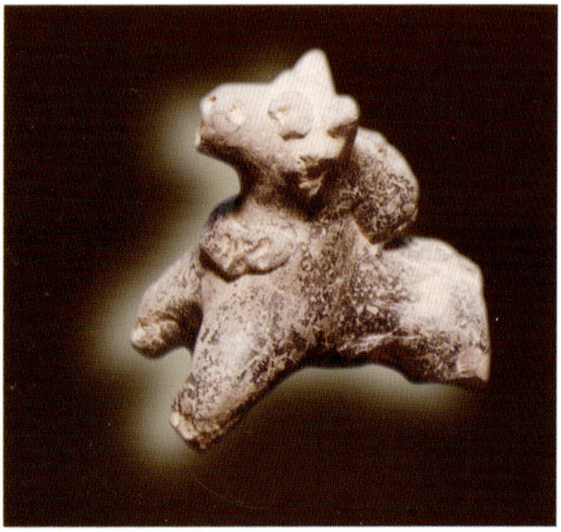

fig. 89

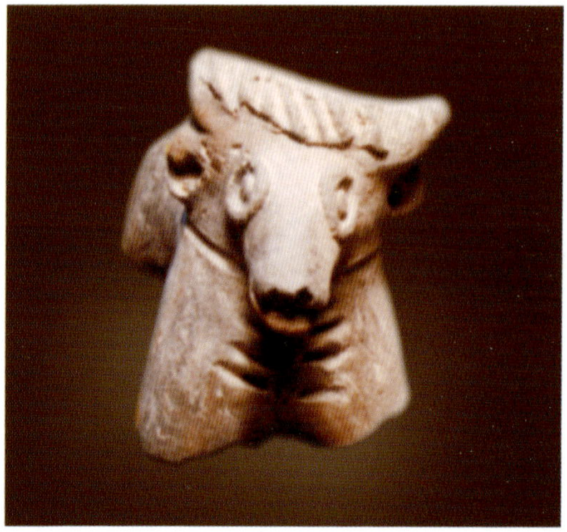

fig. 90

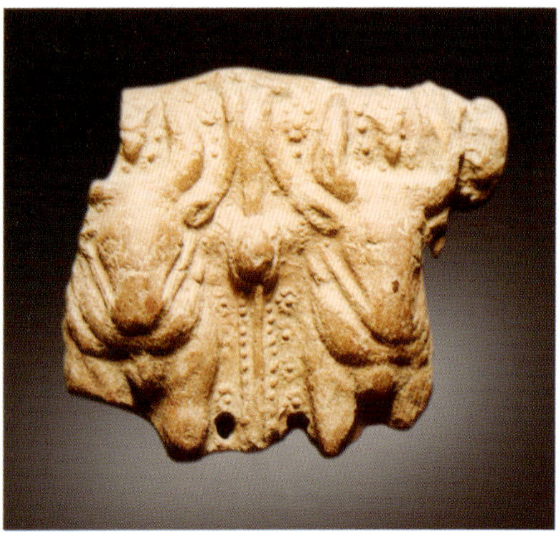

fig. 98

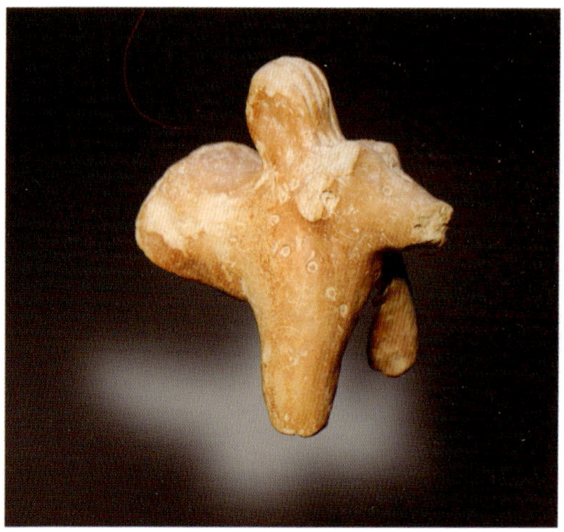

fig. 99

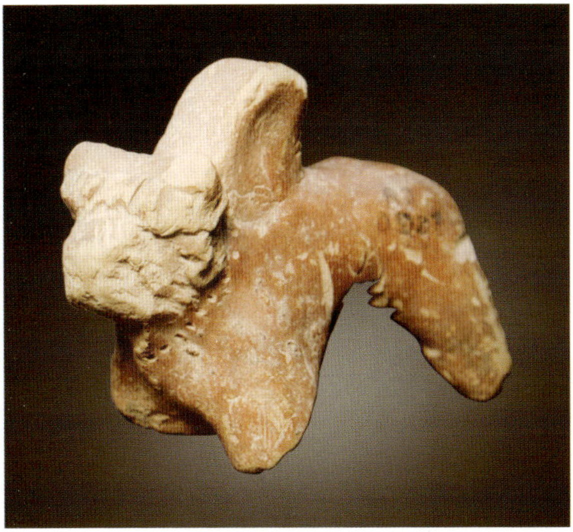

fig. 100

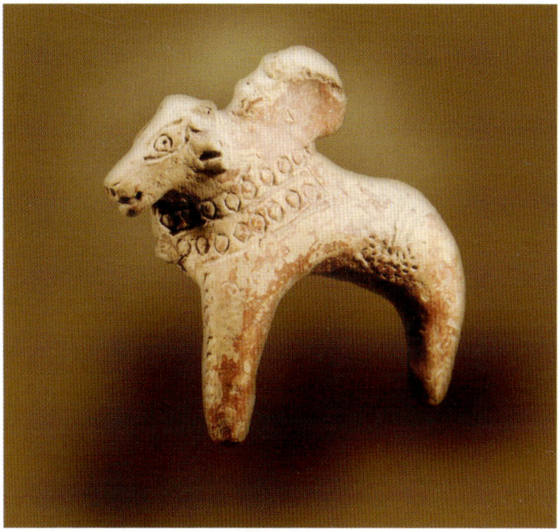

fig. 101

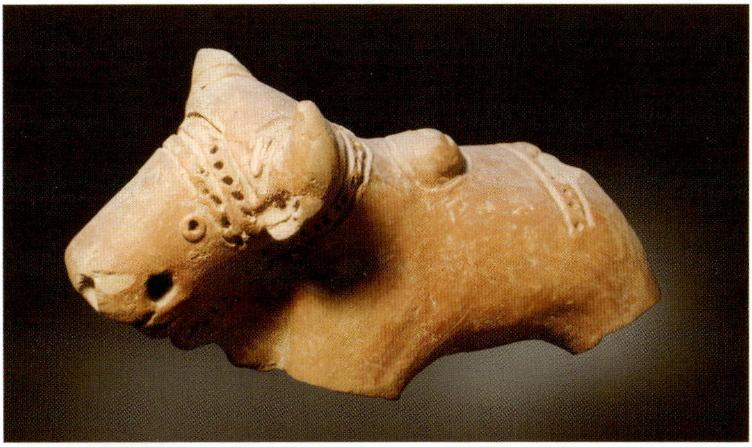

fig. 102

fig. 103

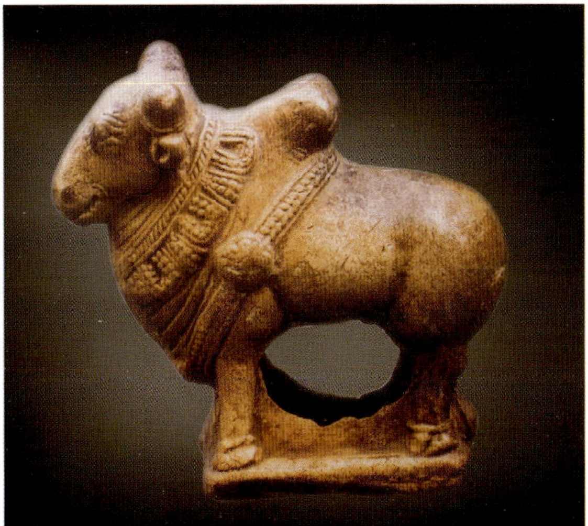

fig. 105

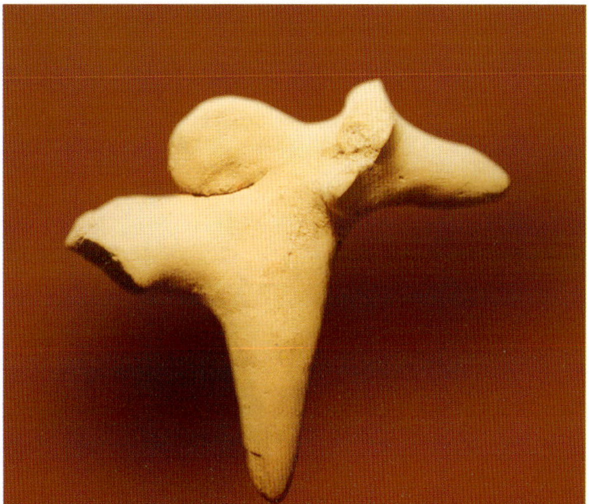

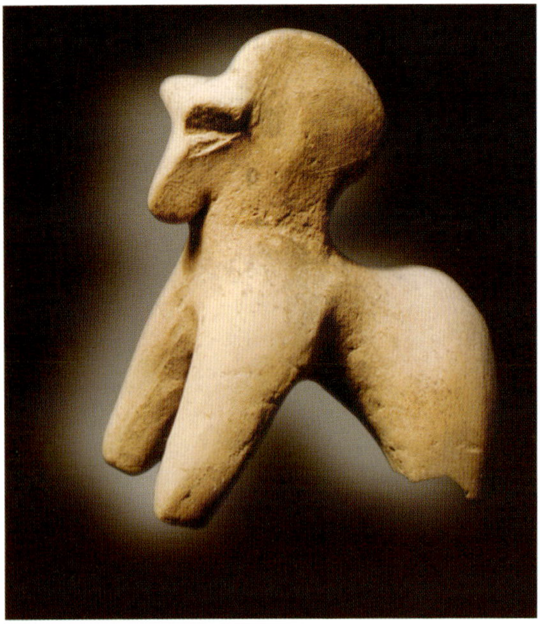

fig. 106

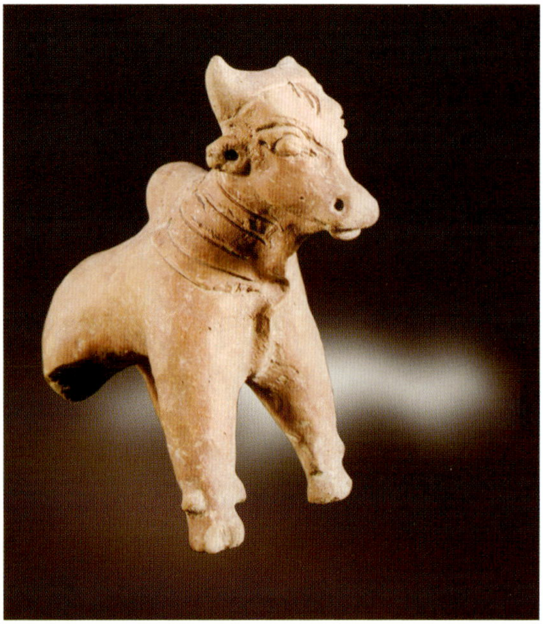

fig. 107

fig. 108

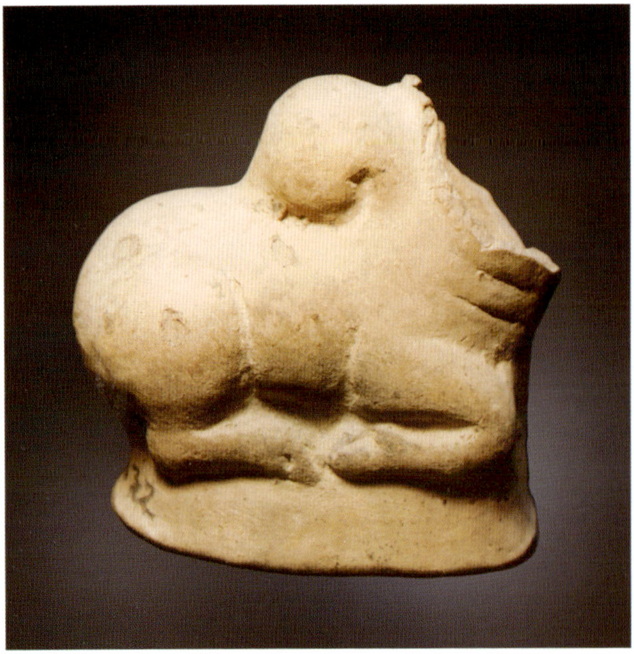

fig. 109

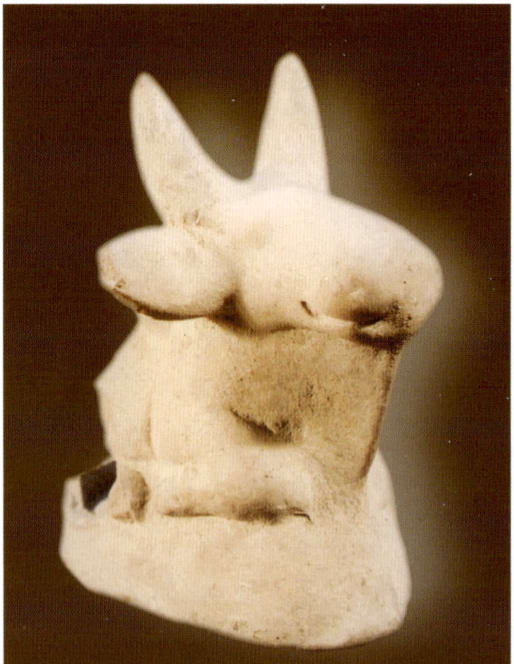

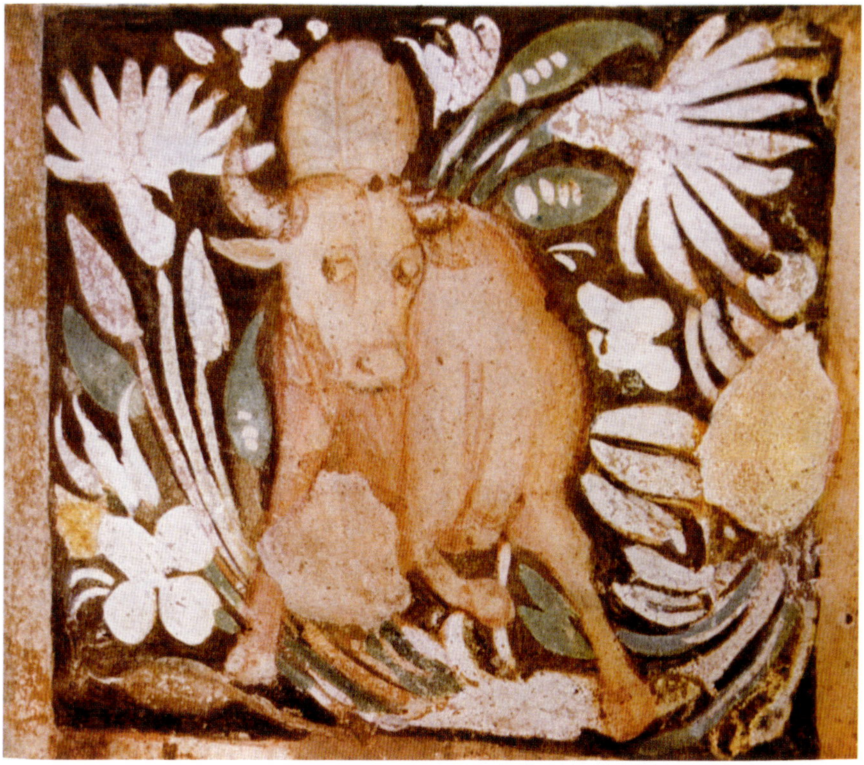

fig. 145

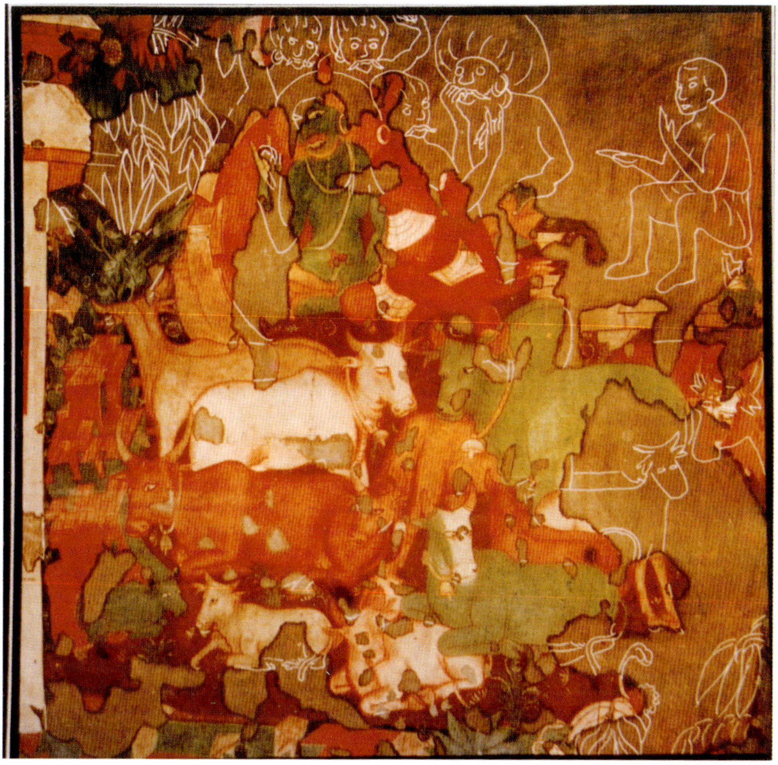

fig. 146

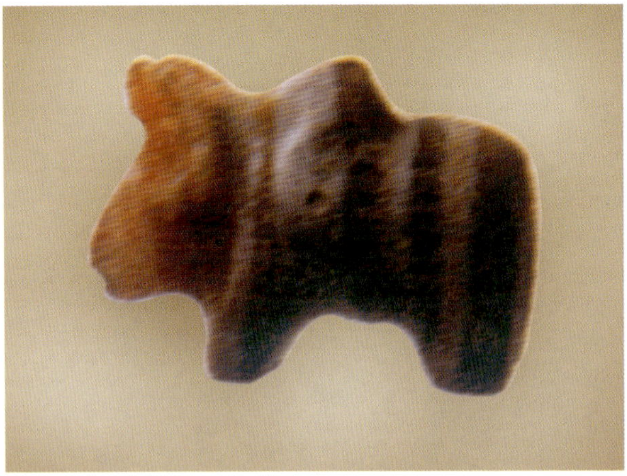

fig. 147

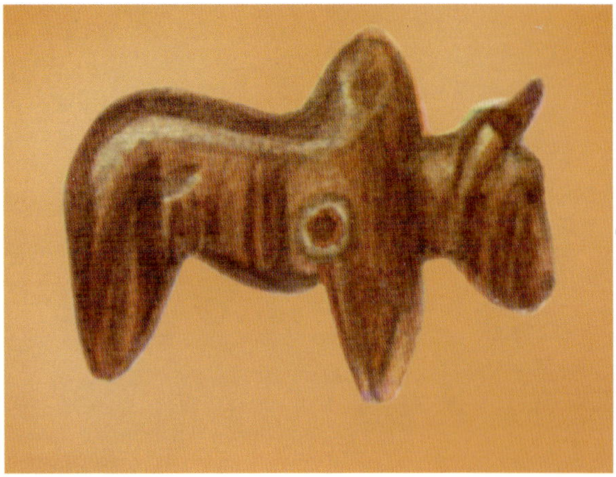

fig. 150

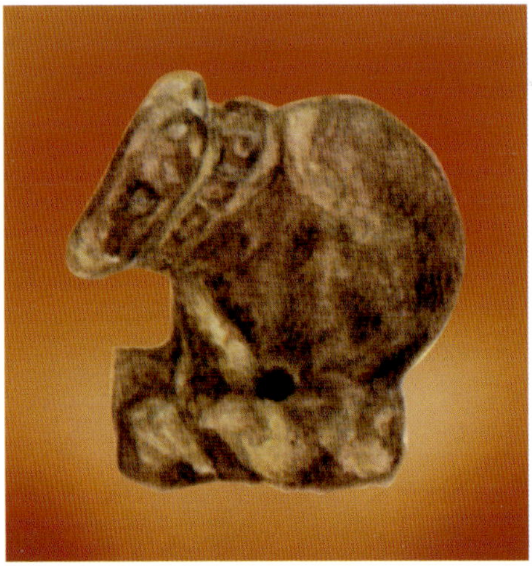

fig. 151

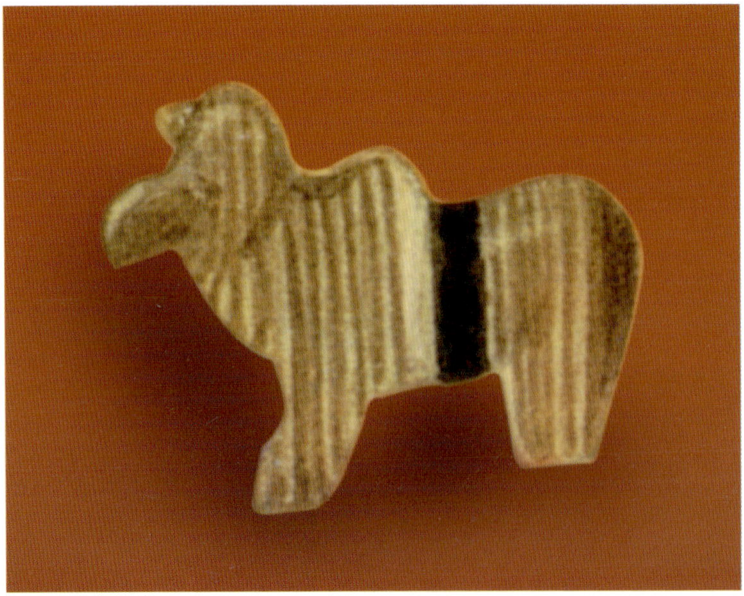

fig. 152

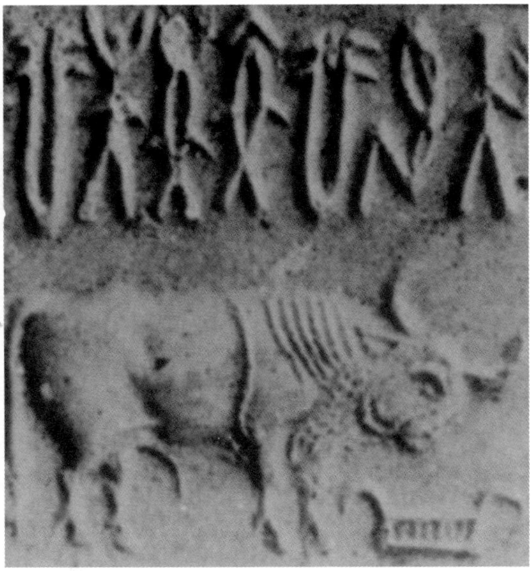

fig. 2

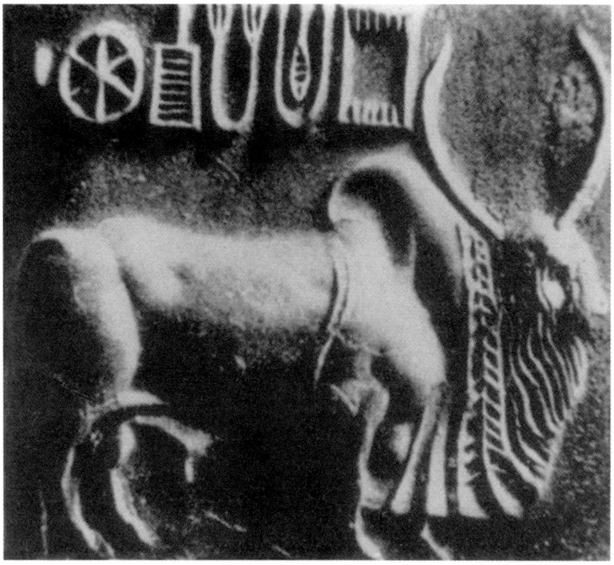

fig. 3

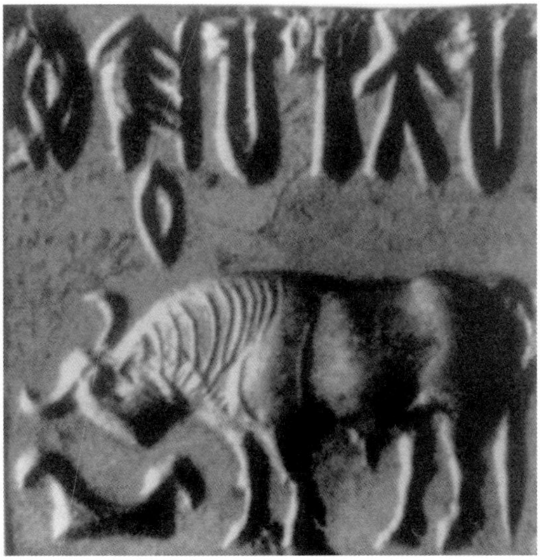

fig. 4

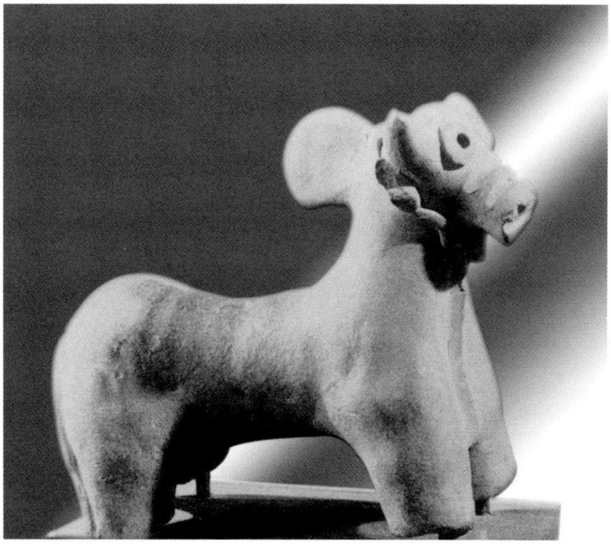

fig. 5

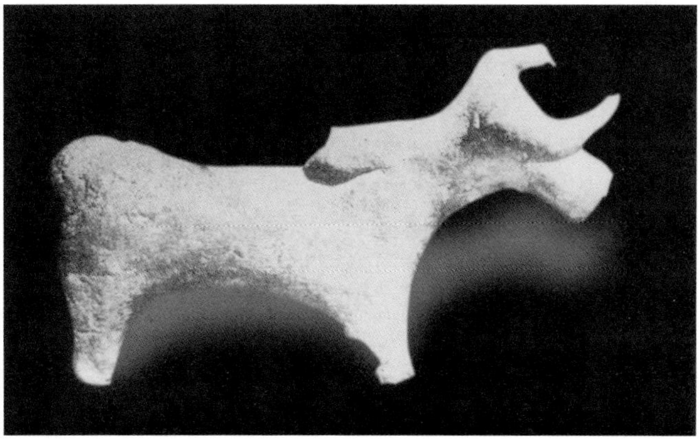

fig. 9

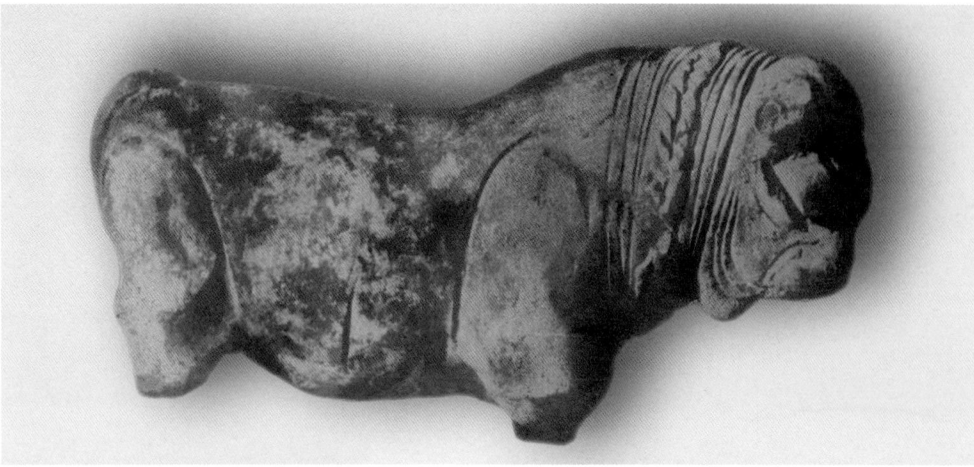

fig. **11**

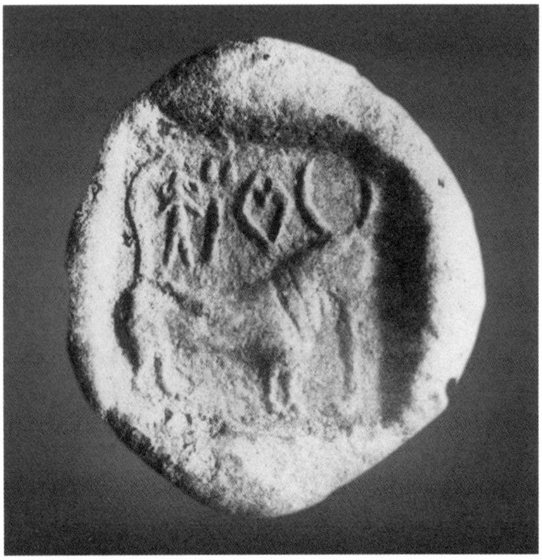

fig. **12**

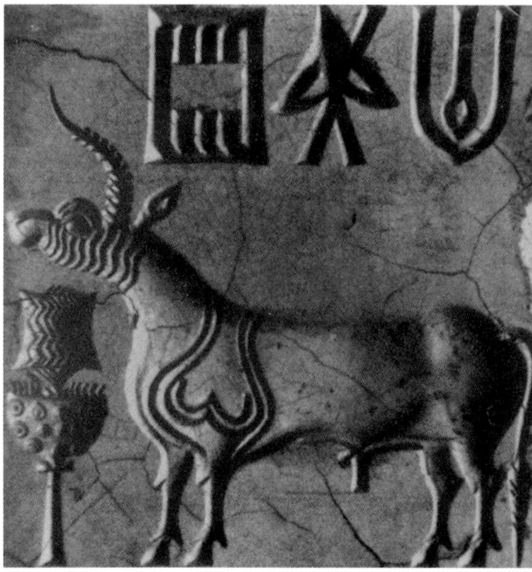

fig. **13**

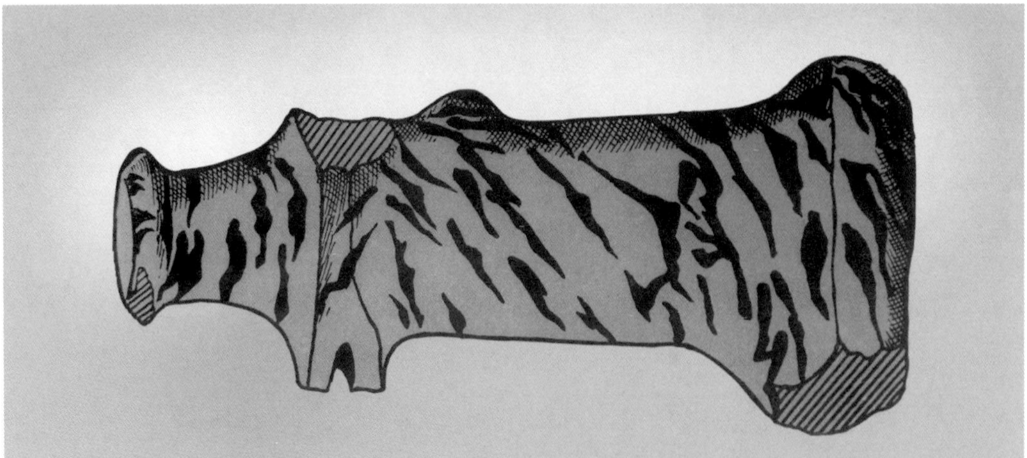

fig. **14**

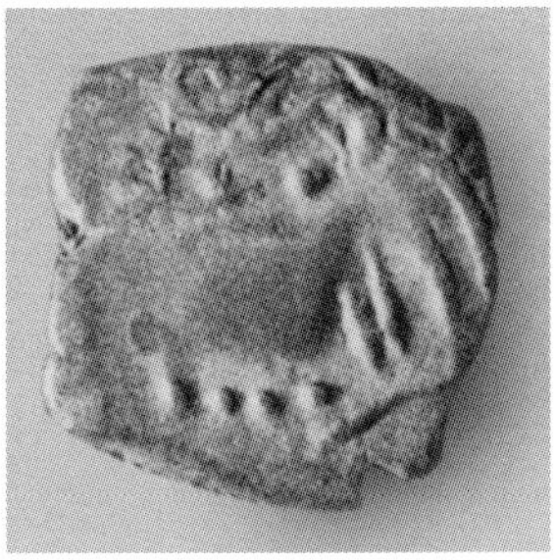
fig. 44

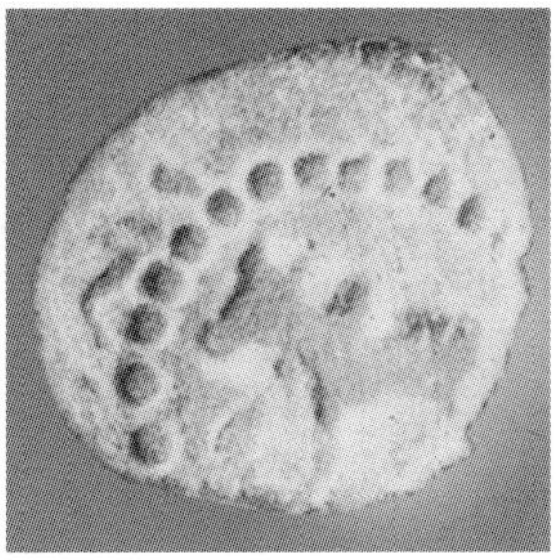
fig. 45

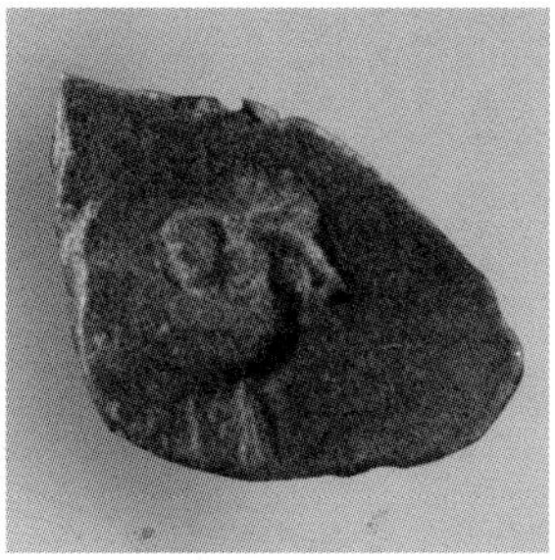
fig. 46

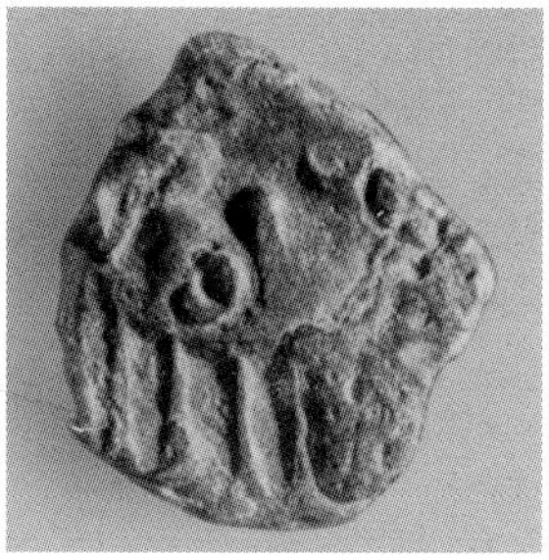
fig. 47

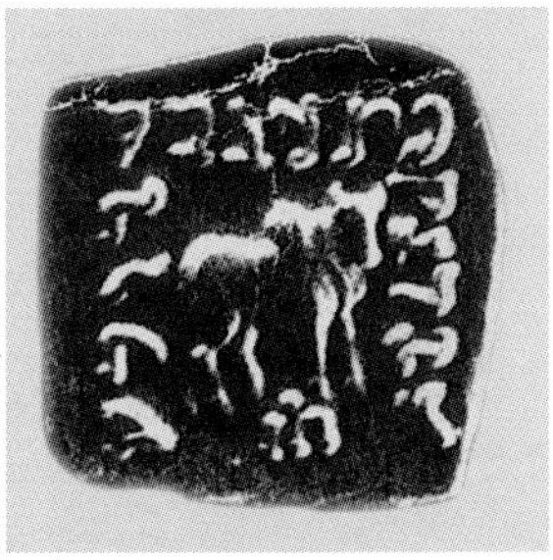
fig. 48

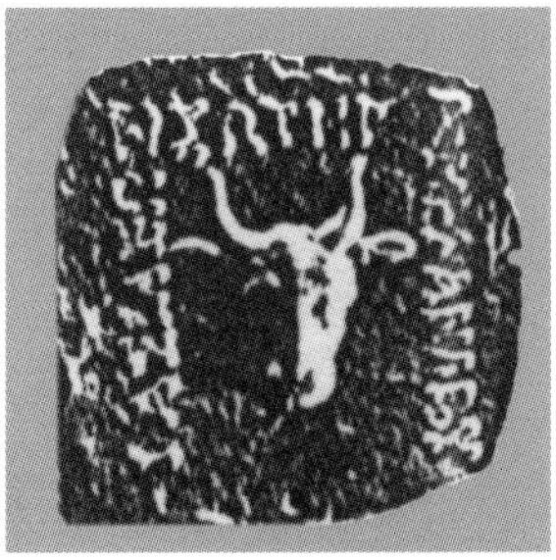
fig. 49

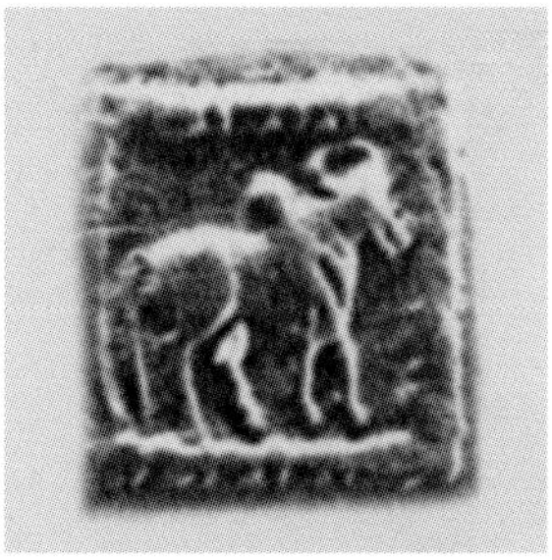
fig. 50

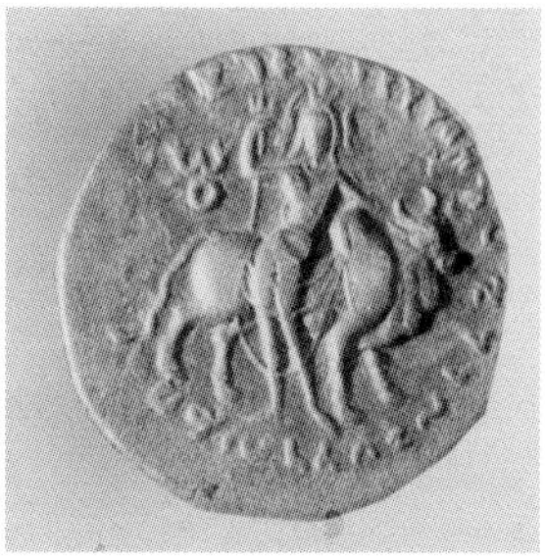
fig. 53

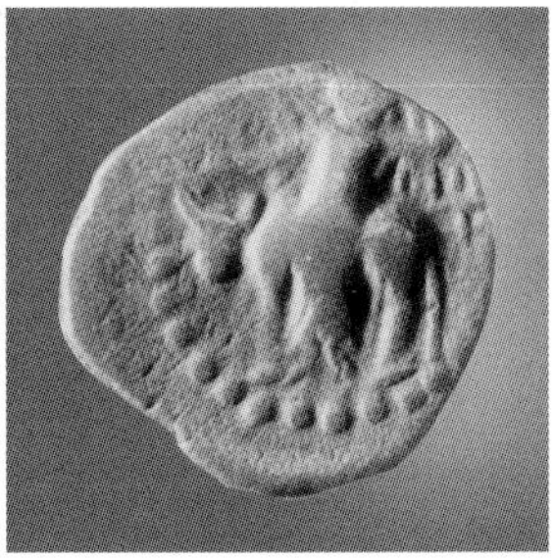
fig. 68

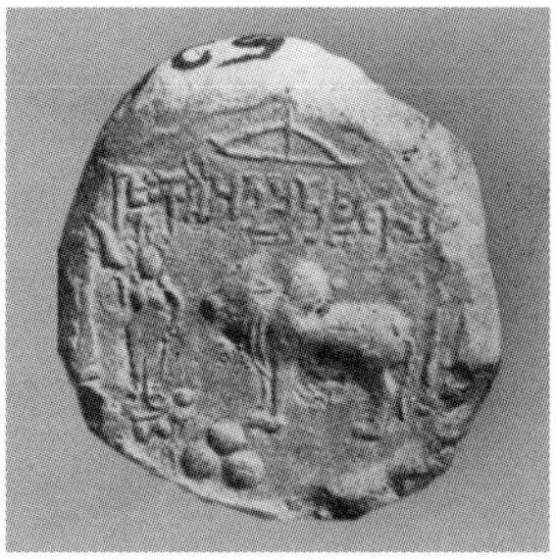
fig. 72

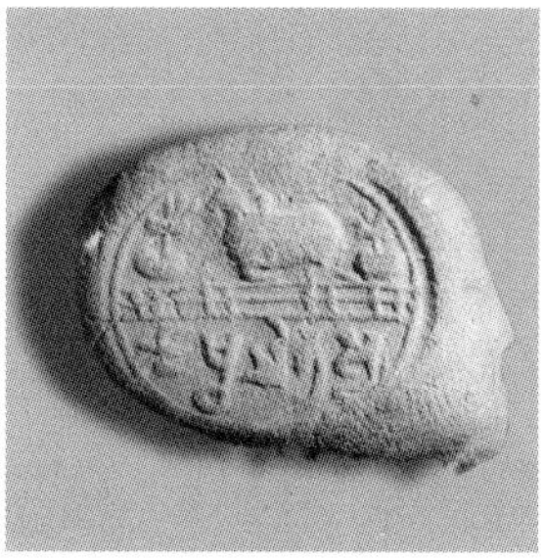
fig. 73

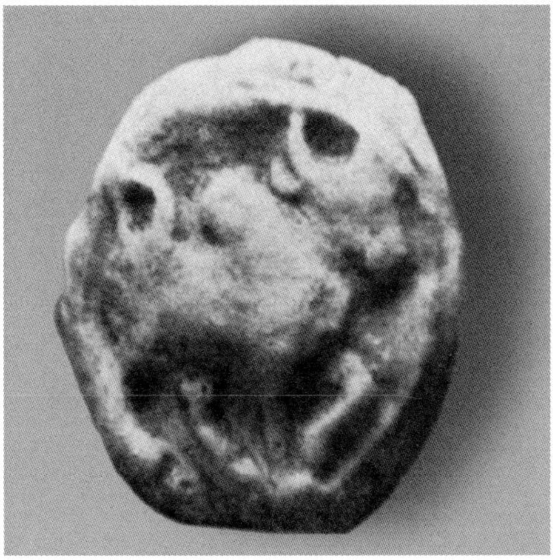
fig. 74

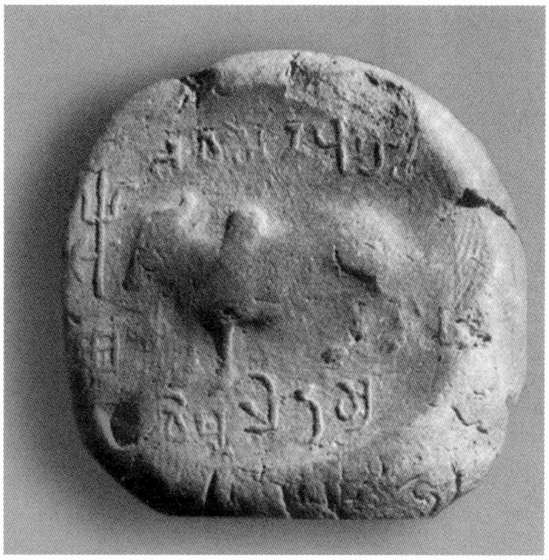
fig. 75

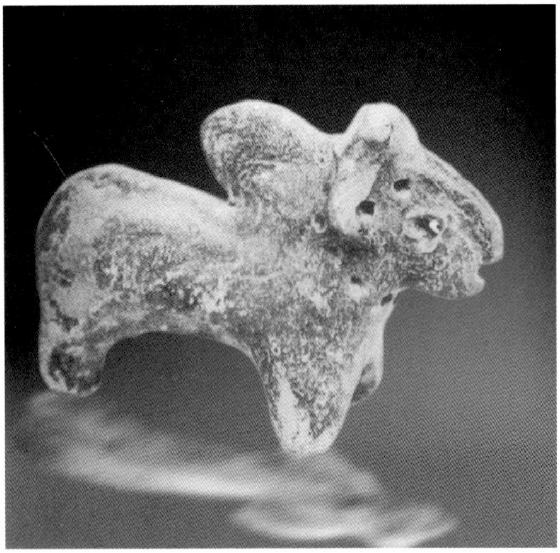

fig. 86

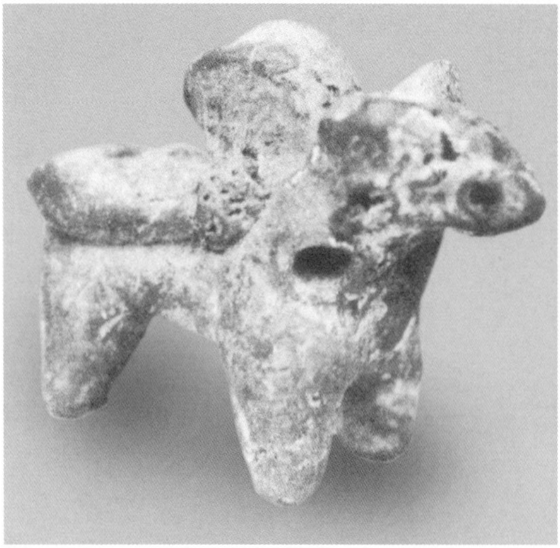

fig. 87

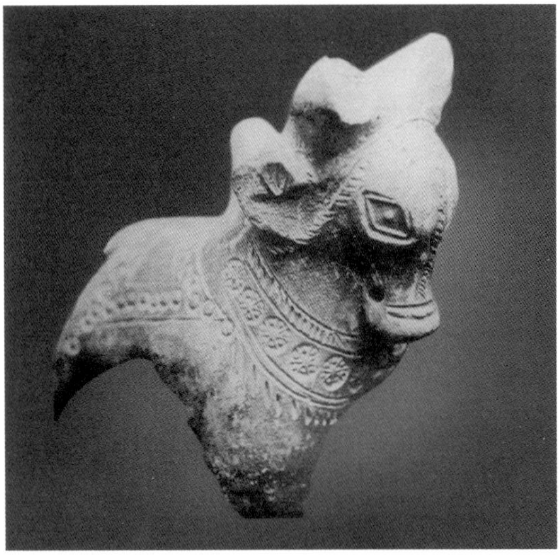

fig. 88

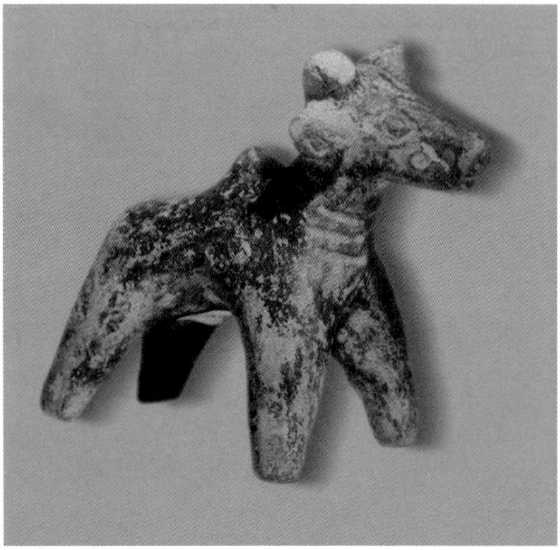

fig. 91

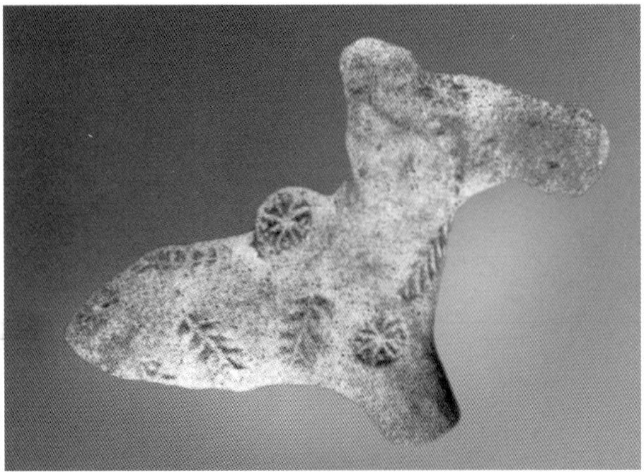

fig. 92

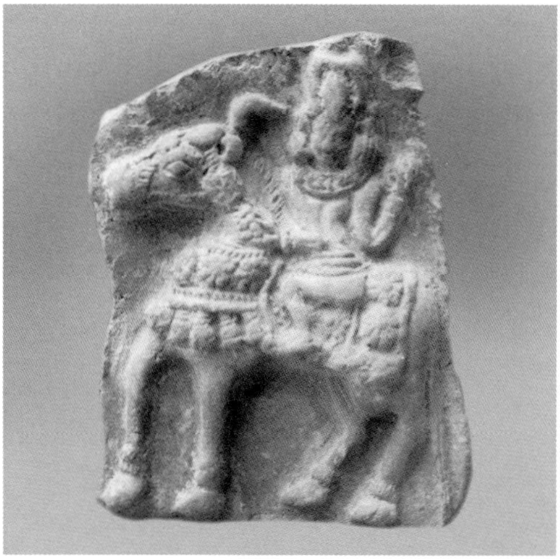

fig. 93

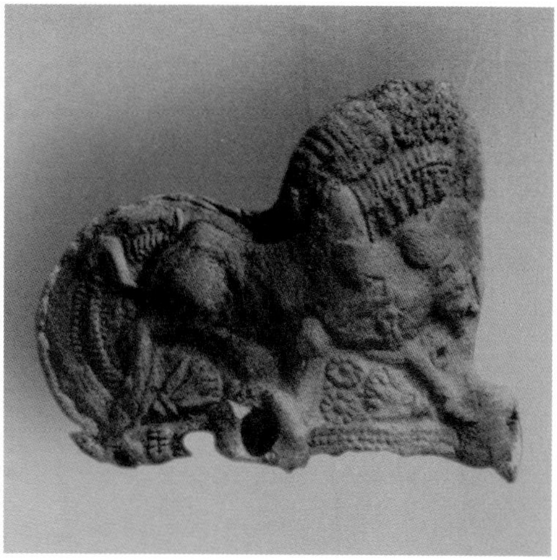

fig. 94

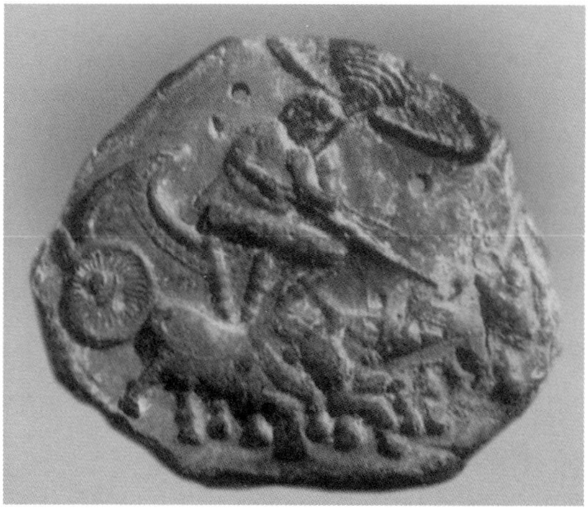

fig. 95

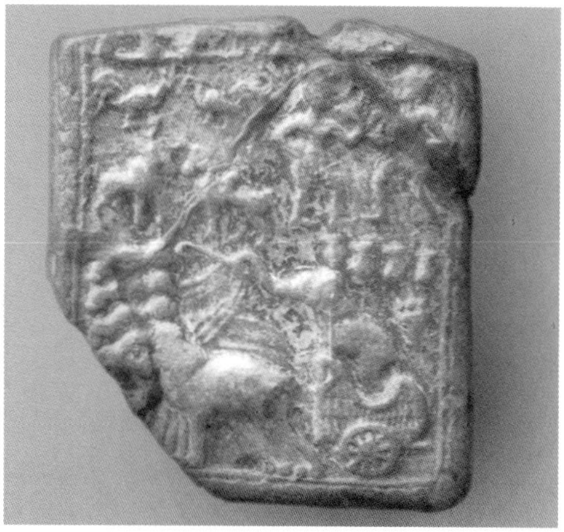

fig. 96

fig. 97

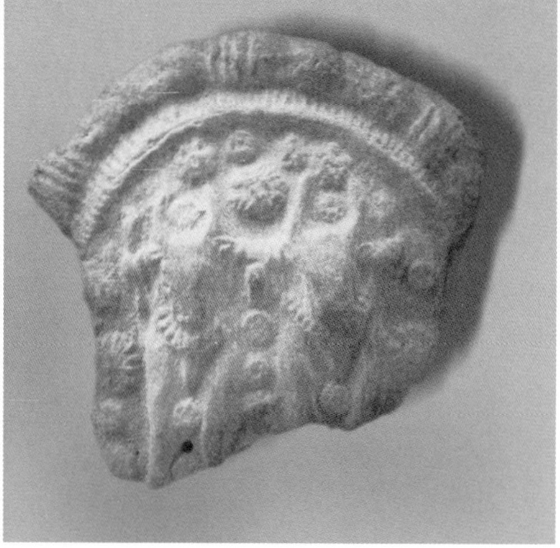

fig. 104

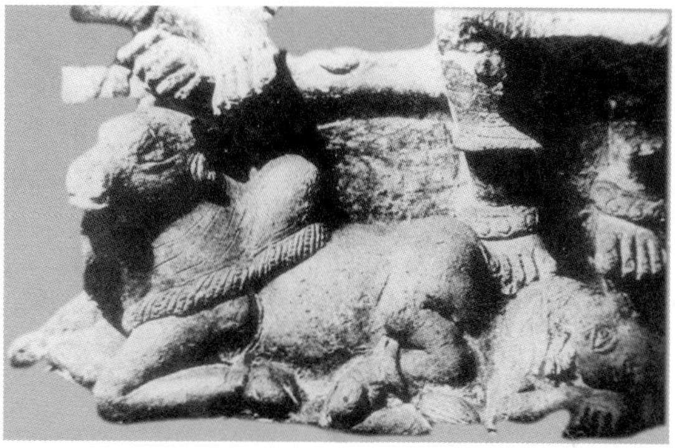

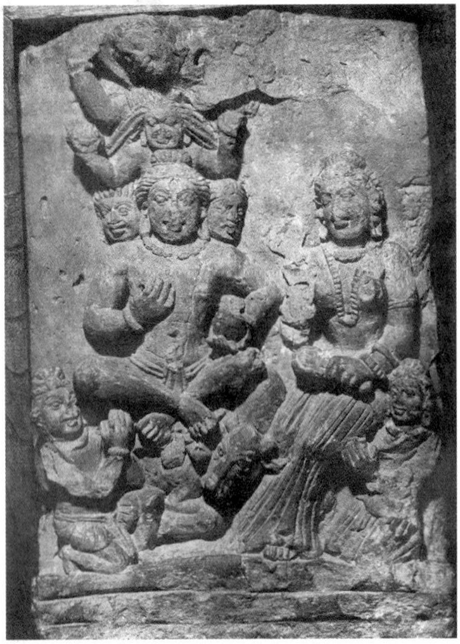

fig. 110

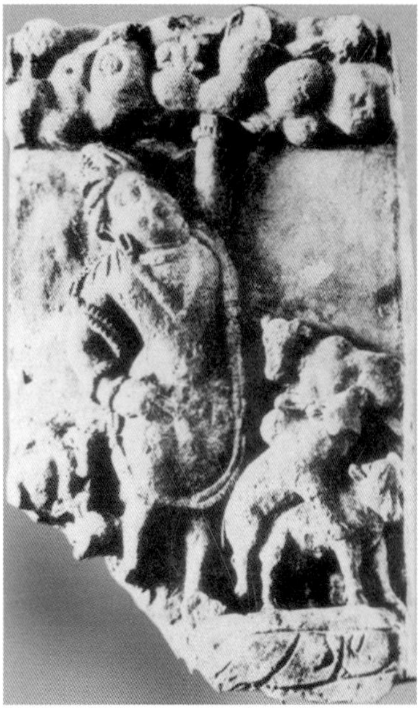

fig. 111

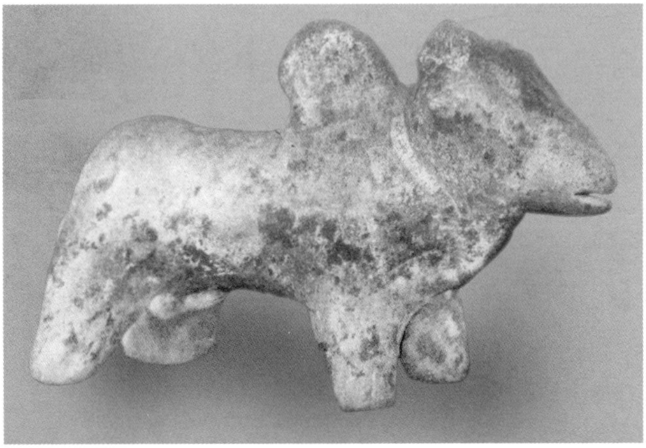

fig. 112

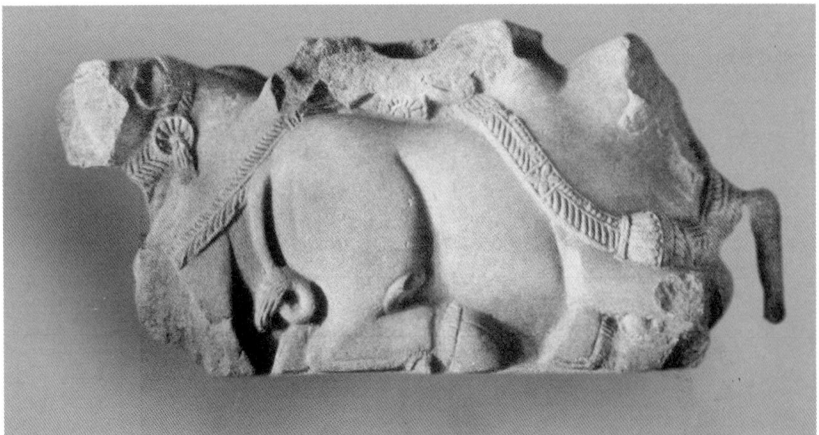

fig. 113

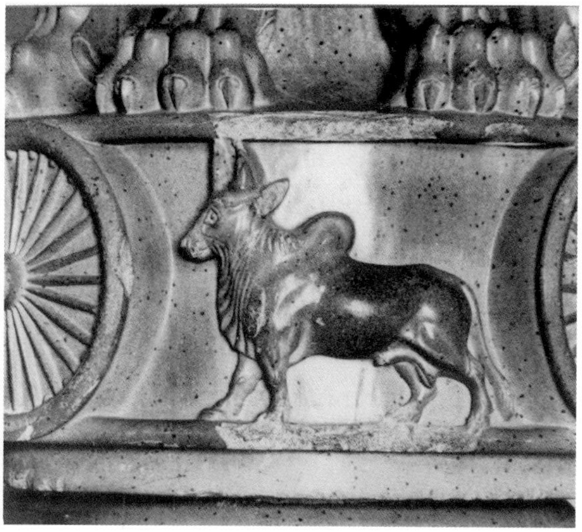

fig. 114

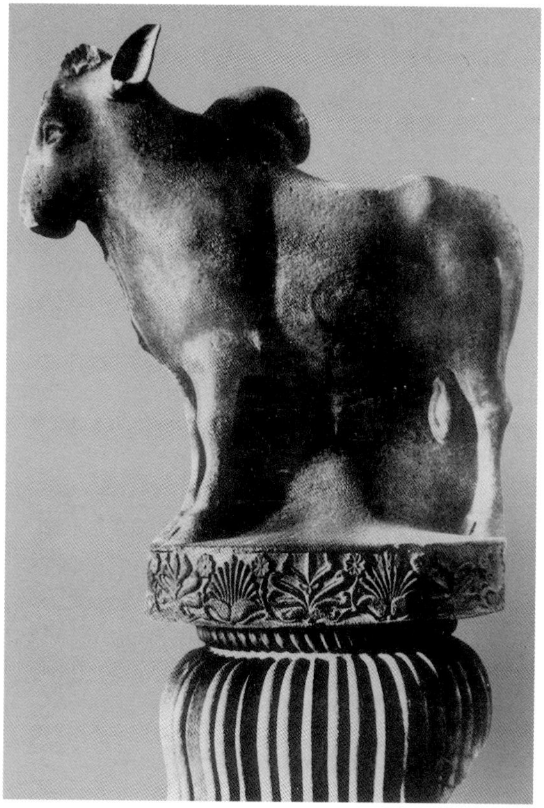

fig. 115

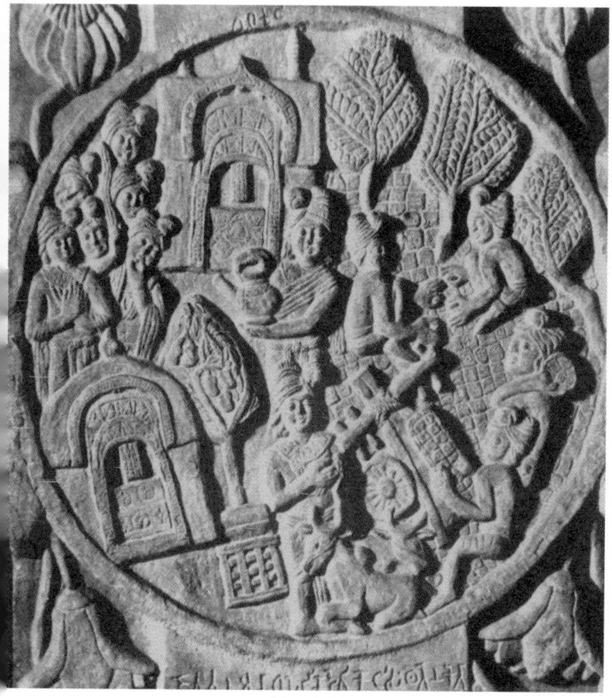

fig. 116

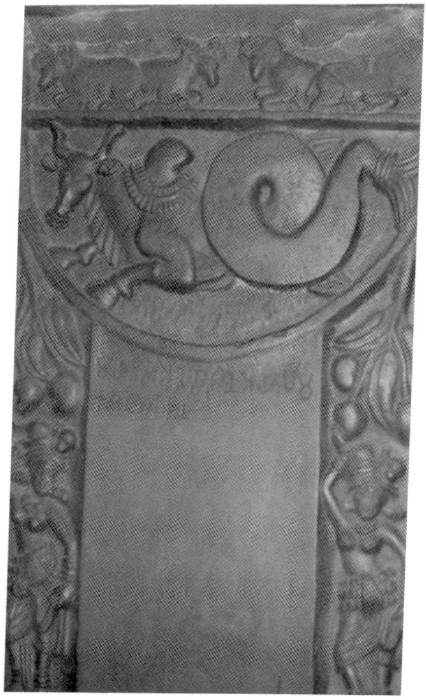

fig. 117

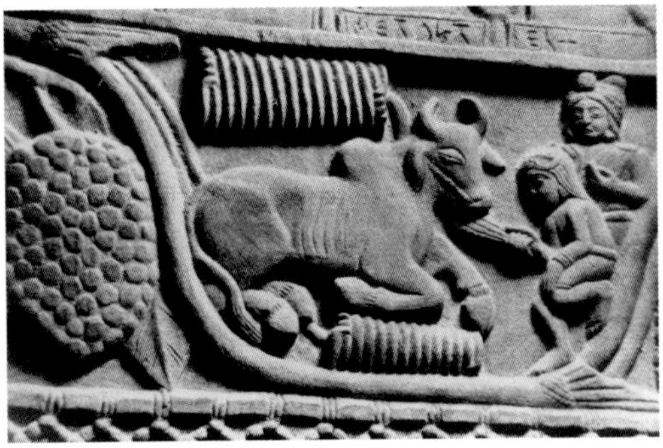

fig. **118**

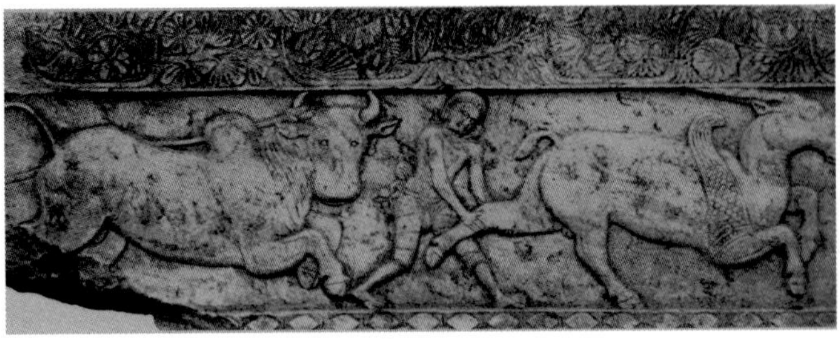

fig. **119**

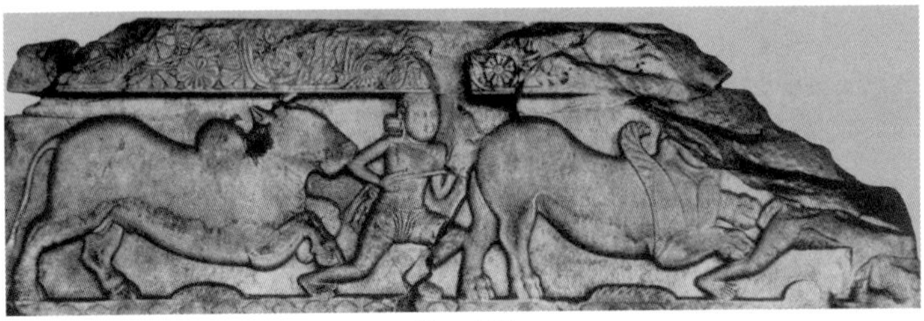

fig. **120**

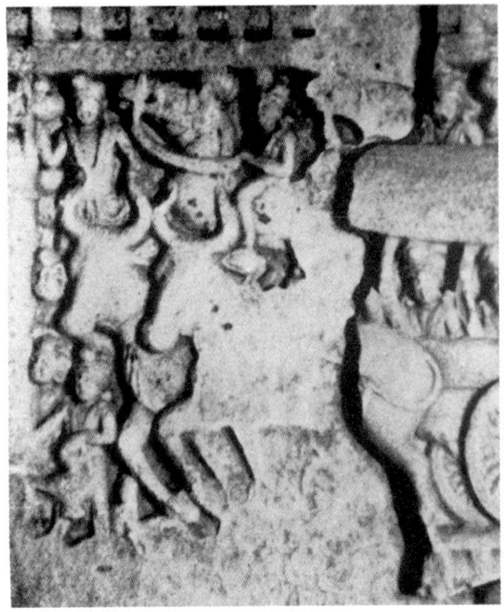

fig. **121**

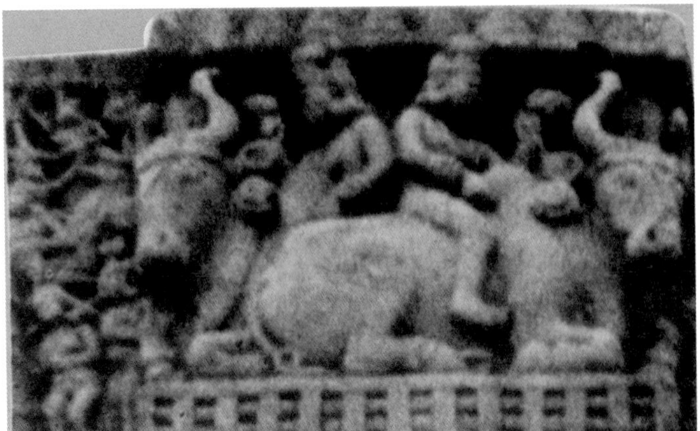

fig. **122**

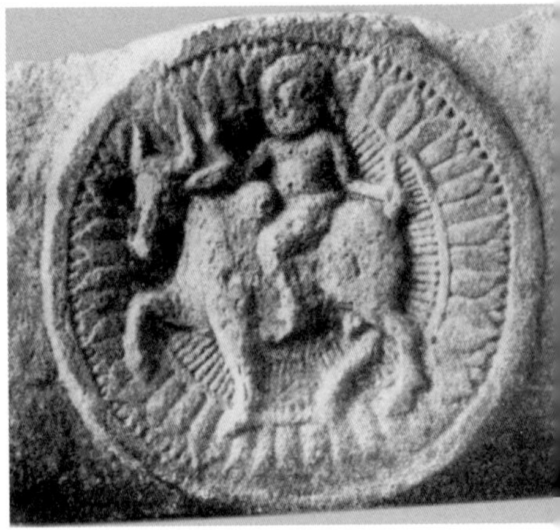

fig. **123**

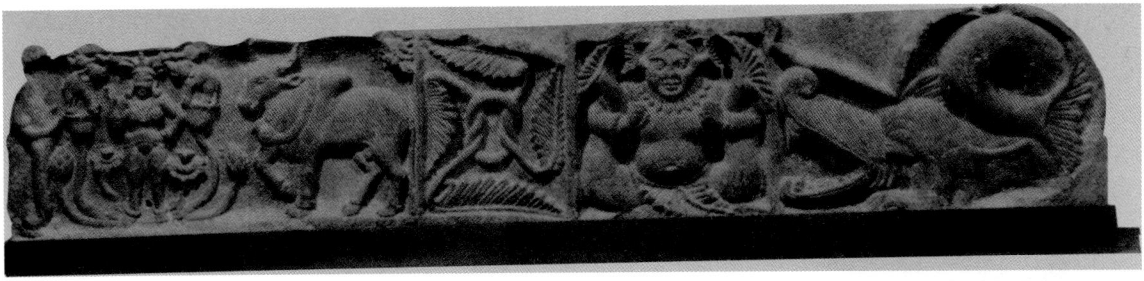

fig. 124

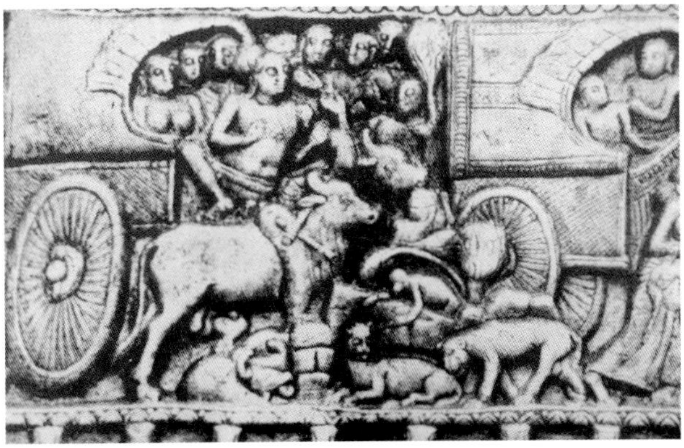

fig. 125

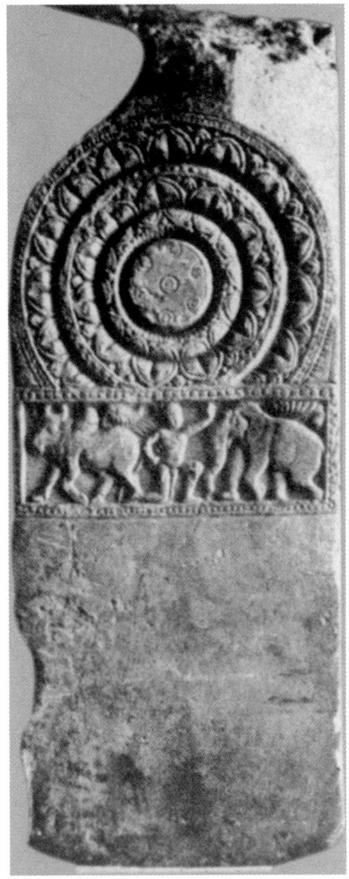

fig. 126

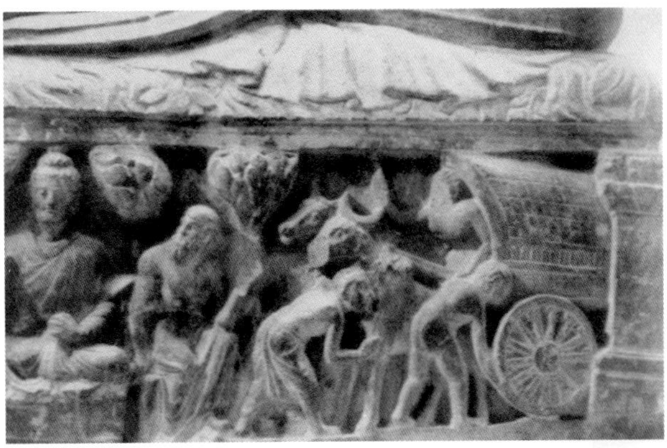

fig. 127

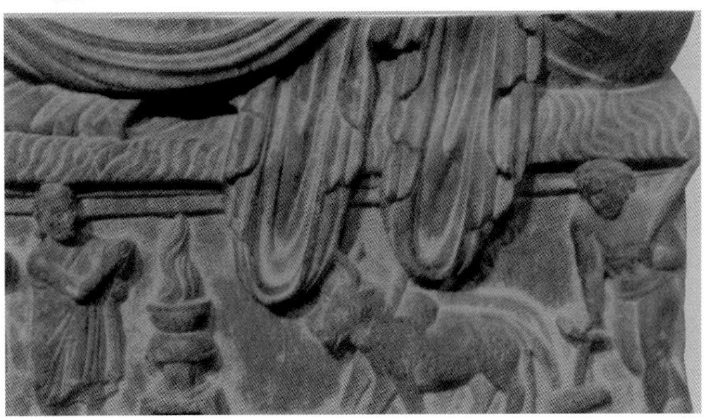

fig. 128

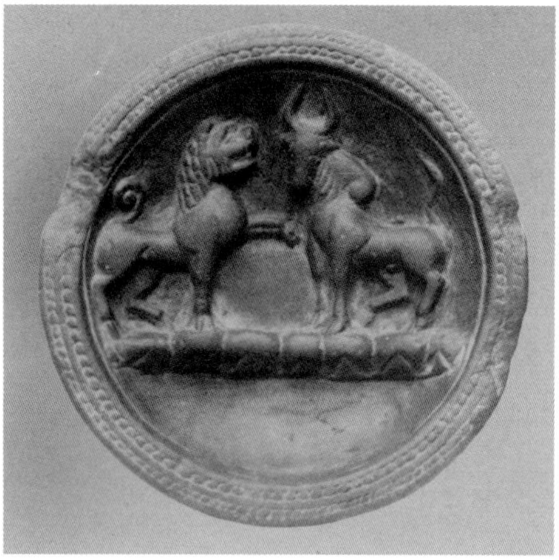

fig. 129

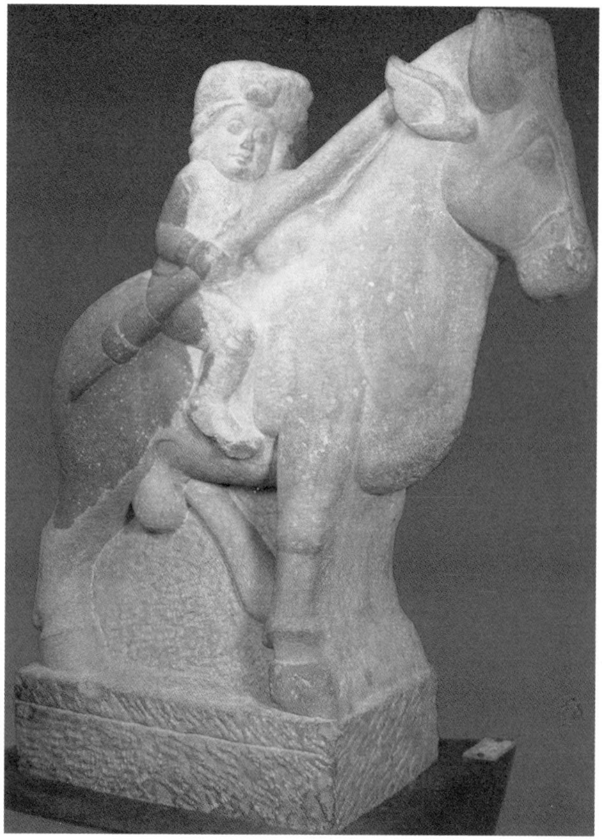

fig. 130

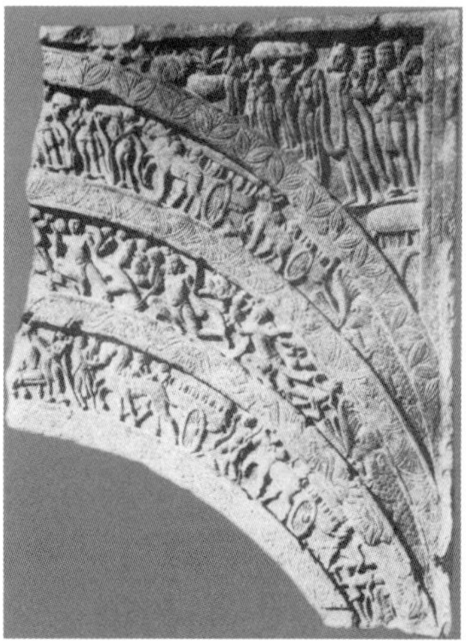

fig. 131

fig. 132

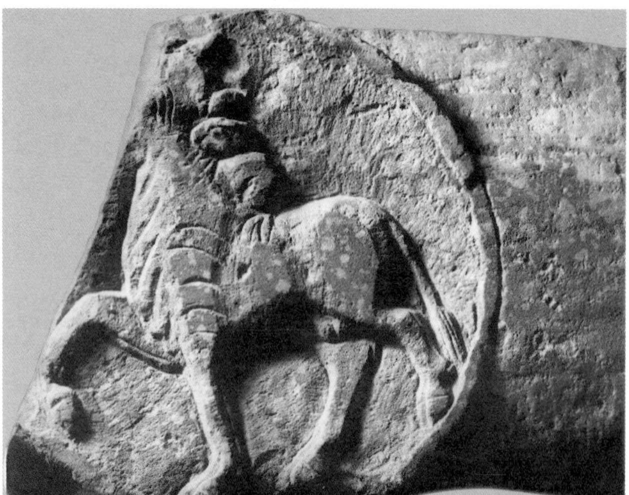

fig. 133

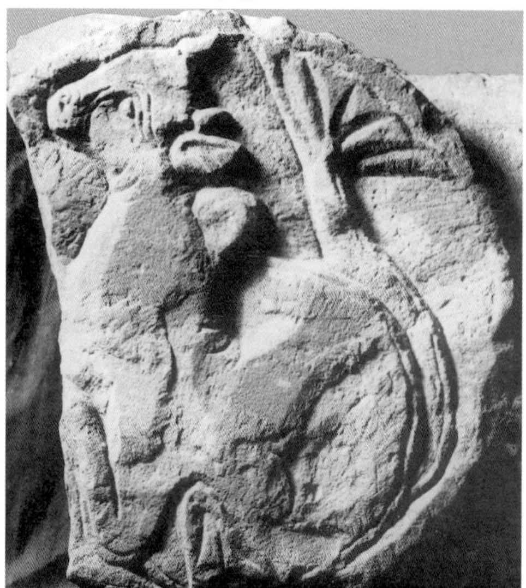

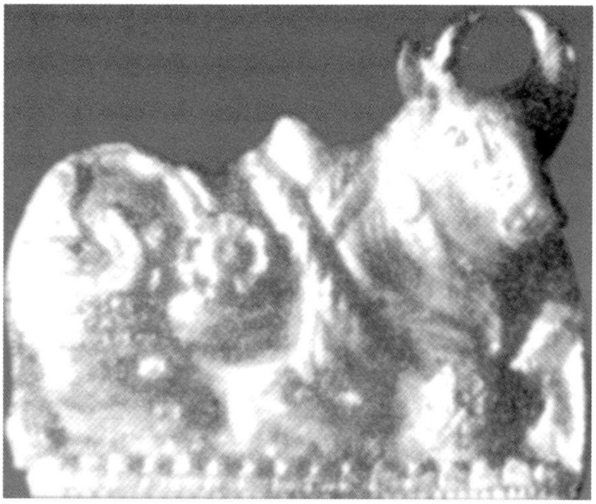

fig. 134

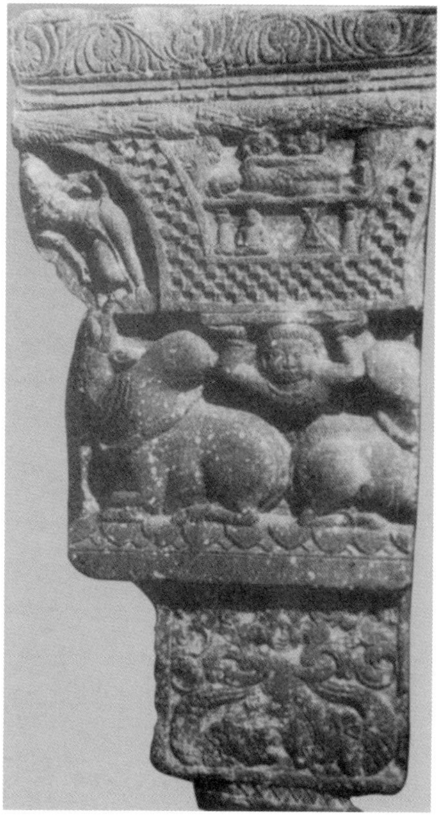

fig. 135

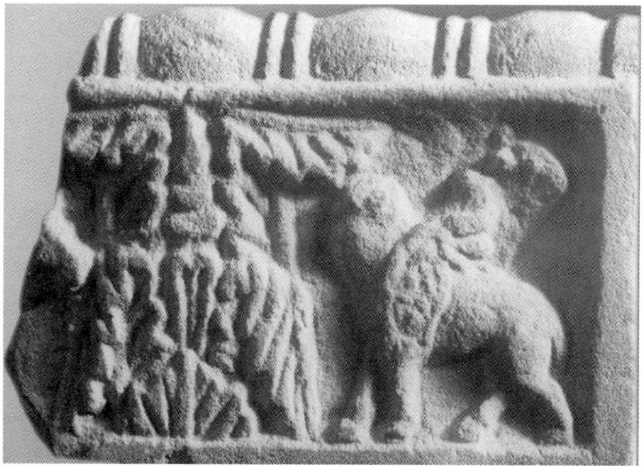

fig. 136

fig. 137

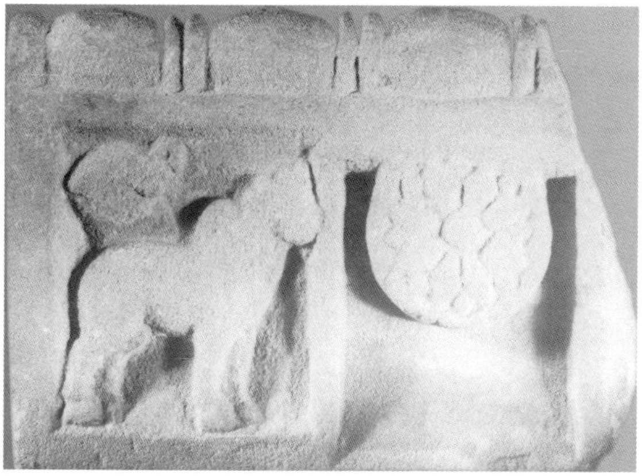

fig. 138

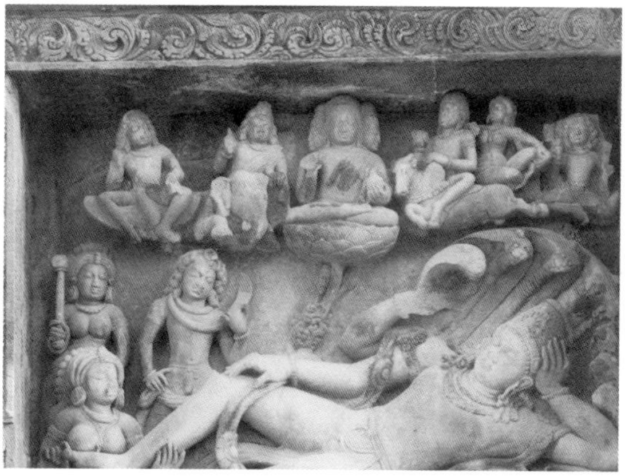

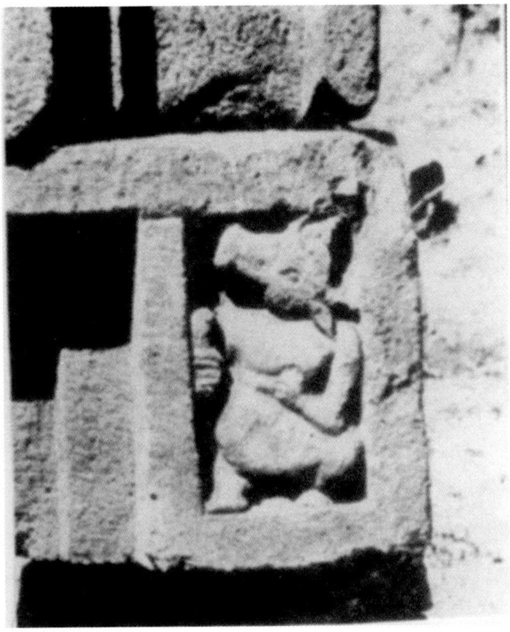

fig. 139

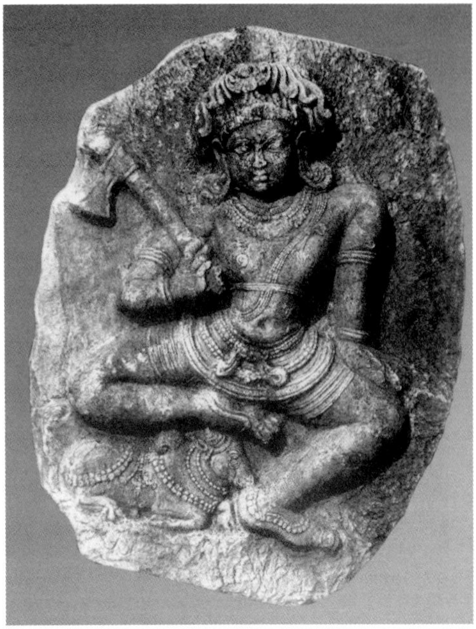

fig. 140

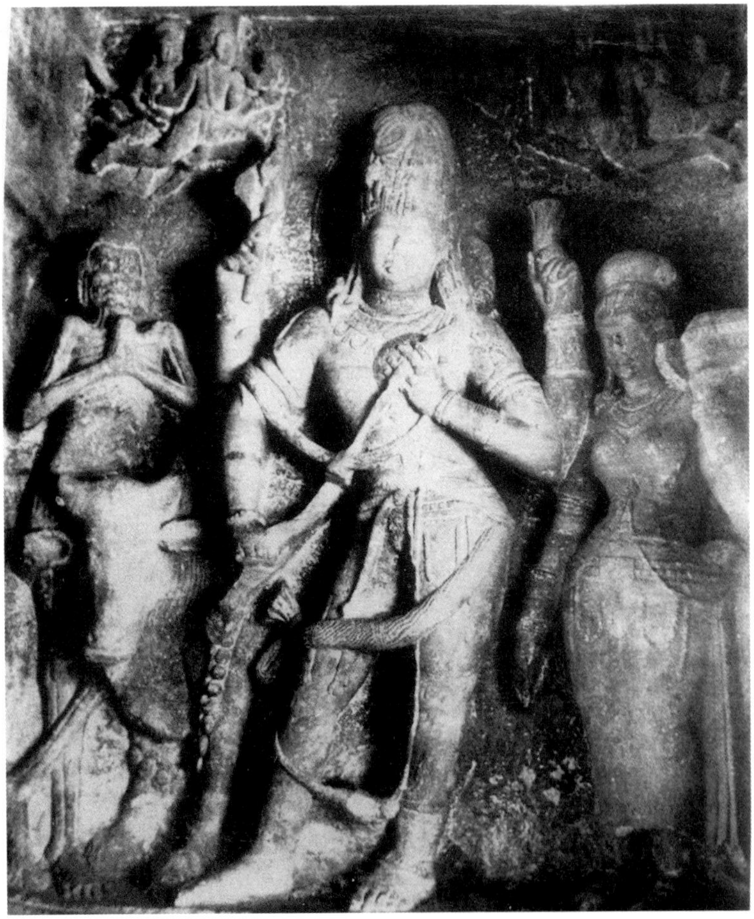

fig. 141

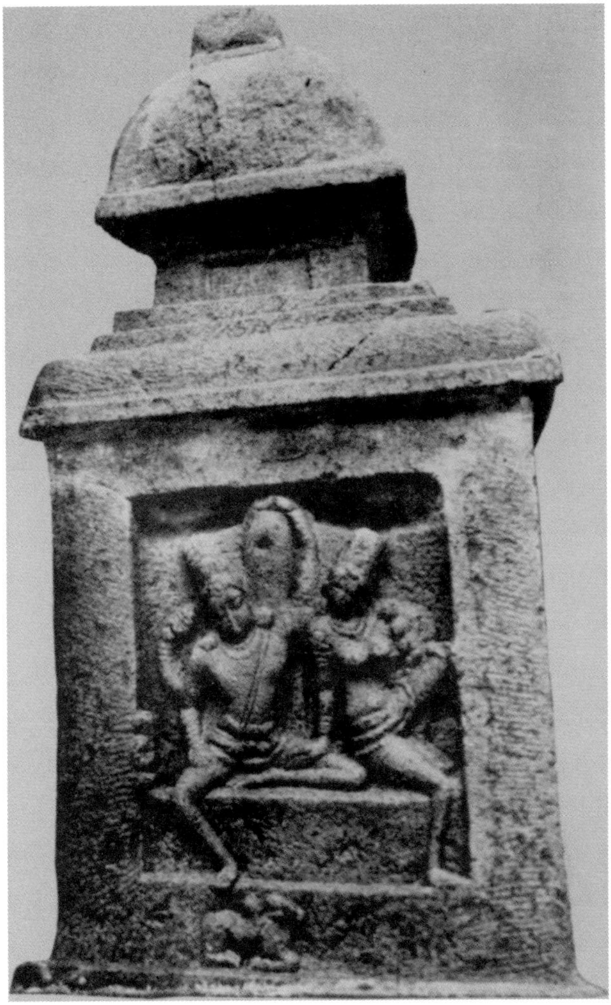

fig. **142**

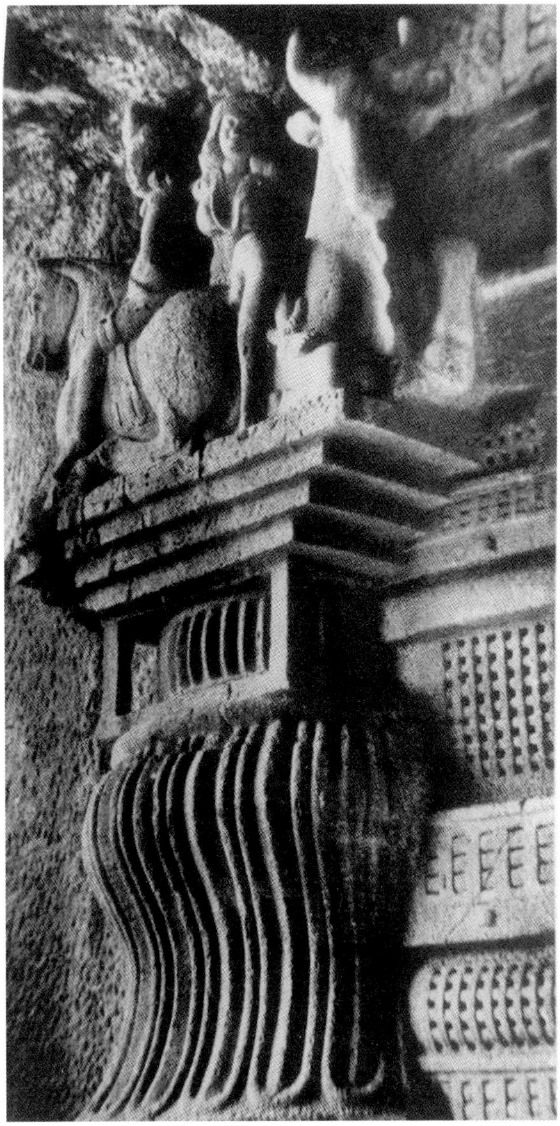

fig. **143**

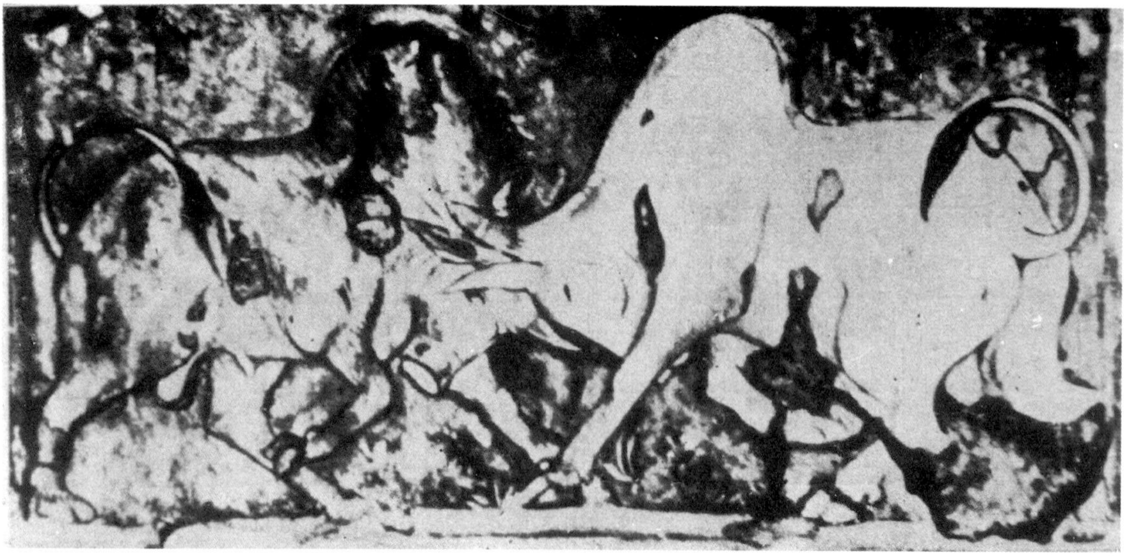

fig. **144**

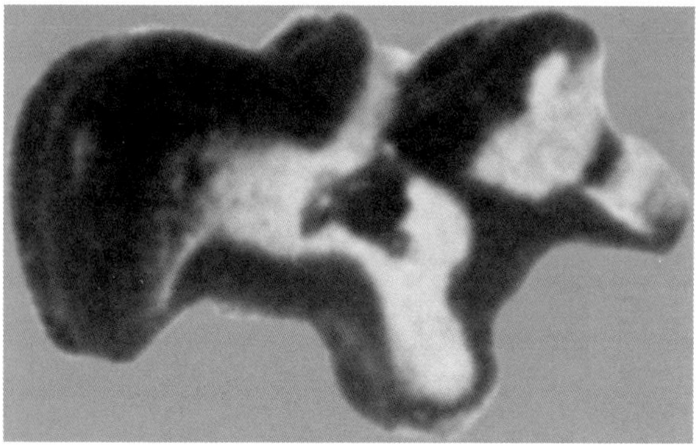

fig. **148**

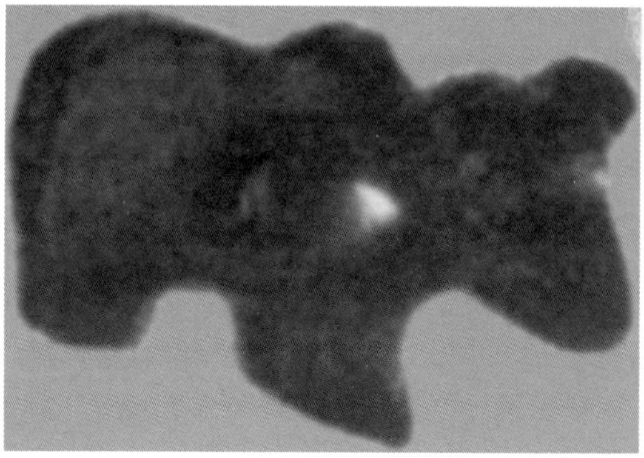

fig. **149**

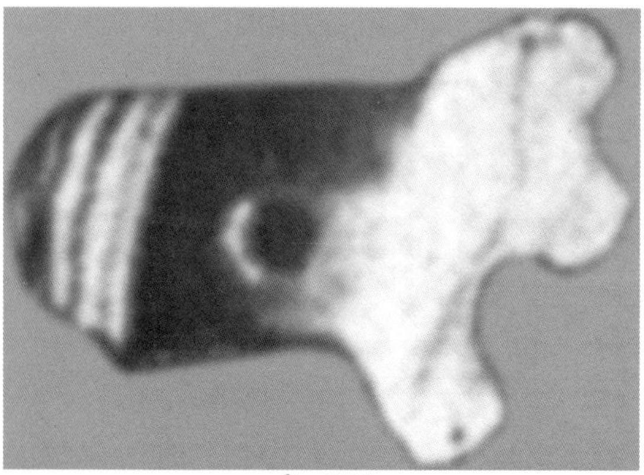

fig. **153**

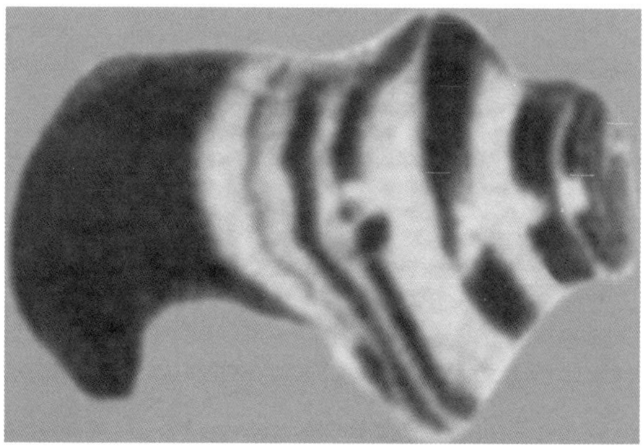

fig. **154**

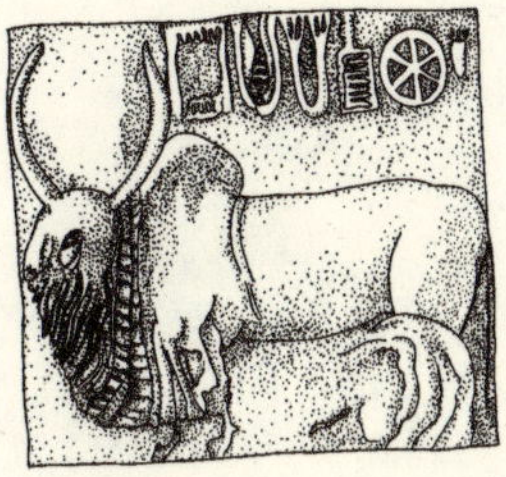

Bibliography

Original Texts

Ṛgveda, ed. with Sāyaṇa's com. F. Max Müller, 2nd edn., 1890-92.

Sāmaveda, ed. Sripad Dandekar Satvalekar, Balsad, 1989.

Atharvaveda, tr. R.T.H. Griffith, Vārāṇasī, 1897, rpt., New Delhi, 1985.

Yajurveda, ed. Sripad Dandekar Satvalekar, Pardi, 4th edn.

Śatapatha Brāhmaṇa, Chandra Dhar Sharma, Vārāṇasī, 1937.

Jaiminīya Brāhmaṇa.

Yāska Nirukta, Chowkhambha Sanskrit Series, Vārāṇasī.

Manu-Smṛti, tr. Gaṇeśa Dutta Pathak, Vārāṇasī, 1947.

Mahābhārata, Poona, 1958.

Rāmāyaṇa of Vālmikī, Geeta Press, Gorakhapur, 1988.

The Jātakas, ed. Cowell, London, 1957.

Mahāmayūrī.

Āvaśyaka Cūrṇi of Jinadasamuni, Ratlam, 1928.

Matsya Purāṇa, Anandasharma Sanskrit Series, Poona, 1907.

Viṣṇu Purāṇa, Venkatesvara Press, 1910.

Vāmana Purāṇa, All India Kashiraj Trust, Vārāṇasī, 1968.

Kūrma Purāṇa, All India Kashiraj Trust, Vārāṇasī, 1971.

Varāha Purāṇa, All India Kashiraj Trust, Vārāṇasī, 1981.

Garuḍa Purāṇa, Venkatesvara Press, rpt. by Nag Publishers, 1984.

Agni Purāṇa, Chowkhamba Prakashana, Vārāṇasī.

Bhāgavata Purāṇa, Gita Press.

Bhaviṣya Purāṇa, Venkatesvara Press.

Skanda Purāṇa, Manasukha Rai More edn.

Nārada Purāṇa, Venkatesvara Press edn.

Śiva Purāṇa, Venkatesvara Press edn.

Āditya Purāṇa.

Devī Bhāgavata, Manasukha Rai More Edn.

Arthaśāstra of Kauṭilya, tr. Vacaspati Gairola.

Mṛcchakaṭika of Śūdraka.

Mahābhāṣya of Pāṇini by Keilhorn.

Pañcatantra, tr. by Motichandra, Bombay.

Kālidāsa Granthāvalī, ed. Sitaram Chaturvedi, Aligarh, 1962.

Śukranitisāra, Chowkhambha Sanskrit Series, Vārāṇasī.

Kirātārjunīya, tr. Aditya Narayan Pandeya, Vārāṇasī, 1961.

Uttara-Rāma-Carita of Bhavabhūti, tr. Tarinish Jha, Allahabad, 1975.

Śiśupālavadha, tr. Hargovind Sastri, Vārāṇasī, 1972.

Bṛhat-Saṁhitā of Varāhamihira, tr. N.C. Iyer, Delhi, 1987.

Viṣṇudharmottara Purāṇa, ed. Mrs. Priyabala Shah, Baroda, 1958.

Vaikhānasāgama.

Mānasāra, ed. Acharya Prasannakumar, London, 1933.

History of Dharmaśāstra, vol. IV, Pandurang Varman Kane, Poona, 1941.

Books and Journals

Agrawala, D.P., *The Copper, Bronze Age in India*, Delhi, 1972.

Agrawala, P.K., *Maurya Kala*, Rajbali Pandeya Smriti Grantha, pp. 271-85.

———, *Early Indian Bronzes*, Vārāṇasī, 1977.

Agrawala, V.S., "Mathurā Terracottas," in *JUPHS*, vol. IX, Pt. II, (July 1936) pp. 27-28.

———, *Handbook of the Sculptures in the Curzon Museum of Archaeology*, Muttra, Allahabad, 1939.

———, *Lalitkala* (Editorial) in *Marg*, vol. IV, no. 2, 1949-50.

———, "A Unique Terracotta plaque from Rajghat," *Bulletin of Prince of Wales Museum of Western India*, no. 2, 1951-52, pp. 82-84.

———, *Mathurā Museum Catalogue*, Pt. IV, Vārāṇasī, 1963.

———, *Matsya Purāṇa — A study*, Vārāṇasī, 1963.

———, *Chakra-Dhvaja*, Vārāṇasī, 1964.

———, *Indian Art*, Vārāṇasī, 1965.

———, *Bhāratīya Kalā*, Vārāṇasī, 1966.

———, *Pāṇini Kālīn Bhāratvarṣa*, Vārāṇasī, 1969.

———, *Gupta Art*, Vārāṇasī, 1977.

———, *Vārāṇasī Seals and Sealings*, Vārāṇasī, 1984.

———, *Masterpieces of Mathurā Sculptures*, Vārāṇasī, 1985.

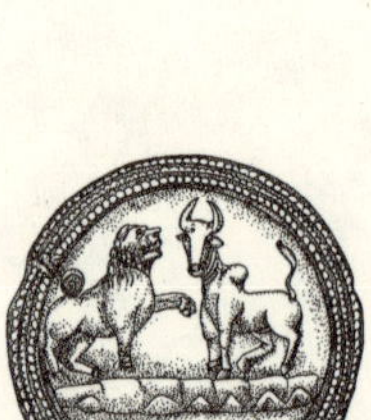

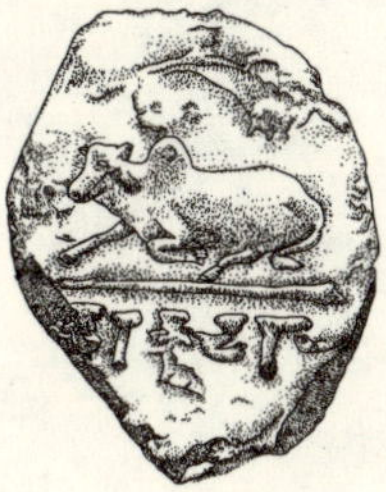

———, *Śiva Mahādeva*, Vārāṇasī, Prithivi Prakashan, 1984.

Alchin, F.R., *Neolithic Cattle Keepers of South India*, Cambridge University Press, 1963.

Allen, John, *Catalogue of Coins of Ancient India*, London, 1936.

Altekar, A.S., *Gupta Kālīn Mudrāen*, Patna, 1954.

Asthana, S., Associate Bhogendra Jha, *Gāndhāra Sculptures of Bharat Kala Bhavan*, Vārāṇasī, 1999.

Awasthi, A.B.L., *Brāhmaṇical Art and Iconography* (Studies in *Skanda Purāṇa*, Part IV), Lucknow, 1976.

Bachhofer, Ludwig, *Early Indian Sculpture*, vol. I, New Delhi, 2nd edn., 1973.

Banerjea, J.N., *Development of Hindu Iconography*, Calcutta, 2nd edn., 1956.

Banerji, R.D., *Temple of Śiva at Bhumara in Memoirs of the Archaeological Survey of India*, no. 16, Calcutta, 1924.

Bangdel, Lain S., *Early Sculptures of Nepal*, New Delhi, 1982.

———, *The Arts of India and Nepal*.

Barret, Douglas, *Sculptures from Amarāvatī in the British Museum*, London, 1954.

Barua, Benimadhaba, *Bharhut*, Book III, Calcutta, 1937.

———, *Gayā and Bodhgayā*, vol. II, 1934.

Bhandarkar, D.R., *The Archaeological Remains and Excavations at Nagri, MASI*, no. 4, Calcutta, 1920.

———, *Aśoka*, Delhi, 1960.

Bhatt, Kaund, *Vaiyakaran Bhusan Sar*, 1947.

Bhattacharya, Ashok. K., *Technique of Indian Painting*, Calcutta, 1976.

Bhattacharya, D.C., *Pratimālakṣaṇa of the Viṣṇudharmottara*, New Delhi, 1991.

Bhattashali, N.K., *Iconography of Buddhist and Brahmanical Sculptures in the Dacca Museum*, Dacca, 1929.

Bisht, R.S., *Excavations at Banawali*, I.A.R., 1986-87 and 1987-88.

Biswas, S.S., *Terracotta Art of Bengal*, Delhi, 1981.

Biswas, T.K. and Bhogendra Jha, *Gupta Sculptures of Bharat Kala Bhawan*, Vārāṇasī, 1985.

Biswas, T.K., *Horse in Early Indian Art*, Delhi, 1987.

Biswas, T.K., Sarnath Lion Capital; its Historians; *Citi-Kithika*, vol. 3, Nos. 1-2, 1997-98; pp 41-54.

Boothlingam, M., *Movement in Stone* (*A study of some Chola temples*),

New Delhi, 1969.

Bosch, F.D.K., *The Golden Cow — An Introduction to Indian Symbolism*, Gravenhage, 1960.

Bridget and Raymond Alchin, *The Rise of Civilization in India and Pakistan*, New Delhi, 1983.

Bunce, Fredrick W., *A Dictionary of Buddhist and Hindu Iconography*, New Delhi, 1997.

Burges, James, *Archaeological Survery of Southern India*, vol. I, The Buddhist Stupas of Amarāvatī and Jaggayapeṭa in the Krishna district, Madras Presidency, surveyed in 1882, (rpt.) Vārāṇasī, 1970.

———, *Notes on the Amaravati Stupa*, New Delhi, 1972.

Chakrabarti, D.K., *The External Trade of the Indus Civilization*, Delhi, 1990.

Chakrabarti, Kanchan, *Society, Religion and Art of the Kuṣāṇas*, New Delhi, 1981.

Chanda, R.P., "The Mathurā School of Sculpture," in *Indian Museum Bulletin*, January 1975, vol. I.

———, "The Beginning of Art in Eastern India with a special reference to Sculpture in the Indian Museum," in *Indian Museum Bulletin*, July 1975, vol. 2.

Chandra, Pramod, *Stone Sculptures in Allahabad Museum*, 1970.

Chattopadhyaya, Bhaskara, *Coins and Icons — A study of Myths and Symbols in Indian Numismatic Art*, Calcutta, 1977.

Chattopadhaya, S., *The Evolution of thematic sects in Ancient India*, Calcutta, 1962.

Chaturvedi, Giridhar Sharma, *Vaidik Vigyan Aur Bharatiya Sanskriti*, Patna, 1960.

Chitakara, Poonam, "Depictions of Cattle Motifs on Amri Pottery," in *Puratattva*, No. 9, 1977-78.

Coomaraswamy, A.K., "Early Indian Terracottas," in *MFAB*, (Boston) vol. XXV, No. 150, 1927, pp. 50-54.

———, *Yakṣas*, I, Washington, 1928.

———, *La Sculptures De Bodhgaya*, Paris, 1935.

———, *La Sculptures De Bharhut*, Paris, 1956.

———, *History of Indian and Indonesian Art*, New Delhi, 1972.

Cattrell, Leomard, *The Bull of Mons*, 5th edn., 1971.

Cunningham, Alexander, *The Stupa of Bharhut — A Buddhist movement — Buddhist legend and history in the third century* BC, Vārāṇasī, (rpt.), 1962.

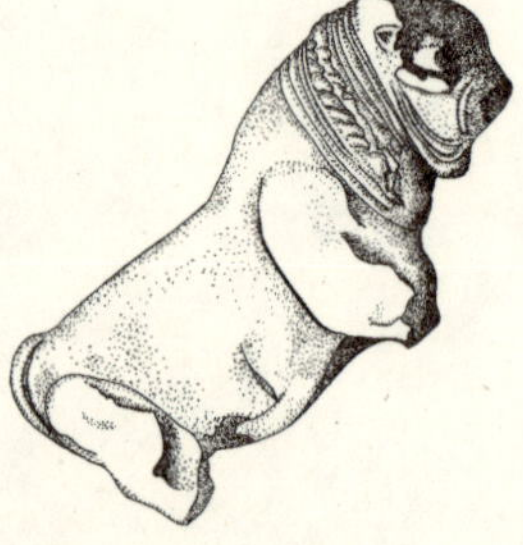

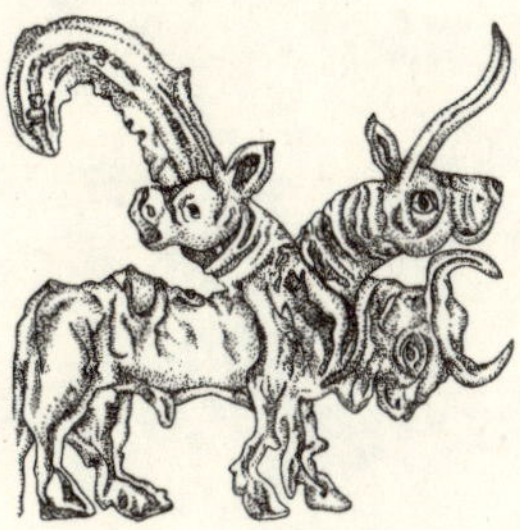

Cunningham, A., and H.B.W. Garrick, *Archaeological Survey of India — Report of Tours in North and South Bihar in 1880-81*, vol. XVI, Calcutta, 1883.

Czuma, Stanislaw J., *Kuṣāṇa Sculptures: Images from Early India*, Cleveland U.S.A. 1985.

Dange, Sadasiva Ambadasa, *Encyclopaedia of Puranic Beliefs and Practices*, vol. I and II, New Delhi. 1987.

Danielou, Alain, *Hindu Polytheism*, New York, 1964.

Dasgupta, Charu Chandra, *Origin and Evolution of Indian Clay Sculpture*, Calcutta, 1961.

Dereck, Margnerite, Marie, *Indian Art*, Hamlyn Publication Ltd. (rpt.), 1970.

Deva, Krisha and S.D. Trivedi, *Stone Sculptures in the Allahabad Museum*, vol. II, New Delhi, 1996.

Dhaky, M.A., *The Vyala Figure on the Medieval Temples of India*, Vārāṇasī, 1965.

———, "The Nandī images of Tamil Nadu and Kannadanad," in *Artibus Asiae*, vol. XXXIV, Separatum M.C.M. LXXII.

Dhavalikar, M.K., *Sanchi : A Cultural Study*, Poona, 1965.

———, *Mathura Art in the Baroda Museum*, Allahabad, 1970.

———, *Masterpieces of Indian Terracottas*, Bombay, 1977.

———, *Proto Pasupati in Western India in East and West*, New Series, vol. 78, no. 1-4, Dec. 1978.

Dikshit, Moresvara, G., *Notes on some Indian Amulet in Bulletin of Prince of Wales Museum of Western India*, no. 2, 1951-52.

Finn, Frank, *Mammalia of India*, Bombay, 1929.

Foucher, A., *The Beginnings of Buddhist Art and other essays in Indian and Central Asian Archaeology*, London 1914.

Frank and Waggol, *Standard Dictionary of Folklore Mythology and Legend*.

Ganguly, O.C., *Andhra Sculpture*, Hyderabad, 1973.

Gaur, R.C., *Excavations at Ataranjikhera*, Delhi, 1983.

Ghosh, A. (ed.), *Ajanta Murals*, New Delhi, 1967.

Glubok, Shirlay, *The Art of India*, 1969.

Goetze, *Animal in Indian Art in German Scholars on India*, 2 vols, Germany 1973.

Graves, Robert, *New Larouse Encyclopaedia of Mythology*, London, 1978.

Grimal, Pierre, *Lurouse World Mythology*, London, 1965.

Gupta, P.L., Sinhavaran Hoard, *et al.*, Ph. D. Thesis unpublished, BHU, 1952.

———, (ed.), *Patna Museum Catalogue of Antiquities*, Patna, 1965.

———, *Gangetic Valley Terracotta Art*, Vārāṇasī, 1972.

———, *Indian Silver Punch Marked Coins*, Nasik, 1985.

Gupta, S.P., The Origin of the Indus Sarasvati Civilization, in *Facets of Indian Civilization*, ed. J.P. Joshi, New Delhi, 1997.

Hackin, J., *et al.*, *Asiatic Mythology*, Cresent Books, New York, 1980.

Handa, Devendra, *Studies in Indian Coins and Seals*, Delhi, 1985.

Harle, J.C., *The Art and Architecture of the Indian Subcontinent*, London, 1986.

Hauks, Jaquetta (ed.), *The World of the Past*, vol. I and II, New York, 1963.

Huntington, Susan, L., *Iconographic Reflections on the Arjuna Ratha*, in Kaladarshan, ed. William Juwana, Bombay, 1981.

———, *The Art of Ancient India*, New York, 1985.

Huyah, Rene, *Lorouse Encyclopaedia of Prehistoric and Ancient Art*, London, 1907.

Ingholt, Harold, *Gandharan Art in Pakistan*, New York, 1957.

Iyer, K. Bharath, *Animals in Indian Sculptures*, Bombay, 1977.

Jayakar, Papul, *The Earthen Drum*, New Delhi, 1980.

Jayaswal, Vidula, "An Archaeological Evidence for tribal tradition in Central India," in *Facets of Indian Civilization*, Pt. I, ed. J.P. Joshi.

Jayaswal, V. and Kalyan Krishna, *An Ethno-Archaeological View of Indian Terracotta*, Delhi, 1986.

Jha, Ramakant and Harihar Jha, *Abhilekhamala*, Vārāṇasī, 1962.

Joshi, J.P. (ed.), *Facets of Indian Civilization, Recent Perspectives*, 3 vols, New Delhi, 1997.

Joshi, J.P. Madhubala and Jassu Ram, "The Indus Civilization: A Reconsideration on the basis of Distribution Map," in *Facets of Indus Civilization*, ed. B.N. Lal and S.P. Gupta, 1984.

Joshi, M.C. & Margbandhu, C., "Some Terracotta from recent excavations at Mathura — A study," in *JISOA*, vol. VIII, 1977.

Joshi, N.P., *Life in Ancient Uttarapatha*, Vārāṇasī, 1967.

———, *Catalogue of the Brahmanical Sculptures in the State Museum*, Lucknow, 1972.

———, *Prācīna Bhāratīya Mūrti Vigyān*, Patna, 1977.

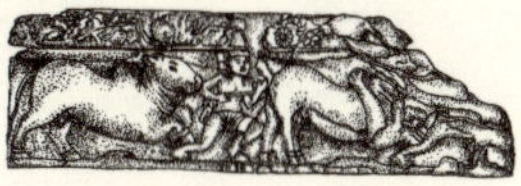

Joshi, N.P. and R.C. Sharma, *Catalogue of Gandhara Sculptures in the State Museum*, Lucknow., 1969.

Kala, S.C., *Terracotta Figurines from Kausambi*, Allahabad, 1950.

———, *Bhāratīya Mṛttikā Kalā*, Allahabad, 1972.

———, *Terracottas in the Allahabad Museum*, New Delhi, 1980.

Khan, F.A., *Preliminary Report on Kot-Diji Excavations*, 1957-58, Mainamati (East Pakistan), Department of Archaeology, Pakistan, 1963.

Khandalawala, K.J., *Herald in Stone, etc., in Buddhist Iconography Sambhata Series*, Delhi, 1989.

———, *Indian Sculpture and Painting*, Bombay.

Knox, Robert, *Amaravati Buddhist Sculpture from the Great Stupa*, British Museum Press, 1992.

Kosambi, D.D., *The Culture and Civilizations of Ancient India.*

———, *Manifestations of Siva*, Philadelphia Museum of Art, 1981.

———, *The Art of India*, Vārāṇasī, 1987.

Krishnamurty, K., *The Gandhara Sculptures.*

Lal, B.B., *Excavations at Hastinapura in Ancient India*, nos. 10 & 11, 1954-55.

———, *The Earliest Civilizations of South Asia*, New Delhi, 1997.

———, "Ṛgvedic Aryans. The debate must go on," in *East and West*, vol. 48, nos. 3-4 (December 1998).

Longhurst, A.H., "The Buddhist Antiquities of Nagarjunikonda," in *MASI*, No. 54, 1938.

Lowery, Susan (ed.), *The Illustrated Encyclopedia of Mammals*, London, 1979.

Macdonald, David (ed.), *The Encyclopedia of Mammals* II, London, 1984.

MacDowall, D.W., *et al.*, (ed.), *Indian Numismatic History, Art & Culture, Essays in Honour of Dr. P.L. Gupta*, Delhi, 1992.

Majumdar, G.P., *Conveyances in Indian Culture*, vol. III, 1935-36, no. II.

Majumdar, R.C. (ed.), *The Vedic Age*, London, 1957.

———, *The Age of Imperial Unity*, 1951.

———, *The Classical Age*, Bombay, 1962, 2nd edn.

Margaret and James Stutly, *A Dictionary of Hinduism*, New Delhi, 1977.

Marshall, Sir John (ed.), *Mohenjo-Dāro and the Indus Civilization*, vols. I-III, London, 1931.

———, *Taxila*, 3 vols., Vārāṇasī (rpt.) 1975.

Mathur, Suman, *Art & Culture Under the Kusanas*, Delhi, 1998.

Mathur, V.K., *Arts and Culture under the Sungas*, Delhi, 1996.

Michal W. Meister, *et al.*, (ed.), *Encyclopaedia of Indian Temple Architecture, North India*, Delhi, 1988.

Mishra, Indumati, *Pratima Vigyan*, Bhopal, 1972.

Mishra, Kesava, *Tarkabhasha*, Vārāṇasī, 1953.

Mishra, T.N., *Ancient Indian Bricks and Brick Remains*, New Delhi, 1997.

Mittal, Prabhudayal, *Braj Kī Kalāon Kā Itihāsa*, Delhi, 1975.

Mitra, Debala, *Buddhist Monuments*, Calcutta, 1971.

Mookerjee, Ajit, *Art of India*, New Delhi, 1952.

Mookerjee, Radha Kumar, *Hindu Civilization*, Pt. I, Bharatiya Vigyan Bhavan, 1957.

Motichandra, *Kāśī Kā Itihāsa*, Vārāṇasī, 1985.

Motichandra and Karl Khandalawala, "A study in the Terracottas from Mirpurkhas," in *Bulletin of PWMWI*, no. 7. 1959-62.

Mukhopadhaya, Biswanath, *Rsabha* in *Visvesvaranad Indological Journal*, vol. XVIII, Pts. I-II, Punjab, University, Hosiarpur, 1980.

Mukhopadhaya, Samir K., "Terracotta toys in Ancient India and their display in Modern Museum," in the *Calcutta Review*, New Series, vol. III, nos. 1 & 2. July-Sept., Oct.-Dec., 1971.

Munshi, K.M., *Indian Temple Sculpture*, Calcutta, 1959.

Murthy, K.K., *Nagarjunakonda: A Cultural Study*, Delhi, 1977.

———, *The Gandhara Sculptures*, Delhi, 1977.

Narayan, A.K. and T.N. Roy, *Excavations at Rajghat*, Pt. II, Vārāṇasī, 1977.

Narayan, A.K. and P.K. Agrawal, *Excavations at Rajghat*, Pt. IV (A-Text), Vārāṇasī, 1978.

Nigam, M.L., *Sculptural Art of Andhra*, Delhi, 1980.

Pandeya, Deena Bandhu, *Devatarccanukirtan, Hindu Deva Pratimā Vigyān*, (Hindi), Varanasi, 1978.

Pandeya, Rajbali, *Hindu Sanskaras* (Hindi), Vārāṇasī, 1949.

Pandeya, S.K., "Indian Rock Paintings — Study in Symbology," in *Marg*, vol. XXVIII, no. 4, Sept. 1975.

Patil, D.R., *The Antiquarian Remains in Bihar*, K.P. Jayaswal Research Institute, Patna, 1963.

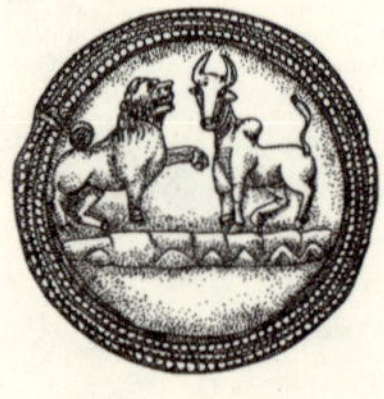

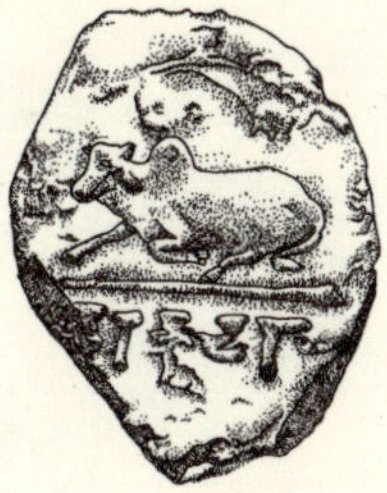

Piggot, S., "The Chronology of Prehistoric North West India", in *Ancient India*, no. 1, 1946.

———, *Prehistoric India to 1000 BC*, Penguin Books, 1950.

Prakash, Pratibha, *Terracotta Animal Figurines in the Ganga-Yamuna Valley (600 BC to 600 AD)*, New Delhi, 1985.

Possehl, G.L. (ed.), *Harappan Civilization*, 1982.

———, (ed.), *Radiocarbon Dates for South Asia Archaeology*, Pennsylvania, Philadelphia, 1990.

———, *History of Research on the Harappan Culture.*

Poster, Ammy G., *From Indian Earth*, Brooklyn Museum, 1986.

Rao, P.R. Ramchandra, *The Art of Nagarjunakonda*, Madras, 1956.

Rao, S.R., "Further Excavations at Lothal," in *Lalit Kala*, no. 11, April 1962, pp. 14-30.

———, *Lothal and the Indus Civilization*, London, 1973.

———, "Lothal A Harappan Port Town (1955-62)," *MASI*, vol. I, no. 78. 1979, New Delhi.

———, "Lothal A Harappan Port Town (1955-62)," vol. II, New Delhi, 1985.

Rao, T.A. Gopinath, *Elements of Hindu Iconography* (2nd edn.), Delhi, 1968.

Ray, Nihar Ranjan, *Maurya and Sunga Art*, Calcutta, 1945.

———, *Maurya and Post Maurya Art*, New Delhi, 1975.

Raychoudhuri, H.C., *The Asoka Chakra — Its symbolism in studies in Indian Antiquities*, Calcutta, 1958, pp. 219-22.

Rene, Huyghe, Larouse, *Encyclopaedia of Prehistoric and Ancient Art*, London, 1907.

Rosenfield, J.M., *The Dynastic Arts of the Kusanas*, University of California Press, 1967.

Roy, Sitaram, Excavations at Balirajgarh, Dist. Madhubani in *Indian Archaeology — A Review, 1974-75*, p. 10.

Rowland, Benjamin, *The Art and Architecture of India*, Great Britain, rpt. 1959.

Sahani, Dayaram, *Catalogue of the Museum at Sarnath*, Calcutta, 1914.

Sali, S.A., *The Harappans of Daimabad in Harappan Civilization*, ed. Possehl, G.L., 1982.

Sankalia, H.D., *et al.*, "Excavations at Ahar: District Udaipur," in *Indian Archaeology Review*, 1961-62, p. 50.

———, *The Prehistory and Proto-history in India and Pakistan*, Poona, New edn., 1974.

———, *Prehistory of India*, Delhi, 1977.

Sankarnarayanan, S., *The Vishnukundins and their times (400-650 AD)*, Delhi, 1977.

Sant, Urmila, *Terracotta Art of Rajasthan (From Pre-Harappan times to Gupta period)*, New Delhi, 1997.

Saraswati, S.K., *A Survey of Indian Sculpture*, New Delhi (2nd edn.), 1975.

Schlingloff, Dieter, *Studies in the Ajanta Paintings*, New Delhi, 1988.

Sen, Asis, *Animal Motifs in Ancient Indian Art*, Calcutta, 1972.

Sewell, Robert, *Report of the Amaravati Tope and excavations on its site in* 1973, New Delhi, 1977.

Shah, Priyabala, *Shri Vishnudharmottara*, Ahmedabad, 1990.

Shah, U.P., "Beginning of Jaina Iconography," in *Bulletin of Museums & Archaeology in U.P.*, June, 1972, p. 6.

———, M.A. Dhaky (ed.), *Aspects of Jain Art and Architecture*, 1975.

Sharma, G.R., *The Excavations at Kausambi (1977-59)*, Allahabad, 1960.

Sharma, I.K., *The Development of Early Saiva Art and Architecture*, Delhi, 1982.

Sharma, O.P., "The Unicorn in Indian Art and Legend," in *JBRS*, vol. XLIII, Sept-Dec. 1957, Parts III & IV.

———, "The Bull In Indian Art and Literature," in *JUPHS*, vol. V (New Series). Pt. I, 1957.

Sharma, Savita, "An uninscribed coin of Shri Lanka," in *Numismatic Digest*, vol. VI, Pts. I & II, June and December, 1982.

———, "Uninscribed copper coins from Ahicchatra," in *JNSI*, vol. XLV (Pts. 1-2). 1982.

———, *Early Indian Symbols, Numismatic Evidence*, Delhi, 1990.

———, *Gold coins of Imperial Kusanas and their successors*, Bharat Kala Bhavan, Vārāṇasī, 1999.

Sharma, Y.D., "Past Pattern in living as unfolded by Excavation at Rupar," in *Lalit Kala*, no. 1-2, April 1955-March 56.

Shastri, Ajayamitra, *Varahmihira's India*, New Delhi, 1996.

Shendge, M.J.,"The formative elements in the Harappan culture," in *Facets of Indian civilization*, ed. J.P. Joshi, 1997.

Shere, S.A., "Stone discs found in Murtjiganj," *JBRS*, vol. XXVII Parts III & IV, Sep-Dec., 1951.

———, *Terracotta figurines in Patna Museum*, Patna, 1961.

Singh, Bhupendra Pal, "Pattern of Faunal Exploitation in

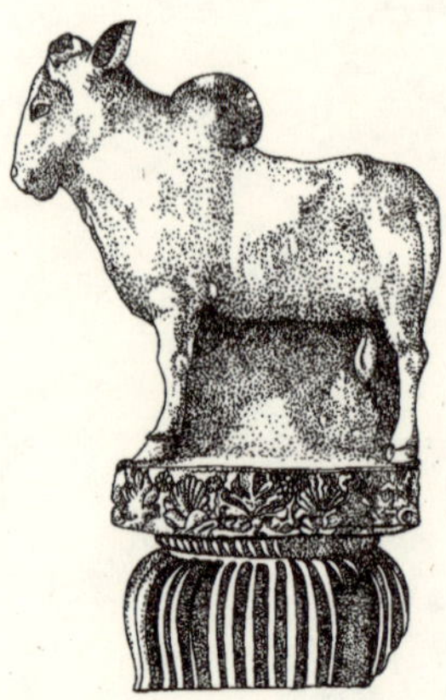

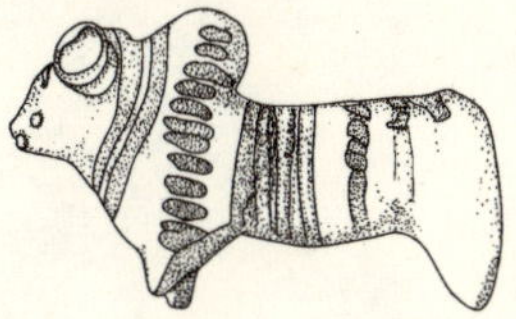

Harappa Culture, Dietery and other implication," in *Bharati — New Series*, no. 1, 1983.

Singh, Purushottam, *Excavations at Narahan (1984-89)*, Delhi, 1994.

Singh, Sheo Bahadur, *Brahmanical Icons in Northern India*, New Delhi, 1977.

Singh, Tahasildar, *Bhavisya Purana and Brhatsamhita on temple Architecture; A Collative study in Puranam*, vol. XXIII, no. 1, January 1981, pp. 69-70.

Singh, B.P. (ed.), *The Comprehensive History of Bihar*, vol. I, Part I, Patna, 1974.

Sinha, Virendra Kumar (tr.), *Bhāratīya Sanskṛti ki Prāgaitihāsik Pṛṣṭhabhūmi* (Hindi), Patna, 1970.

Sircar, D.C., *Inscription of Asoka*, revised edn., Delhi, 1967.

Sivaramamurty, C., *Birds and Animals in Indian Sculpture*, National Museum, New Delhi, 1974.

———, *Chitrasutra of the Vishnudharmottara*, New Delhi, 1978.

Smith, Vincent A., *The Jaina Stupa and other Antiquities of Mathura*, Allahabad, 1901.

———, *The Monolithic Pillars or Columns of Ashoka*, Leipzig, 1911.

Snodgrass, Adrian, *The Symbolism of the Stupa*, Delhi, 1992.

Srinivasan, Doris Math, *Mathura, The Cultural Heritage*, New Delhi, 1989.

Srivastava, A.K., *Indo-Greek Coins in the State Museum*, Lucknow, 1969.

———, *Catalogue of Saka Pahlava coins of North India*, 1972.

Srivastava, A.L., *Life in Sanchi Sculptures*, New Delhi, 1983.

Srivastava, K.M., "An insribed Indus seal from Bahrein," in *Facets of Indian Civilization*, ed. J.P. Joshi, p. 98.

———, *Discovery of Kapilavastu*, New Delhi, 1986.

Srivastava, S.K., *Terracotta in Northern India*, Delhi, 1996.

Stacul, Giorgio, "Excavations at Bhir-Kot-Ghundai (Surat, Pakistan)," in *East and West*, New Series, vol. 18, nos. 1-4, 1978.

Sukla., Dvijendranath, *Pratimā Vigyān* (Hindi), Lucknow, 1956.

Sukla, S.P., "Some Interesting Kosham Terracottas in State Museum, Lucknow," in *Bulletin of Museum and Archaeology in U.P.*, no. 4., Dec. 1969.

Taddai, Maurizia, *Monuments of Civilization — India*, London, 1977.

Takata, Osamu and Taruo Ceno, *The Art of India* (2 vols.), Tokyo, 1966.

Taraporewala, B.D., *Masterpieces of Indian Sculpture.*

Thapar, B.K., *Kalibangan: A Harapan Metropolis Beyond the Indus Valley*, Expedition, Winter, 1975, p. 28.

Thaplyal, K.K., "The symbolism in Sarnath Lion Capital and its purpose," in *JUPHS*, vol. VIII, Pts. I-II, 1960.

———, *Studies in Ancient Indian Seals*, Lucknow, 1972.

Thomas, P., *Epics, Myths and Legends of India*, D.B. Taraporwala and Sons & Co. Pvt. Ltd (12th edn.), 1961.

Tissot, Francise, *The Art of Gandhara*, Paris, 1986.

Tiwari, M.N.P., *Jaina Pratimā Vigyān* (Hindi), Vārāṇasī, 1981.

Toshi, M., "Excavations at Sahari Sokta," in *East and West*, no. 18 (1-2), 1968, p. 54.

Tripathi, Rishi Raj, *Masterpieces in the Allahabad Museum*, Allahabad, 1984.

Tripathi, Vibha & Ajeet K. Srivastava, *The Indus Terracottas*, Delhi, 1994.

Trivedi, C.B., "More Painted Shelter from Madhya Pradesh," in *Facets of Indian Civilization*, ed. J.P. Joshi, Pt. I, p. 46.

Upadhayaya, V.S., *Bhāratīya Vyakti Kośa* (Hindi), New Delhi, 1976.

Vats, Madho Sarup, *Excavations at Harappa*, 2 vols., Calcutta, 1940.

Verma, T.P., "Rajghat Sealings and their bearing on the Religious History of Varanasi," in *JNSI*, XLIX, 1987, pp. 60-67.

Verma, V.S., "Importance of Chirand," in *JBRS*, vol. XLV, Pts. 1-4, 1959, p. 320.

Wacchter, John, *The making of the Past-Man before History*, ed. Margaret Histed, Elsevier Phaidon.

Wakankar, V.S., "Pro-Historic, Cave Paintings", in *Marg*, vol. XXVIII, no. 4. Sept. 1975.

Wheeler, R.E.M., *The Indus Civilizations*, 2nd edn., Cambridge, 1960.

———, *Civilizations of Indus Valley and beyond*, England, 1966.

Williams, Joana, *Kala Darshana* (A.I.I.S.), New Delhi, 1981.

Zimmer, H., *The Art of Indian Asia*, 2 vols., U.S.A., 1955.

———, *Myths and Symbols in Indian Art and Civilization*, ed. Joseph Campbell, Washington, 1963.

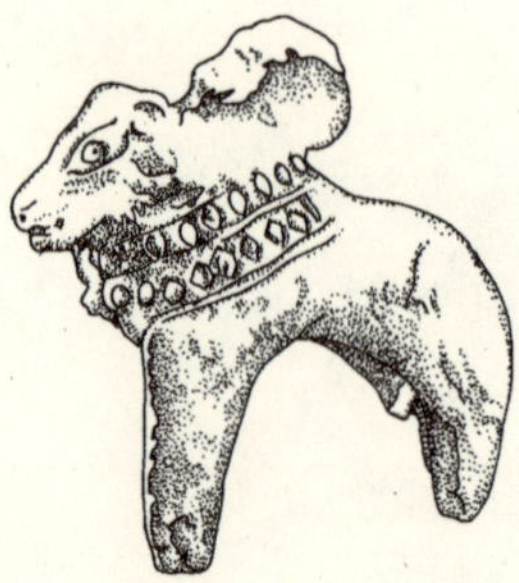

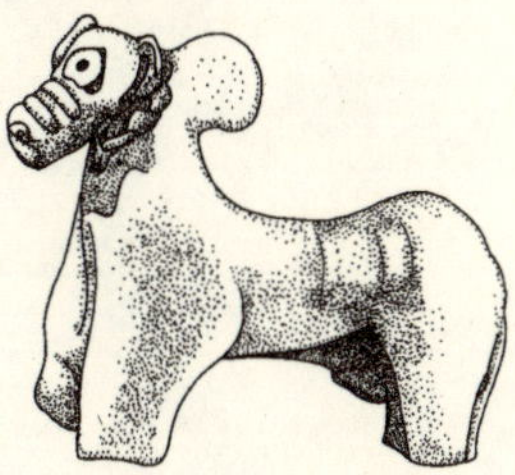

Index

Aghnyā, 37
Agnicayana, 38
Agni Purāṇa, 46
Ahar Culture, 11
Ahicchatra, 62
Ahicchatra T.C., 80
Aitareya Upaniṣad, 39
Ajantā, 120-21
Amarāvatī, 108-10
Anataṭṭa lake, 44
Appolodotus I, 63
Arthaśāstra, 51
Aśokan Pillar, 95-102, 119-20
Atarañjikherā, 74-75
Atharvaveda, 38
Atithigva, 37
Auḍumbara coins, 63
Ayodhyā coins, 63
Ayodhyā Seals, 66-67

Babyloniā, 14
Bādāmī, 121-23
Baluchistan, 13
Balukoṭa, 30
Banwālī, 30
Baudhāyana Śrauta-Sūtra, 39
Beads, 121-23
Bellari, 10
Bhagalpur T.C., 76
Bhāgavat Purāṇa, 45-46
Bharhut sculpture, 102-04
Bhaviṣya Purāṇa, 46-47
Bhīmbeṭakā, 8-9
Bhītā seals, 68
Bhumarā, 119
Bodh-Gayā, 104
Boss-Indicus linn, 13, 24
Brahmāṇḍa Purāṇa, 50-51
Bṛhadāraṇyaka Upaniṣad, 39
Bṛhat-Saṁhitā, 53-54
Bronze chariot, 22
Bull fight, 23, 46, 51, 53-54
Bull Man, 18
Bull sacrifice, 17
Bullock cart, 11, 13, 40, 42

Candoli, 10
Composit bull, 21
Copper bull, 20-21

Daburkoṭ, 11
Dāimābād chariot, 22
Damb-sadat, 12
Devagarh Temple, 118-19
Dhanadeva, 62
Divyāvadāna, 43

Enkiḍu, 14

Gāndhāra Sculpture, 112-14
Garuḍa Purāṇa, 49
Gilgameṣa, 9, 14
Gombiguda, 10
Gomukha, 42

Gomukha yakṣa, 44
Govṛṣa, 41
Gupta coins, 64
Gupta sculpture, 117-20
Gupta terracotta, 86-90

Harappan culture, 13-14
Hastināpur terracotta, 14
Hissar, 30
Homa, 14
Humpless bull, 17

Ināmgāon, 10
Indo-Greek coins, 63
Īśopaniṣad, 39

Jātaka, 43
Jorwe culture, 10

Kālibaṅgan, 12, 23
Kālidāsa, 52-53
Kālikā Purāṇa, 45
Kapgolu, 10
Kātyāyana Śrauta-Sūtra, 39
Kauśāmbī, 61
Kayathā, 11
Kayathā terracotta, 63-64
Kirātārjunīya, 53
Kośala, 61
Kulli, 11-12, 28
Kuṇāl, 29
Kuṣāṇa coins, 63-64
Kuṣāṇa sculptures, 110-17
Kuṣāṇa terracottas, 83-86

Lal Gairik, 10
Lothal, 12

Magha Dynasty, 63
Mahābhārata, 41-42
Mahābhāṣya, 51
Mahāmayūrī, 43
Mandesri, 10
Mānasāra, 55-58
Manu-Smṛti, 40
Mārkaṇḍeya Purāṇa, 46
Mathurā coins, 63
Mathurā sculptures, 107, 114-16, 118
Mathurā terracotta, 77, 99
Matsya Purāṇa, 48-49
Mauryan sculpture, 94-102
Mauryan terracotta, 76-79
Mehi, 11
Mehi Damb, 12
Minander, 63
Mohenjo-Dāro, 14

Nāgārjunikoṇḍa, 109-10
Nal ware, 28
Nandī, 39, 42, 83
Nandīśvara, 41
Narhan, 76
Nārada Purāṇa, 50
Neolithic culture, 10
Nevāsā, 10
Nīlavṛṣa, 42, 47
Nirvāṇa Kālikā, 45

Pañcamarhī, 9
Punch-marked coins, 60-61
Pāṇini, 51
Pāraskara Gṛhya-Sūtra, 39
Paśupati, 18
Piklihal, 10, 73
Pillar capital, 95-102
Potteries, 26-31
Prehistoric art, 8
Protohistoric art, 11
Puṣkalāvatī, 63

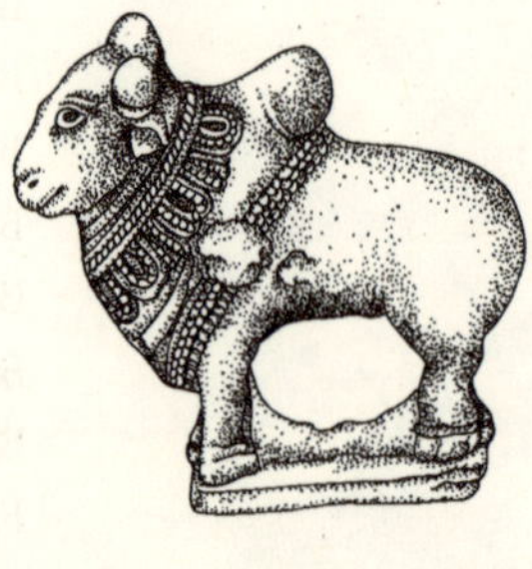

Quetta Valley, 13

Raichur, 10
Rājghāṭ sealings, 67
Rājghāṭ terracottas, 75-77, 80-81
Rāmāyaṇa, 42
Ṛgveda, 37
Ṛgvedīya Puruṣasūkta, 36
Ringstone, 95
Ṛṣabha, 35
Ṛṣabhanāth, 44

Sahari Sokhta, 13
Sāñcī, 105-07
Śatapatha-Brāhmaṇa, 39
Seals, 65-69
Short-horned bull, 21
Śiva Purāṇa, 50
Skanda Purāṇa, 47
Śrāvastī, 74
Śuṅga sculpture, 102-10
Śuṅga terracotta, 79-83
Surkotdar, 12

Thoban, 9
Three-headed bull, 16-17

Ukṣaṇ, 35
Unicorn, 16
Upper Paleolithic period, 9
Ur, 14

Vāmana Purāṇa, 48
Varāha Purāṇa, 50
Vāyu Purāṇa, 45
Vijayawāḍā, 120
Viṣṇu Purāṇa, 45
Vṛṣa, 40
Vṛṣabha, 35, 40
Vṛṣabha dhenu, 38
Vṛṣal, 40
Vṛṣākapi, 41
Vṛṣotsarga, 41, 49

Zhob, 11-12

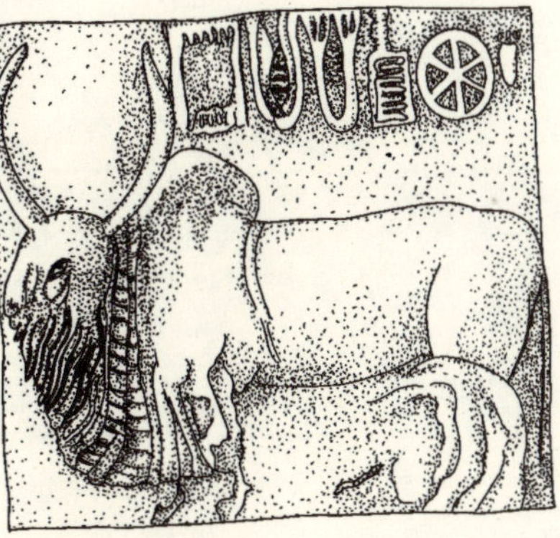